# CONTEND EARNESTLY FOR THE FAITH

## *A SURVEY OF CHRISTIAN APOLOGETICS*

by

# Phil Fernandes, Ph.D.

**PUBLISH AMERICA**

PublishAmerica
Baltimore

First printing

Unless otherwise indicated, Scripture quotations are from the NEW AMERICAN STANDRAD VERSION BIBLE. Copyright The Lockman Foundation 1960, 1962, 1963, 1968, 1971, 1972, 1973, 1975, 1977. Used by permission.

PublishAmerica has allowed this work to remain exactly as the author intended, verbatim, without editorial input.

Hardcover 978-1-61582-081-8
Softcover 1-60474-024-8
PAperback 978-1-4512-4280-5
Hardback 978-1-4512-5976-6
Price Edition 978-1-4560-7625-2
PUBLISHED BY PUBLISHAMERICA, LLLP
www.publishamerica.com
Baltimore

Printed in the United States of America

## DEDICATION

With all my love,
To my wife Cathy,
My best friend next to Jesus.

# ACKNOWLEDGMENTS

I am extremely grateful for the efforts of those who aided me in the completion of this book. Dr. Rick Walston of Columbia Evangelical Seminary read this manuscript and made numerous helpful suggestions. I appreciate the Institute of Biblical Defense research staff; they have sharpened my argumentation through hours of discussion (Proverbs 27:17). Without the encouragement and support of Conrad Clayton and his family, this present work would still be a dream. Special thanks go to my congregation at Trinity Bible Fellowship—they have allowed their pastor to spend hours studying the Word. I praise God that He blessed me with a father, Joseph Fernandes, who set a noble example for me by studying the writings of Augustine and Thomas Aquinas long before I even knew Jesus. I am also thankful for the diligent study and writings of the leading Christian apologists who have greatly influenced my thought: Gary Habermas, Norman Geisler, J. P. Moreland, and William Lane Craig. I thank God for my grandson, Nathan Michael Smith, with whom I have spent hours discussing the philosophical and theological implications of *Star Wars* and *Lord of the Rings*. I pray that God will use his young mind for the glory of God's Kingdom. I will always appreciate the love, patience, and encouragement of my wife, Cathy. When no one believed in me, she did, and I am forever grateful. And, finally, I can never repay the gift of eternal life given to me by my Lord and Savior, Jesus Christ. It is my prayer that this work is pleasing in His sight.

# TABLE OF CONTENTS

## PART ONE
## AN INTRODUCTION
## TO APOLOGETICS

## PART TWO
## TESTIMONIAL APOLOGETICS

## PART THREE
## PRESUPPOSITIONAL APOLOGETICS

# PART FOUR
## PSYCHOLOGICAL APOLOGETICS

# PART FIVE
## PHILOSOPHICAL APOLOGETICS

# PART SIX
## HISTORICAL APOLOGETICS

# PART SEVEN
## SCIENTIFIC APOLOGETICS

# PART EIGHT
## COMPARATIVE RELIGIOUS APOLOGETICS

# PART NINE
## CULTURAL APOLOGETICS

**APPENDIXES**

**BIBLIOGRAPHY**

# INTRODUCTION

I wrote this book to help Christians defend their faith. Originally, the main portion of this book comprised my 1996 doctoral dissertation for Greenwich University of Hilo, Hawaii. Part IX, dealing with cultural apologetics, was added in 2007.

The first part of this book introduces the reader to Christian apologetics. Apologetics is defined and a biblical justification for apologetics is given. I survey a brief history of Christian apologetics and explain why apologetics is needed.

Part II deals with testimonial apologetics—using how God transforms lives and answers prayer as evidence for the truth of Christianity. In Part III, I discuss the presuppositional apologetic methodologies of Christian thinkers Gordon Clark and Cornelius Van Til. Part IV touches upon the topic of psychological apologetics. This deals with arguing for God from man's search for meaning and man's thirst for God.

Part V reviews the topic of philosophical apologetics. This section gives an overview of the traditional arguments for God's existence. Non-Christian world views are refuted and the problem of evil is discussed. I also provide the reader with a refutation of moral relativism and an argument for the possibility of miracles.

In Part VI, I comment on historical apologetics. The historical reliability of the Old and New Testaments is defended, while evidence is presented for Christ's resurrection and deity, as well as the inspiration of the Bible. Scientific apologetics is examined in Part VII of this work. A scientific case for creation and against evolution is presented.

In Part VIII, I expose the reader to comparative religious apologetics. A refutation of non-Christian world religions, cults, the occult, and the New Age Movement will be given. Finally, in Part IX, I will give examples of cultural evidence for the Christian world view. I will briefly comment on the impact of different religions on human governments as well as the consequence of Western Civilization's flight from God.

It is my prayer that God will use this book in two ways. First, I pray that God will use this work to equip Christians to rationally defend their faith when witnessing to their unsaved friends. Second, I hope God will use this book to reach the hearts of unsaved readers who are open to the truth claims of Christianity.

# PART ONE

# AN INTRODUCTION TO APOLOGETICS

# CHAPTER 1
# APOLOGETICS: ITS DEFINITION

For many Christians, apologetics is a forgotten art. Though Christian laymen and ministers usually know how to share their faith, they are often unable to defend it. Due to the anti-Christian climate currently prevalent in America, believers need to be informed about this discipline.

Before examining the branch of theology known as apologetics, the term must be defined. Apologetics comes from the Greek word *apologia*, meaning "a verbal defense, a speech in defense."[1] Therefore, apologetics is that branch of Christian theology that is dedicated to defending the beliefs of biblical Christianity.

Apologetics is a biblical concept. The word *apologia* is found in Peter's first epistle. Peter declares, "sanctify Christ as Lord in your hearts, always being ready to make a defense to everyone who asks you to give an account for the hope that is in you, yet with gentleness and reverence" (3:15).[2] In this passage, the word *apologia* is translated "defense."[3]

Since apologetics is one branch of theology, its relationship to the other main branches of theology must be shown. Theology simply means "the study of God." Of course, when studying God, His work of creation and redemption must also be included. Hence, theology entails the study of all Christian doctrines.[4] The main branches of theology are 1) exegetical theology, 2) biblical theology, 3) systematic theology, 4) historical theology, 5) practical theology, 6) polemics, and 7) apologetics.[5]

## EXEGETICAL THEOLOGY

*Exegetical theology* is the branch of Christian theology which deals with the direct study of the biblical text. Exegetical theology attempts to arrive at the true meaning of the biblical passage being studied. This type of theology encompasses the study of biblical introduction, biblical languages, and archaeology.[6] Hermeneutics, the science of how to properly interpret the scriptures, is utilized within exegetical theology.[7]

Exegetical theology forms the basis for all other branches of Christian theology. This is due to the fact that the Bible is the sole authority from which orthodox Christians draw their beliefs. If a student of the Word of God wrongly interprets biblical passages, it will damage his theological system of thought.

## BIBLICAL THEOLOGY

*Biblical theology* studies God as He has progressively revealed Himself throughout the scriptures.[8] The Old Testament does not immediately reveal Jesus Christ as the Savior of mankind. Instead, God related the account of His creation of the universe (Genesis 1 and 2). This was followed by the fall of mankind into sin (Genesis 3). God then promised to send a Savior to defeat the serpent (Genesis 3:15). Man is commanded to perform animal sacrifices when seeking to approach God (Genesis 4). These animal sacrifices pointed forward to the day when the Savior of mankind would come and die for the sins of the world (Hebrews 10:4; 9:22; John 1:29; 1 Corinthians 5:7).

When the earth increased in wickedness, God judged the world by bringing upon it a flood that destroyed all mankind. Only Noah and his family were saved (Genesis 6-9). As humans once again multiplied, they united in their rebellion against God. God divided mankind by causing them to speak different languages. This resulted in the beginning of the nations (Genesis 11).

God then selected one man named Abraham and produced from him a nation (Genesis 12). From this nation the world's Savior would someday come. This chosen nation was Israel. Through Moses, God gave Israel His Law (Exodus, Leviticus, Numbers, and Deuteronomy). The Law was never intended to save anyone. Its purpose was to show men that they fell short of God's holy standards, and that they need to trust in the coming Savior (Galatians 3:24).

The Old Testament contains the history of the nation Israel, some of its inspired poetry, and messages from its prophets. In short, the Old Testament points forward to the coming of the Savior.

The New Testament begins with the four Gospels (Matthew, Mark, Luke, and John). The Gospels record eyewitness testimonies of the life, teachings, and works of the Savior when He came to earth. The book of Acts gives an account of the history of the apostolic church, while the epistles teach how Christians should live. The Bible culminates with the book of Revelation. This book predicts the return of Jesus the Savior to the planet earth in the last days.

As one examines this brief survey of God's revelation called the Bible, it becomes clear that God did not reveal Himself and His salvation plan all at once. He did so progressively over a period of more than 1,500 years. Biblical theology takes note of this and seeks to study God's unveiling of Himself as He progressively did so. Therefore, biblical theology picks up where exegetical theology leaves off.

## SYSTEMATIC THEOLOGY

*Systematic theology* groups the teachings of the Bible into a system that makes sense.[9] It seeks to display a "total picture" of God's revelation to man.[10] There are several divisions in systematic theology.

*Prolegomena* deals with introductory matters, while *Theology Proper* discusses what the Bible teaches about God Himself. *Bibliology* contains the truths that the Bible declares about itself. *Angelology* spells out the scriptural doctrines about spirit beings called angels. The study of fallen angels is called *Demonology*. The leader of the fallen angels is called Lucifer or Satan. The doctrine about this vile being is called *Satanology*. *Pneumatology* deals with the study of the Holy Spirit, the third Person of the Trinity. *Christology* is the study of Jesus Christ, the second Person of the Trinity. *Anthropology* is the doctrine of man, while *Hamartiology* is the doctrine of sin. The doctrine of salvation is discussed in *Soteriology*. *Ecclesiology* is the study of the biblical teachings about the church. Finally, *Eschatology* is the study of the last days.

Systematic theology picks up where exegetical and biblical theology leaves off. Once it is determined what a given biblical text means (exegetical theology), one can proceed to study how God progressively revealed Himself in His Word (biblical theology). After this, the teachings of the Bible must be grouped into a system that makes sense (systematic theology).

## HISTORICAL THEOLOGY

*Historical theology* studies the progressive development of systematic theology throughout the history of the Christian church.[11] This branch of theology examines the many different creeds and statements of faith that were drawn up by the church throughout the centuries. Much focus is placed upon the thought of great theologians, e.g., Augustine, Aquinas, Luther, Calvin, and Wesley.

Historical theology often directs its attention to the thought of one or more of the different eras of church history. Important time periods would include the apostolic age, the early church fathers, the medieval period, the reformation, and the rise of modern theology.[12] Different periods of church history focused on different areas of theology, mainly for purposes of combating doctrinal errors. For example, the early church fathers devoted much of their effort and time to christological issues, while reformation theologians specialized in soteriology. Much can be learned through a study of historical theology.

## PRACTICAL THEOLOGY

*Practical theology* is the practical application of the teachings of the Bible to one's life.[13] *Regeneration* is the first issue that needs to be applied. The Bible teaches that a person must be born again to see God's Kingdom (John 3:3). This new birth comes only through faith in Christ as Savior (John 3:16-18).

Once a person is saved, *sanctification* comes into play. This deals with the daily life of the believer as God sets him apart for His purposes (Romans 6 and 7). Practical theology also includes issues such as living a life of service, studying the Word, worship, prayer, and evangelism.

Practical theology builds upon the accomplishments of the other four theological branches mentioned above. It seeks to apply the truths of God to one's daily life. This branch of theology moves the theologian from a mere "head knowledge" of the truths of the Bible to a personal relationship with the God of the Bible. When one partakes of practical theology in the fullest sense, he moves from a life of study to a life of service.

## POLEMICS

*Polemics* is the often overlooked branch of theology that specializes in the refutation of heresies that develop within the professing church.[14] Hence, polemics is the function of "good" theology whereby it protects itself from "bad" theology.

Throughout church history, false doctrines have risen within the church. These heresies have been continually refuted by theologians who sought to protect the essential teachings of the Bible. At times, heretics accepted correction and recanted of their erroneous views. On other occasions, however, some heretics had to be excommunicated from the church in order to protect the essential teachings of the Christian faith.

Often, unrepentant heretics started their own religions or cults. This was exactly the case concerning Islam and Mormonism.

Though their founders claimed to be returning Christianity to its purest form, both Islam and Mormonism were actually heretical offshoots of Christianity. Once the heretical movement is clearly separated from true Christianity, polemics (which deals only with internal heresies) is no longer used against it. Instead, apologetics is called upon to enter the theological battle for truth.

## APOLOGETICS

As was already mentioned, *Apologetics* is that branch of Christian theology which devotes itself to the defense of the gospel. Unlike polemics, which refutes internal heresies, apologetics defends the essential teachings of the Bible against external attacks. Whereas polemics refutes false teachers who claim to be proclaiming Christian truths, apologetics enters into debate with those who openly claim to be opposed to historic and biblical Christianity.

Apologetics has two functions.[15] Negatively, it refutes belief systems that oppose Christianity, and, positively, it defends the essential truths of the Christian faith.

## CONCLUSION

As the table on this page shows, one can easily see where apologetics fits into Christian theology. The first four branches of theology (exegetical, biblical, systematic, and historical) attempt to arrive at the truths of the Bible. The fifth branch (practical theology) attempts to help the believer live these biblical truths. The sixth theological branch (polemics) protects Christian truth from internal errors. And, finally, the seventh branch of theology (apologetics) defends Christian truth from outside attacks.

All seven branches of Christian theology are needed. For the truth must first be found. Then it must be lived, protected, and defended. The church will suffer if it neglects any of these seven branches.

Apologetics is vital to the Christian church today. Those who share the gospel must also defend the gospel. People are seeking answers to their questions. Through apologetics we can find those answers. We can remove intellectual stumbling blocks that stand between lost souls and Christ. We can communicate the gospel in such a way that the "modern" man will understand it. We must, as the inspired writer instructs us, "contend earnestly for the faith" (Jude 3).

## THEOLOGY
(the study of God)

### 1) EXEGETICAL THEOLOGY
*direct study of the biblical text, attempting to arrive at the true meaning of the passage in question.*

### 2) BIBLICAL THEOLOGY
*studying God as He progressively revealed Himself through the Scriptures.*

### 3) SYSTEMATIC THEOLOGY
*grouping the teachings of the Bible into a system that makes sense.*

### 4) HISTORICAL THEOLOGY
*studying the development of systematic theology throughout the history of the church.*

## 5) PRACTICAL THEOLOGY
*applying the teachings of the Bible to one's daily life.*

## 6) POLEMICS
*refuting heresies that arise within the professing church.*

## 7) APOLOGETICS
*defending the essential teachings of the Bible against external attacks.*

## ENDNOTES

1W.E. Vine, *Expository Dictionary of New Testament Words* (Grand Rapids: Zondervan Publishing House, 1952), 61.

2*New American Standard Bible* (La Habra: The Lockman Foundation, 1973). All biblical quotations are taken from the NASB unless otherwise noted.

3*The Zondervan Parallel New Testament In Greek and English* (Grand Rapids: Zondervan Bible Publishers, 1975), 691.

4Henry Clarence Thiessen, *Lectures In Systematic Theology* (Grand Rapids: William B. Eerdmans Publishing Company, 1979), 1-2.

5Walter A. Elwell, ed. *Evangelical Dictionary of Theology* (Grand Rapids: Baker Book House, 1984), 68, 1066.

6Thiessen, *Lectures in Systematic Theology*, 19-20. (Although Thiessen includes biblical theology as part of exegetical theology, an argument can be advanced for biblical theology as a separate branch.)

7Ibid.

8Charles C. Ryrie, *Basic Theology* (Wheaton: Victor Books, 1986), 14.

9Ibid.

10Ibid.

11Millard J. Erickson, *Christian Theology* (Grand Rapids: Baker Book House, 1985), 25.

12Ryrie, *Basic Theology*, 13.

13Thiessen, *Lectures In Systematic Theology*, 20.

14Earle E. Cairns, *Christianity Through the Centuries* (Grand Rapids: Zondervan Publishing House, 1981), 105.

15Ibid.

# CHAPTER 2
# APOLOGETICS: ITS BIBLICAL BASIS

In the previous chapter, apologetics was defined as the branch of Christian theology that specializes in the defense of the Christian faith. Also noted was how apologetics relates to the other main branches of Christian theology. In this chapter, the biblical basis of apologetics will be examined.

Some scholars believe that the gospel should not be defended. These scholars are called fideists.[1] They maintain that one's beliefs should not be rationally defended. Instead, according to this school of thought, one should accept his or her theological views by a leap of blind faith. One should not look for or provide evidence for religious beliefs. To do so, according to fideists, is to elevate human reason above divine revelation.

If fideism is true, then apologetics is an unbiblical exercise. However, if the practice of apologetics is found to be based in the scriptures, then fideism is an unbiblical system.

## THE BIBLE COMMANDS BELIEVERS TO DEFEND THE FAITH

The Bible clearly teaches that Christians are to defend the faith. In fact, believers are commanded to do apologetics. The apostle Peter instructs believers to always be "ready to make a defense" of the Christian hope (1 Peter 3:15).

Jude, the half-brother of Christ, also commands Christians to defend the faith. He tells believers to "contend earnestly for the faith which was once for all delivered to the saints" (Jude 3).

The apostle Paul states that those who are appointed as elders or overseers of local churches should be able to do more than just teach sound biblical doctrine. Paul states that those who hold this office must also be able "to refute those who contradict" the teachings of the Bible (Titus 1:9). In Paul's letter to the Colossian believers, he made the following statement:

Conduct yourselves with wisdom toward outsiders, making the most of the opportunity. Let your speech always be with grace, seasoned, as it were, with salt, so that you may know how you should respond to each person (Colossians 4:5-6).

From these biblical passages, it becomes sufficiently clear that the Word of God commands believers to defend the faith. Therefore, the accusations of the fideists are false. Apologetics is biblical.

## THE BIBLE SPEAKS OF NATURAL REVELATION

The Bible not only commands Christians to defend the faith, but also speaks of God revealing Himself in nature.[2] This is called *natural revelation*. Natural revelation is also known as general revelation since it gives evidence of God's existence to all mankind.[3] When God made Himself known to man in the Bible, He miraculously had to guide human authors to record His Word without error. This is why the Bible is called *supernatural revelation* (also known as special revelation). However, in natural revelation no supernatural work of God is needed. God has given evidence of His existence in the universe He created. The Bible declares the following regarding God's revelation of Himself in nature:

The heavens are telling of the glory of God; and their expanse is declaring the work of His hands. Day to day pours forth speech, and night to night reveals knowledge (Psalm 19:1-2).

For the wrath of God is revealed from heaven against all ungodliness and unrighteousness of men, who suppress the truth in unrighteousness, because that which is known about God is evident within them; for God made it evident to them. For since the creation of the world His invisible attributes, His eternal power and divine nature, have been clearly seen, being understood through what has been made, so that they are without excuse. For even though they knew God, they did not honor Him as God, or give thanks; but they became futile in their speculations, and their foolish heart was

24

darkened. Professing to be wise, they became fools...(Romans 1:18-22).

These passages teach that though no one has ever seen the invisible God, the visible work of His hands can be seen in His creation. If someone finds a watch, he knows a watchmaker must exist, though he has never seen him.[4] Therefore, when man sees the beauty and order of the universe, he knows that it must have been caused by an intelligent and powerful Being.

Since God has revealed Himself in nature, Christians can argue from the effect (the universe) to its cause (God). To gaze at the starry sky on a clear night and still believe that the universe is a product of chance is an insult to human reason.

Another aspect of natural revelation deals with the fact that God has revealed His law in the conscience of each person. The apostle Paul affirms this in the following words:

For when Gentiles who do not have the Law do instinctively the things of the Law, these, not having the Law, are a law to themselves, in that they show the work of the Law written in their hearts, their conscience bearing witness, and their thoughts alternately accusing or else defending them...(Romans 2:14-15).

Because God has given all men a glimpse of His moral law in their consciences, believers can argue from this moral law to the existence of the moral Lawgiver. Since the moral laws are above all men, the moral Lawgiver must also be above all men. Since evidence for God can be found in nature, philosophical apologetics (which argues for God's existence from the evidence of nature) is a biblical practice.

## THE BIBLE SPEAKS OF HISTORICAL EVIDENCES

As mentioned above, the Bible teaches that God has revealed Himself to man in nature. However, besides this evidence in nature, the Bible declares that evidence for the Christian faith can also be found in history.[5] While attempting to prove the resurrection of Christ from the dead, as well as the future resurrection of all believers, the apostle Paul lists the eyewitnesses of Christ's post-resurrection appearances:

For I deliver to you as of first importance what I also received, that Christ died for our sins according to the Scriptures, and that He was buried, and that He was raised on the third day according to the

Scriptures, and that He appeared to Cephas, then to the twelve. After that He appeared to more than five hundred brethren at one time, most of whom remain until now, but some have fallen asleep; then He appeared to James, then to all the apostles; and last of all, as it were to one untimely born, He appeared to me also (1 Corinthians 15:3-8).

From this passage it is clear that the apostle Paul was willing to refer to the evidence of eyewitness testimony in order to provide a defense for the truth of the gospel. Therefore, there is a biblical basis for historical apologetics. Historical apologetics utilizes historical evidences to argue for the truth of the Christian faith.

## THE EARLY CHURCH DEFENDED THE FAITH

The Bible commands believers to do apologetics. The scriptures speak of both natural revelation and historical evidences. And, finally, the early church did apologetics. The apostles defended the gospel.

*The apostle Peter* defended the faith. On the day of Pentecost, Peter preached his famous sermon. Three thousand people were saved and added to the church. During that sermon Peter stated, "This Jesus God raised up again, to which we are all witnesses" (Acts 2:32). Peter often defended the faith during his sermons by appealing to eyewitness testimony (Acts 3:15; 5:30-32; 10:39-41).

*The apostle John* also defended the faith. In fact, he claimed that the main purpose for writing his Gospel was to provide eyewitness accounts of Christ's miraculous life in order to persuade others to believe (John 20:30-31).

*Luke* willingly shared proof of Christ's claims. When Luke wrote the book of Acts, he stated that Christ "presented Himself alive, after His suffering, by many convincing proofs, appearing to them over a period of forty days" (Acts 1:1-3). Luke shared with Theophilus, the person to whom the book of Acts was addressed, eyewitness evidence of the post-resurrection appearances of Christ. Thus, Theophilus would not have to exercise blind faith in order to believe. Luke knew that biblical faith is based upon evidence, not an irrational leap.

*The apostle Paul* was also a defender of the faith. The scriptures say that he kept "confounding the Jews who lived at Damascus by proving that this Jesus is the Christ" (Acts 9:22). Paul's custom was to enter various synagogues and reason with the Jews from the scriptures (Acts 17:1-3; 18:4). If the Jews rejected the gospel message, he would then go and proclaim it to the Gentiles:

And he entered the synagogue and continued speaking out boldly for three months, reasoning and persuading them about the kingdom of God. But when some were becoming hardened and disobedient, speaking evil of the Way before the multitude, he withdrew from them and took away the disciples, reasoning daily in the school of Tyrannus. And this took place for two years, so that all who lived in Asia heard the word of the Lord, both Jews and Greeks (Acts 19:8-10).

While in Athens, Paul stood on Mars Hill and preached one of his greatest sermons (Acts 17:16-34). There, he was confronted by Greek philosophers: the Epicureans and the Stoics. The Epicurean philosophers believed that God did not exist, while the Stoic philosophers equated God with the universe.

Paul noticed that the Athenians had devoted a statue to "an Unknown God." Paul then claimed to personally know this God of whom they were ignorant. Twice he quoted from the works of ancient Greek poets to establish his case as he began to share the gospel. Finally, when Paul spoke of God raising Jesus from the dead, many of the Greek philosophers sneered, while others asked Paul if he would be willing to speak to them again. Though the idea of a bodily resurrection had been repugnant to the Greeks since the days of Plato (427-347BC),[6] some Greeks were willing to give Paul a second hearing. This was probably due to the fact that he had proved himself to be well-read in Greek philosophy, even though he held the belief of Christ's bodily resurrection.

As demonstrated in Paul's case, apologetics enables a person to speak to the "intellectual elite." Paul chose to "become all things to all men" (1 Corinthians 9:19-22). He chose to use anti-Christian philosophies in order to refute the false beliefs of his listeners and to lead them to Christ. No defender of the faith can do less.

And, finally, *Apollos* used apologetics. He was a great defender of the faith. Luke records this about him:

Now a certain Jew named Apollos, an Alexandrian by birth, an eloquent man, came to Ephesus; and he was mighty in the scriptures...for he powerfully refuted the Jews in public, demonstrating by the scriptures that Jesus was the Christ" (Acts 18:24-28).

## CONCLUSION

Apologetics is taught in the Bible. The Bible commands us to defend the faith. The scriptures also speak of natural revelation and historical evidences for the Christian faith. And finally, the early church defended the faith. Apologetics is squarely based in the Bible.

## ENDNOTES

1Norman L. Geisler, *Christian Apologetics* (Grand Rapids: Baker Book House, 1976), 58-59.

2Thiessen, *Lectures*, 7-8.

3Ibid.
4John Hick, ed. *The Existence of God* (New York: The Macmillan Company, 1964). 99-103.

5Ibid., 8-9.

6William S. Sahakian. *History of Philosophy* (New York: Harper Perennial, 1968). 55-56.

# CHAPTER 3
# A HISTORY OF APOLOGETICS:
# ITS DEFENDERS AND ANTAGONISTS

Christian apologetics is not new. In the last chapter it was shown that the apostles themselves utilized apologetics on numerous occasions. In this chapter, it will be demonstrated that apologetics has continued throughout church history. Before discussing the history of Christian apologetics, three points need to be stressed.

First, some of the apologists (those who defend the faith against external threats) that will be discussed in this chapter were not orthodox in all areas of their theology. Still, they professed faith in Christ and defended some orthodox aspect of the faith. Therefore, they deserve mention here.

Second, some of these defenders of the faith could be classified as apologists, while others did polemical work (they refuted heresies that developed within the professing church). Since some of the heresies refuted by the polemical scholars were later revived as apologetic issues, both types of defending the faith will be discussed in this chapter.

Third, several non-Christian thinkers greatly influenced the history of Christian apologetics. Therefore, mention will be made concerning their views despite the fact that they did not profess faith in Christ. Keeping these three points in mind, a brief overview of the history of the defense of the Christian faith will be given. This will establish the fact that apologetics (as well as polemics) has always been practiced by the church.

## THE FIRST CENTURY

As was mentioned in the last chapter, the apostolic church defended the faith. Peter often used eyewitness evidence to defend the resurrection of Christ from the dead. John used his own eyewitness accounts of Christ's miracles to persuade others to believe. Luke referred to the post-resurrection appearances of Jesus to establish his case. Paul reasoned with both Jews and Greeks in his attempts to lead them to Christ. And, Apollos debated Jews and proved that Jesus was the Christ (the one anointed by God to redeem Israel).

## THE SECOND CENTURY

Ignatius, the Bishop of Antioch, was martyred early in the second century (between 110 and 115AD).[1] During this time he wrote seven letters. In his letters to Smyrna and Talles, he condemned a gnostic heresy called Docetism.[2] Gnosticism made salvation dependent on secret knowledge.[3] The Gnostics believed that all matter was evil while spirit was good.[4] Docetism was the gnostic view that since matter is evil, Jesus only *appeared* to have a body. He was actually only a spirit being without a real body. Docetists believed that only a phantom died on the cross. Ignatius refuted this view by declaring Jesus to be "truly" of human flesh and stating that He was "truly" put to death in the flesh for our sins.[5]

Justin Martyr (100-165) was converted to Christianity from paganism. In his writing entitled *Dialogue With Trypho*, he answered Trypho's accusations that Christians violate the Mosaic Law since they worship a human being.[6] Justin Martyr argued from Old Testament passages that Jesus is God and He fulfilled the Mosaic Law.

Aristides, Tatian, Athenagoras, and Theophilus all argued that Christianity is superior to the pagan religions.[7] *The Epistle to Diognetus* and *The Epistle of Barnabas*, both by unknown authors, presented rational defenses of the Christian faith and presented Christ's death as adequate for salvation.[8]

Irenaeus became the Bishop of Lyons in 177AD.[9] He wrote a work entitled *Against Heresies*. In this work, he refuted Gnosticism by teaching that 1) evil is not co-eternal with God, 2) matter is not evil, and 3) Jesus rose bodily from the dead.[10] Irenaeus also wrote *Proof of the Apostolic Preaching.* In this writing, he demonstrated that Jesus fulfilled Old Testament prophecies.[11]

### THE THIRD CENTURY

Tertullian wrote between 196 and 212AD. In *Apology,* he defended Christian beliefs against heresy and argued that Christians should be tolerated, not persecuted.[12] Tertullian also wrote five books called *Against Marcion.* In these works, he defended the use of the Old Testament by Christians and the oneness of God.[13] In another work, *Against Praxeas,* Tertullian defended the doctrine of the Trinity (God eternally exists as three equal Persons).[14]

Origen (185-254) wrote *Against Celsus,* in which he answered pagan objections to the Christian faith.[15] Unfortunately, Origen himself taught the heretical doctrines of the preexistence of souls and universal salvation and was later condemned by the church.[16]

### THE FOURTH CENTURY

Athanasius (300-373) refuted Arius, a heretic who taught that Jesus was a created being and a lesser god than the Father.[17] Athanasius rightly taught that Jesus is equal with the Father and existed from all eternity with Him. The church ruled in favor of the Athanasian view and condemned the Arian heresy.[18] This was eventually made clear in the Nicene Creed.

Ambrose (339-397) helped to complete the overthrow of Arianism in the Western Church.[19] Unfortunately, it has been revived in modern times by the Jehovah's Witnesses.

Basil the Great (330-379) also opposed Arianism. He defended the Trinity by affirming the Deity of the Holy Spirit. He helped to define the Trinity as one in substance but three in persons.[20]

### THE FIFTH CENTURY

Augustine (354-430) was the Bishop of Hippo in North Africa. Many people consider him to be the greatest church leader between the apostle Paul and Martin Luther. Early in his life, Augustine had accepted a dualistic religion called Manicheanism.[21] This religion taught that God (light) and matter (darkness) are both eternal.[22] The Manicheans believed that both good and evil existed throughout all eternity. This, they reasoned, removed any responsibility from God for the evil that exists in the universe.

Under the preaching of Ambrose, Augustine became a Christian.[23] He began to see that evil was not coexistent with God. Rather, God alone is eternal, and all that He created is good. Yet, by giving angels and men free will, God permitted evil to come into existence. Therefore, evil is a privation (a lack of the good that should be there). Evil does not exist on its own, but must exist in something good (just as rust cannot come into existence without the metal it corrupts). Therefore, Augustine concluded, evil exists as a corruption or perversion of God's perfect creation.[24] God created the universe perfect, but angels and men brought evil into the universe through their free choices.

As one of the greatest theologians in the history of the church, Augustine wrote many works defending Christianity. He provided evidence for God's existence,[25] attempted to reconcile faith and reason,[26] and correctly saw and defended the fact that mankind has inherited a corrupted nature from Adam.[27]

Augustine's most famous debate was with a monk named Pelagius. Pelagius believed that each person is born in the same state in which Adam was created. Thus, each person is *not* contaminated by Adam's sin.[28] In Pelagius' view, Adam merely set a bad example for his offspring. It is possible for man to live without sin. Augustine refuted Pelagius by pointing out that the scriptures teach that each person inherits Adam's sin nature. Therefore, no one can please God through human effort.[29] Man must rely on God's grace to be saved.

Though Augustine rightly defended both divine sovereignty and human free will, his later writings exhibited an extreme view of predestination that seemed to cancel out any real human freedom in the area of salvation.[30] Man, in Augustine's view, believes in Christ only because God predestined him to do so.

In his writings Augustine defended the doctrine of the Trinity, the deity of Christ, and salvation by God's grace. Augustine's two greatest works were *Confessions* and *The City of God*. *Confessions* is an autobiographical work detailing Augustine's conversion. *The City of God* was Augustine's view of history. It represented his greatest philosophical and apologetic work. For Augustine, the city of God consists of all angels and men who love and serve God, while the city of the Devil is comprised of those angels and men who oppose the God of the Bible.

## THE SIXTH CENTURY

Boethuis (480-524) was educated in both the philosophies of Plato and Aristotle. He wrote five books in defense of Christianity. Boethuis, long before Thomas Aquinas did, applied Aristotle's logic to Christian theology.[31]

## THE EIGHTH CENTURY

Alcuin (735-804) was an Anglo-Saxon scholar who led the battle against Adoptionism in Spain.[32] Adoptionism is the heresy that teaches that Jesus was only a man whom God adopted as His son. At His baptism, Christ was given special powers by God. After God raised Jesus from the dead as a reward for His good works, God adopted Jesus into the Godhead.[33] Alcuin refuted this view by proclaiming the biblical teaching that Jesus is fully God and fully man. Jesus always existed as God, but also took a human nature upon Himself at some point in time.

## THE ELEVENTH CENTURY

Anselm (1033-1109) was the archbishop of Canterbury. He was an early scholastic theologian. Scholasticism dates from the eleventh century to the end of the fourteenth century. Scholasticism was an attempt by medieval Christian scholars to use reason to reconcile orthodox Christianity and the philosophy of Aristotle.

Anselm is famous for his ontological argument for God's existence.[34] Anselm believed that God's existence could be proven by reason alone. He concluded that God must exist since His nonexistence is inconceivable. For God is, by definition, the greatest conceivable being. The greatest conceivable being must exist. If He did not exist, then one could conceive of a being greater than Him who did exist. But then this being would be God. Hence, according to Anselm's reasoning, God must exist.[35]

Anselm had another way of stating his ontological argument.

He declared that since God is by definition the most perfect being, He must lack no perfection. Since Anselm believed that existence was a perfection, he reasoned that it is impossible for God to lack existence.

Therefore, God must exist.[36] Most philosophers today reject the ontological argument for God's existence. Still, it has provoked much thought and debate even in this modern era.

It should also be noted that Anselm did not limit his apologetics to the ontological argument for God's existence. Anselm also used the cosmological argument when attempting to prove God's existence. He argued from the existence of good things in the world to the existence of the supreme Good.[37]

## THE TWELFTH CENTURY

Peter Aberlard (1079-1142) was a Catholic monk. He was a brilliant lecturer and debater.[38] He attempted to reconcile faith and reason. It was his conviction that true Christianity was reasonable and consistent.[39]

## THE THIRTEENTH CENTURY

Albert the Great (1206-1280) was a Catholic theologian who utilized the philosophy of Aristotle in his system of thought. His most famous student was Thomas Aquinas. Albert saw a distinction between theology (the study of that which God has supernaturally revealed) and philosophy (the use of human reason to find truth). Still, he recognized the need for both disciplines.[40] One of Albert's greatest contributions to apologetics was his promotion of the study and use of philosophy in Christian thought.[41]

Albert argued for God's existence from the motion in the universe. He, like Aristotle, concluded that there must be an unmoved Mover as the cause of all motion in the universe.[42] Albert was well read in Greek, Jewish, and Arabian philosophy.[43] Still, he remained true to orthodox Christianity and held many beliefs in common with Augustine (though Augustine utilized the philosophy of Plato rather than that of Aristotle).

Albert's thought was never a completed system. What he began was completed by his great student Thomas Aquinas.[44] Aquinas took Aristotle's philosophical thought and produced a complete synthesis with Christian theology.

Thomas Aquinas (1225-1274) was the greatest scholastic thinker of the middle ages.[45] He was born in Aquino, Italy. As mentioned above, he studied under Albert the Great in Paris and Cologne. Aquinas, like Albert, utilized Aristotle's philosophy in structuring his theological thought, but, unlike Albert, Aquinas developed a complete system.

Aquinas rejected the ontological argument for God's existence. He believed that all human knowledge begins in the senses and that the human mind begins life as a "blank slate" upon which nothing is written.[46] He taught that everything in the mind was first in the senses except the mind itself.[47] In other words, we start life with no data in our minds, though our minds have the innate ability to draw information from sense experience.[48] The mind has the capacity to draw more out of sense data than sense data itself. The mind does this by reasoning and making judgments on the information gained through sense experiences.[49] Still, knowledge must begin with sense experience. Therefore, one cannot argue from the idea of God to His existence (the ontological argument).[50] Instead, one must argue from the elements of the physical world to its ultimate Cause.[51] This is why Aquinas used the cosmological and teleological arguments for God's existence. The cosmological argument reasons that finite things such as the universe need an infinite Cause. The teleological argument concludes that design and order in the universe is evidence for the existence of an intelligent Designer of the universe.

Aquinas is famous for his five ways to prove God's existence.[52] The first four ways are cosmological arguments, while the fifth way is a teleological argument. In his first way to prove God's existence, Aquinas argued from the movement or change in the universe to an unmoved Mover.[53] Second, Aquinas argued from effects in the universe (which cannot account for their own present existence) to their uncaused Cause.[54] Third, Aquinas argued that the existence of beings that have the possibility of nonexistence must have their existence grounded by a Being which has no possibility of nonexistence.[55] Fourth, Aquinas reasoned that since there are different degrees of perfections among beings, there must be a most perfect Being.[56] And, in Aquinas' fifth way he concluded that since non-intelligent nature progresses towards a definite goal, it must be directed towards this goal by an intelligent Being.[57]

Aquinas also attempted to solve the problem of evil.[58] He agreed with Augustine that God did not create evil, but that evil is merely a corruption of God's good creation. God did however, according to Aquinas, create the possibility for evil by giving man and angels free will. Fallen men and angels brought evil into the universe by choosing to rebel against God. Aquinas reasoned that God allows evil for the purpose of a greater good. Evil is necessary in order for man to have free will. Since God is all-good and all-powerful, He will one day defeat evil. He accomplishes this through the atoning work of Christ.

Aquinas solved the problem of religious language. Aquinas rejected univocal knowledge of God. Words used of the infinite God cannot mean exactly the same when used and applied to finite man. For God's existence far transcends man's existence. On the other hand, if words used of man have totally different meanings when applied to God, then man can have no knowledge of God whatsoever. This rules out equivocal knowledge of God. Aquinas settled this dilemma by his doctrine of analogical language. A term used both of God and man will be defined the same. Still, the term will be not be attributed to man and God in exactly the same way. The terms will be infinitely applied to God, but finitely applied to man. We must remove all limitations from terms before attributing them to God.[59]

Aquinas believed that God has revealed Himself in both nature and the scriptures.[60] Some truths can be proven by reason, but others (like the doctrine of the Trinity) are above reason and must be accepted by faith alone.[61] Still, there is much evidence for accepting the Bible as God's Word. In fact, miracles and philosophical arguments confirm the truth of Christianity.[62]

Aquinas spent much time philosophically defending the orthodox attributes of God. In Aquinas' thought, God is immutable, eternal, simple (not composed of parts), one, and infinite.[63]

Thomas Aquinas was one of the greatest defenders of the Christian faith of all time. To this day, many scholars rely heavily upon his thought. Whether Catholic or Protestant, scholars who utilize his system of apologetics are called Thomists.

Bonaventure (1221-1274) was a contemporary of Thomas Aquinas. Bonaventure used many different arguments for God's existence. He reasoned that our idea of imperfections assumes the existence of the Perfect (by which the imperfections are compared).

Bonaventure argued that since beings that are produced exist, there must exist a first Cause of their existence. The existence of changeable beings declares the existence of an unchangeable Being. Bonaventure stated that since from nothing, nothing can come, there must be a self-existent Being as the ground of all other existence. Beings which have the possibility of nonexistence necessitates the existence of a Being which cannot not exist.[64]

Bonaventure believed that God's existence is self-evident to all men. God's existence is a truth that is naturally implanted in the human mind. Still, he viewed this knowledge to be dim and implicit, rather than obvious and explicit. He considered the atheist to be one who has chosen not to reflect upon this truth. Thus, God's existence can be doubted by men.[65]

Bonaventure also utilized Anselm's ontological argument for God's existence. Since God is the greatest conceivable being, He must exist. For if He did not, one could conceive of a being greater than Him, a being that did exist. Therefore, God must exist.[66] Bonaventure borrowed from Augustine as well. He reasoned from the existence of eternal truths to the existence of an eternal Mind.[67]

Bonaventure, however, had a major disagreement with Thomas Aquinas. Aquinas believed that it was philosophically possible for the universe to be eternal, while Bonaventure believed it could be philosophically proven that the universe had a beginning. Both men agreed that the universe was created and was not eternal. This was clear from the scriptures. However, Aquinas agreed with Aristotle that there is nothing logically contradictory with an eternal universe. To refute this view, Bonaventure showed that it is impossible to both add to an infinite number and to pass through an infinite series. For if the universe is eternal, then present events would be adding to the infinite number of past events. But the infinite cannot be added to since it is already infinite. Also, if the universe is infinite, then one could never reach the present moment since one would have to pass through an infinite series of past events to arrive at the present. This is impossible due to the fact that no matter how many past events are crossed, there will always be an infinite number more to pass through before the present moment can be reached. Therefore, Bonaventure showed in convincing fashion that it is philosophically contradictory to hold to the possibility of an eternal universe.[68]

John Duns Scotus (1265-1308) argued that if any being cannot cause its own continued existence, then it cannot ground the existence of another being. Therefore, there must exist a totally independent Being who is the ground of all dependent existence.[69] Scotus, like Aquinas before him, was not arguing for the cause of the beginning of the existence of dependent beings. Rather, he argued for the cause of the continuing existence of dependent beings.

## THE FOURTEENTH CENTURY

William of Ockham (1290-1384) was a Franciscan monk. He denied rational proofs for God's existence. He taught that God was known by faith alone. Man could not reason to God.[70] This led to a decline in philosophical apologetics that culminated in the thought of Kant, Hegel, and Kierkegaard. Kant denied that man could know reality as it exists in itself. Man could only know reality as it appeared to him.[71] Hegel taught that all contradictory views would be reconciled, thus denying that truth is absolute.[72] Kierkegaard declared that religious beliefs were nonrational and must be accepted through a leap of blind faith.[73] Since Kant, Hegel, and Kierkegaard have greatly influenced contemporary thought, William of Ockham's impact on current religious and secular dialogue should not be underestimated. Ockham is also famous for his principle, called "Ockham's razor," which declares the simplest explanation as the best explanation.[74] This principle has been used by many later scientists to rule out in advance any supernatural causes since natural causes are thought to be less complex explanations.

## THE SIXTEENTH CENTURY

Martin Luther (1483-1546) was the great German reformer. He posted his famous 95 theses on the church door in Wittenberg. This was to protest what Luther felt were abuses in the Roman Catholic Church. Luther opposed the sale of indulgences and excessive church wealth. He denied the supremacy of the pope and considered the Bible alone to be the final authority for the church.

Though this work was mainly polemic in thrust, Luther also defended the doctrine of salvation by grace alone through faith alone in Christ alone.[75] Since salvation by grace is an essential doctrine of Christianity, its defense falls squarely in the field of apologetics.

John Calvin (1509-1564) was the famous Geneva reformer.[76] Like Luther, he broke from the Roman Catholic Church. He defended the scriptural doctrine of salvation only by God's grace through faith in Christ.[77] At a time when the Roman Catholic Church was elevating human effort in the attaining of salvation, Calvin, like Luther before him, stressed God's grace in salvation.[78]

Other great reformers include Huldreich Zwingli (1484-1531), William Tyndale (1494-1536), and John Knox (1514-1572). These men primarily defended the sole authority of the scriptures and salvation by grace through faith.[79]

### THE SEVENTEENTH CENTURY

Rene Descartes (1596-1650) was a Roman Catholic philosopher.[80] He decided that something was not worth believing unless one could be certain about it.[81] He decided to reject any beliefs that could be doubted. In this way, he would attempt to find a belief that could not be doubted. This belief would be his point of certainty. From this belief, he would attempt to build an entire system of thought.[82] As Descartes searched for this starting point, he began to doubt more and more beliefs. He became skeptical about all things. Finally, he found what he believed to be this point of certainty. For, the more he doubted, the more he became certain of the existence of the doubter (himself). Descartes coined his famous phrase *"Cogito ergo sum"* (I think, therefore I am). From the starting point of his own existence, he attempted to build his system of thought. Descartes utilized Anselm's ontological argument for God's existence, as well as cosmological type arguments.[83]

Blaise Pascal (1623-1662) was a great French thinker like Descartes. Pascal died while working on a defense of Christianity. It was later published in its incomplete form as *Pensees* (Thoughts). Pascal argued that God could only be known through faith in Christ and that reason is limited and fallible—it cannot, by itself, decide theological issues. We cannot reason to God in an unbiased manner.[84] He concluded that faith is needed—a choice must be made.

Pascal is famous for his "wager" argument for God's existence. He reasoned that since the odds for and against God's existence are even (before examining the evidence for or against God), we cannot reason to God. We must use our will. We must either choose God or reject

Him. Pascal concluded that if we wager that God exists and we find that He does in fact exist, we gain eternal happiness. But if God exists and we reject Him, we have lost everything. On the other hand, if God does not exist, we would still lose nothing by wagering that He does. Pascal stated that when a person wagers on God, he will either win or lose. If the person loses, he loses nothing. But if the person wins, he wins everything. Therefore, the wise man will wager that God exists.[85]

Gottfried Wilhelm Leibniz (1646-1716) was a German Protestant.[86] Due to his extreme confidence in the abilities of human reason, he made use of the ontological argument for God's existence.[87] Leibniz also utilized the cosmological argument for God's existence.[88] He rested his form of this argument on the principle of sufficient reason. This principle states that everything that exists needs an explanation or reason for its existence. Dependent beings, such as human beings, need explanations outside of themselves for their existence. For example, one's existence cannot be explained without reference to his parents, the food that he eats, the air that he breathes, and so on. Leibniz concluded that eventually one must arrive at a Being which is totally independent. This Being contains within itself the reason for its own existence. Leibniz reasoned that if there is no such Being, then there is no ultimate explanation for the existence of dependent beings.

Baruch Spinoza (1623-1677) was a Jewish philosopher.[89] Although he was a proponent of the ontological argument, he used it in an attempt to prove the existence of an impersonal God. Spinoza was a pantheist—he believed that the universe is God.[90] In this way, he argued against the God of the Bible.

Spinoza believed that the science of his day had proven that the laws of nature could not be violated. Since he viewed miracles as violations of the laws of nature, he considered miracles impossible.[91] Up to that point in history, scholars had for the most part assumed the Bible to be a reliable document. However, from Spinoza on, thinkers began to question the reliability and authenticity of the Bible. Human reason became the ultimate authority. It stood above the Bible as its judge. Men began to decide which portions of the

Bible were inaccurate. Spinoza was the forerunner of the eighteenth century thinkers who were extremely critical of the veracity of the scriptures.

Spinoza dealt a devastating blow to Christian apologetics. If apologetics was ever to be revived, it must place more emphasis on scientific and historical evidences (the two areas thought to disprove the claims of Christianity).

## THE EIGHTEENTH CENTURY

David Hume (1711-1776) was a Scottish philosopher and skeptic.[92] He was extremely skeptical about all areas of life. He was an empiricist, believing that truth could be found only through the five senses. Therefore, he believed that it was impossible to prove the existence of the self. He questioned the principle of causality (which forms the basis for the cosmological argument). This principle states that every effect needs an adequate cause. Since Hume doubted this principle, he questioned the validity of the traditional arguments for God's existence (although he did give some weight to the teleological argument).[93] Following in the footsteps of Spinoza, Hume also questioned the possibility of miracles. He, like Spinoza, considered miracles violations of natural laws. Hume believed that the wise man bases his decisions upon the evidence. Since natural laws are based upon the uniform experience of mankind, the wise man will never believe in miracles.

Immanuel Kant (1724-1804) was a German philosopher. He taught that the thing in itself cannot be known by man. All man can know is the thing as it appears to him.[94] Man cannot know objective reality; all he can know is his own subjective views about reality. Kant's view took Christianity outside the realm of the objectively verifiable. He claimed that the traditional arguments for God's existence were flawed. Still, he felt that the moral nature of man made it practical to assume God's existence. For if there is no God, then there can be no after-life and no rewards. Therefore, in order to make sense of man's moral nature, we must posit the existence of God.[95] Although the moral argument was to become an effective tool for Christian apologists, the damage Kant had done far outweighed the good. Hegel and Kierkegaard would later pick up where Kant left off. They would inflict Christian apologetics with more serious wounds.

William Paley (1743-1805) was the Archdeacon of Carlisle. Despite the widespread skepticism of his day, he was an aggressive defender of the Christian faith. He wrote several apologetic works. His most famous contribution to Christian thought was his teleological argument for God's existence.

Paley's teleological argument is called the "watchmaker."[96] In this argument, Paley reasoned that if one found a watch in the wilderness, he would have to conclude that there must have been a watchmaker who designed it. Even if he had never seen a watch before, one would recognize the obvious design, order, and complexity of the watch and conclude that it was designed. Paley then asks his readers to consider the design in the universe and conclude with him that it also needs an intelligent Designer.

## THE NINETEENTH CENTURY

Georg Wilhelm Friedrich Hegel (1770-1831) was a German philosopher who also dealt a devastating blow to Christian apologetics. Up to his day, men had viewed reality in terms of antithesis (opposites).[97] If something was true, its opposite must be false. Mankind accepted this law of non-contradiction. However, things began to change with Hegel.

Hegel accepted the view of the ancient Greek philosopher Heraclitus.[98] Heraclitus believed that everything is changing; nothing remains the same. Change was viewed by Heraclitus as the fundamental feature of reality. Hegel saw this change as a dialectical process; reality is progressively developing through a threefold process. This process consists of a thesis which is followed by its antithesis (its opposite, a contradiction of the thesis), and then by a synthesis (the reconciling of the two opposites).[99] Therefore, in Hegel's philosophy, truth is relative. Contradictions can be reconciled. In short, the idea of absolute truth was discarded in Hegelian thought.

The result of this view upon Christian apologetics is obvious. The defense of the truth becomes futile because contradictions or opposites can both be true. Much of modern philosophy is based upon this denial of absolutes, despite the fact that the denial of absolute truth is self-refuting. For if the denial is true, then it would be an absolute truth.

Soren Kierkegaard (1813-1855) was a famous Danish philosopher who took modern thought one step beyond that of Hegel. Kierkegaard is known as the "father of modern existentialism." Existentialism is the philosophical school that either denies or de-emphasizes objective meaning while elevating subjective feelings and beliefs to a position of primacy.

The existentialism of Kierkegaard did not deny the existence of objective truth. However, Kierkegaard viewed subjective truth as of greater importance. Truth is viewed as something personal, not merely propositional. One's subjective beliefs are of greater importance than the objective truth.[100]

Applying this line of thought to religion, Kierkegaard held that religious beliefs could not be defended. One accepts something as true by an act of the will, not by reason. One accepts a religious truth by a leap of blind faith into the non-rational realm.[101] Faith and reason are worlds apart. Never shall the two meet. This view is called fideism. Fideism is opposed to Christian apologetics. It teaches that the defending of one's religious beliefs is useless. The distaste for apologetics harbored by many contemporary theologians can be directly traced to a Kierkegaardian influence.

Charles Darwin (1809-1882) published his famous work *The Origin of Species* in 1859. In this work, he attempted to present evidence for his view of evolution called natural selection (survival of the fittest).[102] Darwin's theory of evolution denied any need for God as the designer of the universe. Instead, the impersonal laws of nature were proposed to explain the origin of first life and of complex life forms. Life was thought to have evolved from non-life. Complex life forms supposedly evolved from simple life forms. Finally, modern man, who wanted so desperately to be free from God's rule over his life, had no intellectual need to see God as the designer of the universe.[103] Belief in God was viewed as anti-intellectual.

Ludwig Feuerbach (1804-1872) believed that only the material realm exists. He reasoned that only the objects of sense are real. Therefore, he concluded that God and all religious values were created by man's imagination.[104] God is the imaginary fulfillment of man's wishes to transcend his own nature. In short, God did not create man; man created God.

Friedrich Nietzsche (1844-1900) accepted the atheistic evolutionary theory. This German philosopher concluded that since "God is dead," all traditional values died with Him.[105] In other words, man has philosophically and scientifically outgrown the outdated myths of religion. Modern man now recognizes that God is nonexistent. But, if the God of the Bible does not exist, then the morality taught in the Bible is no longer relevant. Nietzsche called

for a race of "supermen" who would have the courage to go "beyond good and evil" and create their own moral values.[106] He recommended that the "soft" values of Christianity be replaced with the "hard" values of the "supermen."

## THE TWENTIETH CENTURY

A very important point concerning apologetics is that by the start of the twentieth century the atheistic bias was extremely prevalent among "intellectuals." This was true to the extent that it was thought that no educated person could be a Christian. Dialogue between orthodox Christians and secular leaders became almost nonexistent. Christian apologetics needed to be revived in the midst of this antagonistic climate. Scientists, philosophers, and historians had attacked the Bible so thoroughly in the nineteenth century that Christian apologetics would have to start once again from the ground floor.

*Liberal theology* was extremely popular at the start of the twentieth century. Liberal theology denied the inspiration and inerrancy of the scriptures and salvation only through Christ. Jesus was reduced to merely a wise man. Liberalism stressed the universal brotherhood of all men, the basic goodness of man, and the possibility of achieving world peace through human effort. However, two world wars effectively crumbled the foundations of liberalism.

The American reaction against liberalism was seen in the emergence of *fundamentalism*. The fundamentalists defended the orthodox doctrines of the Christian faith. They held to the inspiration and inerrancy of the Bible, the deity and resurrection of Christ, and salvation only through Him. Leading fundamentalists were B. B. Warfield, H. C. G. Moule, and James Orr.[107] They published a work in 1909 listing an entire series of orthodox beliefs which they held. Though fundamentalism is still strong today, it has come under much attack and has been accused of being anti-intellectual. Therefore, many Christians who hold to the fundamentals of the faith today, would rather be called "evangelicals."

Karl Barth (1886-1968) wrote his commentary on Romans in 1919. This marked his break from liberalism. His theological school of thought is called Neo-orthodoxy. Barth held that man was sinful and that God was "wholly other" than man.[108] However, he kept many liberal assumptions. He viewed the Bible as a human book that contained errors. Rather than the Bible objectively being God's inspired word, Barth believed that it becomes God's Word to the individual when the individual is encountered by God at the moment of crisis.[109] In effect, Barth introduced a heavy existential emphasis into the professing church. The propositional truths of Scripture were questioned. All that mattered was one's own personal encounter with God. Therefore, Barth was an extreme fideist. The fideism of Barth is still prevalent in the church today.

Rudolf Bultmann (1884-1976) was also a Neo-orthodox theologian. He used a method called form criticism to find what he felt were the oral traditions behind the written scriptures. He removed the supposed "myths" from God's Word.[110]

Despite the decline of Neo-orthodoxy that began in the 1950s, in its place, more secular and humanistic types of theology began to emerge. Any Christian theology that denies the essentials of the faith will eventually redefine Christianity in terms of its own secular culture. This was fully actualized when the "God is dead" theologies (so called "Christian atheism") were introduced in the 1960s.[111] The lessons of history have taught the church that a "watered-down" Christianity is no Christianity at all. Christian apologists found themselves defending the faith not only against the attacks of anti-Christian thinkers, but against professing Christians as well.

Yet, in the midst of this madness, a British scholar named C. S. Lewis (1898-1963) was converted from atheism to Christianity in 1931. He then became the most famous defender of orthodox Christianity in the English-speaking world until his death.[112] His writings provide rational arguments for the existence of God, the possibility of miracles, and the truth of the Christian faith. He also attempted to answer the question as to how an all-good and all-powerful God could allow evil and human suffering. With Lewis, the revival of Christian apologetics had begun. Many defenders of the faith were to follow in his footsteps.

Frederick Copleston, a Roman Catholic scholar, defended God's existence in a debate against the famous British philosopher Bertrand Russell in 1948.[113] Copleston is also the author of the nine-volume work *A History of Philosophy*.

Gordon Clark (1902-1985) and Cornelius Van Til (1895-1987) popularized the presuppositional school of apologetics.[114] They presupposed Christianity to be true rather than arguing for it. However, their willingness to refute non-Christian belief systems was enough to separate presuppositionalism from fideism. For fideists are opposed to all apologetics. A fideist will neither provide evidence for Christianity, nor refute non-Christian beliefs.

Edward John Carnell (1919-1967) also presupposed the truth of Christianity when he did apologetics. But, unlike Clark and Van Til, he believed that one's presuppositions could be tested.[115]

Francis Schaeffer (1912-1984) reached many "intellectual dropouts" with the gospel through his writings, films, and lectures.[116] He managed to present the gospel at a philosophical level which touched the hearts and minds of many thinkers who were disenchanted with modern thought. Schaeffer's approach to apologetics was much like that of Carnell.

John Warwick Montgomery is a Lutheran scholar who gained notoriety in the 1960s for his lectures, books, and debates in defense of the Christian faith. Montgomery focused primarily on historical evidences for the Christian faith.[117]

Walter Martin (1928-1989) established himself as the foremost authority on refuting non-Christian cults in 1965. It was then that his book The Kingdom of the Cults was published.[118]

Today, there are many articulate defenders of the faith. Battling on the front lines are Christian philosophers Norman Geisler, William Lane Craig, Gary Habermas, and J. P. Moreland, as well as theologian R. C. Sproul. Christian apologetics is clearly making a comeback.

## ENDNOTES

1Tim Dowley, ed., *The History of Christianity* (Oxford: Lion Publishing, 1977), 83.

2J. B. Lightfoot and J. R. Harmer, eds., *The Apostolic Fathers* (Grand Rapids: Baker Book House, 1984), 148,156.

3Cairns, 68.

4Ibid.

5Lightfoot and Harmer, 156.

6Dowley, 94.

7Cairns, 68.

8Ibid., 75-76.

9Ibid., 110.

10Ibid.

11Ibid.

12Dowley, 112.

13Ibid.

14Ibid.

15Ibid., 107.

16Ibid.

17Ibid., 145.

18Cairns, 134.

19Dowley, 149.

20Ibid., 175.

21Ibid., 206.

22Ibid., 98.

23Ibid., 206.

24St. Augustine, *City of God* 14.11., 22.1.

25Norman L. Geisler, ed., *What Augustine Says* (Grand Rapids: Baker Book House, 1982), 19-22.

26Ibid., 13-31.

27St. Augustine, *City of God* 14.6-14.15.

28Cairns, 137.

29Ibid., 137-138.

30Sahakian, 91.

31Dowley, 229.

32Ibid., 241.

33Everett F. Harrison, *Baker's Dictionary of Theology* (Grand Rapids: Baker Book House, 1960), 26.

34Dowley, 284.

35William Lane Craig, *Apologetics, An Introduction* (Chicago: Moody Press, 1984), 62.

36R. C. Sproul, John Gerstner, and Arthur Lindsley, *Classical Apologetics* (Grand Rapids: Academie Books, 1984), 102.

37Norman Geisler and Winfried Corduan, *Philosophy of Religion* 2nd ed., (Grand Rapids: Baker Book House, 1988), 155.

38Dowley, 288-289.

39Ibid.

40Frederick Copleston, *A History of Philosophy* Book One, Vol. 2 (New York: Image Books, 1985), 295.

41Ibid., 296.

42Ibid.

43Ibid., 299.

44Ibid., 298.

45Dowley, 292.

46Norman L. Geisler, *Thomas Aquinas: An Evangelical Appraisal* (Grand Rapids: Baker Book House, 1991), 86.

47Ibid.

48Ibid.

49Ibid., 87.

50Geisler and Corduan, 127.

51Copleston, 338-339.

52St. Thomas Aquinas, *Summa Theologiae.* ed. Timothy McDermott. (Westminster: Christian Classics, 1989), 12-14.

53Geisler and Corduan, 158-159.

54Ibid., 159.

55Ibid.

56Ibid., 159-160.

57Geisler, *Thomas Aquinas* 121-122.

58Ibid., 153-162.

59Ibid., 40.

60Ibid., 37.

61Ibid., 38.

62Ibid.

63Ibid., 103.

64Copleston, 251-252.

65Ibid., 252-253.

66Ibid., 255-256.

67Ibid., 256-257.

68Ibid., 262-265.

69Geisler and Corduan, 160-162.

70Sahakian, 116.

71Ibid., 172.

72Ibid., 188.

73Ibid., 346-348.

74Sahakian, 116.

75Martin Luther, *Commentary on Romans*, trans. J. Theodore Mueller (Grand Rapids: Kregel Publications, 1976), 76-80, 88-89.

76Dowley, 368-369.

77John Calvin, *On the Christian Faith: Selections From the Institutes, Commentaries, and Tracts*. ed. John T. McNeill (Indianapolis: The Bobbs-Merrill Company, 1957), 82-88.

78Ibid., 21-22.

79Dowley, 379, 390, 398.

80Ibid., 486-487.

81Sahakian, 135.

82Ibid.

83Geisler and Corduan, 127-131, 163.

84Dowley, 488.

85Craig, 33-36.

86Dowley, 489.

87Geisler and Corduan, 131-132.

88Ibid., 164-165.

89Dowley, 487-489.

90Geisler and Corduan, 132-133.

91Norman L. Geisler, *The Battle For the Resurrection* (Nashville: Thomas Nelson Publishers, 1989), 67.

92Dowley, 490-491.

93David Hume, *Dialogues Concerning Natural Religion.* ed. Henry D. Aiken. (New York: Hafner Publishing Company, 1948), 95.

94Gordon H. Clark, *Thales to Dewey* (Jefferson: The Trinity Foundation, 1985), 402.

95Geisler and Corduan, 109-110.

96Hick, ed., *The Existence of God*, 99-104.

97Francis A. Schaeffer, *The Complete Works of Francis A. Schaeffer.* Vol. 1 (Westchester: Crossway Books, 1982), 13-14.

98Sahakian, 190.

99Ibid., 191-192.

100Norman L. Geisler and Paul D. Feinberg, *Introduction to Philosophy: A Christian Perspective* (Grand Rapids: Baker Book House, 1980), 46.

101Ibid.

102Sahakian, 225.

103Ibid.

104Ibid., 202.

105Ibid., 231.

106Ibid.

107Dowley, 611-612.

108Cairns, 444-445.

109Ibid.

110Ibid., 446.

111Ibid., 446-447.

112Dowley, 621.

113Hick, 167-191.

114Gordon R. Lewis, *Testing Christianity's Truth Claims* (Lanham: University Press of America, 1990), 100-150.

115Ibid., 176-284.

116Cairns, 454.

117John Warwick Montgomery, *History and Christianity* (Minneapolis: Bethany Book House, 1965).

118Walter Martin, *The Kingdom of the Cults* (Minneapolis: Bethany Book House, 1985).

# CHAPTER 4
# APOLOGETICS: WHY IT IS NEEDED

Having discussed the definition, biblical basis, and history of apologetics, the issue of why apologetics is needed must now be examined. In this chapter, seven reasons why Christians need to defend the faith will be given. Though more reasons could be listed, these seven will suffice to demonstrate that Christian apologetics is a necessary discipline in the church.

### GOD CREATED MAN TO THINK
Man was created by God to think. Man was created a rational being.[1] God wants man to use all that He has given him for His glory (1 Corinthians 10:31). God has given each man a mind; God wants him to use his mind.

God calls out to the unsaved and invites them to reason with Him that they might be saved (Isaiah 1:18). But God also commands the believer to love Him with all his mind (Mark 12:30). Whether saved or unsaved, God wants man to think and use his mind. For this reason, believers are to reason with others concerning the gospel (Colossians 4:5-6). God never meant for His gospel message to be considered "anti-intellectual." Therefore, the first reason why apologetics is needed is that God created man to think; He wants people to use the minds He gave them.

## TO CONFIRM THE FAITH OF BELIEVERS

A second reason why apologetics is needed is to strengthen or confirm the faith of believers.[2] It is necessary to answer the many intellectual doubts that believers often have.

Our society enthusiastically promotes such ideologies as atheistic evolution and moral relativism. Because of this, Christians are often ridiculed. Born-again believers are often called old-fashioned or dull. It is often said that Christians believe outdated myths or fairy tales. This type of verbal persecution and peer pressure often lead believers to doubt their faith. For this reason, apologetics is needed. It helps answer the doubts a believer may develop in an anti-Christian society.

## TO PERSUADE NONBELIEVERS

A third reason why apologetics is needed is that it can and has been used to persuade nonbelievers to accept Christ.[3] This is done by removing intellectual stumbling blocks that often keep a person from Christ.[4]

Some believers disagree with this particular point. They are quick to point out that arguments cannot lead people to Christ. For only the Holy Spirit can lead a person to Christ. Several things must be mentioned here. First, it is true that only the Holy Spirit regenerates (John 3:3-6). Second, Jesus commands believers to share their faith (Matthew 28:19-20). Third, the Bible commands believers to defend the gospel (1 Peter 3:15). And, fourth, the people who make this objection still share their faith. This shows that they believe that though only the Holy Spirit regenerates, He has chosen to use believers as His instruments. And they are correct at this point. But their position is mistaken in that they fail to realize that the same God who told Christians to share their faith also commanded them to defend it. In other words, just as the Holy Spirit uses believers' sharing of the gospel, He can also use believers' defending of the gospel. Very few Christians, if any, actually believe that the Holy Spirit will lead people to Christ without using believers. Though He has the power to do so, He has chosen to use Christians in both the sharing and the defending of the faith.

It should also be noted that many people were led to Christ through apologetics. Josh McDowell, C. S. Lewis, Walter Martin, and John Warwick Montgomery are just a few outstanding Christian leaders who came to Christ through apologetics.

Those who don't do apologetics must stop witnessing when objections to the gospel are raised, for they do not believe in providing evidence for the gospel. But Christians who do apologetics can continue to witness. Defenders of the faith can attempt to answer those objections. And, if Christians really love their fellow man, they should be willing to answer his objections if possible.

### TO REFUTE SYSTEMS OF FALSE BELIEF

A fourth reason why apologetics is necessary is that heretical movements must be refuted. If the truth is to be protected, then errors must be exposed and countered. The apostle Paul made it clear that pastors of local churches must be able to "refute those who contradict" the truths of the Bible (Titus 1:9).

If Christians refuse to do battle with belief systems that oppose Christianity, then non-Christian cults and religions will proclaim their false teachings without opposition. Many people who thirst for God will be led astray. Though most Christians shy away from confrontation, they must be willing to boldly combat the false teachings that they encounter. As the Lord confronted the legalistic and hypocritical Pharisees (Matthew 23), His followers must be willing to refute those who promulgate error.

If the Christian church does not oppose false religions and cults, then the essential differences between truth and error will be blurred. Therefore, apologetics is needed to refute non-Christian belief systems.

### TO IMPROVE THE MORAL HEALTH OF AMERICA

Fifth, apologetics is needed to help improve the moral well-being of America.[5] The increase in crime, sexual promiscuity, and abortion have plagued this nation. Apologetics can be used to reverse these trends. This can be done in two ways. First, believers may lead others to Christ through apologetics. This will effect the behavior of these new converts. They will begin to live by biblical morality as opposed to the morality which the world promotes (James 2:26). Second, through the use of apologetics, Christians can defend biblical morality even when dealing with nonbelievers.

America needs moral direction. The Christian can encourage a return to traditional values through the use of apologetics. Christian thinkers should engage in public debates and dialogues with non-Christian thinkers concerning ethical issues. In this way defenders of the faith can argue for the superiority of Christian morality.

### TO SHOW THE WORLD CHRISTIANITY IS NOT IRRATIONAL

A sixth reason why apologetics is needed is to declare to the world that the Christian faith is not a contradictory system of thought. The world must be shown that one does not have to throw away his or her mind to become a Christian. Many intelligent and educated people have been Christians in the past. Intelligent and educated people can still be Christians today.

Defenders of the faith need to engage in public debate with non-Christian thinkers. Even if no one is persuaded through apologetics (which is usually not the case), at least it will be shown that the Christian faith can be intelligently defended in the world of ideas. The Church must not allow others to call the gospel an outdated myth without responding to this accusation. Therefore, apologetics is needed to show the world that Christianity is not irrational.

### TO STAND UP FOR WHAT IS RIGHT EVEN IF NO ONE IS LISTENING

Seventh, apologetics is needed to stand up for what is right even if no one is listening. God demands that Christians stand up for His truth even if it is rejected by all others. The apostle Paul preached the same gospel regardless of whether his listeners applauded him or stoned him (1 Corinthians 9:16; 2 Corinthians 11:23-33; Philippians 4:11-13; Galatians 1:10). The prophet Jeremiah's message was extremely unpopular to the people of Judah. Still, he proclaimed it (Jeremiah 37:15-17). Just because others may harden their hearts to the message, this does not relieve the Church from defending the faith.

In the midst of an immoral culture, someone must stand up for what is right. In the midst of an idolatrous society, someone must contend for the one true God. Anything less is to ignore the responsibilities entrusted to the Church. Paul stated, "I am appointed for the defense of the gospel" (Philippians 1:16) and "woe is me if I do not preach the gospel" (1 Corinthians 9:16). All Christians must proclaim and defend the gospel even if no one is listening.

## CONCLUSION

In conclusion, apologetics is needed for several reasons. First, God created man to think. Therefore, the Church should be able to give reasons for why she believes what she believes. Second, apologetics helps to strengthen the faith of believers. Third, it is instrumental in persuading nonbelievers to accept Christ. Fourth, it is necessary since false belief systems must be refuted. Fifth, apologetics can help improve the moral health of society. Sixth, apologetics is needed to show the world that Christianity is not irrational. And, seventh, apologetics is needed since God calls His followers to stand up for what is right even if no one else is listening.

## WHY APOLOGETICS IS NEEDED

1) Because God created man to think

2) To confirm the faith of believers

3) To persuade nonbelievers

4) To refute systems of false belief

5) To improve the moral health of America

6) To show the world Christianity is not irrational

7) To stand up for what is right even if no one else is listening

ENDNOTES

1John R. W. Stott, *Your Mind Matters* (Downers Grove: InterVarsity Press, 1972), 14-15.

2Gary R. Habermas, *The Resurrection of Jesus* (Lanham: University Press of America, 1984), 16.

3Ibid., 17.

4J. P. Moreland, *Scaling the Secular City* (Grand Rapids: Baker Book House, 1987), 12.

5Ibid.

# CHAPTER 5
# APOLOGETICS: ITS PROPER FOUNDATION

In order for the defender of the faith to achieve maximum results, he must have the proper foundation in place before he sets out on the apologetic task. This chapter will be devoted to examining this foundation. Many apologists of the past have not had a solid base from which to work. Because of this deficiency, their apologetic system was inadequate in those areas where they fell short.

There are five components that make up the proper foundation for apologetics: 1) regeneration, 2) thorough Bible study, 3) sound theology, 4) a knowledge of non-Christian thought, and 5) a genuine love for others. If any of these components is missing, one's defense of the faith will be greatly handicapped.

## REGENERATION

A person has no business trying to defend the Christian faith if he or she is not a true believer. Jesus asked, "A blind man cannot guide a blind man, can he? Will they not both fall into a pit?" (Luke 6:39). The Bible teaches that nonbelievers are spiritually blind (John 9:39-41; 2 Corinthians 4:3-4). If a nonbeliever attempts to defend the faith, he will only lead others further from the truth. In fact, this is exactly what Jesus accused some Jewish religious leaders of His day of doing. Christ rebuked them, "Woe to you, scribes and Pharisees, hypocrites, because you travel about on sea and land to make one proselyte; and when he becomes one, you make him twice as much a son of hell as yourselves" (Matthew 23:15).

Jesus taught that, "unless one is born again, he cannot see the kingdom of God" (John 3:3). He stated that, "If you abide in My word, then you are truly disciples of Mine; and you shall know the truth..." (John 8:31-32). In order to adequately defend the truth, one must first know it. And Christ taught that only born-again believers know the truth.

For a person to be given the new birth, he must trust in Jesus alone for salvation (John 3:16-18; Ephesians 2:8-9). At the moment a person first believes, the Holy Spirit regenerates him (John 3:5-8; Ephesians 1:13-14; Titus 3:5-6). Jesus referred to Himself as the "light of the world" (John 8:12). Those who reject Him walk in spiritual darkness; they can be of no help to others in the area of apologetics.

THOROUGH BIBLE STUDY

Before embarking on the apologetic task, a born-again believer must be grounded in God's Word. Paul told Timothy to "be diligent to present yourself approved to God as a workman who does not need to be ashamed, handling accurately the word of truth" (2 Timothy 2:15). Without thorough study of the Bible, a defender of the faith will be ineffective.

Paul also told Timothy that "all Scripture is inspired by God and profitable for teaching, for reproof, for correction, for training in righteousness; that the man of God may be adequate, equipped for every good work" (2 Timothy 3:16-17). Therefore, the defender of the faith must spend much time and effort studying the Word of God to prepare himself for the "good work" of defending the faith.

The apostle Paul warned believers that the real battle is not against "flesh and blood," but against demonic spirit beings who influence the ideas and actions of men (Ephesians 6:10-12). Because of this, Paul commands believers to wear the "full armor of God" (Ephesians 6:10-18). The only offensive weapon in this armor is the "sword of the Spirit, which is the Word of God" (Ephesians 6:17). Just as a Roman soldier had to master his ability to effectively use his sword, believers must master the content of the Bible. Otherwise, Christians will go into battle unarmed.

## SOUND THEOLOGY

The apostle Paul predicted that the time would come when many professing Christians would not "endure sound doctrine" (2 Timothy 4:3). Paul knew that some of these people would rise to positions of leadership in the church and introduce falsehoods into the body of accepted Christian doctrines.

Many Christian apologists of the past limited their effectiveness because their theology was not completely sound (free from errors in important Christian doctrines). C. S. Lewis is an example of this. Though he successfully refuted atheism, he was a theistic evolutionist. He believed that God used evolution to bring about mankind.[1] He denied special creation by God. Though Lewis

did defend miracles in the New Testament, he referred to the Old Testament miracles as "myths."[2]

It is true that Lewis was one of the greatest defenders of the faith in the twentieth century. However, his theology should have been more sound. When one attempts to defend the truth, he must make sure it is the truth that is being defended. Lewis defended the essential Christian beliefs, still he was weak on other important doctrines.

There are nine doctrines that the defender of the faith must adhere to if he is to be sound in his theology. Though a denial of some of these beliefs may not declare the apologist a heretic, it will greatly limit his defense of Christianity.

### THE DOCTRINE OF THE TRINITY

First, *the doctrine of the Trinity* is essential to the apologetic task. The Bible clearly teaches that there is only one God (Isaiah 43:10; 44:6; 46:9; 1 Timothy 2:5). The Father is referred to as God (Galatians 1:1; 1 Peter 1:1). However, the Son (Jesus) and the Holy Spirit are also called God (John 1:1; 5:18; 10:30-33; Titus 2:13; 2 Peter 1:1; Acts 5:3-4; 1 Corinthians 3:16). Because of these passages, some students of the Bible assume that the Father, Son, and Holy Spirit are the same person. However, this is opposed to what the scriptures teach, for the Bible affirms that the Father, Son, and Holy Spirit are three separate persons (Matthew 3:16-17; John 14:16-17, 26; 15:26). When all this biblical data is gathered, the doctrine of the Trinity becomes evident. This doctrine teaches that there is only one true God, and that this one true God eternally exists as three equal Persons (the Father, Son, and Holy Spirit).[3]

Though this doctrine is not self-contradictory, it is above human understanding as to how one being (God) could be three Persons. Still, an illustration may be helpful. A single-celled animal has one cell and is one being. Though a man is also only one being, he has more than ten million cells that comprise his body.[4] If a single-celled animal had understanding, it would probably have difficulty believing that one being (a man) could be more than one cell. This is analogous to man's relationship to God. Since man is only one being and only one person, it transcends his limited understanding as to how God could be only one being, yet three Persons.

Still, the Bible teaches this doctrine, and, as will be shown later, there is much evidence that the Bible is God's inerrant word. Therefore, though it is above human reason, defenders of the faith should humbly accept the doctrine of the Trinity. It is only reasonable that certain aspects of God's nature go beyond human reason. For the unlimited Creator's existence itself transcends the limited existence of His creatures.

## CREATION BY GOD

Second, *creation of the universe and man by God* should be upheld by defenders of the faith. Though theistic evolutionists can be saved and often are, evolution was proposed by scientists in an attempt to explain away any need for God's existence. If it can be shown that God exists, evolution becomes an unnecessary belief system. Also, the supposed evidence for evolution is very unconvincing (as will be shown in a later chapter). In reality, evolution is only one way to interpret the evidence; it is not what the evidence demands.

If an apologist accepts evolution, then many problems arise. For the Bible declares that God formed Adam from the ground (Genesis 2:7). Adam did not, according to the Bible, evolve from apes. Nor did his wife Eve, for the scriptures declare that God formed her from Adam's side (Genesis 2:21-22). Since all mankind came from this couple, there is no room for a theistic-evolutionary interpretation of man's origin. Once must choose between the biblical account of creation or atheistic evolution. They are mutually-exclusive.

Scriptures declare death to be a consequence of the fall (Genesis 2:16-17; Romans 5:12; 6:23), for all that God created was good (Genesis 1:31). The creation was not cursed until after the fall of man (Genesis 3:17-19; Romans 8:18-22). But, if evolution is true, there would be death and suffering before the fall of man. This appears inconsistent with the concept of a perfect creation before the fall. Though defenders of the faith may disagree as to whether the earth is old or young, to accept evolution would be to contradict the Bible's account of both creation and the fall. Therefore, the defender of the faith should reject evolution entirely.

## BIBLICAL INSPIRATION AND INERRANCY

The third belief that the defender of the faith should accept is the doctrine of *biblical inspiration and inerrancy*. The Bible clearly teaches that it itself is the Word of God (2 Timothy 3:16-17). All that God says is true (Proverbs 30:5-6; John 17:17). God guided human authors to record His word without errors. The apostle Peter made it clear that the Bible is not a book that records the mere speculation of men. He stated that, "no prophecy was ever made by an act of human will, but men moved by the Holy Spirit spoke from God" (2 Peter 1:20-21). Jesus taught that not only are the ideas of the Bible inspired, but so are the words themselves (Matthew 5:18). For the apologist to take any lesser view of Scripture would greatly hinder his effectiveness.

## SALVATION BY GOD'S GRACE THROUGH FAITH IN CHRIST ALONE

Fourth, the apologist should accept the doctrine of *salvation by God's grace through faith in Christ alone*. The Bible teaches that salvation cannot be earned. For all men are sinners who cannot save themselves (Romans 3:10, 23; Matthew 19:25-26). Jesus is the only way for man to be saved (John 14:6; Acts 4:12). A person must put his trust in Jesus as Savior if he is to escape the eternal flames of hell (John 3:16-18; 11:25-26; Ephesians 2:8-9; Revelation 20:15). It must also be noted that a person cannot accept God the Father if he rejects God the Son (1 John 2:23; Luke 10:16). There is no such thing as a person who believes in the true God but rejects the true Savior. Though a Christian is not saved by good works, true faith will produce good works in his life (James 2:26; Romans 3:31). This doctrine of salvation by God's grace through faith in Christ alone is essential. One cannot be a true believer if the biblical view of salvation is denied.

### THE VIRGIN BIRTH OF CHRIST

Fifth, the defender of the faith should believe in *the virgin birth of Christ*. Though this is not essential to salvation, those who reject this doctrine usually reject other teachings which are essential (such as the deity of Christ). The Bible teaches that Jesus had no human father. He was born of the virgin Mary through the miraculous work of the Holy Spirit (Isaiah 7:14; Matthew 1:18-25; Luke 1:35). If God managed to create the universe out of nothing, He would have no problem making a baby without the agency of a man. If Jesus had two human parents, His claim to be God would seem questionable, for how would He be different from any other man since each had two parents as well? But if Jesus had one human parent, He would still be fully human (for His human nature would have been inherited from his human parent). And if God was His Father, Jesus could be fully God (He would share the divine nature of His Father). When one denies the virgin birth, the deity of Christ usually falls as well.

### THE DEITY OF CHRIST

Sixth, Christian apologists must accept *the deity of Christ*. This doctrine is essential for salvation. A person cannot be saved while rejecting Christ's deity (John 8:23-24).

There are many Bible passages which teach that Jesus is God. The Old Testament prophets teach that the Jewish Messiah is God (Isaiah 7:14; 9:6; Zechariah 14:5; Micah 5:2), and the New Testament confirms that Jesus is the Jewish Messiah (Mark 14:61-62; John 4:25-26). The apostles Matthew, John, Thomas, Peter, and Paul clearly referred to Jesus as God (Matthew 1:23; John 1:1, 14; 20:26-29; 2 Peter 1:1; Philippians 2:5-6; Colossians 2:9; Titus 2:13). Even God the Father called Jesus God (Hebrews 1:8).

On numerous occasions, Jesus claimed to be God (John 5:17-18; 8:23-24, 58-59; 10:28-33; 14:9). He accepted worship (Matthew 2:11; 28:9, 17; John 9:35-38) and expected the same honor for Himself that was due God the Father (John 5:22-23). He claimed to have shared the Father's glory with Him before the world was created (John 17:5). Jesus forgave sins (Mark 2:5-12) and was crucified for claiming to be

God (Mark 14: 61-64). No true defender of the faith can deny that Jesus is God.

## THE BODILY RESURRECTION OF CHRIST

Seventh, the Christian apologist must believe in *the bodily resurrection of Christ*. Paul states that a person must believe that

Jesus rose from the dead if he is to be saved (Romans 10:9). Paul included Christ's resurrection as an essential component of the gospel he preached (1 Corinthians 15:1-4). Though many cultists deny that Christ rose bodily from the dead, the Jewish concept of resurrection always entailed a raising of the same body that had previously died.[5] Since the Christian concept of resurrection was derived from Jewish thought, this argues strongly for Christ's bodily resurrection.

New Testament evidence for Christ's bodily resurrection is abundant. Jesus appeared numerous times to witnesses after His death and resurrection (1 Corinthians 15:3-8). Jesus gave these witnesses convincing evidences that He had risen in the same body in which He had died (John 20:24-29; Luke 24:36-43). In fact, at an earlier time, He had predicted He would raise His own body from the dead (John 2:19-21).

Though He was raised in the same body in which He had died, this body was glorified and received powers it had not previously possessed (1 Corinthians 15:35-54). The apostle Paul stressed the importance of the resurrection by declaring that if Jesus had not risen from the dead, then faith in Him and preaching the gospel is worthless. If Jesus did not rise, then Christians will die in their sins (1 Corinthians 15:14, 17).

## THE BODILY AND VISIBLE RETURN OF CHRIST

Eighth, the defender of the faith should accept *the bodily and visible return of Christ*. The Bible is very clear that Jesus will someday return to the planet earth (Matthew 24:29-31; John 14:2-3). Christ's return will be visible (Revelation 1:7) and bodily (Acts 1:10-11; Zechariah 12:10). Jesus will return to gather believers (John 14:1-3; 1 Thessalonians 4:13-18) and to judge nonbelievers (Revelation 19:11-21; 2 Thessalonians 1:6-10). Jesus will bring the Kingdom of God to earth (Revelation 11:15).

The bodily and visible return of Christ to earth is important for two reasons. First, it is the blessed hope of the church (Titus 2:13). Christian apologists must continue to remind believers that our hope is not founded in the things of this world. Second, Peter predicted that in the last days mockers would come denying Christ's return (2 Peter 3:3-4). These mockers must be confronted; their false teachings must be refuted.

## THE SUBSTITUTIONARY DEATH OF CHRIST

Ninth, the Christian apologist must hold to *the substitutionary death of Christ*. This is an essential Christian belief. To deny it is to deny the faith. Jesus did not die on the cross to merely set an example for others or to encourage others to live moral lives. The significance of His death goes far beyond this. Jesus died on the cross for the sins of mankind (Matthew 1:21; John 1:29; 2 Corinthians 5:21). He took the punishment that man deserves (1 Peter 2:24; 3:18). Since God is totally just, He can only forgive sin if it has been paid for in full. Jesus, through His death on the cross, paid the price for the sins of mankind (Mark 10:45; 2 Peter 2:1). He took the penalty man deserves; He substituted Himself for man. Because of Jesus, those who put their faith in Him are no longer under the judgment of God (1 Corinthians 5:7).

If a defender of the faith denies any of these nine doctrines, it will greatly reduce his effectiveness. Indeed, some of these doctrines (the Trinity, salvation by grace through faith in Christ, the deity and bodily resurrection of Christ, and His substitutionary death) are essential to orthodox Christianity. A denial of any of these teachings would place a person outside true biblical Christianity. Without a sound theology, no one should begin the apologetic task.

TABLE 3

SOUND THEOLOGY

1) The Trinity

2) Creation of the Universe and Man by God

3) Biblical Inspiration and Inerrancy

4) Salvation by Grace through Faith in Christ Alone

5) The Virgin Birth of Christ

6) The Deity of Christ

7) The Bodily Resurrection of Christ

8) The Bodily, Visible Return of Christ

9) The Substitutionary Death of Christ

## KNOWLEDGE OF ANTI-CHRISTIAN THOUGHT

To be effective in apologetics, one must know anti-Christian thought. The Christian apologist must not only know how to defend the truth, he must also be able to refute error. Effective apologists will often be called upon to refute evolution or other arguments against God's existence. However, before one can refute the arguments of another, one must know what those arguments are. Real communication cannot take place if the apologist does not understand the other person's world view.

This point is especially important when dealing with non-Christian cults (heretical offshoots of Christianity). These cults often redefine common Christian terms in such a way that an intelligent exchange of ideas is impossible until the apologist learns the cultist's meanings of the terms.

The apostle Paul commanded believers to use wisdom when dealing with the unsaved. He stated that the believer should know how to respond to the objections raised against the gospel by nonbelievers (Colossians 4:5-6). Paul was himself very knowledgeable of Greek philosophy and displayed this when preaching to Greek philosophers on Mars Hill (Acts 17:16-34). He quoted from some of the ancient writings of Greek poets (Acts 17:28). Therefore, like Paul, defenders of the faith should have a strong knowledge of anti-Christian thought.

GENUINE LOVE

Finally, all defenders of the faith should have genuine love for the unsaved. Jesus commands His followers to love their neighbors as themselves (Mark 12:31). He also commands Christians to love their enemies (Matthew 5:43-48). The apostle Paul commands believers to speak the truth in love (Ephesians 4:15). The apologetic task should never be practiced for the purpose of bringing attention to the apologist's intelligence. It should only be practiced out of love for the lost.

God desires all men to be saved (2 Peter 3:9; 1 Timothy 2:1-6). God loves all mankind (John 3:16; Romans 5:8). Therefore, defenders of the faith should also love all men and seek their salvation. Jesus has died for all mankind (1 John 2:2; 2 Corinthians 5:15). Therefore, it is the responsibility of the church to share the gospel message with all mankind (Matthew 28:19-20). And, when necessary, Christians must defend the faith. Still, love must be the primary motivation. Without a genuine love for people, one should not engage in the apologetic task.

The apostle Paul said it best:

> If I speak with the tongues of men and of angels, but do not have love, I have become a noisy gong or a clanging cymbal. And if I have the gift of prophecy, and know all mysteries and all knowledge; and if I have all faith, so as to remove mountains, but do not have love, I am nothing. And if I give all my possessions to feed the poor, and if I deliver my body to be burned, but do not have love, it profits me nothing (1 Corinthians 13:1-3).

CONCLUSION

In short, an effective defender of the faith must 1) be born again, 2) be grounded in God's Word, 3) have a sound theology, 4) know the philosophical thought of anti-Christian thinkers, and 5) genuinely love the lost and seek their salvation. Only with this fivefold foundation can a person begin the apologetic task.

TABLE 4

Our apologetics must be built upon the proper foundation:

*APOLOGETICS*

*GENUINE LOVE*

*KNOW ANTI-CHRISTIAN THOUGHT*

*SOUND THEOLOGY*

*REGENERATION*

ENDNOTES

1C. S. Lewis, *Mere Christianity* (New York: Collier Books, 1952), 65.

2C. S. Lewis, *Miracles* (New York: Collier Books, 1960), 134.

3Charles C. Ryrie, *The Ryrie Study Bible* (Chicago: Moody Press, 1978), 1936. For a more in-depth discussion of the doctrine of the Trinity see Millard J. Erickson, *God in Three Persons* (Grand Rapids: Baker Book House, 1995).

4*The World Book Encyclopedia* (Chicago: World Book, Inc., 1985), vol. 3, "Cell" by Irwin Rubenstein.

5Merrill C. Tenney, ed. *The Zondervan Pictorial Bible Dictionary* (Grand Rapids: Zondervan Publishing House, 1967), 713, "Resurrection" by James Oliver Buswell, Jr.

# CHAPTER 6
# FIDEISM:
# THE ENEMY OF APOLOGETICS

Fideism is the belief that religious faith cannot be defended through the use of philosophical, historical, or scientific evidences. Religious faith is viewed as a leap of faith into the non-rational realm. One makes an ultimate commitment apart from any evidence. Objective truths are not considered as important as a person's subjective beliefs. Religious truth is viewed as personal, not propositional.[1]

Obviously, fideism is the antithesis of apologetics. Apologetics is the defense of the Christian faith; fideism claims that the Christian faith cannot be defended. It can only be believed. For this reason, fideism is the enemy of apologetics. They cannot both be true. In this chapter, the views of several men whose ideas are associated with fideism will be discussed. This chapter will close with a critique of the fideist position.

## TERTULLIAN
Though Tertullian, a second century Christian thinker, was a great defender of the faith, he has often been mistaken for a fideist. Tertullian stated, "I believe because it is absurd."[2] However, Norman Geisler and Paul Feinberg point out that Tertullian was not saying that he held to the idea that contradictions are true. Rather, he merely meant that he accepted the gospel as true even though the world

considered it foolishness.[3] In other words, Tertullian was merely echoing the teachings of the apostle Paul (1 Corinthians 1:18-31).

Tertullian also stated, "What indeed has Athens to do with Jerusalem?"[4] Obviously, he was contrasting Greek philosophy and Christian theology. Still, he was probably not opposed to all philosophy, since he often used reason to defend the faith. Tertullian was simply opposed to all anti-Christian philosophy. He refused to judge the gospel by human reason. Rather, he judged the reason of men by God's revelation in the Bible. Still, this did not make him a fideist. He believed that the truth of Christianity had been proven by the blood shed by Christian martyrs.[5] In other words, he accepted the evidence of eyewitness testimonies as establishing the truth of the Christian revelation. That being proven, he then judged the philosophies of men by God's wisdom.

Hence, Tertullian was not a fideist. Still, he is often quoted out of context to promote fideism. For that reason, he has been discussed here.

### BLAISE PASCAL

Blaise Pascal (1623-1662) was not a complete fideist. He argued for the truth of the Christian faith, something a fideist would not do. However, it is the way that Pascal defended the faith that moved him closer to fideism. This was due to the fact that he criticized rationalism to the point that he questioned the reliability of man's reasoning processes—at the very least, he stressed the limitations and fallibility of human reason. In Pascal's thinking, to a certain degree, man must submit his reason to his will.[6] The mind must bow to the heart.

Pascal did not consider Christianity to be against reason. He merely emphasized the point that God cannot be found through human reason alone.[7] It was here that Pascal developed his famous "wager argument" for God's existence. Pascal considered the rational evidence for or against God's existence to be even. Reason cannot decide. One must choose with one's will whether or not to believe that God exists since the odds are even. The mind must give way to the will. Each person must decide to choose or not to choose God. Pascal pleads with his readers to choose God. If his readers choose God and He does not really exist, they will have lost nothing. But, if his readers choose God and He does exist, they gain eternal life. On the other hand, if his readers wager against God and win, they win nothing, but if they lose, they lose everything.[8]

Though many have found this argument convincing, it has opened the door to fideism. For Pascal declared that man must test truth with his heart, not merely with his mind.[9] Future believers went far beyond what Pascal proposed. Subjective beliefs were beginning to surpass objective truth in importance in the history of philosophical thought.

## GOTTHOLD EPHRAIM LESSING

Gotthold Ephraim Lessing (1729-1781) was a critic of the Bible who denied biblical inerrancy. He taught that religious beliefs could not be proven through reason or historical evidences.[10] He was a fideist in the truest sense. He held that faith rested on subjective experience rather than on objective evidence. He believed that religions should be judged by their effect on the moral conduct of its followers.[11] Evidence for or against religious truth claims were irrelevant.

Lessing imagined an "ugly ditch" between faith and historical facts.[12] This ditch could not be crossed. No one can know for sure if the Jesus of the gospels is in fact the true Jesus of history. Religious beliefs could not be defended by appealing to objective facts. Only practical results could be used to determine the worth of a religious system. Testing religious truths is a subjective, inward task. Any appeal to objective evidence is futile.

## SOREN KIERKEGAARD

Soren Kierkegaard (1813-1855), the famous Danish philosopher, is known as the "father of modern existentialism." Kierkegaard believed that there were three stages of life: the aesthetic, the ethical, and the religious.[13] Each stage is separated by a feeling of despair. Also, each stage can only be crossed by a leap of faith.[14]

A person lives in the aesthetic stage when he exists for his own pleasure. In this stage, the person is *self-centered*. Through a leap of faith, a person can enter into the ethical stage. Here, duty comes first. This person is *law-centered*. But when the overwhelming feeling of despair and futility comes, the person can, through another leap of faith, arrive at the religious stage. In this stage, the person is *God-*

*centered.*[15] Kierkegaard believed religious truth is personal and subjective, not propositional and objective. He felt that subjective truth is of greater importance than objective truth. To leap into the religious stage, one must leave the realm of reason. Kierkegaard is not saying that religious faith is irrational. He merely means that it is nonrational. Reason does not apply. It is an act of the will that is necessary. A leap of blind faith (apart from reason) is needed to accept religious truth.

For Kierkegaard, God's existence cannot be proven.[16] Religious faith comes from the heart, not the mind. An act of the will is needed, not an act of the intellect. Since religious truth is subjective and personal, there is no test for truth which can be applied.[17]

## KARL BARTH

Karl Barth (1886-1968) rebelled against liberal theology and started neo-orthodoxy. He rejected the liberal view that man was basically good.[18] Barth, though accepting a critical view of the Bible, recognized that man is limited and sinful. He taught that God is "wholly other" than man. He considered the Bible a human book which contains errors. However, it becomes revelation from God to the individual in the moment of crisis. This crisis is the crisis of faith. It is that moment when a person recognizes God's condemnation of all human effort and that deliverance comes only through God. At this moment, the Holy Spirit uses the Bible as His instrument to bring about a personal encounter between the individual and God. During this encounter, no communication of information takes place. In Barth's eyes, revelation is personal encounter with God, not the making known of information.[19]

Barth taught that sin blinds man from finding the truth. Only the Holy Spirit can open man's spiritual eyes so that he can see God. The divine-human encounter is purely a subjective experience.[20] In this encounter, man encounters God. However, man does not encounter any objective truths about Him.[21]

In Barth's thought, man is incapable of receiving any revelation from God through nature.[22] Man's spiritual blindness can only be removed by a contact sovereignly initiated by the Holy Spirit.[23] Obviously, Barth is opposed to apologetics. There is no need to defend the divine-human encounter since it cannot even be expressed. There is also no need to defend the Bible since it is a human book with errors. Therefore, for Barth and all other fideists, Christianity is to be accepted by faith. It should not be defended.

CONCLUSION

In chapter two of this work, apologetics was shown to be biblically based. First, it was concluded that the Bible commands believers to do apologetics (1 Peter 3:15; Colossians 4:5-6; Titus 1:7-9; Jude 3). Second, the Scriptures speak of God revealing Himself in nature (Psalm 19:1; 94:9; Romans 1:18-22; 2:14-15). Third, God's Word speaks of historical evidences for the Christian faith (1 Corinthians 15:3-8). And, fourth, the early church defended the faith. Examples were given: Peter, John, Luke, Paul, and Apollos. In short, by showing that apologetics is biblically based, fideism has been proven unscriptural.

Still, there is a lesson one can learn from fideists. Though Thomas Aquinas was one of the greatest defenders of the faith, his thought was often misinterpreted as equating faith with intellectual assent to doctrines that could not be proven by reason.[24] This misinterpretation of Aquinas placed faith into the head with reason, rather than in the heart. The biblical concept of faith as a personal trust in Christ for salvation was lost. In reality, Aquinas taught that there was a clear distinction between "faith that" (intellectual assent) and "faith in" (personal trust in Christ). Still, even though misunderstanding of Aquinas' thought prevailed, the fideists must be credited for reemphasizing the aspect of personal commitment and trust. However, in the process, they have de-emphasized reason. Though a personal relationship with Jesus must be stressed, before one can believe *in* the Jesus of the Bible, one must believe the facts *about* Him. Revelation without content is no revelation at all.

If one's apologetics is to be biblical, one must learn this lesson from the fideists. The defense of the faith can lead a person to give intellectual assent to the facts of the gospel. Still, the person must *choose*, by an act of his or her *will*, to personally appropriate the truths of the gospel. Mere head knowledge will save no one. A decision of the heart is needed. Though belief in the claims of Christ is necessary for salvation, one must still personally trust in Christ to be saved. One must never turn the gospel into a mere creed by removing the personal, experiential aspects of Christianity. Even so, the fideist has faltered on the other extreme by removing the intellectual content from the gospel. When this has been done, there is no gospel left at all. Gospel means *good news*. There can be no gospel if there is no *news*.

The Christian faith contains both objective and subjective elements. Effective defenders of the faith will proclaim both. To neglect one at the expense of the other is to move away from historical Christianity.

## ENDNOTES

1Geisler, *Apologetics*, 58-59.

2Ibid., 47.

3Geisler and Feinberg, *Introduction to Philosophy*, 262.

4Geisler, *Apologetics*, 47.

5Dowley, ed., *The History of Christianity*, 112.

6Geisler, *Apologetics*, 48.

7Ibid.

8Ibid., 49.

9Ibid., 50.

10Frederick Copleston, *A History of Philosophy* (New York: Doubleday, 1960), book 2, vol. 6, 126-131.

11Ibid.

12Millard J. Erickson, *The Word Became Flesh* (Grand Rapids: Baker Book House, 1991), 115.

13Sahakian, 343.

14Geisler, *Apologetics*, 50.

15Ibid.

16Ibid., 52-53.

17Ibid., 53.

18Cairns, 445.

19Ibid.

20Ibid.

21Geisler, *Apologetics*, 53-56.

22Ibid, 55.

23Ibid.

24Craig, *Apologetics An Introduction*, 9-10.

# CHAPTER 7
# APOLOGETICS: ITS WIDER SCOPE

Many defenders of the faith fail to see apologetics in its wider scope. They often focus only on one apologetic methodology, neglecting the other methodologies. Though choosing to specialize in only one type of apologetics is often admirable, ignorance of the contributions of the other methodologies is unfortunate.

In this chapter, an attempt will be made to examine the entire spectrum of the apologetic discipline. There are basically eight distinct apologetic methodologies. They are 1) testimonial apologetics, 2) presuppositional apologetics, 3) psychological apologetics, 4) philosophical apologetics, 5) historical apologetics, 6) scientific apologetics, 7) comparative religious apologetics, and 8) cultural apologetics.

## TESTIMONIAL APOLOGETICS
Testimonial apologetics is used when a person defends the faith by appealing to evidence from either his own testimony or that of another person. Testimonial apologetics contends for the truth of Christianity by employing evidences from transformed lives and/or divine intervention in one's life.

Evidence from transformed lives deals with providing to others the information about how Jesus has changed the lives of those who have trusted in Him for salvation. Divine intervention pertains to documenting how God has intervened in the lives of people. Examples of divine intervention would include answers to prayer and genuine episodes of miraculous healing. Regardless of what position a person takes in reference to the continuance or cessation of the spiritual gifts of healings, most Christians would agree that God does at times still heal in answer to prayer.

Many people who consider themselves opposed to the practice of apologetics unknowingly use testimonial apologetics. When they evangelize others, resistance to the gospel is often countered by utilizing testimonial apologetics. The use of testimonial evidences is as much a part of apologetics as any other evidences.

## PRESUPPOSITIONAL APOLOGETICS

Presuppositional apologetics denies the validity of all other apologetic approaches. This technique for defending the faith teaches that a believer must assume or presuppose the truth claims of Christianity rather than argue for them. On this point presuppositional apologetics is in agreement with fideism. However, presuppositionalists specialize in tearing down anti-Christian belief systems, something true fideists do not do. The presuppositional methodology is vital to the apologetic task. Still, presuppositionalists need to appreciate the other forms of apologetic argumentation. Presuppositional apologetics is an effective way to defend the faith, but it is not the only way.

## PSYCHOLOGICAL APOLOGETICS

Psychological apologetics focuses on man's psychological need for the God of the Bible. This approach appeals more to the will and the emotions of the person than to his or her intellect. This methodology deals with issues such as the meaningless of life without God. It attempts to explain the dilemma of man (man is both great and cruel). Psychological apologetics targets the thirst within man to transcend his present earthly experience.

This seldom-used approach can be very effective when dealing with modern man. Today's secular thinkers have generally lost confidence in the power of human reason to find ultimate truth. Yet, modern man has not been able to quench his thirst for meaning. It is here that Christianity has much to offer. For, the gospel makes sense of life and gives meaning to human existence. Without the God of the Bible, mankind is without any real purpose. However, if one assumes the existence of the God of the Bible, then man has eternal significance. What one does or does not do in this life really does matter. Only Christianity can quench modern man's thirst for transcendence.

## PHILOSOPHICAL APOLOGETICS

Philosophical apologetics provides rational argumentation for the truth of Christianity. This methodology has been extremely effective in the past. It can also be very successful today among those who have not lost faith in man's reasoning ability to find answers of ultimate importance.

Philosophical apologetics serves several purposes. It can be utilized in refuting atheism and other anti-Christian world views, providing evidence for God's existence, proposing solutions to the problem of evil, and establishing the possibility of miracles. Philosophical apologists also argue for the existence of universal moral laws.

Those defenders of the faith who use this apologetic methodology often use both the reasoning processes of the mind and the facts of experience to prove the case for Christianity. Philosophical apologists, when they have completed their task, often move on to historical apologetics.

## HISTORICAL APOLOGETICS

Historical apologetics provides evidence for the historical claims of the Christian Faith. Evidence is provided for the historical reliability and authenticity of the New Testament manuscripts, Christ's resurrection and deity, and the inspiration and inerrancy of the Bible.

Christianity is a religion that makes historical truth claims. The truth of Christianity depends on the reality of these assertions. Therefore, it is essential that evidences from history be used to establish the veracity of these claims.

## SCIENTIFIC APOLOGETICS

Scientific apologetics provides modern scientific evidence that confirms certain truths of Christianity. This method of defending the faith also exposes the weaknesses of the evolutionary model. The Big Bang model, the expansion of the universe, and the second law of thermodynamics (energy deterioration) are often employed to establish the case for the beginning of the universe and its need for a supernatural Cause. The highly complex information found in even the most simple life forms is used to prove that the supernatural Cause of the universe must possess intelligence.

## COMPARATIVE RELIGIOUS APOLOGETICS

Comparative religious apologetics specializes in the investigation of opposing religions and cults. Evidence is provided to demonstrate that these other belief systems contradict Christianity on essential issues. The comparative religious apologist will attempt to establish both the truth of Christianity and the falsehood of any non-Christian faiths. Often, the refutation will be based upon an appeal to biblical data. Still, philosophical, historical, or scientific evidences are at times called upon to disprove these false belief systems.

## CULTURAL APOLOGETICS

Finally, cultural apologetics attempts to prove the superiority of the Christian world view by pointing out the positive consequences of applying Christian principles to a society, as well as the negative consequences of either rejecting the Christian world view or accepting other belief systems. The impact of different religions (including Christianity) on governments and societies will be examined. I will also argue that the rejection of God by Western Civilization will lead to devastating consequences for the West, and that, apart from repentance, Western Civilization will crumble. The cultural apologetics of Christian thinkers C. S. Lewis and Francis Schaeffer will be discussed.

## CONCLUSION

Defenders of the faith often suffer from one of two common misconceptions. First, many Christians verbally oppose the entire field of apologetics. However, unknown to themselves, they often do this while making use of one of the lesser known apologetic approaches (usually testimonial, presuppositional, or psychological).

Second, many apologists refuse to acknowledge a methodology other than the one they choose to employ. It has rightfully been said that "all truth is God's truth." Therefore, evidences for the Christian faith should not be limited to one area of knowledge. Apologetics can draw from the wealth of information in many different fields (philosophy, history, science, psychology, etc.). Apologists from each methodology should respect the efforts of other defenders using different approaches. Christians can never succeed in the apologetic task by arguing among themselves. Many philosophical apologists (i.e., Geisler, Moreland, Craig, etc.) also utilize historical and scientific evidences. This combinational methodology is a healthy approach for the apologist to take.

TABLE FIVE

CHRISTIAN APOLOGETICS

(8 methodologies)

*TESTIMONIAL APOLOGETICS*

*PRESUPPOSITIONAL APOLOGETICS*

*PSYCHOLOGICAL APOLOGETICS*

*PHILOSOPHICAL APOLOGETICS*

*HISTORICAL APOLOGETICS*

*SCIENTIFIC APOLOGETICS*

*COMPARATIVE RELIGIOUS APOLOGETICS*

*CULTURAL APOLOGETICS*

# PART TWO

# TESTIMONIAL APOLOGETICS

# CHAPTER 8
# TRANSFORMED LIVES

As stated earlier, many Christians who consider themselves opposed to apologetics actually defend the faith by sharing their testimonies. Testimonial apologetics is a type of pragmatic argument for the Christian Faith. It provides evidence to show that Christianity works; it changes lives.

Alone, the testimony of transformed lives does not provide an adequate defense of the gospel, for there are those who claim that another religion has changed their lives for the better. Therefore, it is better to argue for Christianity through other means first, and then use testimonial apologetics to strengthen one's case.

Still, there are people who do not need intellectual arguments to come to Christ. Instead, they are more likely to come to Christ through hearing how Jesus has changed another person's life for the better. They long to have their lives changed as well, and they find through another person's testimony that Christ can do this for them.

In this chapter, the evidence of how Jesus Christ changes lives will be examined. If Jesus is truly alive today, then He is still in the business of changing lives. In the next chapter, divine intervention (the other aspect of testimonial apologetics) will be discussed.

When using evidence from changed lives, three things should be noted. First, there must be *thorough transformation*. The changes in the life of the person using testimonial apologetics must be so thorough that it could not have been produced through human will power alone. If a person quit smoking cigarettes due to accepting

Christ, this is not enough. Many non-Christians have given up smoking without conversion. Evidence from other areas of the Christian's life must be shared as well.

Second, there must be *genuine transformation*. Often, a person's testimony is later discovered to be filled with lies and exaggerations. This can only push people further away from Christ.

Third, there must be *permanent transformation*. Too often new converts are called upon to publicly share their testimonies. Then, a short time later, these supposed converts are once again practicing their old lifestyles. A sufficient amount of time is needed to assure others that the changes are of a permanent nature.

BIBLICAL SUPPORT

The Bible supports the practice of testimonial apologetics. First, it teaches that Jesus changes the lifestyles of those He saves. James tells us that "faith without works is dead" (James 2:26). Thus, true saving faith will produce good works in the life of a believer. After listing many sins of the unrighteous, the apostle Paul states, "And such were some of you; but you were washed, but you were sanctified, but you were justified in the name of the Lord Jesus Christ, and in the Spirit of our God" (1 Corinthians 6:11). Paul also taught that "we are His workmanship, created in Christ Jesus for good works" (Ephesians 2:10). Jesus declared that "not everyone who says to Me, 'Lord, Lord,' will enter the Kingdom of heaven; but he who does the will of My Father who is in heaven" (Matthew 7:21).

Second, the Bible records the apostle Paul sharing his testimony on two separate occasions to provide evidence for the truth of Christianity (Acts 22:1-21; 26:1-23). Therefore, testimonial apologetics should not be ignored when discussing ways to defend the faith. Still, it must be remembered that it is not the only way to provide evidence for the faith.

The remainder of this chapter will provide several brief examples of lives that had been transformed by Jesus Christ. First, the lives of two apostles will be discussed. Then the lives of other Christians will also be examined.

## THE APOSTLE PETER

This Jewish fisherman had sat under the teachings of Jesus for over three years. Still, when Christ was arrested, he became fearful and three times denied knowing Christ (Matthew 26:69-75).

After Jesus rose from the dead, Peter confessed his love for Jesus three times (John 21:15-17). Just before He ascended to heaven, Jesus promised to send the Holy Spirit to empower Peter and the other apostles (Acts 1:8-9). The Holy Spirit came upon Peter, the apostles, and the rest of the church ten days later (Acts 2:1-4). Filled with the power of the indwelling Holy Spirit, Peter boldly proclaimed Christ's salvation message despite opposition from the Jewish religious leaders. No longer was he overcome with fear. Three thousand people accepted Christ as their Savior due to Peter's first message (Acts 2:14-42).

The courage that Peter had in that day, due to the transforming work of Christ, continued to be evident throughout his life. This apostle suffered great persecution for the Christian faith (Acts 4:1-3; 5:40-42). Eventually, Peter was martyred for preaching the gospel. He was crucified (possibly upside down).[1]

## THE APOSTLE PAUL

Paul was schooled in the Old Testament from his youth. At a young age he became a Pharisee, a Jewish religious leader specializing in teaching the Old Testament (Philippians 3:4-6). His greatest desire was to serve the God of Israel. However, he mistook Jesus of Nazareth for an impostor and a false messiah. Therefore, he dedicated his energies to persecuting the church which he thought to be heretical.

When Paul was on the road to Damascus (attempting to persecute more Christians), he encountered the risen Christ. Falling to the ground and blinded by the light of Christ's glory, he realized that Jesus was who He claimed to be...the Jewish Messiah and Savior of the world. Christ then commissioned Paul to be the apostle to the gentiles (Acts 9:1-22; 22:3-16; 26:9-18).

From that day forth, Paul, who had previously led the persecution against the church, became the greatest missionary of the early church. Despite the horrible persecution he was to suffer, he managed to spread the gospel of Jesus Christ throughout the Roman Empire. He was stoned, scourged, shipwrecked, beaten, and mocked (2 Corinthians 11:24-33). But nothing could deter him from his mission. His life was totally devoted to the one he had met on the road to Damascus.

This persecutor of the church had been transformed into one of the church's greatest assets. He loved his Messiah and faithfully served Him until death. He was beheaded for sharing the gospel sometime after 65AD.[2]

### AUGUSTINE

Saint Augustine (354-430AD) spent his early life seeking to find fulfillment in sexual immorality. Finding no true joy there, he accepted the Manichean teaching (matter is evil and co-eternal with God), but later found this inadequate. He then began to despair. How could evil exist if all that God created is good? He doubted that he would ever find ultimate truth. All during this time, his Christian mother prayed for his salvation.[3]

Eventually, he was exposed to the teachings of Ambrose, a Christian philosopher. Ambrose taught that evil exists only as a corruption or perversion of God's perfect creation.[4] This and other teachings of Ambrose answered much of the philosophical doubt that Augustine had in regards to the Christian Faith. In 386AD, while in a garden meditating on his spiritual thirst for God, Augustine heard a neighbor's voice stating, "Take up and read." Augustine, taking this to be a sign from God, opened his Bible to Romans 13:13-14 and began to read. This passage commands one to depart from sexual immorality and to appropriate the work of Jesus Christ to one's life. Augustine immediately broke off his immoral relationship with a woman and became a Christian.[5]

Augustine became one of the greatest scholars of church history. His many writings are still widely read by Catholics and Protestants alike. This great thinker's quest for truth led him to accept Jesus Christ as his Savior. His life of sexual immorality was replaced by a life of holiness.

## JOHN NEWTON

John Newton (1725-1807) sought lustful pleasures throughout his early life. He was also a man of extreme violence and was a ruthless slave-trader. However, this man who victimized men and women himself became a victim. His life collapsed as he himself was sold into slavery. In the midst of his despair he called out to Jesus for salvation. Once saved, his life was totally transformed. After his conversion, he was ordained to the ministry.

Today, we do not remember John Newton as one of the vilest men who ever lived. Instead, we remember him as the man who penned the words, "Amazing grace, how sweet the sound that saved a wretch like me. I once was lost, but now am found; was blind, but now I see."[6]

## NICKY CRUZ

Nicky Cruz grew up on the streets of New York. He was the leader of a gang called the Mau Maus. His life was filled with violence. He trusted in his own strength to solve his problems. But when a persistent preacher proclaimed the gospel message in his presence, the heart of this street warrior began to melt. He accepted Christ as his Savior, and his life has never been the same.

Now he speaks publicly throughout America, leading many city youths to faith in Christ. Because of Cruz's testimony, hundreds of youths have been directed off the path of destruction that he once traveled.[7]

## CHUCK COLSON

Chuck Colson was one of the most powerful men in America.

He was one of the top political figures in the country. He worked directly under the leadership of President Richard Nixon. But the Watergate Scandal brought down the kingdom Chuck Colson had built. Soon, he was just another inmate in just another prison. However, this man was set free from the spiritual imprisonment of his soul. As he read a book written by the Christian apologist C. S. Lewis, he came to know Jesus Christ as his Savior.

Chuck Colson no longer seeks power over other men. Currently, he not only spreads the gospel, but also leads the fight for prison reform throughout the world.[8]

## FRANK MORISON

Frank Morison was a journalist who set out to disprove Christ's resurrection. He proceeded to research the historical evidence in great detail. But, having examined the evidence, the skeptic was alarmed with his own conclusion: Christ had actually risen from the dead! Though reluctant at first, he decided to accept the evidence. He accepted Christ as his Savior and is now a defender of the gospel he once tried to destroy.[9]

## CONCLUSION

These are just a few examples of how Jesus Christ has transformed lives throughout history. Many others could be given. These testimonies speak loudly of Christ's ability to make good come out of the worst of situations. Jesus is alive, He saves, and He is still in the business of changing lives.

Paul E. Little speaks of the transforming power of Christ:

> The late Harry Ironside was preaching, some years ago, when a heckler shouted, "Atheism has done more for the world than Christianity!" "Very well," said Ironside, "tomorrow night you bring a hundred men whose lives have been changed for the better by atheism, and I'll bring a hundred who have been transformed by Christ." Needless to say, his heckler friend did not appear the next night.[10]

Although many people claim that only ignorant people become Christians, this is not the case. People from different walks of life have become Christians. They have had different levels of education. Some have been poor; some have been rich. Some were successful; others were failures. Some Christian apologists have even suggested that there is more evidence for atheists fitting into a tightly defined group than there is for Christians.[11] Many leading atheists throughout history have had either absent or passive fathers.[12] It can be argued that atheists deny God's existence because of their desire to kill the father image.[13]

It seems that a merely psychological explanation for a conversion to Christianity is unacceptable. The transformed lives of Christians who have come from many different backgrounds provide strong confirmation for the life-changing power of Jesus Christ.

ENDNOTES

1Carsten P. Thiede, *Simon Peter* (Grand Rapids: Zondervan Publishing House, 1988), 190.

2F. F. Bruce, *Paul Apostle of the Heart Set Free* (Grand Rapids: William B. Eerdmans Publishing Company, 1977), 450.

3Cairns, 146.

4Dowley, 206-207.

5Cairns, 146.

6Ibid., 396.

7Nicky Cruz, *Run Baby Run* (Plainfield: Logos Books, 1968), entire book.

8Shirl Short, "Exclusive Interview with Chuck Colson." *Moody Monthly* (Chicago: Moody Bible Institute, Feb., 1976).

9Frank Morison, *Who Moved the Stone?* (London: Faber and Faber, 1958), entire book.

10Paul E. Little, *Know Why You Believe* (Wheaton: Victor Books, 1967), 145-146.

11Moreland, *Scaling the Secular City*, 229.

12Ibid.

13Ibid.

# CHAPTER 9
# DIVINE INTERVENTION

Testimonial apologetics deals not only with evidence from transformed lives. It also appeals to evidence from cases of divine intervention. These are circumstances in which God intervenes, either directly or indirectly, in the daily affairs of people. This divine intervention can take many different forms. Healings and answers to prayer are two well-known types of divine intervention. Divine intervention can be a *miracle* or an act of *special providence*. A miracle is when God supersedes the laws of nature (the regular and usual way the world operates) by directly intervening in the affairs of mankind. An act of special providence is when God works through natural laws to bring about His will. God here indirectly intervenes.[1]

The debate concerning whether or not certain spiritual gifts (tongues, prophecy, miracles, healing, etc.) have ceased is irrelevant for our present purposes. Those who believe that miracles no longer occur still believe that God may heal someone or answer a prayer through special providence.

EVIDENCE FROM MIRACLES

The Bible is filled with eyewitness accounts of miracles. These miracles could not be explained away. Unlike many current reports of supposed miracles, the miracles in the Bible were verifiable and could not be explained by other means. Two examples will suffice.

In the ninth chapter of his gospel, the apostle John records the healing of a man born blind. After Jesus healed this man, the

Pharisees decided to thoroughly investigate this miracle claim. They questioned the blind man who had his sight restored. Even after talking with him, they were not convinced. They therefore interrogated his parents who confirmed that he had been born blind. Even though the Pharisees were the enemies of Christ, they could not deny that a supernatural event had occurred. Instead, though admitting the healing was genuine, they accused Christ of breaking the Sabbath (the healing took place on a Sabbath day). The point is that the miracle could be verified through investigation. It could not be explained by natural causes alone. The healed man used this miraculous work of Christ to testify to Christ's own enemies concerning the power of Jesus. He witnessed that Jesus must be from God (John 9:30-33).

In the eleventh chapter of John's gospel, another miracle of Christ is discussed. Here, Jesus raised Lazarus from the dead. Lazarus had been dead for four days. Eyewitnesses at his funeral and the stench of his body could attest to this fact. At Jesus' command, Lazarus rose from the dead and came out of the tomb (John 11:43-44). Because of this great miracle, many people believed in Jesus (John 11:45; 12:17-19). The Jewish religious leaders again could not deny or refute the miracle. Therefore, being envious of Christ, they sought to kill both Jesus and Lazarus (John 11:53; 12:10-11).

Many miracle claims made today would not pass the close scrutiny that these two examples were put through. No one can adequately explain away the restoring of sight to a man born blind. Nor could the raising of a man who was dead for a period of four days be viewed as a natural event. If present-day miracle claims are used as evidence for the Christian faith, they should be well documented. Written statements of eyewitnesses should be used to confirm the truth of the miracle in question. If a healing has occurred, it should be documented with statements from the doctors involved. Evidence must be produced to prove both the initial sickness (blindness, deafness, etc.) and the subsequent healing.

## EVIDENCE FROM SPECIAL PROVIDENCE

As mentioned above, cases of special providence do not supersede the laws of nature. Instead, God works through the laws of nature to bring about a result that He desires. An example of special providence is given in the sixteenth chapter of Acts. Paul and Silas had been arrested in Philippi for doing God's work. At midnight, while they sang hymns of praises to God, a great earthquake occurred which freed the prisoners (Acts 16:23-26). Though the prisoners chose not to escape, the event was used by Paul to lead the Philippian jailer to Christ (Acts 16:27-34).

In this case, the earthquake could be explained by the laws of nature alone. However, it stretches the imagination to claim that the loosing of Paul and Silas was merely a coincidence. God had obviously intervened. However, He had chosen to use the laws of nature rather than supersede them.

When documenting episodes of special providence, emphasis should be placed on the role of God. If God's role is minimized, the event will seem like a mere coincidence. For example, I know of someone who was in desperate need of $5,000. In his despair he called out to God in prayer. Days later, he received a check in the mail from his father who lived on the other side of the country. The amount was for $5,000. The man in need had never informed his father of his need. The father had sold his house and bought a less expensive one. He then decided to divide the profit he had made among his four children. Though he was a man who always provided for his family, the father was not wealthy. He stated that he felt bad he was never able to put his children through college. This was the first time in his life he had given a gift of this amount. The gift he gave was the exact amount his son had prayed for, yet his son had told no one else (except his wife) of his need. God's role was evident. He had answered the man's prayer. The man's wife was also aware of the situation; she confirmed his report.[2]

If God had dropped the money out of heaven, it would have been a miracle. Instead, in the case mentioned above, He chose to work through natural means by persuading the heart of the father to give a gift of that size. It was an act of special providence. And though this does not lessen the merit of the father's generosity, it was an act of God in answer to prayer.

CONCLUSION

Whether through miracles or acts of special providence, God still intervenes in the affairs of men. This can be used as evidence for the truth of Christianity. In fact, the apostle John wrote his gospel for this very reason. He stated that, "Many other signs therefore Jesus also performed in the presence of the disciples, which are not written in this book; but these have been written that you may believe that Jesus is the Christ, the Son of God; and that believing you may have life in His name" (John 20:30-31).

## ENDNOTES

1Norman L. Geisler, *Miracles and the Modern Mind* (Grand Rapids: Baker Book House, 1992),124-125.

2The recipient of this generous gift is the author of this work.

# PART THREE

# PRESUPPOSITIONAL
# APOLOGETICS

# CHAPTER 10
# GORDON CLARK

Gordon Haddon Clark (1902-1985) was the Chairman of the Philosophy Department at Baylor University for 28 years.[1] He and Cornelius Van Til were the two greatest proponents of the presuppositional method of apologetics. In this chapter, Clark's apologetic views will be examined, and the strengths and weaknesses of these views will be discussed.

## CLARK'S REJECTION OF TRADITIONAL APOLOGETICS

Gordon Clark rejected the idea that unaided human reason could arrive at truths about God. Due to this fact, he rejected traditional apologetics. Clark stated that "The cosmological argument for the existence of God, most fully developed by Thomas Aquinas, is a fallacy. It is not possible to begin with sensory experience and proceed by the formal laws of logic to God's existence as a conclusion."[2] After listing several reasons why he rejected the Thomistic arguments for God's existence, Clark added that even if the arguments were valid, they would only prove the existence of a lesser god. They would not prove the existence of the true God of the Bible.[3]

Clark not only despised the use of philosophical arguments to provide evidence for God's existence, but he also deplored the utilization of historical evidences in defense of Christianity. Clark reminded his readers that the facts of history do not come with their own built-in interpretation. He states that "Significance, interpretation, evaluation is not given in any fact; it is an intellectual judgment based on some non-sensory criterion."[4]

Clark declared that while the conclusions of science constantly change, Scriptural truth remains the same.[5] Therefore, believers should not rely on observable facts to prove Christianity. Instead, Christians must presuppose the truth of God's Word and allow revelation to interpret the facts of history for them.[6]

The reason behind Clark's distaste for traditional apologetics was his belief that unaided human reason could never discover any truth, religious or secular. This, Clark believed, should convince one of his need to presuppose the truth of the Christian revelation.[7] Without this presupposition, man cannot find truth. Clark emphasized this point at the conclusion of his textbook on the history of philosophy. He stated, "Does this mean that philosophers and cultural epochs are nothing but children who pay their fare to take another ride on the merry-go-round? Is this Nietzsche's eternal recurrence? Or, could it be that a choice must be made between skeptical futility and a word from God?"[8]

## CLARK'S REJECTION OF EMPIRICISM

Empiricism is the attempt to find truth through the five senses. This school of thought believes "that all knowledge begins in sense experience."[9]

According to Clark, Thomas Aquinas was an empiricist. Aquinas believed that "all knowledge must be abstracted out of our sensations."[10] Aquinas believed that each person begins life with his mind as a blank slate. He held that "everything that is in the mind was first in the senses, except the mind itself."[11] Although Aquinas believed that God created man's mind with the innate ability to know things and draw rational conclusions from sense data, Clark does not seem to do justice to this aspect of Aquinas' thought.[12] Instead, he merely attacks the idea that man could argue from sense data to the existence of God.

Clark turns next to William Paley. Paley argued from the evidence of design in the universe to the existence of an intelligent God as its Cause. Therefore, he, like Aquinas, began with sense experience and then argued to the existence of God. Clark agreed with the criticisms made by David Hume concerning the teleological argument (the argument for God's existence from design). Hume stated that experience cannot determine if there was one God or several gods who designed the world. Second, since the physical world is finite, nothing in man's experience tells him that its designer must be infinite. And third, since human experience includes such things as natural disasters, might not the world's designer be an evil being?[13]

Clark pointed out that Hume himself was an empiricist. But Hume was consistent in his thinking. Therefore, he realized that the principle of cause and effect, the existence of external bodies, and the reality of internal selves could not be proven through sense data alone. Therefore, Hume admitted that his empiricism inevitably led to skepticism.[14]

Clark emphasized the point that there is a wide gap between basic sense experience and the propositional conclusions made by empiricists.[15] Sense data (the facts of experience) do not come with their own built-in interpretation. Rational conclusions cannot come from sense experience alone. Empiricism, therefore, fails as a truth-finding method. Next, Gordon Clark turned his attention to rationalism.

## CLARK'S REJECTION OF RATIONALISM

Rationalism is the attempt to find truth through reason alone. Though Clark admitted that Augustine was not a pure rationalist, he discussed his views of reason.[16] At a time when Greek philosophy was dominated by skepticism, which argued against the possibility of attaining knowledge, Augustine attempted to find a base for knowledge that could not be denied.[17] Augustine declared that "the skeptic must exist in order to doubt his own existence."[18] Augustine therefore reasoned that even the skeptic should be certain of his existence. Augustine also showed that skeptics could not live like knowledge was impossible.[18]

Augustine also held that the laws of logic were universal, eternal, and unchanging truths. Since the human mind is limited and changing, it could not be the ultimate source of these eternal truths. Hence, there must be an eternal and unchanging Mind as their source. Obviously, this eternal Mind is God.[19]

Clark critiqued the views of Anselm. Anselm was even more rationalistic in his thought than Augustine. He believed that the existence of God could be proven through reason alone. Anselm referred to God as the greatest conceivable Being. Therefore, if God does not exist, then one could conceive of a being greater than Him, a being that has the same attributes but does exist. But then this would be the greatest conceivable Being. Therefore, God (the greatest conceivable Being) must necessarily exist.[20] This is called the ontological argument for God's existence.

Clark wrote that Rene Descartes, also a rationalist, viewed sensation and experience as very deceptive. He attempted to find a single point of certainty by doubting everything until he found something he could not doubt. Through this process, he realized that the more he doubted, the more certain he became of the existence of himself, the doubter.[21]

Descartes borrowed Anselm's ontological argument for God's existence. Clark stated Descartes' version of this argument as follows: "God, by definition, is the being who possesses all perfections; existence is a perfection; therefore God exists."[22]

Clark related that Spinoza also used the ontological argument for God's existence. But Spinoza's version of the argument did not conclude with the God of the Bible. Instead he "proved" the existence of a god who is the universe (the god of pantheism).[23] However, this raised questions as to rationalism's claim to prove the existence of God with certainty. For Spinoza's god and Descartes' God cannot both exist. Spinoza was also more consistent in his rationalism than was Descartes. Spinoza realized that if all knowledge could be found through reason alone, then supernatural revelation was without value.[24]

Gordon Clark listed several problems with rationalism in his writings. He stated that rationalism has historically led to several contradictory conclusions (theism, pantheism, and atheism).[25] Also, Clark stated that "rationalism does not produce first principles out of something else: The first principles are innate...Every philosophy must have its first principles...Thus a presuppositionless description is impossible."[26] Although Clark made much use of reason in his own defense of the faith, he presupposed his first principles. He contended that without doing this, reason can never get off the ground.[27]

## CLARK'S REJECTION OF IRRATIONALISM

In discussing the history of philosophy, Clark states that "Hume had reduced empiricism to skepticism."[28] Immanuel Kant's views left man with a knowledge of "things-as-they-appear-to-us," but with no real knowledge of "things-in-themselves."[29] Clark emphasized this point with the following words: "In his view the uninformed sense data are entirely incoherent. Order is introduced into them by the mind alone, and what the real world might be like... remains unknowable. The whole Postkantian development from Jacobi to Hegel convicts Kant of skepticism."[30]

Clark added that though Hegel effectively critiqued Kant, Hegelianism also failed to justify knowledge.[31] In Hegel's theory of the unfolding of history, truth was seen as relative. What was true yesterday is not necessarily true today.[32] In short, the greatest minds the world has ever known have failed to escape skepticism. The philosophy of man cannot even prove that man can know anything. Empiricism and rationalism have both failed. This has caused some thinkers to accept irrationalism as the method of finding meaning to life. One such thinker was Soren Kierkegaard.

Kierkegaard denied the effectiveness of both reason and sense experience in finding truth. He believed that a man must stop reasoning. Only through a blind leap of faith can man find true meaning in life. An individual's subjective passion is of more importance than objective truth. Kierkegaard believed that the doctrines of Christianity were absurd and contradictory. Still, he chose to believe against all reason.[33]

Clark rejected the irrationalism of Kierkegaard even though it had become so widespread among modern thinkers, both secular and religious. Clark stated of Kierkegaard, "The fatal flaw is his rejection of logic. When once a man commits himself to contradictions, his language, and therefore his recommendations to other people, become meaningless."[34]

As shown above, Gordon Clark rejected empiricism, rationalism, and irrationalism. He taught that they all eventually reduce to skepticism. Man has failed to find truth through these methodologies. Therefore, man, according to Clark, must make a choice between skepticism and a word from God.[36] Clark's method of finding truth is called presuppositionalism or dogmatism.

## CLARK'S VIEW: DOGMATISM

When one finds that Clark saw all of secular philosophy as unable to justify knowledge, one might assume that Clark was himself a skeptic. But this was not the case. Skeptical futility is not the only option left. Clark referred to his view of finding truth as dogmatism. Clark argued that if all other philosophical systems cannot give meaning to life, then dogmatism is worth a try. Clark recommended that one dogmatically presuppose the truth of the teachings of Scripture.[36]

Clark's view may seem to some to be fideism. But this is not so (according to Clark). For everyone, no matter what their philosophical system may be, must presuppose something.[37] The rationalist must presuppose his first principles. Otherwise, he must look for reasons for everything. This would result in an infinite regress, and there would be no real base for knowledge.[38]

The empiricist must assume certain concepts which he cannot prove through sense experience. Such concepts as time, space, equality, causality, and motion are not derived from sense experience. They are brought into one's sense experience in the beginning to aid one in drawing conclusions from the sense data.[39] Logical Positivism is an extreme empirical view. One of its first principles is that truth can only be found through the five senses. However, this first principle refutes itself since it cannot itself be proven through the five senses.[40]

Clark argued that since rationalism and empiricism have failed to make life meaningful, Christian presuppositions should be utilized. For Christian presuppositions do give meaning to life.[41] Clark argued that "Christian Theism is self-consistent and that several other philosophies are inconsistent, skeptical, and therefore erroneous."[42] Clark added that Christianity "gives meaning to life and morality, and that it supports the existence of truth and the possibility of knowledge."[43]

One can see Clark's point more clearly by examining his critique of Kant. In Kant's thinking, there existed no order in sense data. Instead the mind introduces this order into the sense data. Therefore, Kant's view collapses into skepticism since one can only know things-as-they-appear-to-us and not things-as-they-are. One cannot know the real world. One can only know the world as it appears to him.[44]

Clark's response to Kant's dilemma is as follows. Clark presupposes the truth of the revelation found in Scripture. Therefore, Clark presupposes that "God has fashioned both the mind and the world so that they harmonize."[45] If one presupposes the truth of Christianity, then the order that the mind innately reads into the real world is the order which really exists in the real world.

Having discussed Clark's view of obtaining knowledge, one must now consider how Clark defended Christianity. Clark did this by convincing the nonbeliever that he is contradicting himself.[46] Clark was willing to use logic (the law of noncontradiction) to refute the belief systems of others. He did not feel that he was being inconsistent with his presuppositionalism or dogmatism. For Clark believed that God is Logic. In other words, logic is God-thinking. It flows naturally from God's Being.[47] In fact, Clark even translated John 1:1 as, "In the beginning was Logic, and Logic was with God, and Logic was God."[48]

The problem with rationalism is that it lacks sufficient first principles. But, according to Clark, once one presupposes the truth of the Bible, one can use reason to tear down the views of others. Clark spoke of reason in the following manner:

> Therefore I wish to suggest that we neither abandon reason nor use it unaided; but on pain of skepticism acknowledge a verbal, propositional revelation of fixed truth from God. Only by accepting rationally comprehensible information on God's authority can we hope to have a sound philosophy and a true religion.[49]

Clark not only defended the faith by tearing down other belief systems through use of the law of contradiction, but he (after presupposing the truth of Christianity) also was willing to confirm the truth of Christianity in two ways. First, Clark showed that it alone is self-consistent. And second, he appealed to its ability to provide man with meaning to life, moral values, and the genuine possibility of attaining true knowledge.[50] Since all other philosophies have failed to obtain knowledge, one must choose between skepticism and presupposing Christian revelation.[51]

Still, Clark seemed to revert back to fideism. This was due to his hyper-Calvinistic theology. He firmly believed that one really cannot convince another of the truth of Christianity, for God alone sovereignly bestows faith upon an individual.[52] When answering the question of why one person presupposes the Bible to be true and not the Muslim Koran, he simply replied that "God causes the one to believe."[53]

## CLARK'S SOLUTION TO THE PROBLEM OF EVIL

In his writings, Gordon Clark attempted to answer the question, "How can the existence of God be harmonized with the existence of evil?"[54] If God is all-good, He would want to destroy evil. If God is all-powerful, He is able to destroy evil. But evil still exists. It seems that God cannot be both all-good and all-powerful. However, Christianity teaches that He is both. This is the problem of evil.[55]

Zoroastrianism attempts to resolve the problem by teaching that there are two gods. One is good while the other is evil. Neither of the two gods is infinite since they have both failed to destroy the opposing god. Plato's views also result in an unresolved dualism. In his thought, God is not the creator of all things. There exists eternal and chaotic space which the Demiurge cannot control.[56]

According to Clark, even Augustine's answer to the dilemma was inadequate. Clark stated that Augustine taught that evil is metaphysically unreal. It does not exist. Therefore, all that God created is good since evil is non-being.[57] (Whether or not Clark treated Augustine's view fairly will be discussed at a later point in this chapter.)

Clark pointed out that Augustine added to his response the doctrine of human free will. Though God is all-powerful, He has sovereignly chosen to give mankind free will. God allows man to make his own choices. Mankind has chosen evil. Therefore, all that God created is good. Evil can be blamed not on God, but on the abuse of free will by man.[58]

But Clark rejected this view of free will. Clark believed that the Bible does not teach that man is free to choose that which is right as opposed to that which is wrong. Clark stated that "free will is not only futile, but false. Certainly, if the Bible is the Word of God, free will is false; for the Bible consistently denies free will."[59]

Though Clark rejected the doctrine of free will, he believed man has free agency. "Free will means there is no determining factor operating on the will, not even God. Free will means that either of two incompatible actions are equally possible."[60] This Clark rejected. On the other hand, "Free agency goes with the view that all choices are inevitable. The liberty that the Westminster Confession ascribes to the will is a liberty from compulsion, coaction, or force of inanimate objects; it is not a liberty from the power of God."[61] Clark argued that a man can still be responsible for his actions even without the freedom to do other than he has done. Clark stated that, "a man is responsible if he must answer for what he does...a person is responsible if he can be justly rewarded or punished for his deeds. This implies, of course, that he must be answerable to someone."[62]

Clark then asked the question, "Is it just then for God to punish a man for deeds that God Himself 'determined before to be done?'"[63] He answered in the affirmative. He stated that, "Whatever God does is just."[64] Man is responsible to God; but God is responsible to no one.

Clark openly admitted that his view makes God the cause of sin. For, in his thinking, "God is the sole ultimate cause of everything."[65] But, while God is the ultimate cause of sin, He is not the author of sin. The author is the immediate cause of an action. Man is the immediate cause of his sin. But he was not free to do otherwise. For God is the ultimate cause of sin.[66]

Clark stated that, "God's causing a man to sin is not sin. There is no law, superior to God, which forbids him to decree sinful acts. Sin presupposes a law, for sin is lawlessness."[67] Clark explained that "God is above law" because "the laws that God imposes on men do not apply to the divine nature."[68]

Clark stated:

> Man is responsible because God calls him to account; man is responsible because the supreme power can punish him for disobedience. God, on the contrary, cannot be responsible for the plain reason that there is no power superior to him; no greater being can hold him accountable; no one can punish him; there is no one to whom God is responsible; there are no laws which he could disobey. The sinner therefore, and not God, is responsible; the sinner alone is the author of sin. Man has no free will, for salvation is purely of grace; and God is sovereign.[69]

This was Clark's proposed solution to the problem of evil. God is in fact the ultimate cause of sin. But He is not evil, for He committed no sin. And He is not responsible for sin, for there is no one to whom

He is responsible. God is just, for whatever He does is just. Therefore, the creature has no right to stand in judgment over his Creator.

## STRENGTHS OF CLARK'S PRESUPPOSITIONALISM

Gordon Clark, as this study shows, was a very original thinker. Even if one disagrees with much of what he has written, he has made a tremendous contribution to Christian thought that should not be overlooked. There are several strengths which are evident in the thought of Gordon Clark.

*His rejection of pure rationalism.* Clark is absolutely correct when he points out the major deficiency of rationalism. That is, rationalism cannot even get started until certain unproven assumptions are made. Reason cannot prove everything. This would result in an infinite regress, and nothing would be proven. First principles must be presupposed. They are not logically necessary (they cannot be proven with rational certainty).

*His rejection of pure empiricism.* Clark is right when he points out problems with extreme empiricism. Sense data and the facts of history do not come with their own built-in interpretations. They must be interpreted within the context of a person's world view. Empirical data alone cannot give us rational conclusions.

*His rejection of irrationalism.* Clark should be commended for his lack of patience for irrationalism. Once a person denies the law of contradiction, then the opposite of whatever that person teaches can be equally true with those teachings. But all human thought and communication comes to a halt if one allows such an absurd premise. A person who holds to irrationalism cannot even express his view without assuming the truth of the law of contradiction.

*His knowledge of the history of philosophical thought.* Rarely does one read the works of a Christian author who has the insights that Clark had. His knowledge of the thought of the great philosophical minds of the past should encourage all Christians to be more diligent in their own studies. Gordon Clark was a man who had something to say because he was a man who lived a disciplined life of study. Even if one disagrees with the thrust of Clark's thought, one must never dismiss the insights he shared with others concerning the history of philosophy.

*His recognition of the fact that all people have hidden presuppositions.* Too often Christians pretend that they have no biases whatsoever, but this is not the case. Every person, believer and nonbeliever alike, has presuppositions that are often hidden. Clark was right in his view that apologetics is more accurately the seeking of confirmation for our presuppositions than it is the unbiased search for truth.

*His use of the law of noncontradiction.* Clark was justified in his usage of the law of noncontradiction. If two opposite concepts can both be true at the same time and in the same sense, then all knowledge and communication become impossible. Any world view that either is a contradiction or generates contradictions is not worth believing.

*He is very consistent in his Calvinism.* Too often Christians claim to be Calvinists but actually deny or redefine several of the five main points of Calvinism. Clark is not only a strong defender of all five points, but he also consistently holds to the implications of these points. His rejection of human free will and his view of God as the ultimate cause of evil are unpopular concepts, even among Calvinists. Clark is to be credited with having the courage to believe that which is consistent with his system of thought.

*He is right to seek confirmation for his Christian presuppositions.* Many presuppositionalists are content in merely assuming the truth of Christianity. But Clark realizes that, after presupposing biblical truth, one must still seek justification for this assumption. Clark does this by showing that Christianity does what all secular philosophies have failed to do. They failed to give meaning to life, justify moral values, and find truth.

*He is right that man must choose.* Clark recognizes that since all secular philosophies have failed to justify their truth claims, man must make a choice. A person can choose to continue to live with contradictory views. Or a person can choose skepticism and suspend all judgment (except his judgment to be skeptical). Clark even remarks that, for some, suicide is their choice.[70] But Clark pleads with his readers to choose Christianity. If secular philosophies have failed to find truth and give meaning to life, then why not choose Christianity? Whatever the case, man must choose.

## THE WEAKNESSES OF CLARK'S PRESUPPOSITIONALISM

*His denial of the basic reliability of sense perception.* Though Clark is correct when he states that concepts such as moral values, causality, time, and space cannot be derived from sense data alone, he goes too far when he speaks of the "futility of sensation."[71] With Clark's distrust for sense experience, how can he presuppose the truth of the Bible? For he must first use his sense of sight to read the Bible to find out what it is he is going to presuppose. In fact, the Bible itself seems to teach the basic reliability of sense perception. The Mosaic Law places great emphasis on eyewitness testimony, and the eyewitness accounts of Christ's post-resurrection appearances are presented as evidence for the truth of Christ's claims.

*His denial of Thomistic first principles.* While refuting rationalism, Clark stated that it needed first principles. For justification must stop somewhere. He pointed out that since first principles could not be proven through reason alone, rationalism fails to find truth without appealing to something other than reason. The first principles are not logically necessary. In this he is correct. However, Clark accepts the law of contradiction (what Thomists call the law of noncontradiction), though he says it is not logically necessary. He points out that if we do not accept this law, all knowledge and communication would cease. However, this is the same type of argument that Aquinas (and Aristotle long before him) used for his remaining first principles. Besides the principle of noncontradiction, Aquinas utilized the principles of identity, excluded middle, causality, and finality.[72] Aristotle and Aquinas argued that these principles "cannot actually be denied without absurdity."[73] In other words, they are actually undeniable (though not logically necessary). But this is very similar to what Clark claims for one of his first principles, the law of contradiction. If Clark is justified in using this principle, then the other Thomistic first principles of knowledge may likewise be justified. If one accepts the principle of causality (every effect has an adequate cause), then one can reason from the effect (the finite world) to its cause (the infinite Creator). This would deal Clark's entire system a lethal blow since it would justify the use of traditional arguments for God's existence. This would eliminate presuppositional apologetics as the only way for a Christian to defend his faith.

*His downplaying of historical evidences for the Christian Faith.* Clark rightly criticized deriving knowledge from sense data alone. Because of this, he minimized historical evidences. For facts of history, like sense data, do not come with their own built-in interpretations. However, if one accepts Thomistic first principles (because they are actually undeniable), then one can attempt to make sense of the facts of history. If a man claimed to be God and rose from the dead to prove His claim true, then one is not justified in explaining this resurrection in purely naturalistic terms. For every event must have an adequate cause. And no naturalistic explanation has succeeded to account for the resurrection.[74] Only a supernatural cause is sufficient in this case.

*He gives no credit to probability arguments.* Clark points out that other systems of philosophy do not have a starting point based on certainty. They must presuppose their first principles. However, Clark's own first principles are also not based on certainty; they too must be presupposed. It seems that Clark is judging his own philosophical system in a more lenient fashion than he does other schools of thought. It is true that Clark finds confirmation for the Christian presupposition that is lacking in other presuppositions. Still, this is after the fact. And, as Clark admits, this confirmation itself only makes Christianity more probable than other views; it does not establish its certainty. It seems that more credit should be given to arguments for first principles based upon a high degree of probability. Why should an argument be rejected when its premises and conclusion are very probable, while opposing views are unlikely?

Other philosophers have settled for less than certainty but still have solid systems of thought. Some might argue from premises that they believe are "beyond all reasonable doubt." Norman Geisler, following in the tradition of Thomas Aquinas, uses the principle of "actual undeniability."[75] Some things cannot be denied without contradiction and therefore must be true. For instance, if I deny my existence I must first exist to make the denial. For nothing is nothing. Nothing cannot deny anything. Only an existent being can deny something. Therefore, it is actually undeniable that I exist.[76]

Charles Hodge (1797-1878) based his philosophical arguments on what he believed were "self-evident truths." Though these truths could be denied by others, their denial is "forced and temporary." Once a philosopher finishes lecturing or debating, he returns to the real world and no longer denies self-evident truths such as his existence, the existence of others, and the reality of moral values.[77] He can deny moral values in the lecture hall, but once he is at home, he calls the police when he is robbed.

It seems then that Clark is mistaken. Christians can discover truths that are either "self-evident" or "actually undeniable." They can then dialogue with nonbelievers using these premises as common ground. Clark was wrong not to give proper due to first principles based upon a high degree of probability. This leaves the door open for traditional apologetics.

*His attacks on traditional apologetics.* Clark's attack on traditional apologetics is unfounded. This can be shown from his treatment of the Thomistic cosmological argument for God's existence. Aquinas argued that all existent beings which could possibly not exist need a cause or ground for their continuing in existence. In other words, all dependent existence must rely for its continued existence on a totally independent Being, a Being which is uncaused and self-existent.[78]

Clark comments that Aquinas has not ruled out the possibility of an infinite regress of dependent beings.[79] However, Clark is mistaken. For Aquinas is not arguing indefinitely into the past. He is arguing for the current existence of a totally independent Being. Aquinas is arguing for the cause of the continued and present existence of dependent beings, not just the cause for the beginning of their existence.[80] Aquinas is pointing out that if one takes away the independent Being, then there is nothing to sustain the existence of all dependent beings. Every dependent being relies directly on the independent Being for preserving it in existence. The causality is simultaneous, just as a person's face simultaneously causes the existence of its reflection in a mirror. At the exact moment the person moves his face, the reflection is gone.

Clark raises another objection against the Thomistic cosmological argument. He states that even if the argument is valid, it would not prove the existence of the God of the Bible. Clark seems to imply that unless we prove every attribute of God, then it is not the identical God.[81] However, if Aquinas proves the existence of the Uncaused Cause of all else that exists, how could this possibly not be the God of the Bible? If Clark can refer to God as "Truth" and "Logic" and still

114

be talking about the Triune God of the Bible, then Aquinas can identify God with the "Unmoved Mover."

Finally, Clark accuses Aquinas of using the word "exist" with two completely different meanings.[82] When Aquinas speaks of God, he speaks of God existing infinitely. But when he speaks of man, he speaks of man existing finitely. God *is* existence; man merely *has* existence. Though Clark's critique may seem valid, it is not. Aquinas would define existence as "that which is" whether it referred to God or man. True, Aquinas would apply the term "existence" to God infinitely, but to man only finitely. Still, the fact remains that whether Aquinas speaks of God or man, the meaning of existence remains the same.

Apparently, Clark misunderstands Aquinas' view of analogical language. Aquinas taught that we cannot have univocal (totally the same) knowledge of God. Still, our knowledge of God is not equivocal (totally different) since that would be no knowledge at all. Instead, according to Aquinas, our knowledge of God is analogical (similar). By this Aquinas did not mean that the concepts used of God and man have similar meanings. He meant that they have identical meanings, but that they must be applied only in a similar way. All limitations must be removed from a concept before it is applied to God. However, the concept itself continues to have the same meaning throughout.[83]

Not only did Clark express distaste for the cosmological argument for God's existence, he also disliked the teleological argument (the argument from design).[84] He accepted Hume's criticism of this argument. Hume concluded that it proved the existence only of a finite god or gods, and that this god or gods may be evil (due to the evil in the world). However, if one argues for the existence of one infinite God through the cosmological argument, and then finishes the argument with the teleological premises, the argument from design will add the attribute of intelligence to the Uncaused Cause. The problem of evil could also be dealt with as a separate issue. In short, Clark's attempt to destroy traditional apologetics has failed.

*His failure to refute the Islamic Faith.* After destroying secular philosophy through the use of the law of contradiction, Clark does not apply this law to Islam. Instead, he merely states that God causes some to accept the Bible when answering the question, "Why does one man accept the Koran and another the Bible?"[85] Apparently, after all is said and done, Clark's system relies on God alone to cause the person to believe. One wonders why Clark went to such trouble to refute secular philosophies. Could not the same response be given to them?

*His misrepresentation of Augustine and Aquinas.* While dealing with the problem of evil, Clark accused Augustine of denying the reality of evil. He stated that Augustine taught that "all existing things are good" and that "evil therefore does not exist—it is metaphysically unreal."[86] Clark represented Augustine as reasoning that since evil does not exist, God cannot be the cause of evil.[87] In this way, Clark makes it sound as if Augustine is in agreement with the Christian Science view of evil as an illusion. Clark, is misrepresenting Augustine on this point.

Augustine did teach that God created everything that exists and that all that God created is good. However, evil is a perversion of that good brought about by the free choices of rational beings (fallen angels and men). Evil is a privation. It is a lack of a good that should be there.[88] An illustration of this would be rust. God did not create rust. Still it exists, but only as a corruption of something that God created (metal). Therefore, evil is real, but it must exist in some good thing that God created. All that God created is good. God did not create evil. He created the possibility of evil (free will). Fallen rational beings actualized evil by abusing a good thing (free will) God gave them.

Clark also misrepresents Aquinas by implying that Aquinas is a strict empiricist. It is true that Aquinas believed all knowledge comes through sense experience; he taught that God created man's mind with the innate ability to draw rational conclusions from sense data. Aquinas spoke of both the active mind (this innate ability to arrive at universals from particulars) and the receptive mind (the aspect of the mind which receives data from sense experience). Clark seems to view Aquinas as only holding to the existence of the receptive mind. He chooses to ignore Aquinas' teaching about the active mind (also called the agent intellect).[89]

*His proposed solution to the problem of evil.* Clark's answer to the problem of evil is inadequate. He stated that God is not responsible for evil simply because there is no one above Him to whom He is responsible. Since Clark denied human free will (man could not choose to do otherwise), Clark made God the ultimate cause of evil.

The Augustinian approach, in the opinion of many Christian philosophers, is to be preferred. Augustine held that God gave man the freedom to disobey His commands. Therefore, God permitted sin; it was not part of His perfect will for man. A free will theodicy (attempting to propose a reason why God permitted evil) or a free will defense (attempting to merely show that it is not impossible for an all-good and all-powerful God to coexist with evil) is a much more plausible solution to the problem of evil than the solution Clark proposed.[90] Of course, since Clark denied genuine free will, these options were not open to him.

*He does not allow for the use of secular material during evangelism.* Clark states, "in evangelistic work there can be no appeal to secular, non-Christian material."[91] However, this is exactly what the apostle Paul did on Mars Hill. When speaking to Stoic and Epicurean philosophers, he quoted from the writings of two ancient Greek poets to find common ground with his hearers (Acts 17:16-34). If one must choose between the evangelistic approach of Gordon Clark and that of the apostle Paul, then one should choose Paul.

*No Christian can show that every non-Christian system of thought is inconsistent.* Clark claims that since every non-Christian philosophy has failed, people should presuppose the truth of the Christian world view. However, it is impossible for Clark, or any other person, to thoroughly examine every non-Christian system of thought.[92] Even if it were possible for Clark to expose the contradictions in every non-Christian world view today, there is no guarantee that a totally consistent non-Christian world view will not be produced in the future.93

CONCLUSION

Clark's presuppositional approach to apologetics, with minor adaptations, is a worthy apologetic. Uncovering contradictions in non-Christian belief systems is a necessary component in one's defense of the faith. However, Clark's presuppositional approach is not the only method Christians can use when defending the faith.

Although Clark successfully demolishes several secular philosophies, traditional apologetics survives his assault.

## ENDNOTES

1Gordon H. Clark, *Clark Speaks From the Grave* (Jefferson: The Trinity Foundation, 1986), 2.

2Gordon H. Clark, *Religion, Reason and Revelation* (Jefferson: The Trinity Foundation, 1986), 35.

3Ibid., 37.

4Clark, *Clark Speaks From the Grave*, 54.

5Ibid., 55.

6Ibid., 57.

7Geisler, *Apologetics*, 37.

8Gordon H. Clark, *Thales to Dewey* (Jefferson: The Trinity Foundation, 1989), 534.

9Geisler and Feinberg, 431.

10Gordon H. Clark, *Three Types of Religious Philosophy* (Jefferson: The Trinity Foundation, 1989), 60-61.

11Geisler, *Thomas Aquinas*, 86.

12Ibid.

13Clark, *Three Types of Religious Philosophy*, 64-70.

14Ibid., 71,76-78.

15Ibid., 91.

16Ibid., 27.

17Ibid., 28-29.

18Ibid., 31.

19Ibid., 32.

20Ibid., 33-35.

21Clark, *Religion, Reason and Revelation*, 50-51.

22Clark, *Three Types of Religious Philosophy*, 35.

23Clark, *Thales to Dewey*, 332.

24Clark, *Religion, Reason and Revelation*, 53.

25Clark, *Three Types of Religious Philosophy*, 56.

26Ibid., 117-118.

27Ibid., 120.

28Ibid., 93.

29Clark, *Religion, Reason and Revelation*, 62.

30Gordon H. Clark, *A Christian View of Men and Things* (Jefferson: The Trinity Foundation, 1991), 315-316.

31Clark, *Religion, Reason and Revelation*, 63-68.

32Ibid., 98.

33Clark, *Three Types of Religious Philosophy,* 101-105.

34Ibid., 114.

35Clark, *Thales to Dewey,* 534.

36Clark, *Three Types of Religious Philosophy,* 116.

37Ibid., 118.

38Ibid., 51-52.

39Ibid., 70-91.

40Ibid., 118-119.

41Clark, *A Christian View of Men and Things,* 324.

42Ibid.

43Ibid.

44Ibid., 315-316.

45Ibid., 316.

46Clark, *Three Types of religious Philosophy,* 140-142.

47Sproul, Gerstner, and Lindsley, 76.

48Ibid.

49Clark, *Religion, Reason and Revelation,* 87.

50Clark, *A Christian View of Men and Things,* 324.

51Clark, *Religion, Reason and Revelation,* 109-110.

52Clark, *Three Types of Religious Philosophy,* 138.

53Ibid., 139.

54Clark, *Religion, Reason and Revelation,* 195.

55Ibid.

56Ibid., 195-196.

57Ibid., 196.

58Ibid., 199.

59Ibid., 206.

60Ibid., 227.

61Ibid.

62Ibid., 231.

63Ibid.

64Ibid., 232-233.

65Ibid., 237-238.

66Ibid., 237-239.

67Ibid., 239-240.

68Ibid., 240.

69Ibid., 241.

70Clark, *Thales to Dewey*, 534.

71Clark, *Three Types of Religious Philosophy*, 91.

72Geisler, *Thomas Aquinas*, 72-74.

73Ibid., 78-79.

74Habermas, 26-33.

75Geisler, *Christian Apologetics*, 143.

76Ibid., 143-144.

77Charles Hodge, *Systematic Theology* (Grand Rapids: Eerdmans Publishing Company, 1989), vol. 1, 210.

78Thomas Aquinas, *Summa Theologiae*, 1a. 2,3.

79Clark, *Religion, Reason and Revelation*, 36-37.

80Craig, *Apologetics*, 63-65.

81Clark, *Religion, Reason and Revelation*, 37-38.

82Ibid., 38-39.

83Geisler, *Thomas Aquinas*, 40.

84Clark, *Three Types of Religious Philosophy*, 64-70.

85Ibid., 139.

86Clark, *Religion, Reason nand Revelatio*, 196.

87Ibid.

88Augustine, *The City of God*, 22.1.

89Geisler, *Thomas Aquinas*, 86.

90Alvin C. Plantinga, *God, Freedom, and Evil* (Grand Rapids: Eerdmans Publishing Company, 1974), 28-31.

91Clark, *Three Types of Religious Philosophy*, 139.

92Gordon R. Lewis, 119.

93Ibid., 119-120.

# CHAPTER 11
# CORNELIUS VAN TIL

Gordon Clark was not alone in his use of presuppositional apologetics. Another Calvinist scholar named Cornelius Van Til (1895-1987) also used this methodology. Despite the fact that both thinkers were presuppositionalists, they differed on many things. Clark's presuppositionalism could be called dogmatic presuppositionalism,[1] whereas Van Til utilized what could be called transcendental presuppositionalism.[2] Still, their thought systems had much in common.

## REJECTION OF TRADITIONAL APOLOGETICS

Like Clark, Van Til was opposed to traditional methods of apologetics. Van Til taught that because of man's Fall in the garden "every one of fallen man's functions operates wrongly."[3] Van Til stated that "on account of sin man is blind with respect to truth wherever truth appears."[4] Van Til taught that without the correct view about God, man cannot have the correct view of himself and the world.[5]

According to Van Til, the unsaved man is biased against God; he presupposes his own autonomy.[6] The unsaved man believes he can start with himself and find truth without aid from God. There is therefore no neutral ground between believers and nonbelievers[7] The nonbeliever presupposes human autonomy; the believer presupposes the existence of God.

However, there is common ground: all mankind must live within God's universe.[8] All men live in the real world of reason and moral values. Because of this common ground, believers can reason with nonbelievers. Still, with the absence of neutral ground, traditional apologetics cannot even get started. People are not unbiased observers who allow the facts to determine their world view. Instead, people interpret the facts by their preconceived world view (their presuppositions or biases).[9] Therefore, all apologetics must be by way of presupposition.[10]

Van Til disagrees with Roman Catholicism for declaring the autonomy of human reason. Roman Catholicism "ascribes ultimacy or self-sufficiency to the mind of man."[11] When Arminians, Evangelicals, and "less consistent" Calvinists defend the faith, they take the side of the Roman Church by assuming the mind of the unsaved man can of itself rise to a proper understanding of the Triune God.[12] Only a consistent Calvinistic position rightly denies the nonbeliever the ability to reason correctly (without faulty biases).

Van Til adds that traditional apologetics would never prove the existence of the Triune God of the Bible. Instead, traditional apologetics only proves the existence of a finite god.[13] Van Til states that Roman Catholicism would never desire to prove the existence of an infinite God who controls whatever comes to pass. The Roman Church, according to Van Til, wants to protect man's self-sufficiency.[14]

Van Til believed the root of the problem is found in the fact that all nonbelievers suppress their knowledge of the true God (Romans 1:18-22). Concerning the unsaved man, Van Til states that "deep down in his mind every man knows that he is a creature of God and responsible to God. Every man, at bottom, knows that he is a covenant-breaker. But every man acts as though this were not so."[15] By using traditional apologetics, believers mistakenly assume that the unsaved man honestly needs proof that the God of the Bible exists. Instead, Christians should directly confront the nonbeliever by proclaiming the gospel message from the start.[16]

According to Van Til, traditional arguments are also misguided in that they use inductive arguments for Christianity. Inductive arguments are probabilistic; they do not prove their conclusions with certainty. Therefore, traditional arguments give nonbelievers an excuse for rejecting the truth of Christianity. For if Christianity is only probably true, then it is also possibly false. Van Til believed that what was needed was not a probabilistic argument for Christianity, but an argument that proved the impossibility of the contrary. Van Til believed that his transcendental argument alone proved Christianity to be true with certainty.[17]

The traditional arguments for God's existence are therefore useless. The nonbeliever must be confronted with the gospel. Only in this direct approach will the believer find a point of contact with the nonbeliever. It should not be assumed that the nonbeliever is an honest, neutral seeker of truth.[18]

## REASONING BY PRESUPPOSITION

After rejecting traditional apologetics, Van Til unveils his own method of defending the faith. He states that "a truly Protestant apologetic must therefore make its beginning from the presupposition that the Triune God...speaks to him with absolute authority in Scripture."[19] Now that believers stand on Christian foundations, they can see "the futility of reasoning on non-Christian foundations..."[20] Thus, rather than argue to the existence of the Triune God who has spoken to man through His Word, apologists must presuppose His existence.

Van Til sees no middle ground at this point. Two opposing presuppositions are competing for a person's allegiance. The nonbeliever presupposes that he himself is the final or ultimate reference point in all human thought, but the believer rightly presupposes the final or ultimate reference point in human thought to be the Triune God who speaks to man through His infallible Word.[21] There is no neutral ground here.

If humans were really products of chance as the nonbeliever assumes is the case, then there would be no possibility of knowing the world, ourselves, or anything else.[22] But human thought and knowledge is possible because man is who the Bible declares him to be, a being created by God.[23]

Van Til does engage in refuting the beliefs of others. For the sake of argument, believers may "place themselves with the unbeliever on his presupposition" in order to expose the contradictions which the nonbeliever holds.[24] However, even the law of noncontradiction is not presupposed by the Christian. It is only borrowed from the nonbeliever's system of thought and used by the Christian to show the internal inconsistencies of the anti-Christian thought.

In Van Til's apologetic system, only the "Triune God revealed in Scripture" is presupposed.[25] Not even nature or the laws of logic are presupposed. For man to start with himself rather than with God would be to deny his utter dependence on God. One cannot argue for Christianity. Instead, the validity of the gospel must be presupposed. However, Van Til will allow believers to utilize the presuppositions of nonbelievers in order to refute their views.

## CIRCULAR REASONING

Cornelius Van Til stated that "all reasoning is, in the nature of the case, circular reasoning."[26] By this he meant that "the starting-point, the method, and the conclusion are always involved in one another."[27] In other words, when attempting to prove something, a person must first assume the conclusion to be true before proving it to be true. Van Til was claiming that every argument contains its conclusion in its initial premise.

Philosophers refer to circular reasoning as "begging the question." It has long been considered an informal fallacy by logicians. To assume what you are attempting to prove has historically been considered to be an illegitimate form of argumentation. Most believers and nonbelievers agree on this point.

It is interesting that Van Til chooses to refer to "all reasoning" as circular. The point he is stressing is that we argue from our presuppositions, not to them.[28] Apart from regeneration by the Holy Spirit, a person will not presuppose the truth of Christianity.[29] Here, Van Til's Calvinism is evident.

## PARADOX

Van Til does not believe that the law of contradiction can be found in God's being.[30] Whereas Gordon Clark viewed this law as an expression of God's very being, Van Til considers this law a human limitation that does not apply to God. He believed that Clark, and those who agree with him, make God subject to a human law. Van Til warns that the rational man will allow his reason to sit in judgment over God's Word. He will not allow the Bible to rule his life.[31]

Van Til goes so far as to speak of God's Word as seemingly contradicting itself. Though he states that God does not actually contradict Himself, he adds that God's communication to man often appears contradictory to finite human minds.[32] But, Van Til cannot have it both ways. Either God cannot contradict Himself and the law of contradiction flows from His nature, or God can contradict Himself and the law is merely a human limitation.

If by paradox Van Til simply means an apparent contradiction, then even Clark would agree with his premise. Therefore, any criticism that Van Til made of Clark on this point would also apply to Van Til himself. However, if his usage of the term paradox does mean an actual contradiction, then nothing could be known of God, for God could both love mankind and not love mankind at the same time and in the same sense. It seems that Van Til should have withdrawn his criticism of Clark in this area and admitted that the law of contradiction flows naturally from God's being.

## THE TRANSCENDENTAL ARGUMENT

Though Van Til rejected traditional apologetics, he was willing to do more than refute the nonbeliever's world view. Van Til was willing to use one argument for the truth of Christianity. He believed it to be the only valid argument for the true God. He called this argument the transcendental argument.

The transcendental argument attempts to uncover the hidden presuppositions of the nonbeliever. These hidden presuppositions are the necessary preconditions for human thought.[33] Van Til argued that all human thought and moral judgments would be impossible if the Christian God did not exist. Van Til claimed that if God did not exist, then man would know nothing. Even for man to be conscious of his own existence presupposes a consciousness of God's existence. When a nonbeliever argues against God's existence, he must first presuppose God's existence just to argue at all.[34]

For the sake of argument, a believer can place himself within the unbeliever's world view to show that the unbeliever has to presuppose the truth of Christianity just to raise an objection against Christianity.[35] Only Christianity justifies man's ability to reason. Only Christianity gives meaning to life. All other world views lead to irrationality and chaos.[36] In fact, scientific induction makes no sense in a universe without God. For, only the Christian God guarantees the uniformity and order of nature necessary for scientists to argue from the particulars of nature to general conclusions about the world in which he lives.[37]

## COMPARISON WITH GORDON CLARK

When comparing the thought of Cornelius Van Til with that of Gordon Clark, one finds several points of agreement as well as several areas of disagreement. First, some points of agreement between these two men will be examined.

*Both were serious and consistent Calvinists.* Because they both believed that no one could freely choose Christ apart from the Holy Spirit's regenerating work, direct attempts to persuade nonbelievers were thought to be counterproductive.

*Both agreed that the gospel should be presupposed and not argued for.* Van Til and Clark felt that to defend the truth of the gospel was to deny the Calvinist doctrine of the total depravity of man. They both believed that man's reason was damaged due to the Fall and that direct argumentation for the truth of Christianity would be useless. Still, both were willing to refute the beliefs of the nonbeliever and provide indirect confirmation for the truth of Christianity.

*Both agreed that secular philosophy was a complete failure.* Clark taught that all non-Christian philosophy eventually reduced to skepticism. Van Til believed that secular philosophy was futile since human reason was fallen. In his view, without presupposing the God of the Bible, no knowledge was attainable. However, Van Til believed that even nonbelievers presuppose God's existence (though they suppress this truth) in order to find truth.

*Both agreed that traditional apologetics is unbiblical and useless.* Throughout their writings, Clark and Van Til belittled the traditional method of defending the faith. They believed that there was no neutral battle ground between the believer and nonbeliever where Christianity could be defended. The gospel was to be presupposed rather than defended. They saw no use for the classical arguments for God's existence or for traditional usage of historical evidences for the Christian Faith.

Besides these points of agreement between Clark and Van Til, there were areas of disagreement. The following examples will illustrate this.

*They disagreed about circular reasoning.* Van Til believed that all reasoning is circular. The conclusion of one's arguments can always be found in one's premises. However, Clark was more rationalistic in his thinking. He considered circular reasoning a logical fallacy. Because of this, Clark dogmatically presupposed his first principle (the existence of the God of the Bible) and then deduced his beliefs from this first principle.

*They disagreed about the status and use of the law of contradiction.* Clark believed that the law of contradiction flowed from God's nature. He taught that God is logic. Therefore, when he presupposed the Triune God who revealed Himself in the Bible, he also presupposed the law of contradiction. He would then use this law to destroy the belief systems of nonbelievers.

Van Til, however, believed this law to be a human limitation which Clark forced upon God. Van Til believed that Clark had subjected God to this law. Though Van Til would use this law to refute other belief systems, it was only because he chose to use the "enemy's own ammunition to defeat the enemy in battle." In fact, Clark's view of the law of noncontradiction is probably what caused the widest gap between the thought of these two men. Clark presupposed the law of noncontradiction when doing apologetics. Van Til refused to do so.

## STRENGTHS OF VAN TIL'S SYSTEM

In the presuppositional apologetics of Cornelius Van Til there is much to be commended. The following examples will make this clear.

*He stresses the sinfulness of man.* Too often, defenders of the faith tend to de-emphasize the effects of the Fall on mankind. But this is not true of Van Til. If Van Til can be accused of any fault in this area, it would be overkill. For, due to his Calvinism, man is not free to accept Christ; regeneration precedes faith.

*He stresses man's suppression of God's truth.* Many apologists assume that the reason why nonbelievers do not come to Christ is merely an intellectual one. Van Til rightly shows that men willfully suppress whatever knowledge of the true God they have. Van Til is correct in his view that the problem is ultimately that of a moral choice rather than an intellectual one. God has proven his existence to all men through His visible creation (Romans 1:18-22). Therefore, man has no excuse for rejecting Him.

*He stresses God's work in salvation.* Even non-Calvinists should commend Van Til for his focus on God's work in salvation. Apart from God's grace, no man would be saved. Traditional apologists often imply that they can lead people to Christ through argumentation alone. More emphasis is needed on the inward persuasion of the Holy Spirit concerning those to whom apologists witness. God can use traditional argumentation. Still, it is God who does the saving. The apologist can remove intellectual stumbling blocks to the faith, but only God can persuade one to turn to Christ.

*He stresses the importance of faith over reason.* Van Til emphasizes that one must believe in Christ to be saved. Without Christ, even the wisest man in the world will be eternally lost.

Though traditional apologists are right in that man can reason to the true faith (Van Til disagrees with this), once a person through reason finds the true faith, he must submit his reason to it.

*He is willing to tear down the belief systems of those who oppose the gospel and use an indirect argument for Christianity.* If it were not for this point, Van Til would probably be classified as a fideist. Though he rejects traditional apologetics (like the fideist), he is willing to refute non-Christian views and give one argument for his beliefs (unlike the fideist). Van Til's transcendental argument goes beyond refuting non-Christian world views; it presents positive evidence for the Christian faith. Still, it does so in an indirect manner, rather than in the direct fashion found in traditional apologetics.

## WEAKNESSES OF VAN TIL'S SYSTEM

Despite the many good things that could be said about Van Til's apologetics, there are many weaknesses in his thought. A few of these weaknesses are mentioned below.

*He denies that man has the ability to test revelation-claims.* Given Van Til's system, there seems to be no way to decide whether the Bible or the Koran is the Word of God. Yet the Bible frequently commands us to test the spirits, the prophets, and the messages they proclaim (1 Jn 4:1; Deut 18:20-22; Mt 7:15-23; Gal 1:8-9).[38] Also, God provided ample evidence for His revelation-claims by performing miracles through His spokesmen and by raising Jesus from the dead (Jn 20:30-31; 1 Cor 15:3-8). It seems that God has given even fallen man the ability to test revelation-claims. Whether or not man uses this ability wisely is another question. Again, Van Til's Calvinism can be seen. For without regeneration by the Holy Spirit, no one will accept the Bible as God's Word.

*His view that all reasoning is circular.* It is true that much of Van Til's thought is circular. It is not true that all thought is circular. Even though all men have presuppositions, they can be tested just as scientific hypotheses are tested. One does not have to sneak one's presuppositions into the premises of one's arguments. Any argument that uses circular reasoning is fallacious, regardless of whether or not the conclusion is true.

*His rejection of the law of noncontradiction being universally valid.* Though Van Til claimed that he only used the law of noncontradiction for the sake of argument when he shared his faith with nonbelievers, he often criticized many of his colleagues for being inconsistent Calvinists.[39] Though Van Til implied that this law is a man-made principle, he diligently labored to keep his system free from contradictions. Van Til should have realized that there could be no thought or communication whatsoever without the law of contradiction. Even God cannot contradict Himself. And, since God is not subject to anything outside Himself, Clark was right to view this law as naturally flowing from God's being.

*Van Til's transcendental argument is not the only valid argument for Christianity.* Even John Frame, a former student of Van Til, saw problems with Van Til's transcendental argument.[40] Although Frame recognized the worth of this argument for apologetics, he did not believe it was the only valid argument for Christianity.

First, Frame doubts that the transcendental argument could be persuasive without "the help of subsidiary arguments of a more traditional kind."[41] Second, Frame thinks Van Til was wrong in his assertion that the traditional arguments proved something less than the God of the Bible.[42] Third, Frame believes that some traditional arguments often work despite the fact that the traditional apologist might wrongly assume that their arguments do not themselves presuppose a Christian world view.[43] Fourth, Frame doubts that the whole of the Christian faith can be established by a single argument which stands alone.[44] Fifth, if Van Til is right in his claim that the apologist must prove the whole biblical doctrine of God rather than just one or a few of His attributes, then the transcendental argument also fails. For the God of the Bible is more than the source of meaning, morality, and rationality. Even the transcendental argument must be supplemented by other arguments.[45] And, sixth, Frame believes that any argument (including the transcendental argument) can be rejected. Hence, further argumentation may be needed to defend the original argument.[46] Therefore, though the transcendental argument of Van Til may be a good argument for the God of the Bible, it is not the only good argument for the God of the Bible. The traditional arguments (cosmological, teleological, moral) for God's existence may also be used by the apologist.

*His rejection of traditional apologetics.* Finally, Van Til was wrong to reject traditional apologetics. The Bible commands believers to defend the faith (1 Pt 3:15; Col 4:5-6). The apostles used historical evidences to lead others to Christ (1 Cor 15:3-8). Even Van Til admits that man suppresses the truth that God has given him in nature (Romans 1:18-22). If this is the case, then why shouldn't apologists use traditional arguments to attempt to dislodge these truths from the nonbelievers' subconscious mind? As the last chapter showed, traditional apologetics is on much more solid ground than the presuppositional apologetics of either Van Til or Clark would admit.

## ENDNOTES

1Gordon H. Clark, *Three Types of Religious Philosophy*, 115-142.

2John M. Frame, *Apologetics to the Glory of God* (Phillipsburg: Presbyterian and Reformed Publishing, 1994), 69-75.

3Cornelius Van Til, *Christian Apologetics* (Phillipsburg: Presbyterian and Reformed Publishing Co., 1976), 43.

4Ibid., 42.

5Cornelius Van Til, *The Defense of the Faith* (Phillipsburg: Presbyterian and Reformed Publishing Co., 1967), 73.

6Ibid., 34.

7Ibid., 298.

8Ibid.

9Gordon R. Lewis, 128.

10Van Til, *Defense of the Faith*, 34, 99-105, 179-180, 195, 197.

11Ibid., 90.

12Ibid., 78-79.

13Ibid., 77.

14Ibid., 78.

15Ibid., 92, 94, 231.

16Ibid., 94.

17Ibid., 103.

18Ibid., 94.

19Ibid., 99-105, 179-180, 195, 197.

20Ibid., 180.

21Ibid.

22Ibid.

23Ibid.

24Ibid.

25Gordon R. Lewis, 131.

26Van Til, *The Defense of the Faith*, 101.

27Ibid.

28Ibid.

29Ibid., 299.

30Ibid., 298.

31Lewis, 133.

32Ibid.

33Van Til, *The Defense of the Faith*, 60, 150, 180, 298.

34Frame, 69-75.

35Van Til, *The Defense of the Faith*, 180.

36Ibid.

37Ibid.

38Gordon R. Lewis, 144.

39Ibid., 146.

40Frame, 69-75.

41Ibid., 71.

42Ibid.

43Ibid., 71-72.

44Ibid., 72.

45Ibid., 73.

46Ibid.

# PART FOUR

# PSYCHOLOGICAL APOLOGETICS

# CHAPTER 12
# THE ABSURDITY OF
# LIFE WITHOUT GOD

Psychological Apologetics attempts to deal with the whole man, not just his reason. The will and emotions of man are taken into account. Man desperately needs meaning in life. Apologists who use this methodology often focus on this fact. They point to the fact that if there is no God, then life is absurd and without ultimate meaning.

Psychological apologists also focus on man's innate thirst to transcend this earthly experience (chapter 13), and the paradox of man—that man is both wonderful and cruel (chapter 14). An adequate world view must offer a viable explanation for these three phenomena (the absurdity of life without God, the thirst for transcendence, and the paradox of man). Psychological apologists argue that Christianity provides a better answer in these areas than any other world view.

## KING SOLOMON

This chapter will examine the argument for God's existence based on the absurdity of life without God. Though this argument is popular today, it is not new. In fact, King Solomon of Israel used this argument as far back as 935BC. This is rather strange since most historians place the start of philosophy at about 585BC.[1] However, there were wise thinkers at a much earlier time. As Solomon began his reign, he prayed for wisdom and knowledge (2 Chronicles 1:10-

12). God answered his prayer and his wisdom surpassed that of all other men of his day. People came from remote parts of the earth just to ask him "difficult questions" (1 Kings 4:29-34). The biblical account of Solomon's wisdom is as follows:

Now God gave Solomon wisdom and very great discernment and breadth of mind, like the sand that is on the seashore. And Solomon's wisdom surpassed the wisdom of all the sons of the east and all the wisdom of Egypt. For he was wiser than all men, than Ethan the Ezrahite, Heman, Calcol and Darda, the sons of Mahol; and his fame was known in all the surrounding nations. He also spoke 3,000 proverbs, and his songs were 1,005. And he spoke of trees, from the cedar that is in Lebanon even to the hyssop that grows on the wall; he spoke also of animals and birds and creeping things and fish. And men came from all peoples to hear the wisdom of Solomon, from all the kings of the earth who had heard of his wisdom (1 Kings 4:29-34).

Solomon's two philosophical writings are *Proverbs* and *Ecclesiastes*. In *Proverbs*, Solomon teaches wisdom that can be applied to daily life. It can be viewed as a manual on practical living. In *Ecclesiastes*, Solomon shows that a man's life is totally useless until he recognizes his relation to God.

Solomon begins his work sounding like a modern-day existentialist. He cries, "Vanity of vanities! All is vanity" (Ecclesiastes 1:2). He expresses the view that life is futile and that man is thrust into a state of deep despair. However, Solomon makes this bleak assessment of human existence only when he considers the human condition "under the sun" (1:9). Solomon is attempting to find purpose in life without any appeal to man's relation to God. Take the God of heaven out of the equation, Solomon says, and life has no meaning. Man, viewed strictly from an earthly perspective, has no hope or purpose.

Solomon proclaims that "...in much wisdom there is much grief, and increasing knowledge results in increasing pain" (1:18). The human situation is such that the more that is known of it, the less hope there is (so long as man is viewed in isolation from God).

Solomon attempts to find meaning and purpose in life apart from God. He finds none. Apart from God, life is futile. Solomon surveys a list of candidates that might bring meaning to life apart from God.

But he finds in them only frustration and "striving after the wind" (1:14). The attainment of human wisdom is vain (1:17-18). It brings no lasting satisfaction. Laughter and pleasure-seeking are vain (2:2,10). There is no genuine satisfaction in the drinking of wine (2:3) or engaging in building projects (2:4). The accumulation of wealth is without lasting significance (2:8). Music and women can provide only temporary pleasure (2:8). Even popularity amounts to nothing (2:9). Solomon's conclusion is that "everything is futility and striving after the wind" (2:17).

Though Solomon grieves for all that is "under the sun," he also begins to acknowledge God's purposes in the affairs of this world (3:1-11). He states that God has placed eternity in the hearts of men (3:11). Though man cannot fully understand the ways of God, he has an innate longing for the eternal things of God. Without appealing to these eternal matters, man will be damned to a life of despair and frustration. But if man acknowledges his God and serves Him, life has meaning and eternal significance.

Solomon closes Ecclesiastes with these words. "The conclusion, when all has been heard, is: fear God and keep His commandments, because this applies to every person. For God will bring every act to judgment, everything which is hidden, whether it is good or evil" (12:13-14).

Man's search for satisfaction and meaning in life is futile if he only looks "under the sun." Life without God is useless and absurd. Despair is inevitable for all who recognize the futility found in the temporary pleasures of life. True satisfaction can only be found in God. Once man acknowledges God's existence, the works of man are no longer meaningless. What we do on earth takes on eternal significance. For we must all give an account to God for our actions. And God alone gives genuine meaning to life.

Many modern thinkers have rejected the existence of God. But they also recognize that life is without meaning if there is no God. Still, they live lives of despair (or escape this despair through an existential leap) rather than submit to God who can give meaning to life. Solomon calls upon these modern thinkers to make a choice. Blind leaps into the irrational realm to find meaning are not open to honest thinkers. Man must choose God or despair. There is no other choice.

## BLAISE PASCAL (1623-1662)

The Christian thinker Blaise Pascal revolted against the idea that reason alone should settle religious truth questions. Pascal realized that there is more to the decision-making processes of man than mere thought. Man's choices are also influenced by his emotions and will. "We know the truth not only through our reason but also through our heart."[2] Therefore, Pascal set out to develop a defense of the Christian Faith that appealed to these aspects in man.

Pascal stated, "Being unable to cure death, wretchedness and ignorance, men have decided, in order to be happy, not to think about such things."[3] Men "have a secret instinct driving them to seek external diversion and occupation, and this is the result of their constant sense of wretchedness."[4] "...it makes a man happy to be diverted from contemplating his private miseries by making him care about nothing else but dancing well..."[5]

Pascal saw in man a tendency to focus his attentions on temporary pleasures rather than on his own wretched state and certain death. If a man could amuse himself with these temporary pleasures, he could ignore and deny the more important issues of life that cause him fear. But Pascal warns man that there is no genuine satisfaction in this world. He says, "in this life there is no true and solid satisfaction" and that "all our pleasures are mere vanity."[6] Pascal concludes "that the only good thing in this life is the hope of another life."[7]

According to Pascal, "there are only two classes of persons who can be called reasonable: those who serve God with all their heart because they know him and those who seek him with all their heart because they do not know him."[8] Pascal considered the possibility of life after death to be of such great importance that he considered those who were not concerned about investigating this issue to be without feeling.[9] Pascal graphically describes the human situation apart from God:

Imagine a number of men in chains, all under the sentence of death, some of whom are each day butchered in the sight of others; those remaining see their own condition in that of their fellows, and looking at each other with grief and despair await their turn. This is an image of the human condition.[10]

All men face their own inevitable death. As they go through life, they seek to hide this dreadful fact from themselves through temporary pleasures. But, as far as Pascal is concerned, this is a meaningless existence. Man can only find genuine meaning in life if he finds the God of the Bible. Apart from God, life is absurd.

Pascal calls his readers to make a choice. It is foolish for them to go on deceiving themselves. They must admit that without God and eternal life, human existence is without hope. Man must choose between despair and God. If a person wagers on God and loses, the person loses nothing. But if a person wagers on God and wins, the person wins everything. If, however, one wagers against God there is no hope of winning. If that person wins, he wins nothing. But if one bets against God and loses, one loses everything. Pascal concludes that the wise man will therefore wager on God.[11] Pascal, contrary to popular belief, is not attempting to prove God's existence with his wager argument. Instead, he is attempting to persuade others to desire and seek God with all their hearts. Pascal believed that if a person seeks God with all his heart, he will find Him (Jeremiah 29:13).

### FRANCIS SCHAEFFER (1912-1984)

Christian thinker Francis Schaeffer effectively argued that life is absurd without the existence of the God of the Bible. He believed that modern man had thrust himself into a state of despair. Schaeffer saw three key philosophers as leading man away from reason and into this feeling of meaningless existence.

Immanuel Kant (1724-1804), the first of these key thinkers, brought secular philosophy to a halt. His thought concluded that man could only know reality as it appeared to him (phenomena) and not reality as it is (noumena). Man's mind could not bridge the gap between the two. When one begins with unaided human reason, the phenomena and noumena never meet.[12] At this point, secular philosophers gave up their attempt to find "a unified rationalistic circle that would contain all thought, and in which they could live."[13]

The next thinker emphasized by Schaeffer was Hegel (1770-1831). Before him, philosophers for thousands of years had attempted to find truth based on antithesis. This meant that they held to the idea of absolute truth. Something could not be both true and not true at the same time and in the same sense. But Kant had shown that unaided human reason within the boundaries of antithesis led to skepticism about the real world. Hegel therefore concluded that man must try a new method. He recommended abandoning absolutes. His dialectical approach allowed for the synthesizing of contradictory statements.[14] This shift in the concept of truth from antithesis (absolute truth) to synthesis (truth is relative) resulted in modern man's new way of viewing reality.[15] At this point, modern man faces great despair. For there is no longer any hope of man finding true meaning to life. There are no absolutes. Truth is relative.

The third philosopher Schaeffer discusses is Soren Kierkegaard (1813-1855). With the rejection of absolutes, modern man was left without meaning in life. Despair seemed to be the only alternative. But this is where Kierkegaard enters the scene. Schaeffer states that Kierkegaard realized that "Man has no meaning, no purpose, no significance" in the rational realm. "There is only pessimism concerning man as man." But if man takes a leap of blind faith into the nonrational realm, says Kierkegaard, this nonreasonable faith gives man optimism.[16]

Schaeffer sees modern man as facing a choice between despair and a false, nonrational hope. Schaeffer's method of evangelizing the modern man is to show him that he must reason with absolutes. For the only way to deny absolutes is to assume there are absolutes.[17] The Kierkegaardian leap into the nonrational realm is therefore not an option. If the modern man refuses to turn to the God of the Bible, he is damned to a meaningless life of despair (that is, if he has enough courage to refrain from a nonrational leap). Only when a person accepts the existence of the God of the Bible can life have true meaning. Without God, life is absurd. Without God, the reasonable man will wallow in despair.

### GORDON LEWIS

In his work entitled *Testing Christianity's Truth Claims*, Gordon Lewis approvingly discusses the psychological apologetics utilized by Edward John Carnell and Vernon C. Grounds. Lewis recognizes the fact that Christianity alone is able to relieve man's deepest anxieties. Science and Philosophy can offer no substitute for God's unconditional love.[18] All people long for loving acceptance, peace, and significance. Only in Jesus can these needs be met. Jesus loves each person unconditionally. He will never stop loving any individual (though each person has the freedom to reject His love and suffer the consequences). Trusting in His promises gives man peace in the midst of trials. One can find true significance in human existence only if he recognizes that all people were created by God for the purpose of eternal fellowship with Him.

Man desperately needs forgiveness to remove his guilt and hope to obliterate his despair. But without Christ's atoning death on Calvary, there is no forgiveness. And without Christ's resurrection from the dead, there can be no genuine hope for man. Only in Christianity can man's deepest psychological needs be met.[19]

The stresses of modern life inflict multitudes with anxiety and despair. Modern man is crying out for help. Psychologists often correctly diagnose the problems, but seldom provide any real solutions. The source of man's anxiety stems from his alienation from God, and only the gospel of Jesus Christ can remedy this. The world desperately seeks joy and peace. However, joy and peace can only be found in Christ, and the church must make this known.

### LAWRENCE J. CRABB JR.

Christian psychologist Lawrence Crabb states that modern psychology has rightly concluded that one of man's most basic needs is personal worth.[20] Crabb states that there are two required inputs to make a person feel worthy. The two inputs are significance and security.[21]

To feel significant, each person must have a sense of purpose and a feeling of importance. One's life must be meaningful. One must have a definite impact on his world. To feel secure, a person must know he is loved unconditionally and eternally. If he does not feel eternally accepted, he will not feel secure.[22] Man longs for everlasting acceptance; temporary acceptance will not satisfy him.

Crabb argues that Adam and Eve had significance and security before the Fall, but once they alienated themselves from God through sin, they no longer felt significant and secure.[23] Since the Fall, significance and security have alluded man. Man has lost his sense of personal worth. Because of this, each person pretends to be someone he or she is not. Man also seeks significance and security in other people and in temporary pleasures, but inevitably true personal worth always evades man.

However, Crabb finds the solution to this dilemma of man in the gospel. Once a person is saved, his needs for personal worth are met in Christ. Man is significant because God has given each person an eternal mission. The King of the universe has given every person a job to perform. He has called each individual to minister to others in His power and love.[24]

Man can also be secure for God loved man enough to send His Son to die for him. God loves all people unconditionally. He loves all people just as they are, and He will never stop loving them.[25] Only in Jesus Christ can man find true personal worth.

CONCLUSION

Modern man seems more concerned with feelings than he does with reason. Because of this, psychological apologetics can be a very effective method of defending the faith in the present cultural climate.

If the God of the Bible does not exist, there is no hope for mankind. Man cannot experience true peace and joy knowing that he will someday cease to exist. There can be no genuine meaning to life, if God does not exist.

If God does not exist, objective moral values are nonexistent. Right is wrong and wrong is right. If there is no moral Lawgiver above man, there can be no moral law above man. Without life after death and a final judgment, it does not matter if one lives like Hitler or Mother Theresa. A million years from now, it will make no difference.

All men acknowledge the existence of evil (at least in their practice if not in their beliefs). But nothing less than the God of the Bible can guarantee the ultimate defeat of evil.

In short, if the God of the Bible does not exist, man is damned to a life of meaningless existence. To hide from this fact, a person can focus his attention on Pascalian diversions, or maybe a Kierkegaardian leap into the nonrational realm will be one's choice. But for those with the courage to deal with reality head on, a choice must be made between despair and the God of the Bible. As Pascal has said, the wise man will wager on God.

## ENDNOTES

1Gordon H. Clark, *Thales to Dewey*, 3.

2Blaise Pascal, *Pensees* trans. A. J. Krailsheimer (New York: Penguin Books, 1966), 58.

3Ibid., 66.

4Ibid., 69.

5Ibid., 71.

6Ibid., 157.

7Ibid.

8Ibid., 160.

9Ibid., 156.

10Ibid., 165.

11Ibid., 149-155.

12Schaeffer, *Complete Works*, vol. 5, 178.

13Ibid., vol. 1, 10.

14Ibid., 232-233.

15Ibid., 10.

16Ibid., 238.

17Ibid., 229.

18Gordon R. Lewis, 231-236.

19Ibid., 253.

20Lawrence J. Crabb Jr., *Effective Biblical Counseling* (Grand Rapids: Zondervan Publishing House, 1977), 61.

21Ibid.

22Ibid.

23Ibid.

24Ibid., 70.

25Ibid.

# CHAPTER 13
# CONTEMPORARY MAN'S
# THIRST FOR GOD

In the last chapter the absurdity of life without God was discussed. A similar aspect of psychological apologetics deals with contemporary man's thirst for God. Though many people currently deny or ignore the existence of the God of the Bible, their lives display a vacuum only He can fill.

ALL MEN THIRST FOR GOD

Christian philosophers Norman Geisler and Winfried Corduan argue that all "people sense a basic need for God."[1] The fact that Sigmund Freud attempted to explain this phenomena away shows that even he recognized this need for God in himself and others. (Of course, Freud denied that God exists.) Freud admitted that man feels powerless and insignificant in the face of the vast universe in which he finds himself.[2] According to Freud, man invents God through his imagination to calm his fears.

Friedrich Schleiermacher taught that all people have a feeling of absolute dependence, even though they do not all explain it in the same way. Both believers and nonbelievers alike recognize their absolute dependence on something that transcends their earthly experience.[3]

Martin Heidigger viewed man as a "being-unto-death."[4] Man finds himself thrown into the world. He has no say about his being here. He knows not why he is here, but there is one thing he does know. He knows he is destined for nothingness. Man had no control over his birth, and he can have no control over his death. He must die. Man finds himself thrust into this world enroute to extinction. He is without a ground for his being. Man desperately needs a ground for his being.[5]

Paul Tillich recognized that man is limited and dependent. Man needs a ground for his being, something to anchor him in existence. Tillich spoke of this need as man's "ultimate concern."[6]

Jean-Paul Sartre, a French atheist, admitted his need for God. Sartre taught that man needs God to give his existence definition and meaning. But, since Sartre rejected God's existence, he felt that the entire project was absurd.[7] Man has a need for God, but there is no God who can meet this need.

Walter Kaufmann referred to man as the "God-intoxicated ape."[8] Friedrich Nietzsche considered his own atheistic views to be so unbearable that he wished he could be convinced he was wrong. He felt a strong thirst for God, but rejected the possibility of God's real existence.[9]

Geisler and Corduan, after surveying the above list of non-Christian thinkers, arrived at the following conclusion:

That people generally, if not universally, manifest a need for the Transcendent seems incontestable. The sense of contingency, the feeling of cosmic dependence, the need to believe in some sort of Transcendent is apparently present in all men. The residual but most essential question is this: Is there any basis in reality for this God-need which both believers and nonbelievers have confessed to having?[10]

The evidence indicates that all men sense a need for the God of the Bible. Even atheists and other non-Christians have expressed this need. Still, as Geisler and Corduan have noted, it must be shown that this need points to the actual existence of God.

## THE FREUDIAN EXPLANATION
Though both atheists and Christians alike recognize the universal thirst for God, atheists deny that God actually does exist. Instead, they speculate as to why so many people believe that He does exist. An example of this kind of speculation is found in the thought of Sigmund Freud.

Freud was convinced that God did not exist. But if atheism is true, then why do so many people believe in God? Freud tried to answer this question. Freud suggested that primitive man felt extremely threatened by nature (due to storms, floods, earthquakes, diseases, and ultimately death).[11] Man had no control over nature. He was totally helpless in this regard. Primitive man was completely at the mercy of nature. There was nowhere man could turn for help. Freud theorized that primitive men therefore decided to personalize nature. In this way, man could attempt to plead with or appease nature.[12] Imagining nature to be a personal being enabled man to offer sacrifices to nature in hope that nature would be kind to him in return.

Freud's speculation did not stop there. He also promoted another theory of early human society. He assumed that originally mankind banded together in small groups. These clans consisted of a male, his several wives, and their offspring. Freud believed that, early in life, male children desired to have sex with their mothers. They therefore became extremely jealous of their father. Though they loved their father since he was their protector, they began to hate him due to their jealousy. Eventually, they banded together and murdered their father. After the murder, they ate the flesh of their father in a ritual meal. Soon, the male children were overcome with feelings of guilt. As a result, they deified the father image and began offering sacrifices to him as a god.[13]

Freud taught that God is nothing but a product of man's imagination. God did not create man. Instead, man created God. Man personalized nature due to his fear of nature. The guilt he felt for murdering his father also caused him to project the father image onto this personalized nature. In this way, reasoned Freud, the belief in the Father-God was originated by man's wishful thinking.

This highly speculative theory does not do justice to mankind's universal thirst for God. This theory appears to be "wishful thinking" on the part of Freud. Whatever the case, Freud's proposed explanation deserves a response.

## A CHRISTIAN RESPONSE

Christian theologian R. C. Sproul is quick to point out that Freud's line of reasoning does not disprove God's existence. Instead, it presupposes His nonexistence. In other words, Freud was not trying to answer the question, Does God exist? Rather, he was attempting to answer the question, "Since God does not exist, why do so many people believe that He does?"[14]

Therefore, this speculation by Freud should not be viewed as a disproof of God's existence. It is simply a desperate attempt to explain away strong evidence for God's existence. It is an endeavor which focuses on answering the question, "If atheism is true, why are there so few atheists?" Freud answers the question by accusing all who disagree with him of being deluded.

Sproul points out that Freud's speculation explains how men use their imaginations to invent idols (false gods), but not the God of the Bible. For the God of the Bible is far too demanding. No one would wish for the existence of a Being that requires the submission and obedience demanded by the Christian God. The gods of other religions are attractive candidates for projection. But the Holy God of the Scriptures is the type of Being from whom men run. No one would invent Him through wishful thinking.[15]

Christian philosopher J. P. Moreland states that "atheism is a result of a desire to kill the father figure (in Freudian language) because one wishes to be autonomous."[16] Man's two greatest drives are his thirst for God and his desire to be autonomous. Man has a void that can only be filled by God. Still, man wants to be his own king. The Christian chooses God over autonomy. The atheist, on the other hand, chooses his own autonomy.

Moreland adds that even if Freud was right, his argument would still be guilty of what philosophers call the genetic fallacy.[17] The genetic fallacy claims that a belief can be shown to be false just by showing its origin is unreasonable. But this is not the case. Even if mankind, due to fear and guilt, originated the idea of God, this does not prove that God does not exist. God might still exist even if people arrived at this conclusion through faulty reasoning.

Christian philosophers Norman Geisler and Winfried Corduan argue that what people really need actually exists.[18] Humans need food and water. Food and water exist. Even if a person dies of thirst or hunger, the fact is that food and water do exist. It is just that the person did not find them. Geisler and Corduan argue that all men really need God. The thirst for God is universal. As shown above, even many atheists admit to this fact. God is not something people merely desire. He is something people need. And since whatever man needs exists, then God exists.[19] This would be true even if a person does not find God (as some people do not find food or water). This argument is not meant to be an air-tight proof, but it does seem to have a high degree of probability (everything else man needs does in fact exist).

CONCLUSION

If all men have a void that only God can fill, then one would expect the Bible to address this issue, and this, of course, is the case. Jesus said, "Man shall not live on bread alone, but on every word that proceeds out of the mouth of God" (Matthew 4:4). Man is more than a physical being. He is also a spiritual being. Not only does man need physical nourishment, he also needs spiritual nourishment from the true God.

Jesus proclaimed, "I am the bread of life; he who comes to me shall not hunger, and he who believes in me shall never thirst" (John 6:35). Only Jesus can quench our thirst for God.

Unfortunately, most people attempt to quench this thirst with unworthy substitutes which can never meet man's most ultimate needs. The Word of God declares, "For My people have committed two evils: they have forsaken Me, the fountain of living waters, to hew for themselves cisterns, broken cisterns, that can hold no water" (Jeremiah 2:13). Rather than turn to Christ, most people look elsewhere to find fulfillment in life. For some, their "broken cistern" is a false religion. For others, it is material wealth. Many people try sexual immorality, drugs, or alcohol. But there is no worthy substitute for the true living water. Only Jesus can meet man's deepest needs.

As mentioned earlier, the two strongest drives in man are his thirst for God and his desire for autonomy (he wants to be his own king). Jesus was aware of this. He addressed this issue during His conversation with Nicodemus. Jesus stated:

And this is the judgment, that the light is come into the world, and men loved the darkness rather than the light; for their deeds were evil. For everyone who does evil hates the light, and does not come to the light, lest his deeds should be exposed. But he who practices the truth comes to the light, that his deeds may be manifested as having been wrought in God (John 3:19-21).

Those who place their need for God above their desire to be in complete control of their lives will find Christ. On the other hand, those who continually refuse to surrender their autonomy to God will never come to Jesus. Because the thirst for God resides within the hearts of all men, we must offer them living water. Man will never find ultimate fulfillment in life without trusting in the Lord Jesus Christ. Only then will his thirst for God be quenched. As Augustine has prayed, "…you made us for yourself and our hearts find no peace until they rest in you."[20]

## ENDNOTES

1Geisler and Corduan, 69.

2Ibid., 69-70.

3Ibid., 70.

4Ibid.

5Ibid., 70-71.

6Ibid., 71.

7Ibid., 71-72.

8Ibid., 72.

9Friedrich Nietzsche, *The Portable Nietzsche*, ed. Walter Kaufmann (New York: Penguin Books, 1982), 441.

10Geisler and Corduan, 72-73.

11Sigmund Freud, *The Future of an Illusion,* trans. W. D. Robson-Scott (New York: Doubleday, 1964), 20.

12R. C. Sproul, *If There's a God, Why are There Atheists?* (Wheaton: Tyndale House Publishers, 1978), 42-44.

13Ninian Smart, *The Religious Experience of Mankind* (New York: Charles Scribner's Sons, 1976), 40.

14Sproul, 49.

15Ibid., 12, 58, 101.

16Moreland, *Scaling the Secular City,* 229.

17Ibid.

18Geisler and Corduan, 74.

19Ibid., 74-75.

20Saint Augustine, *Confessions,* trans. R. S. Pine-Coffin (London: Penguin Books, 1961), 21.

# CHAPTER 14
# MAN'S GREATNESS
# AND WRETCHEDNESS

Psychological apologetics has been used to remind man that though he is great and noble, he is also wretched and cruel. Defenders of the faith must show that Christianity alone offers an adequate explanation for this dilemma of man. Man was created in God's image (man's greatness) but he has fallen (man's wretchedness).

### BLAISE PASCAL

Pascal taught that neither man's greatness, nor his wretchedness should be overlooked. He stated, "It is dangerous to explain too clearly to man how like he is to the animals without pointing out his greatness."[1] Pascal added, "It is also dangerous to make too much of his greatness without his vileness."[2] "It is still more dangerous to leave him in ignorance of both, but it is most valuable to represent both to him."[3]

Pascal declared that "Man's greatness comes from knowing he is wretched: a tree does not know it is wretched."[4] He reasons that, "All these examples of wretchedness prove his greatness. It is the wretchedness of a great lord, the wretchedness of a dispossessed king."[5] Pascal concludes that man "must have fallen from some better state which was once his own. Who indeed would think himself unhappy not to be a king except one who had been dispossessed?"[6]

Pascal describes the current state of man when he says that men "retain some feeble instinct from the happiness of their first nature..." and that they are "plunged into the wretchedness of their blindness and concupiscence, which has become their second nature."[7] Pascal states:

> Man is only a reed, the weakest in nature, but he is a thinking reed. There is no need for the whole universe to take up arms to crush him: a vapor, a drop of water is enough to kill him. But even if the universe were to crush him, man would still be nobler than his slayer, because he knows that he is dying and the advantage the universe has over him. The universe knows none of this. Thus all our dignity consists in thought.[8]

Pascal challenges his readers with the following words:

> Man's greatness and wretchedness are so evident that the true religion must necessarily teach us that there is in man some great principle of greatness and some great principle of wretchedness. It must also account for such amazing contradictions...Let us examine all the religions of the world on that point and let us see whether any but the Christian religion meets it.[9]

Pascal detected in man a greatness not found in the animal kingdom. But he also found in man a wretchedness that he shared with animals. Pascal believed that the true religion, whatever it is, must explain this dilemma of man. He concluded that Christianity alone adequately treats this issue.

## FRANCIS SCHAEFFER

Francis Schaeffer states that "Anyone with sensitivity and concern for the world can see that man is in a great dilemma. Man is able both to rise to great heights and to sink to great depths of cruelty and tragedy."[10] Schaeffer speaks of the "nobility of man" as well as man's "cruelty." Schaeffer declares, "So man stands with all his wonder and nobility, and yet also with his horrible cruelty that runs throughout the warp and woof of man's history."[11]

Schaeffer, in his attempt to explain the fact of man's nobility and cruelty, suggests that the only answer to the dilemma is the Christian answer. Man was created perfect and in God's image. But man has fallen into sin. Schaeffer states:

> In the area of morals, we have nothing of these answers except on the basis of a true, space-time, historic Fall. There was a time before the Fall, and then man turned from his proper integration point by choice; and in so doing, there was a moral discontinuity—man became abnormal.[12]

Schaeffer, in the tradition of Pascal, sees Christianity as the only solution to the dilemma of man. Without the doctrines of creation and the Fall, there would be no explanation for the cruelty and wretchedness of man.

## WEAKNESSES OF THE EVOLUTIONARY EXPLANATION

Many atheists have proposed the evolution hypothesis as another possible explanation for man's nobility and cruelty. Still, there are two weaknesses with the evolutionary hypothesis that cause it to fall short of offering an adequate explanation of man's dilemma. First, evolution implies that man is moving towards greatness, not away from it. Man, according to this view, is getting better. But the wars of the twentieth century have been the bloodiest of all time. There is much talk of peace, but men continue to war with one other. If anything, man is getting worse.

Second, man's greatness does not appear to be merely the next stage in animal development. Rather, it seems to be distinctly that which separates men from the animals. There seems to be a gap at this point that cannot be traversed. As one examines the animal kingdom, there is an advancement from one species to another that cannot be denied (although the evolutionary doctrine of common ancestry can be called into question). However, the advancement between man and animal is too great. The greatness of man is not a point of continuity with the animal kingdom. It is a point of discontinuity. It argues against evolution, not for it.

## CONCLUSION

Pascal and Schaeffer were both right to point out the greatness and wretchedness of man. Man's greatness can be seen in many ways. His unselfish acts of heroism, charitable giving, and caring for the less fortunate all attest to the greatness of man. Still, the builder of hospitals is also the builder of torture chambers. The history of mankind is filled with more than just acts of heroism. It records horrible murders. For every act of charity, there may be several acts of thievery.

Pascal and Schaeffer are also correct in declaring Christianity to be the only religion that deals adequately with man's greatness and his wretchedness. All other world religions downplay the wretchedness of man by teaching that man is good enough to save himself. There is an overemphasis on man's greatness and an underemphasis on man's wretchedness. Only Christianity offers the proper balance.

The argument for Christianity which begins with the greatness and wretchedness of man can be very effective. However, its effectiveness will depend on how well the apologist uncovers the deficiencies of all other proposed solutions offered by non-Christian belief systems. The Christian must show that man's greatness can only be explained if man was created perfect and in God's image. The believer must also show that only the Fall adequately deals with man's wretchedness.

ENDNOTES

1Pascal, *Pensees*, 60.

2Ibid.

3Ibid.

4Ibid., 59.

5Ibid.

6Ibid.

7Ibid., 77.

8Ibid., 95.

9Ibid., 76.

10Schaeffer, *Complete Works*, vol. 1, 109.

11Ibid., 293.

12Ibid., 304.

# PART FIVE

# PHILOSOPHICAL APOLOGETICS

# CHAPTER 15
# THE FAILURE OF ATHEISM

Philosophical Apologetics deals with the rational defense of the Christian Faith. Philosophy means the love of wisdom.[1] One of the functions of philosophy is the attempt to describe the true nature of reality.[2] Philosophy of religion (a branch of philosophy) and apologetics (a branch of theology) overlap in certain areas.[3] Arguments for God's existence, the philosophical problem of evil, the possibility of miracles, and the nature of morality are common to both philosophy of religion and apologetics. These topics will be examined in this section.

## ATHEISM AND AGNOSTICISM

Atheism is the belief that it can be proven that God does not exist.[4] Agnosticism, on the other hand, is the belief that man cannot know whether or not God exists.[5] It is possible to hold weaker forms of either view.[6] However, this chapter is only concerned with refuting the more dogmatic forms of atheism and agnosticism. Only the stronger forms, if proven, would defeat theism. The weaker forms leave open the possibility of theism. However, both atheism and agnosticism, in their strongest forms, are self-refuting.

In order for one to disprove God's existence (atheism), he would have to be all-knowing.[7] One would need to have the ability to see and know all things in the physical and spiritual realms. In short, one would have to be God to disprove God's existence. Of course, this is absurd.

Agnosticism is also self-defeating. One must know something about God to know that nothing can be known about God.[8] Obviously, this statement refutes itself. Therefore, agnosticism, like atheism, is a self-refuting view.

Many agnostics say that since man is finite (limited), he can never attain knowledge of an infinite (unlimited) Being. It is true that the finite cannot find the infinite on its own. However, this ignores the possibility that the infinite Being may choose to reveal Himself to finite beings. This is exactly what Christianity claims. The Bible teaches that God reveals Himself through both nature (Romans 1:18-22; Psalms 19:1) and the scriptures (2 Timothy 3:16-17; 2 Peter 1:20-21).

### DID MAN INVENT GOD?

Throughout history thinkers proclaimed their belief that God was a product of man's imagination. Ludwig Feuerbach (1804-1872) taught that man, due to his fear of death, wishes God into existence. Man recognizes his limitations and fears. God is projected to calm these fears. In short, God is what man wishes to be.[9]

Sigmund Freud (1856-1939) saw two separate causes for man's belief in God. First, Freud believed that each boy desires to have sexual relations with his mother. Because of this, he becomes jealous of his father and develops a hatred for him. Second, since man could not fully understand the forces of nature, he began to fear nature. Freud concluded that due to these two factors (man's guilt for hating his father and man's fear of nature), mankind deified nature and personalized it into a Father God.[10]

It should be understood that the speculation of Feuerbach and Freud was never meant to be used as an argument against God's existence. Instead, these two thinkers believed that God's existence had already been proven false by the advances of modern science. Their views were promoted not to disprove God's existence. Rather, they were promoted as a desperate attempt to explain why nearly all of mankind believes in a non-existent God. Therefore, the ideas of Feuerbach and Freud should not be considered evidence against God's existence. Instead, their theories were merely attempts to explain away some of the evidence against their views.[11]

Freud's own theories can be used against him. For it seems more likely that atheism is caused by the desire to kill the father image, rather than theism being caused by man's guilt for wanting to kill his father.[12] In man's attempt to be autonomous, he wishes God out of existence.

Whatever the case, the speculation of Feuerbach and Freud seems itself to be wishful thinking by atheists. If men were to invent a God, it is doubtful that it would be the demanding God of the Bible.[13] Man would create a more permissive god, much like the gods of the pagan religions. In short, the theories of Feuerbach and Freud offer a more adequate explanation for atheism and idolatry than they do for Christianity.[14]

## A. J. AYER AND LOGICAL POSITIVISM

In the first half of this century, A. J. Ayer and his colleagues popularized their view of logical positivism. Logical positivism was based upon the verification principle. This principle declared that for a statement to be meaningful, it has to be either true by definition or verifiable by one or more of the five senses.[15] This meant that all discussion about God should be considered meaningless.[16]

If true, this view would be very damaging for theism. Though it would not prove God's nonexistence, it would make all talk about God meaningless.[17] If one cannot meaningfully talk about God, one cannot speculate about his possible existence.

The problem with the verification principle is that it is itself not true by definition or verifiable by one or more of the five senses.[18] In other words, the verification principle is self-refuting. If the verification principle is true, then it is itself meaningless, for it fails its own test.[19]

If atheism is to deliver a fatal blow to theism, it will have to look elsewhere. Logical positivism has failed to render discussion about God meaningless.

## IS RELIGIOUS LANGUAGE EQUIVOCAL?

Some have maintained that all talk about God is equivocal.[20] In other words, they believe that terms used to describe God have totally different meanings than when they are used in connection with finite beings such as man. If this is true, then man cannot know anything about God. If someone says God is holy, he has uttered a meaningless statement. For man knows what holiness means only when it refers to a man. Man has no idea of what holiness means when applied to God. What holiness means in reference to an infinite being (God) cannot be known by finite beings. If the theist is justified in his or her claims to know something about God, then this objection must be answered.

Some theists have argued that terms used to describe God are univocal.[21] This means that they have totally the same meaning when used to describe both God and man. The problem with this view is that it is hard to believe that God is holy in the same way that man can be holy. For God is infinitely holy, whereas man is only finitely holy. Can holiness have the exact meaning for both man and God? It seems not.

Other theists contend that religious language is analogical.[22] They hold that terms used of God and man are not equivocal (totally different meanings) or univocal (totally the same meanings). Instead, terms used of God and man are only analogical (similar meanings). However, this view is also problematic. For if God-talk is analogical, then theologians are still using meaningless terms about God. For terms like "holiness" still lack the same meaning they hold when used of men. We can only know what holiness means when it is applied to man. It appears that there must be some univocal element to God-talk if it is to be meaningful.[23]

The answer to this dilemma is to hold the view of Thomas Aquinas. He reasoned that words have the same meaning (univocal) when applied to either God or man. However, Aquinas taught that they can only be applied in a similar (analogical) way.[24] Therefore, holiness means the same thing for both man and God. Still, it must be applied finitely to man and infinitely to God. Therefore, God-talk is not equivocal. Theists can meaningfully talk about God.

## JEAN-PAUL SARTRE AND EXISTENTIALISM

Jean-Paul Sartre was a famous French philosopher and existentialist. He argued that if the theist persists in his assertion that everything needs a cause, then even God needs a cause. Therefore, the theist, according to Sartre, must argue that God caused His own existence. But, this would make God a self-caused being, which is impossible.[25] For a being to cause its own existence, it must exist before it existed in order to bring itself into existence. However, it is absurd to say that a being existed before it existed. Therefore, reasoned Sartre, since God is a self-caused being, He cannot exist.

However, no informed theist believes that everything (including God) needs a cause. Only dependent beings (beings that have a beginning) need a cause. Since God is an independent and eternal being, He does not need a cause.[26] God is not a self-caused being. He is an uncaused being. His existence needs no cause for He always existed.

Sartre also contended that since man is free, God cannot exist. In his view, if man is free (and Sartre believed so), then there could be no sovereign God. If a sovereign God exists, then men are robots.[27]

There have been two ways that theists respond to this argument. One can take a hyper-Calvinistic position and deny human free will.[28] Or, one can simply maintain that God sovereignly chose to make man free.[29] Still, man is not absolutely free. He is free to disobey God and reject Christ, but he is not free to escape the God-ordained consequences of his actions. In short, neither of Sartre's objections presents insurmountable problems for theism.

### BERTRAND RUSSELL

The great British philosopher and mathematician Bertrand Russell reasoned that if everything needs a cause, then so does God. But if God doesn't need a cause, then neither does the universe.[30] As mentioned above, the theist responds to this by pointing out that not everything needs a cause. Only that which has a beginning needs a cause. Since God does not have a beginning, He needs no cause.[31]

Secondly, there is both scientific and philosophical evidence that the universe had a beginning. Scientific evidence consists in the second law of thermodynamics (energy deterioration) and the big bang model. The second law of thermodynamics shows that the amount of usable energy in the universe is running down. Therefore, the universe will eventually cease to exist when all its energy is used up. But if the universe will have an end, it had to have a beginning. This means that the universe began with all its energy in a usable state. Hence, the universe had a beginning.[32]

## THE BIG BANG MODEL

The big bang model reveals that the universe is expanding at an equal rate in all directions. This is much like the effects of an explosion which blows debris in all directions. If one goes back in time, the universe would become more and more dense until the entire universe would be compressed into an infinitely small point. This would mark the beginning of the universe.[33]

The scientific evidence for the beginning of the universe does not stand alone. Philosophical evidence can be found as well. For if the universe is eternal, there would be an infinite amount of actual events in the past. But then it would be impossible to reach the present moment. For no matter how many events one traverses, there will always be an infinite amount of events left. Hence, the present moment could never be reached. But the present moment has been reached. This reveals that there is only a finite amount of events in the past. Therefore, the universe had a first event. In other words, the universe had a beginning.[34]

Bertrand Russell's objection therefore loses its force. The universe cannot be eternal. It must have a cause. Eventually one must arrive at a first cause, a being that needs no cause. This uncaused being is what the theist calls God.

## ALBERT CAMUS

The French existentialist Albert Camus authored the novel entitled *The Plague*. In this work, Camus argued that if God allowed the plague to occur, then to fight the plague is to fight God. Therefore, to be religious, one must be antihumanitarian. Only the atheist can be a humanitarian and remain consistent with his beliefs.[35]

However, though God permits the plague (symbolic for evil and human suffering) for the purpose of a greater good, He is nonetheless working to defeat the plague.[36] In fact, the greater good coming from God permitting the plague may include the godly man joining God to battle the plague.[37] Just because God allows something to occur does not make it in itself good. For God could and does allow evil to occur for the purpose of a good that He will bring from the evil.

Therefore, a person can be religious and also be humanitarian without going against his or her beliefs. On the other hand, what is to prevent the atheist from doing whatever he pleases? It seems that the Christian humanitarian is more consistent with his or her beliefs than the atheist is. For in atheism there is no final judgment and moral values are mere human inventions. Atheists are not being consistent with their world view whenever they condemn an action as wrong.

### ANTONY FLEW

British philosopher Antony Flew claims that since there is no way to falsify God's existence, to assert that He does exist is an incoherent statement.[38] Flew is famous for his parable of the invisible gardener.[39] In this parable, a believer and a non-believer come upon a garden in the midst of the wilderness. The believer assumes that there exists a gardener who cares for the garden. The non-believer, however, disagrees. He concludes that there is no gardener. They were not able to detect the existence of the gardener though they ran several tests. They did not see or hear him enter the garden. Even bloodhounds could not smell him. Rather than surrender his faith in the gardener, the believer reasons that the gardener must be invisible and unable to be detected by the five senses. The non-believer responds by stating that there is no difference between this invisible gardener and no gardener at all. In other words, if there is no way to falsify a view, then the view is worthless.[40]

Flew declares that just as there is no way to falsify the existence of the invisible gardener, so too the existence of the Christian God cannot be falsified. In short, to claim that God exists is to make a meaningless statement. There is no way to prove it false.

In response to Flew's objection, several things can be noted. First, the believer views the universe as dependent and in need of a cause. If there were no independent God, there would also be no dependent universe. If the universe could be shown to exist independent of any cause, then this would go a long way to falsifying the God hypothesis. However, scientific and philosophical arguments for an eternal and independent universe have not been successful.

Recent thought seems to lead in the other direction.[41] Second, the God of the Bible is not a silent God who is unable to be detected. The Judeo-Christian scriptures are filled with prophecies that were fulfilled hundreds of years after they were recorded.[42] If these prophecies had failed, then the God of the Bible would be falsified.

Third, Christianity claims that the God of the Bible has become a man (John 1:1,14). The invisible gardener has taken visible form. Jesus claimed to be God incarnate. Jesus gave persuasive evidence for this claim by performing numerous miracles in the presence of eyewitnesses. His greatest miracle was when He rose from the dead and appeared to many eyewitnesses. If the first century Jewish religious leaders had produced the rotting corpse of Christ, they would have falsified Christ's claims and crushed Christianity in its embryonic form. Despite the fact that the Jewish religious leaders had the desire and to do so, they did not produce the body. In a later chapter, the resurrection will be examined in greater detail. What needs to be noted here is that the belief in the existence of the God of the Bible is open to testing and falsification. Instead of claiming that God is an incoherent concept incapable of being falsified, Flew would do better to examine the supposed evidence for the Christian God and then attempt to prove as false the claim that He exists.

## ARGUMENTS FROM CONTRADICTORY ATTRIBUTES

One attempt to refute the existence of God is to claim that the God of the Bible has certain characteristics that are contradictory.[43] If this can be proven, the Christian God cannot exist. This atheistic endeavor can take its form in several different arguments. Two examples will suffice.

Atheists often argue that if God is all-powerful, then He can do anything. This would include the ability to create a rock so large that even He cannot lift it. But if God cannot lift this rock, He is not all-powerful. Therefore, concludes the atheist, no all-powerful God can exist.[44]

Though the theist agrees that God is all-powerful, he recognizes that there are some things which even an all-powerful being cannot do. Since an all-powerful being will always be able to accomplish whatever He sets out to do, it is impossible for an all-powerful being to fail. The above atheistic argument is arguing that since God is all-powerful He can do anything—even fail. This is like saying that since God is all-powerful He can be not all-powerful. Obviously, this is absurd. An all-powerful being cannot fail. Therefore, God can create a rock of tremendous size, but, since He is all-powerful, He will always be able to lift it.[45]

There are several things that an all-powerful being cannot do: He cannot lie, sin, or change His mind (Numbers 23:19; James 1:13; 1 Samuel 15:29). Anything that indicates failure cannot be credited to God.[46]

It should also be noted that God cannot do whatever is impossible by definition. For instance, God cannot create square circles.[47] He cannot create a human that is non-human. He cannot make something both exist and not exist at the same time.

In short, when one says that God is all-powerful, one means that God is able to accomplish all that He desires to do. It means that God can do everything that is possible.[48] But even an all-powerful being cannot do what is impossible by definition. God can do many things that are humanly impossible. However, there are some things that even an all-powerful being cannot do.

Therefore, since God is all-powerful, He will always be able to master His creation. He will always be able to lift any rock that He creates. And, since all that exists (besides Himself) is His creation, there is no rock, nor will there ever be a rock, that He cannot lift.

A second example of an argument against God from supposed contradictory attributes is as follows. If something is good simply because God wills it, then good is merely an arbitrary concept. But, if God wills it because it is good, then good is a standard above God. Therefore, either good is arbitrary or good is above God.[49]

If the theist concedes either of these two propositions, the concept of God will be damaged. For if good is arbitrary, then calling God good says nothing more than He does what He wills to do. He doesn't do what is right. He simply acts arbitrarily. Whatever He does automatically is considered right for the mere reason that it is an act of God.

If the theist takes the other alternative of the dilemma, the situation is no better. For if God decides to do something because it is good, it appears that there is a standard of right and wrong above God. But then God would not be the ultimate being. A necessary element of the traditional Christian concept of God is that He is the ultimate being. There is no being greater than God. However, God cannot be the ultimate being if there is a standard of right and wrong to which He must submit. The standard itself would be the ultimate being since it would be above God.

Those who use this objection against theism fail to acknowledge that God wills something because it is consistent with His own good nature. Therefore, the standard is not above God; God is the standard.[50] Thus, good is not arbitrary, for it is based upon God's good nature.[51]

### THE PROBLEM OF EVIL

Many atheists believe that the existence of evil is proof that an all-good and all-powerful God does not exist.[52] The significance of this argument requires that an entire chapter of this work be dedicated to its refutation. Therefore, discussion of this objection will be dealt with in a later chapter of this dissertation.

### THE REAL PROBLEM WITH ATHEISTS

According to the Bible, the real problem with atheists is not an intellectual problem. Rather it is a moral problem. It is not that there is not enough evidence for God's existence. Instead, the atheist chooses not to submit to the Creator. The Bible declares that those who act upon the truth will come to the light of Christ (John 3:16-21). On the other hand, those who suppress the truth of God's existence are without excuse. For the invisible God has revealed His existence and power through His visible creation (Romans 1:18-23).

It appears that there are two opposing drives in each person. One is a thirst for God (John 6:35). The other is the drive for human autonomy (Romans 3:10-12). If a person seeks God with all his heart, he will find Him (Jeremiah 29:13). But if he chooses to continually reject the Creator, there is no amount of evidence that will change his mind, unless he chooses to sincerely consider the evidence. All that the Christian apologist can do is provide evidence for the existence of the God of the Bible and to refute arguments for atheism. Once a strong case for Christian Theism is made, the atheist must still choose to accept or reject the evidence. The inward persuasion of the Holy Spirit on the heart of the nonbeliever is necessary, but, in the end, the atheist must choose to follow that persuasion. The ultimate problem is not one of the intellect; it is a moral problem of the will. When all is said and done, one must *choose* God.

## ENDNOTES

1Geisler and Feinberg, 13.

2Ibid., 17.

3Ronald H. Nash, *Faith and Reason* (Grand Rapids: Zondervan Publishing House, 1988), 13-14.

4Geisler and Feinberg, 430.

5Ibid., 429.

6Ibid., 296.

7Geisler, *Apologetics*, 233.

8Geisler and Feinberg, 298-299.

9Sahakian, *History of Philosophy*, 202.

10Sigmund Freud, *The Future of an Illusion* trans. W. D. Robson-Scott (New York: Double Day, 1964), 20-27.

11Sproul, 49-50.

12Moreland, *Scaling the Secular City*, 229.

13Sproul, 58, 145-146.

14Ibid.

15Geisler and Feinberg, 50.

16Ibid.

17Ibid.

18Ibid.

19Ibid.

20Geisler and Corduan, 252-271.

21Ibid., 252.

22Ibid., 253.

23Ibid., 255.

24Ibid., 263-264.

25Geisler and Feinberg, 293.

26Ibid.

27Ibid., 295.

28Ibid.

29Ibid.

30Bertrand Russell, *Why I Am Not a Christian* (New York: Simon and Schuster, 1957), 6-7.

31Geisler and Feinberg, 293.

32Roy E. Peacock, *A Brief History of Eternity* (Wheaton: Crossway Books, 1990), 67-69.

33Hugh Ross, *The Creator and the Cosmos* (Colorado Springs: NavPress, 1993), 19-27.

34Craig, 81.

35Geisler and Corduan, 365.

36Ibid., 365-366.

37Ibid.

38Hick, ed. *The Existence of God*, 224-226.

39Ibid.

40Ibid.

41Craig, 73-95.

42Henry M. Morris, *Many Infallible Proofs* (El Cajon: Master Books, 1974), 181-199.

43Geisler and Feinberg, 294.

44Ibid., 294-295.

45Ibid., 273-274.

46Geisler, *Apologetics*, 229.

47Ibid.

48Ibid.

49Geisler and Feinberg, 226.

50Ibid.

51Ibid.

52Geisler and Corduan, 295-385.

# CHAPTER 16
# THE FAILURE OF OTHER
# NON-THEISTIC WORLD VIEWS

Theism is the view of reality which holds to the existence of a personal God who is separate (transcendent) from the universe though involved (immanent) with it.[1] Christianity, Judaism, and Islam are the three main theistic religions.[2]

It has been shown that atheism, the world view that there is no God, has failed to prove its case. This means that theism may be true. It is therefore possible that God exists. However, before looking into arguments for the existence of the theistic God, discussion of other non-theistic world views is necessary to show that they have also failed to prove their cases.

The non-theistic world views (other than atheism) include pantheism, panentheism, deism, finite godism, and polytheism. If these world views fail as atheism has failed, then the case for theism will become more probable since it is the only remaining major world view. Of course, the case for theism will reach a high degree of probability only if strong arguments can be advanced in its favor.

PANTHEISM
Pantheism is the world view that teaches that God is the universe.[3] Pantheism is based upon monism, the belief that all reality is one being.[4] Hinduism and some adherents of Buddhism are pantheistic in their thought.[5] The New Age Movement (the invasion of Western Society with Hindu thought) is also pantheistic.[6]

Pantheism teaches that God is not a personal being. Instead, God is an impersonal force.[7] Since pantheists believe that all reality is one being and that God is this one reality, they believe that each individual is God.[8] In fact, individual existence is merely an illusion since all reality is one being.[9]

There are several problems for pantheism which cause it to fail as a world view. First, many beings exist, not just one.[10] As Christian philosopher Norman Geisler has pointed out, it is actually undeniable that I exist.[11] For if I attempt to deny my existence, I must first exist to make the denial.[12] For nothing can deny nothing. Only an existent being can deny its own existence. Therefore, I exist. However, if I try to convince others that I alone exist, I must first affirm their own individual and separate existence by communicating with them.[13] In other words, to argue for pantheism is to admit that pantheism is false. To argue with others is to affirm the existence of others, and if more than one being exists, then pantheism cannot be true.

A second problem with pantheism is that there is strong evidence that the universe had a beginning. Both the big bang model and the second law of thermodynamics reveal this.[14] Also, if the universe is eternal, the present moment could never have arrived. But since the present moment has arrived, only a finite number of events could have occurred in the past.[15] Therefore, there was a first event. The universe had a beginning. Since from nothing, nothing comes, everything that had a beginning needs a cause. Hence, the universe needs a cause.[16] But, for pantheism to be true, the universe would have to be eternal and uncaused.

Third, pantheism claims that reality is ultimately impersonal. This is the same as saying that reality is non-intelligent and non-moral.[17] But for someone to deny the reality of intelligence, he must first assume he has the intelligence to make the denial.[18] Even pantheists pass moral judgments on others. In fact, many pantheists have been known to protest violence and the production of nuclear weapons.[19] They have fought for stricter anti-pollution legislation and campaigned for animal rights.[20] It is hard to find a pantheist who is not vocal about his or her moral beliefs. Pantheists must explain where intelligence and morality come from. Could intelligence and morality have been caused by a non-intelligent and non-moral being? It appears more probable that the Ultimate Cause of intelligence and morality must Himself be an intelligent and moral Being.[21]

Fourth, why should anyone accept the pantheistic claim that the world is an illusion? Does not common sense and experience favor the reality of the physical world? Why should anyone embrace pantheism without any evidence when common sense and experience teach otherwise?[22]

For these four reasons it appears that pantheism, as a world view, has failed. If an alternative to theism is to be accepted, one must look elsewhere.

## PANENTHEISM

Panentheism has been described as the belief that the universe is God's body.[23] In this world view, God is conceived of as having two poles to His existence. In His potential pole, He is infinite, unchanging, and eternal. In His actual pole, He is finite, changing, and temporal.[24] Unlike pantheism, panentheism views God as personal.[25]

Panentheism fails for several reasons. First, God cannot be both infinite and finite. This would be the same as saying that God is both unlimited and limited,[26] and this is an obvious contradiction. The Christian concept of God is one of an infinite God in His basic nature.[27] Panentheism, on the other hand, holds the contradictory concept of a God who is both infinite and finite in His basic nature.

Second, panentheism is again contradictory when it declares God to be both eternal (without a beginning) and temporal (with a beginning).[28] One cannot have it both ways. Either God is eternal or God is temporal. In the Christian doctrine of the incarnation, the eternal God added a temporal nature to his eternal nature.[29] This involves no contradiction, but, in the case of panentheism, a contradiction is evident. If the eternal pole of God caused the temporal pole of God to come into existence, then it would make more sense for the panentheist to refer to the temporal pole not as God, but as God's creation. But then the panentheist would cease to be a panentheist. In fact, he would then be a theist.[30]

Third, panentheism teaches that God actualizes His own potentialities. However, this is impossible. No potentiality can actualize itself. For instance, empty cups cannot fill themselves. For a potentiality to become actual, something actual must actualize it. As a result, the panentheistic god, if it existed, would need the theistic God to actualize its potential to exist.[31] Therefore, Panentheism fails as a world view.

## DEISM

Deism is the world view that promotes the belief in a God who created the universe but no longer has any dealings with it.[32] The deist believes that God allows the world to operate on its own in accordance with natural laws that He has set in motion.[33] God does not perform miracles or interrupt the natural course of events.[34]

Thomas Jefferson, Benjamin Franklin, and Thomas Paine were deists of the eighteenth century.[35] Though deism is not as popular as it once was, similar views are held today by many Unitarians and religious humanists.[36]

Several objections to deism deserve mention. First, deists deny a miracle-working God. Yet, they admit one of God's greatest supernatural works when they affirm His work of creation. If God could create the entire universe out of nothing, then could he not perform lesser miracles?[37]

Second, if God cared enough to create the universe, then why doesn't He care enough to be involved with it?[38] And, third, the deistic view of natural laws is outdated. Natural laws are now considered by scientists to be descriptive of the general way nature acts. No longer are natural laws thought to prescribe what can and cannot happen in nature.[39] Natural laws cannot automatically rule out miracles, just as the occurrence of usual events does not disprove the possibility of unusual events occurring.[40]

In the seventeenth and eighteenth centuries, deism was a strong movement.[41] Much of its popularity was due to the belief that the science of that day had proven miracles to be impossible.[42] However, now that this misconception has been overturned, deism is no longer the attractive world view that it once was.

## FINITE GODISM

Finite Godism is a world view that accepts the existence of a god. However, it believes He is limited.[43] Adherents differ as to how God is limited. Some believe He is limited in His power.[44] Others consider Him limited in His knowledge or His goodness.[45]

Devotees of Finite Godism usually promote their world view as the answer to the problem of evil.[46] They reason that an all-good and all-powerful God would not allow evil and innocent humans to suffer in the world.[47] Rabbi Harold Kushner, author of *When Bad Things Happen to Good People*, holds this view. He believes that evil proves God is not perfect and that He is limited in power.[48] For if God could prevent it, reasons Kushner, God would not allow the innocent to suffer.[49] Kushner asks others to forgive God for His failures.[50]

Several responses have been given to those who believe in the existence of a finite God. First, all finite existence needs a cause for its continuing existence.[51] Finite beings are, by definition, limited beings. And limited beings, precisely because of their limitations, must depend on other beings to keep them in existence. In fact, if everything that exists is limited and dependent, then nothing would now exist. For there must exist an infinite Being that is the cause of the continuing existence of all finite and dependent beings. In other words, a finite God would depend on an infinite God for its existence. However, a finite God would not be God after all. Only the infinite Being is God.[52]

Second, a finite God doesn't deserve worship.[53] Only a being that is ultimately worthy is deserving of worship. A God with limitations is surely not ultimately worthy. Only an infinite Being is deserving of worship.

Third, evil does not prove that God must be limited.[54] An all-good and all-powerful God may choose to allow evil and human suffering for the purpose of a greater good. What exactly this greater good may entail in specific cases may remain a mystery to finite beings, but, the wisdom of an infinite Being far transcends the wisdom of finite beings (Isaiah 55:8-9). A child may question the decision of his parents to allow him to receive surgery. But he does not have access to the amount of information that his parents have, and he does not see that the present pain he is enduring is for the purpose of future healing. The relationship of mankind to God is analogous to the relationship of this child to his parents. Also, God may defeat evil in the future (as the Bible teaches). In fact, only an infinite God can guarantee the ultimate defeat of evil. A finite God cannot.[55]

In short, finite godism leaves one with a god who is no God at all. For he, like the rest of the universe, needs a cause. He is not worthy of worship, and he cannot guarantee the defeat of evil. A god who needs help and forgiveness deserves only sympathy, not worship.

## POLYTHEISM

Polytheism is the world view that teaches the existence of more than one god.[56] Many Eastern religions accept the existence of many gods. This includes certain forms of Hinduism, Confucianism, Shintoism, Taoism, and Jainism.[57] Western thought is itself not without polytheistic belief systems. Ancient Greek mythology expressed polytheistic themes.[58] Several cult groups such as Mormonism, Scientology, and the Unification Church spread polytheism in the West today.[59]

Polytheism fails for the following reasons. Either all the gods are finite or at least one of them is infinite. They cannot all be finite. If they are all finite beings, then they would need an infinite Being to ground their existence, but, then this infinite Being would be God.[60]

So there must exist at least one infinite Being. It is not possible that there exist more than one infinite Being. If more than one infinite Being existed, they would limit one another's existence. One infinite Being could prevent the other infinite Being(s) from accomplishing its goals. But then these beings would not be infinite since they would be limited by another's power. Therefore, there must exist one, and only one, infinite Being.[61] This one infinite Being would alone be God. Therefore, Polytheism fails in its attempt to explain reality.

## SKEPTICISM NOT A VIABLE OPTION

All world views, except for theism, have been shown to be failures. They are self-contradictory and fail to explain the available evidence. If theism, the only remaining world view, also fails, then skepticism would be the only possible alternative. However, skepticism also fails.

If one decides to be a skeptic, then he has chosen to suspend judgment on all things. He has failed to suspend judgment on his choice to be a skeptic.[62] This, of course, is contradictory. Also, no one can consistently live like a skeptic. For example, if someone suspended judgment on what he should eat, then he would eventually starve to death.[63]

## CONCLUSION

Therefore, since skepticism fails as all non-theistic world views have failed, then, due to the process of elimination, theism must be true. Still, the following chapters will include a positive defense of theism.

## ENDNOTES

1Norman L. Geisler and William D. Watkins, *Worlds Apart* (Grand Rapids: Baker Book House, 1984), 38.

2Geisler, *Apologetics*, 263.

3Geisler and Watkins, 98-99.

4Geisler, *Apologetics*, 173-174.

5Geisler and Watkins, 78-79.

6Ibid., 94.

7Ibid., 98.

8Ibid., 96.

9Ibid., 99.

10Geisler, *Apologetics*, 187.

11Ibid., 239.

12Ibid.

13Ibid., 241.

14Craig, 81-93.

15Ibid., 81.

16Ibid., 93.

17Geisler, *Apologetics*, 247-249.

18Ibid., 247-248.

19Walter Martin, *The New Age Cult* (Minneapolis: Bethany House Publishers, 1989), 65.

20Ibid.

21Geisler, *Apologetics*, 247-248.

22Geisler and Watkins, 102.

23Ibid., 108.

24Ibid.

25Ibid., 136.

26Ibid.

27Erickson, *Christian Theology*, 272.

28Geisler and Watkins, 139.

29Erickson, 735.

30Geisler and Watkins, 21.

31Geisler, *Apologetics*, 208-209.

32Ibid., 147-148.

33Ibid.

34Ibid.

35Ibid., 148.

36Ibid., 181.

37Ibid.

38Ibid., 182.

39Ibid., 181.

40Ibid.

41Ibid., 148.

42Ibid., 181.

43Ibid., 188.

44Ibid.

45Ibid., 189-190.

46Ibid., 188.

47Ibid.

48Harold S. Kushner, *When Bad Things Happen to Good People* (New York: Avon Books, 1981), 148.

49Ibid., 134.

50Ibid., 147-148.

51Geisler and Watkins, 211-212.

52Ibid., 212.

53Ibid.

54Ibid., 212-213.

55Ibid., 212.

56Ibid., 217.

57Ibid., 218.

58Ibid.

59Ibid.

60Geisler, *Thomas Aquinas*, 130.

61Ibid.

62Geisler and Feinberg, 93-94.

63Ibid., 94.

# CHAPTER 17
# THE ONTOLOGICAL ARGUMENT

Having refuted atheism and other non-theistic world views, it is now time to defend theism. The following four chapters will discuss several philosophical arguments for the existence of the God of theism. In this chapter the ontological argument for God's existence will be examined.

The ontological argument for God's existence is an attempt to prove God's existence solely from the idea or concept of God.[1] It is an attempt to prove God's existence from reason alone. No appeal to the facts of experience is considered. In this way the ontological argument differs from other arguments for God's existence.

All other arguments for God's existence argue from something in existence to the existence of God. The teleological argument argues from the design in the universe to the existence of an intelligent Designer.[2] The moral argument argues from the existence of moral values to the existence of the absolute moral Lawgiver.[3] The cosmological argument reasons from the existence of dependent beings to the existence of a totally independent Being.[4] Only the ontological argument argues from the concept of God to His existence. The ontological argument alone does not begin with the facts of experience.

The ontological argument was originated by Anselm of Canterbury (1033-1109AD). Various forms of this argument has been defended throughout history by great thinkers such as Rene Descartes (1596-1650), Benedict Spinoza (1632-1677), Gottfried

Wilhelm Leibniz (1646-1716). Charles Hartshorne, Norman Malcolm, and Alvin Plantinga are three twentieth century scholars who have also defended this argument.[5] But, the ontological argument has also been opposed throughout history by other great thinkers such as Gaunilo (a contemporary of Anselm), Thomas Aquinas (1225-1274), David Hume (1711-1776), and Immanuel Kant (1724-1804).[6] In short, the ontological argument has been one of the most hotly debated issues in the history of philosophy.

## ANSELM OF CANTERBURY

In Anselm's work entitled *Proslogium*, he introduced this unique argument for God's existence. Though Anselm himself may not have been aware of the fact, he actually gave two different versions of the ontological argument.[7]

In Anselm's first argument, he stated that both believers and unbelievers define God as the greatest conceivable Being. Anselm reasoned that if God does not exist, then a person could conceive of a being greater than the greatest conceivable Being. A person could conceive of a being who had the same attributes as the greatest conceivable Being, but also existed. But, then this would be the greatest conceivable Being. Therefore, concluded Anselm, the greatest conceivable Being must exist.[8]

Another way of stating this first argument is as follows. The greatest conceivable Being would, by definition, be a being who has every possible perfection. Since Anselm held that existence is a perfection, he concluded that the greatest conceivable Being must exist.[9]

Anselm's second form of the ontological argument stated that God, by definition, is a Necessary Being. A Necessary Being is a being that cannot not exist. Therefore, reasoned Anselm, it is a contradiction to say that a Necessary Being does not exist. Hence, concluded Anselm, since God is a Necessary Being, He must exist.[10]

## OBJECTIONS TO THE ONTOLOGICAL ARGUMENT

In Anselm's own lifetime his ontological argument was opposed by a monk named Gaunilo.[11] Gaunilo's main attack on the ontological argument was found in his illustration of a perfect island. Gaunilo reasoned that we have just as much right in concluding that

God exists merely from our idea of a perfect Being as we do in concluding the existence of a perfect island solely from our idea of a perfect island.[12] Anselm responded by stating that the analogy between a perfect island and a perfect Being breaks down. For the idea of a perfect island does not include its existence, while the idea of a perfect Being does entail its existence.[13] Anselm accused Gaunilo of not understanding what Anselm's argument was actually saying. Today, many philosophers agree that Gaunilo did in fact misunderstand Anselm's argument.[14]

Still, this does not mean that Anselm's ontological argument cannot be refuted. Immanuel Kant believed that Anselm's argument was fallacious. Kant stated that the deficiency of Anselm's argument was in Anselm's view that existence is a perfection.[15] The concept of God as a Being who has all perfections does not entail the existence of that Being because existence is not a perfection. Existence does not change in any way the concept of a being, it merely posits actual existence to that being. To say that something has existence is to say that it actually exists outside the mind. The concept of a perfect Being who exists is no greater than the concept of a perfect Being who does not exist. They are both the same concept, though one has existence while the other does not. Therefore, as far as Kant was concerned, it is faulty reasoning to go from the realm of pure thought to the realm of actual existence by treating existence as one of the perfections that the most perfect Being must have.[16]

From Kant's time on, this has become the primary objection to the ontological argument.[17] Still, many philosophers who agree with this criticism believe that it only applies to the first type of Anselm's ontological argument. They believe that Anselm's second argument remains intact despite Kant's critique. Two of these philosophers are Charles Hartshorne and Norman Malcolm.[18]

## RESTATEMENTS OF THE ONTOLOGICAL ARGUMENT

Norman Malcolm defended Anselm's second type of ontological argument. Malcolm reasoned that the existence of a necessary Being can either be necessary (it cannot not exist), impossible (it cannot exist), or possible (it may or may not exist). Malcolm stated that since no one has shown the concept of a necessary Being to be contradictory (logically impossible), then the existence of a necessary

Being is possible. If it is possible for a necessary Being to exist, then it must exist. It is a contradiction to say that a being which cannot not exist (a necessary Being) may or may not exist. Therefore, a necessary being must exist.[19] The heart of Malcolm's argument can be stated as follows. By definition, a necessary Being cannot not exist. Therefore, a necessary Being must exist.[20]

However, Malcolm admits a weakness in his argument. He concedes that he is unaware of any way to prove that there is no contradiction in the concept of a necessary Being. Therefore, it is logically possible that the concept of a necessary Being is contradictory. Hence, it may be the case that it is impossible for a necessary Being to exist. Therefore, at best, Malcolm's ontological argument only shows that it is probable that a necessary Being exists. For it is always possible that someone will someday show that the concept of a necessary Being is contradictory.[21]

Another modern restatement of the ontological argument comes from Alvin Plantinga.[22] After years of examining and critiquing the ontological argument, Plantinga proposed his own version of the argument. Though Plantinga viewed Anselm's argument as problematic, Plantinga considers his own argument as valid.[23]

Plantinga argued that the greatest possible Being would have to be a being that exists as the greatest possible Being in every possible world. Plantinga concludes that since the actual world is a possible world (it is not an impossible world), then the greatest possible being must exist in the actual world.[24]

Though Plantinga's argument appears valid, it ceases to be an ontological argument. Its premises leave the realm of pure reason by assuming the existence of the actual world.[25] By definition, an ontological argument must prove God's existence from the mere concept of God. The other arguments for God's existence begin with something that actually exists and then argue to the existence of God. Plantinga's argument should be classified as a type of cosmological argument. It starts with the existence of the actual world and then argues to God's existence.[26]

Christian philosophers Norman Geisler and Winfried Corduan consider this the downfall of the ontological argument. For it is always logically possible that nothing exists.[27] Therefore, in order for the ontological argument to work, it must start with the premise, "something exists."[28] But, then it is no longer an ontological argument. It starts with actual existence, not pure thought.

## CONCLUSION

An examination of Anselm's ontological argument has produced several observations. First, most philosophers believe that Immanuel Kant has successfully refuted Anselm's first argument. Second, Norman Malcolm's version of Anselm's second ontological argument leaves the realm of logical necessity since he admits he cannot prove that the concept of a necessary Being is not an impossible being. In other words, Malcom admits that it is possible that someone will someday prove that the concept of a Necessary Being involves a contradiction. Therefore, his argument, if successful, could only prove that God probably exists. And, third, Plantinga showed that the only apparent way to rescue the ontological argument is to begin with the cosmological premise that something exists. But, then the ontological argument is no longer ontological; it leaves the realm of pure reason.

Another factor should also be mentioned. Charles Hartshorne and Benedict Spinoza were mentioned earlier as proponents of the ontological argument. But they both denied the existence of a theistic God. Spinoza's God was a pantheistic God (a God who is identical to the universe).[29] Hartshorne utilized the ontological argument to prove the existence of a panentheistic God (a God whose body is the world).[30] Even if the ontological argument is valid (and it seems that it is not), it apparently does not reveal enough about God's nature to show us what kind of God He (or it) is.[31]

At best, apologists should suspend judgment on the ontological argument. At worst, it is a failure. Either way, defenders of the Christian faith should look elsewhere to provide evidence for God's existence.

ENDNOTES

1Craig, 61.

2Ibid., 66.

3Ibid., 70.

4Ibid., 62.

5Geisler and Corduan, 123-149.

6Ibid.

7Ibid., 123.

8Anselm, *St. Anselm: Basic Writings* trans. by S. N. Deane (Lasalle: Open Court Publishing, 1966), 7-8.

9Sproul, Gerstner, and Lindsley, 102.

10Anselm, 8-9.

11Ibid., 145-153.

12Geisler and Corduan, 126.

13Ibid.

14Ibid., 126-127.

15Ibid., 134.

16Ibid., 134-135.

17Ibid., 135.

18Ibid., 142.

19Ibid., 142-144.

20Ibid., 143.

21Ibid., 144.

22Plantinga, 85-112.

23Geisler and Corduan, 146.

24Plantinga, 108-110.

25Geisler and Corduan, 147-148.

26Ibid., 148.

27Ibid.

28Ibid.

29Ibid., 149.

30Ibid.

31Ibid.

# CHAPTER 18
# THE TELEOLOGICAL ARGUMENT

Since the ontological argument appears to have failed in its attempt to prove God's existence through reason alone, Christian apologists must start with the "facts" of experience and argue to God's existence. The ontological argument tried to prove God's existence *a priori* (prior to and apart from experience).[1] It sought to establish God's existence as definitionally true. Rather than trying to deduce God's existence with logical necessity, defenders of the faith should argue inductively. Apologists must argue *a posteriori* (from the particulars of experience to God's existence).[2] Thus, they must aim for conclusions that are probable, though not rationally inescapable.

Inductive arguments argue from particulars to the whole.[3] They, unlike deductive arguments (which argue from the whole to the particular), do not bring conclusions which are logically necessary. Inductive arguments, at best, only bring conclusions which have a high degree of probability.[4] But this is no cause for alarm since almost all of man's knowledge, if not all he knows, is based on probability.[5] The ontological argument (the only deductive argument for God's existence) has apparently failed. Therefore, Christian thinkers should argue inductively for God's existence.

Three of the best known inductive arguments for God's existence are the teleological, the moral, and the cosmological. This chapter will discuss the teleological argument, also known as the argument from design.[6]

## ANCIENT GREEK PHILOSOPHERS

The teleological argument may be the oldest argument for God's existence.[7] Many ancient Greek philosophers reasoned that the the order in the universe could only be accounted for by the workings of an intelligent mind.[8] Plato agreed. He referred to God as the *Demiurge*, which means "hard worker."[9] Still, Plato's Demiurge differs from the God of the Bible. For the Demiurge designed the cosmos out of preexisting chaotic matter.[10] The Demiurge is the designer of the universe, but not the Creator (as He is in Christianity). Plato's student Aristotle also argued for the existence of a divine Being due to the design in the universe.[11]

## THOMAS AQUINAS (1225-1274)

Thomas Aquinas, the great Christian theologian and philosopher of the thirteenth century, is famous for his five ways to prove God's existence.[12] In Aquinas' fifth way to prove God's existence, he argued that some things in nature work towards certain goals despite the fact that they have no knowledge.[13] But things without knowledge do not move towards a goal unless guided by something which has knowledge. Aquinas reasoned that just as an arrow requires an archer, so too everything in nature is guided towards its goal by someone with knowledge (God).[14]

## WILLIAM PALEY (1743-1805)

William Paley is famous for his "watch-maker argument."[15] This is probably the best known teleological argument. Paley stated that if a person who had never seen a watch before was to find one in the wilderness, he would conclude that it is a product of intelligent design.[16] He would see that its several parts were put together for the purpose of producing motion. This motion is so well regulated that it is able to mark the time of the day with precision.[17] The person would see that if there were any small variation in the shape, size, or position of the many parts of the watch, there would either be no motion at all or motion that would not serve the purpose of keeping time.[18] The person would conclude that the watch must have a maker.[19]

Paley then looked at nature and saw evidence of design similar to that of the watch, but to a greater degree.[20] He reasoned that there must be an intelligent Designer of the universe.

Paley's argument is thought to have been refuted by David Hume, but, this does not appear to be the case. Paley wrote his argument thirty years after Hume's supposed refutation was published.[21] The watch-maker argument is not vulnerable to the majority of Hume's criticisms.[22]

## HUME'S CRITICISMS OF THE TELEOLOGICAL ARGUMENT

David Hume (1711-1776) raised objections against the teleological argument for God's existence in his work *Dialogues Concerning Natural Religion*. Several of his objections will be mentioned here. First, Hume reasoned that the Designer of the universe would not have to be infinite. Since the universe is finite, its Designer needs only to be finite.[23] However, if Hume was right and the Designer is only finite, then this Designer would also need a Designer. Eventually one would have to arrive at an infinite Designer. Otherwise, there would be no explanation for the design in the universe. For an infinite regress of designers is impossible (this point will be established in the chapter on the cosmological argument).

Second, Hume speculated that since there is evil in the world, one would be justified in assuming that the Designer of the world is Himself evil.[24] The Christian could here argue that evil exists merely as a privation of that which is good.[25] Hence, for a being to be totally evil, it would have to be non-existent.[26] Therefore, it would be impossible for there to exist an infinite evil being.

Third, Hume reasoned that since ships are designed by multiple designers, the universe may have been designed by multiple designers.[27] Proponents of the teleological argument respond to this criticism by simply emphasizing the unity found in the universe. For it is more probable that the this unity is caused by one Designer rather than several designers.[28]

There is evidence that Hume himself did not find these and other objections to the teleological argument unanswerable. The closing paragraph of Hume's *Dialogues Concerning Natural Religion* implies that he found the teleological argument to be more probable than the objections he raised.[29] Hume's point seems to be that the case for Christianity based upon the teleological argument does not have a rationally certain conclusion.[30] Still, he does express respect for this argument.

## MODERN SCIENCE AND THE TELEOLOGICAL ARGUMENT

It should also be noted that recent advances in modern science have strengthened the teleological argument.[31] Science has uncovered that the highly complex information found in the genetic code of living organisms is similar to that of human language. Since human language is known to have been produced by intelligence, it is reasonable to conclude that living organisms were themselves produced by an intelligent Being.[32]

## CONCLUSION

Defenders of the faith need to recognize that the case for Christian theism does not rest solely on the teleological argument.[33] Rather, a combination of other arguments with the teleological argument strengthens the case for Christianity.[34] In fact, the objections to the teleological argument can be easily bypassed by utilizing the cosmological argument at the outset to prove the existence of one uncaused Cause of all else that exists.[35] Then the teleological argument can be used to show that this uncaused Cause must also be an intelligent Being.[36] Therefore, the teleological argument does have a useful, though supplementary, role in proving the existence of the God of the Bible.[37]

## ENDNOTES

1Geisler and Feinberg, 288.

2Ibid.

3Ibid., 57-58.

4Ibid.

5Ibid., 129-131.

6Craig, 66.

7Ibid.

8Ibid.

9Sahakian, 54.

10Ibid., 55.

11Ibid., 70-71.

12Aquinas, 13-14.

13Ibid., 13.

14Ibid., 14.

15Craig, 68.

16William Paley, *Natural Theology: Selections* edited by F. Ferre (Indianapolis: Bobbs Merrill, 1963), 3-4.

17Ibid.

18Ibid.

19Ibid.

20Ibid., 13.

21Craig, 68.

22Ibid.

23Geisler and Corduan, 98.

24Ibid.

25Augustine, *City of God*, 508.

26Geisler, *Thomas Aquinas*, 154-155.

27Geisler and Corduan, 98.

28Moreland, *Scaling the Secular City*, 65.

29Hume, *Dialogues Concerning Natural Religion*, 95.

30Moreland, 65.

31Geisler and Corduan, 104.

32Ibid.

33Moreland, 65.

34Ibid.

35Geisler, *Apologetics*, 247-249.

36Ibid.

37Ibid.

# CHAPTER 19
# THE MORAL ARGUMENT

The moral argument for God's existence reasons from the existence of universal moral values to the existence of a universal moral Lawgiver.[1] This argument maintains that the source of the objective moral values we experience must be an ultimately good Being.[2]

The apostle Paul stated that Gentiles, who do not have God's written Law, "show the work of the Law written in their hearts, their conscience bearing witness, and their thoughts alternately accusing or else defending them" (Romans 2:15). The Bible declares that God has written His Law on the hearts of all men. This is the basis for defenders of the faith using moral arguments for God's existence.

## THOMAS AQUINAS

Aquinas' fourth way to prove God's existence is his argument from the different degrees of perfection found in finite things.[3] Men commonly judge some things to be more perfect than other things. But judgment concerning the degree of perfection in things only makes sense if there exists a most perfect Being. To say that something is more perfect than something else is to say that it closer approximates the perfect. One cannot determine that something falls short of a perfect standard unless that perfect standard is known. Therefore, the perfect must exist. Whatever contains the most perfection must be the source of all the perfection that exists in other beings. Therefore, concludes Aquinas, there must exist a most perfect Being who is the cause of all the perfections that exist in beings containing lesser degrees of perfection.[4]

## IMMANUEL KANT

Immanuel Kant rejected any attempts to prove God's existence through pure rational argumentation. However, he believed that God's existence must be practically posited in order to make sense of man's moral experience.[5] Kant argued that man must assume the existence of God and life after death if he is to make sense of his desire for happiness and his moral duty.[6] Kant believed that the uniting of man's desire for happiness with man's moral duty could not occur in this life or without God's power. Therefore, reasoned Kant, it is morally necessary (not rationally necessary) to assume God's existence.[7]

It must be remembered that this argument does not prove God's existence. It only states that man must assume God's existence and the afterlife if he is to make sense of his moral life. Kant's argument does not demand that we conclude that God exists; it merely says that man must live as if God does in fact exist.[8]

## C. S. LEWIS (1898-1963)

C. S. Lewis used an advanced form of the moral argument for God's existence in his work *Mere Christianity*.[9] Lewis argued that man's idea of right and wrong is a clue to the meaning of the universe.[10] Lewis reasoned that there must exist a universal moral law for several reasons. First, all moral disagreements between persons imply an appeal to a standard of behavior to which all persons are subject.[11] People accused of doing wrong usually claim that their action did not violate the universal standard, or that they somehow had a special excuse for not submitting to the standard in this particular case.[12] They do not usually deny the standard itself. Second, quarreling often occurs when one person tries to prove that the action of another person is wrong. However, the fact that two people quarrel about whether or not an action was moral implies that they agree that there is such a thing as right and wrong.[13] One person claims the action was right; the other person claims the action was wrong. What they agree upon is the *concept* of right and wrong (the moral law).[14]

Lewis reasons that this moral law could not be mere herd instinct. If it were, then the stronger instinct would always win, but, this is not the case. Often, man suppresses his stronger instinct in order to do what he thinks is right.[15] For instance, when confronted with imminent danger, a man may desire to run for safety but instead chooses to disregard his own well-being to rescue another. Therefore, the moral law is not man's basic instincts. Instead, it judges between these instincts to determine which instinct is to be applied in the specific situation.[16]

Lewis also believed that it is wrong to say that this moral law is merely a social convention.[17] For not everything that man has learned from others is a social convention. Some things, like mathematics, would be true even if it was never taught.[18] The moral law is like mathematics in this respect. It is real regardless of what one's society teaches about it.[19] Social progress makes no sense unless the moral law exists independent of societies.[20] If the moral law is merely invented by society, then one society (America) cannot call the actions of another society (Nazi Germany) wrong.[21]

Lewis declared that the moral law cannot be a law of nature.[22] For a law of nature is descriptive. It describes how nature is, how it usually acts. But, the moral law does not describe how nature is. The moral law is prescriptive; it prescribes how nature ought to be.[23] The moral law stands above man and judges his behavior.

Lewis concluded that there exists a moral law above all men to which they are subject.[24] However, matter could not be the cause of moral laws.[25] Matter gives instructions to no one. Experience shows us that mind is the cause of moral laws.[26] Therefore, this universal moral law that stands above all men must come from a Mind that stands above all men.[27]

CONCLUSION

Each of the three thinkers mentioned in this chapter have contributed valuable aspects to the moral argument. Lewis' argumentation is impressive. A person might arbitrarily deny the existence of the moral law, but the denial is forced and temporary. If that person is wronged, he will appeal to the moral law for justice.

If the moral law is merely subjective, then no one can declare the actions of another to be wrong. If the moral law is produced by nations, then no nation can condemn the actions of another nation. The moral law could not even be the product of world consensus. The world consensus of the twentieth century could not condemn the slavery of the nineteenth, first, or any other century since world consensus favored the practice of slavery during those times.

The moral judgments of men do not make sense unless the moral law stands above all individuals, all nations, and any supposed consensus of the world. The moral law is universal; it applies to all mankind. The moral law is also eternal; it does not change with time. Therefore, there must exist an eternal moral Lawgiver who stands above all men. Prescriptive laws only come from lawgivers.

A variation of Kant's argument can be utilized effectively by apologists. If there exists no God who will someday judge the actions of men, then it makes no difference how one now lives. One million years from now it will make no difference if one lived like Mother Theresa or Adolph Hitler. If God does exist, then how one lives does make a difference. If there is life after death with rewards and punishment, then the moral experience of man makes sense.

Finally, the thought of Aquinas can be used. When a man makes moral judgments he determines some things to be more perfect than other things. This implies the knowledge of something which is the ultimately perfect standard by which all else is judged. No one can determine a line to be crooked without knowledge of a straight line. The Christian believes that this ultimately perfect standard is the all-good God Himself. Without this all-good God, there could be no such thing as evil. For evil is merely the perversion of that which is good. There could be nothing that is good unless there exists an ultimately good Being who is the source of all lesser goods.

Despite the apparent strengths of the moral argument for God's existence, it is susceptible to some of the same criticisms as the teleological argument. Could not there be several moral lawgivers instead of one? Maybe the moral lawgiver is only a finite being?[28] Though these objections can be answered, premises from the cosmological argument for God's existence must be utilized to do so.[29]

Therefore, it is probably best to start one's argument for God's existence with cosmological premises. This will provide evidence for the existence of one Being who is the eternal uncaused cause of all else that exists. Then one can use premises from the moral and teleological arguments to show that this one Being must also be a moral and intelligent Being.

## ENDNOTES

1Geisler and Corduan, 94.

2Craig, 70.

3Geisler, *Thomas Aquinas*, 121.

4Ibid.

5Geisler and Corduan, 109.

6Ibid., 109-110.

7Ibid., 110.

8Ibid.

9C. S. Lewis, *Mere Christianity*, 15-39.

10Ibid., 15.

11Ibid., 17.

12Ibid.

13Ibid., 17-18.

14Ibid.

15Ibid.,  22-23.

16Ibid.,  23.

17Ibid.,  24.

18Ibid.

19Ibid.

20Ibid.,  24-25.

21Ibid.,  25.

22Ibid.,  27-29.

23Ibid.,  28.

24Ibid.,  31.

25Ibid.,  34.

26Ibid.

27Ibid.

28Geisler  and  Corduan,  121-122.

29Ibid.

# CHAPTER 20
# THE COSMOLOGICAL ARGUMENT

The cosmological argument for God's existence reasons for the existence of God from the existence of the universe or some being in the universe.[1] This argument begins with the facts of experience and concludes that there must be a cause or reason to explain these facts.

There are three distinct types of cosmological arguments. Thomas Aquinas (1225-1274) used the argument based on the principle of existential causality (all limited, dependent existence needs a cause for its continuing existence).[2] Bonaventure (1221-1274) used the kalaam cosmological argument (everything that has a beginning needs a cause).[3] Gottfried Wilhelm Leibniz (1646-1716) utilized the principle of sufficient reason (everything that exists must have an adequate explanation for why it exists).[4]

## AQUINAS: EXISTENTIAL CAUSALITY

Thomas Aquinas is famous for his five ways to prove God's existence.[5] In his first way, he argued from the observable movement or change in the universe to the existence of an unmoved Mover. Aquinas' second way reasons that the the causality found in the universe demands the existence of a first, uncaused Cause. His third way concludes with the existence of an independent Being as the cause for the continuing existence of all dependent beings.[6] These first three ways to prove God's existence are cosmological arguments. They all use the principle of existential causality.

Aquinas' fourth and fifth ways to prove God's existence are not cosmological arguments. Aquinas' fourth way (the limited perfections in other beings must be caused by the existence of a most perfect Being), could be classified as a moral argument. His fifth way (the fact that mindless nature moves towards specific goals implies the need for an intelligent Mind to guide these natural processes) is a teleological argument.[7]

Aquinas' first three ways to prove God's existence utilize the principle of existential causality. The thrust of these three arguments is as follows. Aquinas argues that experience shows man that limited, dependent beings exist. These limited, dependent beings need other beings for their continued existence. For example, humans and animals depend on air, water, and food to sustain their existence. However, argues Aquinas, adding limited, dependent beings together will never give someone an unlimited and independent whole. Therefore, the sum total of limited, dependent beings (the universe) is itself limited and dependent. Hence, concludes Aquinas, the ultimate cause of the continuing existence of all limited, dependent beings must itself be unlimited and independent.[8]

Aquinas further argues that there cannot be two or more unlimited and independent beings since, if there were, they would limit one another's existence. But then they would not be unlimited. Therefore, there can only be one unlimited and independent Being.[9]

Aquinas reasoned that this unlimited and independent Being must have all its attributes in an unlimited way. Otherwise, it could not be an unlimited Being.[10] Therefore, this Being must be all-powerful, for He is the source of all the power in the universe.[11] No other power can limit Him. He must be eternal for He is not limited by time.[12] He must be immaterial since He is not limited by matter.[13] This Being must also be all-good since He is not limited by evil.[14] He must also be unlimited in knowledge.[15]

As was mentioned in an earlier chapter, the teleological and moral arguments can be used to compliment the cosmological argument. Therefore, Aquinas' fifth way to prove God's existence (his teleological argument) can be used to provide additional information about the unlimited and independent Being. Since mindless nature works towards goals (such as acorns always becoming oak trees and not something else), there must be an intelligent Designer overseeing natural processes. For without intelligent design and guidance, nature's processes would be left to chance. There would be no orderly patterns that could be described as natural laws. Therefore, this unlimited and independent Being that all finite and dependent existence depends upon for its continued existence, must be an intelligent Being.[16]

Christian philosopher Norman Geisler is a modern proponent of Aquinas' cosmological argument using the principle of existential causality.[17] Winfried Corduan, another contemporary Christian philosopher, also employs this type of cosmological argumentation in his writings.[18]

## BONAVENTURE: THE KALAAM COSMOLOGICAL ARGUMENT

Saint Bonaventure utilized the kalaam cosmological argument for God's existence.[19] Bonaventure argued that whatever began to exist must have a cause. He believed that it could be proven that the universe had a beginning. Therefore, concluded Bonaventure, the universe must have a Cause.[20]

Both Bonaventure and Aquinas believed that the universe had a beginning. They accepted this because it was taught in the Bible. However, Aquinas did not believe that this could be proven philosophically. Bonaventure disagreed. He believed that it could be philosophically proven that the universe had a beginning. Therefore, Aquinas argued for the sustaining Cause of the universe (existential causality), while Bonaventure argued for the Cause for the beginning of the universe (the kalaam argument).[21]

Bonaventure contended that if the universe had no beginning, then there would exist an actual infinite set of events in time. However, Bonaventure reasoned that an actual infinite set is impossible. If an actual infinite set is possible, then contradictions would be generated. For example, Set A contains all the even numbers. It is therefore infinite. But Set B contains all the even and all the odd numbers. Set B would then contain twice as many members as Set A; still, Set A and Set B are equal. For they are both infinite. Bonaventure did not deny potential infinite sets. He only denied infinite sets of *actual* things (such as actual events in time).[22]

Bonaventure also concluded that since it is impossible to traverse an actual infinite set, then the universe could not be eternal. It had to have a beginning. If the universe is eternal, then one could never reach the present moment. For no matter how many moments one passes, one will never pass an infinite set of moments. But, if the universe is eternal, then there are an infinite set of moments in the past. Hence, one would not be able to reach the present moment. But, since mankind has reached the present moment, then the universe had to have a beginning.[23]

In addition to this philosophical evidence, there is now strong scientific evidence for the beginning of the universe as well. Though this evidence was not available in Bonaventure's day, it can be used by the contemporary apologist to strengthen or confirm Bonaventure's cosmological argument. Scientific evidence for the beginning of the universe includes the second law of thermodynamics (energy deterioration) and the big bang model.[24]

The second law of thermodynamics is one of the most firmly established laws of modern science.[25] It states that the amount of usable energy in the universe is running down.[26] This means that someday in the finite future all the energy in the universe will be useless. In other words, if left to itself, the universe will have an end.[27] If the universe is going to have an end, it had to have a beginning.[28] At one time, in the finite past, all the energy in the universe was usable. This would mark the beginning of the universe. However, the universe is winding down; therefore, it must have originally been wound up.[29] Hence, the universe is not eternal; it had a beginning. Since it had a beginning, it needs a cause. For from nothing, nothing comes.[30]

The big bang model also teaches that the universe had a beginning.[31] In 1929, astronomer Edwin Hubble discovered that the universe is expanding at the same rate in all directions.[32] As time moves forward, the universe is growing apart. This means that if one goes back in time the universe would be getting smaller and smaller. Eventually, if one goes back far enough into the past, the entire universe would be what scientists call "a point of infinite density."[33] This marks the beginning of the universe, the big bang.[34]

There have been two main attempts by modern scientists to refute the beginning of the universe. The first is the steady state model.[35]

This view holds that the universe had no beginning. Instead, it always existed in the same state. However, this view (which never gained wide acceptance in modern times) was disproved in 1965 when the radiation background of the universe was discovered. This radiation background indicated that the universe was at one time in an extremely hot and dense state. Thus, the universe has not existed throughout all eternity in a steady-state.[36]

The second attempt to escape the beginning of the universe is the oscillating model.[37] This model teaches that at some point during the universe's expansion, gravity will halt the expansion and pull everything back together again. From that point there will be another big bang. This process will be repeated over and over again throughout all eternity.[38] But the oscillating model fails. First, there is no known principle of physics that would reverse the collapse of the universe into another big bang.[39] Second, current scientific research has shown that the universe is not dense enough for gravity to pull it back together again.[40] Third, even if it could be proven that several big bangs have occurred, the second law of thermodynamics would still require that there was a first big bang.[41] Therefore, since the universe had a beginning, it needs a cause.

What if the cause of the universe needs a cause? Could not an infinite chain of causes and effects exist stretching backwards in time throughout all eternity? The answer is no. It has already been shown that an actual infinite set is impossible. There had to be a first Cause. This first Cause must be uncaused. It could not be caused by another, for then it would not be the first cause. Nor could it be self-caused because it is absurd to say that a being preexisted its own existence in order to cause its own existence.[42] Therefore, only an eternal, uncaused Cause can be the cause of the universe.

Again, the teleological and moral arguments for God's existence can be utilized to complete the cosmological argument. Since intelligent life is found in the universe, the Cause of the universe must be an intelligent Being. No one has ever shown how intelligence could have evolved from mindless nature.[43] Intelligence cannot come from non-intelligence.[44]

Morality also exists in the universe. Without morality, there would be no such thing as right and wrong. The moral judgments people make show that they believe there is are right and wrong,[45] but nature is non-moral.[46] No one holds a rock morally responsible for tripping him. Since nature is non-moral, but morality exists in the universe, the Cause of the universe must be a moral Being.[47]

If morality is relative, then each person can decide for himself what is right and what is wrong.[48] But then no one could condemn the brutal actions of Adolph Hitler. Society also cannot be the cause of moral laws since societies often pass judgment on one another.[49] Therefore, one society, when judging another society, appeals to a moral authority that transcends all societies. Only an absolute moral Lawgiver who is qualitatively above man and societies can be the cause of a moral law that stands above man societies and judges their actions. Therefore, the uncaused Cause of the universe must be an intelligent and moral Being. This means that God must be a personal Being.[50]

## LEIBNIZ: SUFFICIENT REASON

Gottfried Wilhelm Leibniz utilized the principle of sufficient reason to argue for the existence of God.[51] This principle states that there must be a sufficient reason or explanation for everything that exists.[52] Many beings exist that do not contain in themselves the reason for their existence. For instance, a man depends on his parents for his birth, and now he needs air and food to for his continuing existence.[53] Leibniz argued that there cannot be an infinite regress of explanations because then there would be no explanation why anything exists at all.[54] Therefore, reasoned Leibniz, something must exist which contains within itself the reason for its own existence.[55] This Being explains not only its own existence but the existence of all else as well.

Leibniz is not claiming that God is self-caused; this would be absurd. Instead, he is claiming that God is self-explained. God is the explanation for His own existence only because He is an uncaused Being.[56]

## FINDING COMMON GROUND

The cosmological argument for God's existence (in any of its three forms—existential causality, kalaam, sufficient reason) is probably the strongest argument for God's existence.[57] Still, non-Christians often reject that it proves God's existence. Yet, the apologist is not attempting to prove God's existence with mathematical certainty. In fact, very little (if anything) can be known with mathematical certainty about the real world.[58] One can, however, argue to God's existence from premises that are beyond reasonable doubt.[59] The denial of these premises is absurd, forced, and temporary.[60] The premises can be viewed as actually undeniable (each premise must be affirmed in any attempt to deny it).[61] Therefore, God's existence can be proven with a high degree of probability.

Probability arguments can be extremely convincing. The everyday decisions that man must make are rarely (if ever) based on certainty. They are instead based upon a high degree of probability. When a person drives over a cement bridge extended hundreds of feet above the ground, that person is expressing faith that the bridge will support the weight of the vehicle. This is not a blind and irrational faith. There is much evidence for man's ability to build such structures. The person driving across the bridge is basing his faith on the available evidence, though absolute certainty eludes him. In like manner, the existence of God can be proven with a high degree of probability. Because man is limited in knowledge and vulnerable to errors, his knowledge is limited and therefore extends only to the realm of probability.

It should also be noted that a person may know (with a high degree of probability) something to be true, though he or she may not be able to prove it.[62] A suspect of a crime may know he is innocent yet not be capable of proving it. In the same way, many Christians know (with a high degree of probability) that God exists, though they cannot prove that He does.

Having said this, it is now necessary to show that the basic premises of the cosmological argument are beyond reasonable doubt. Once this is shown to be the case, the apologist and the non-theist will share common ground from which the apologist can argue for God's existence.[63]

This common ground (which forms the premises for the cosmological argument) consists of four factors, 1) the law of non-contradiction, 2) the law of causality, 3) the principle of analogy, and 4) the basic reliability of sense perception.[64] All people, whether theist or atheist, must live like these four principles are true.

The law of non-contradiction states that something cannot be both true and false at the same time and in the same way.[65] If something is true, then its opposite must be false. If the non-theist attempts to deny the law of non-contradiction, he must first assume it to be true in order to make the denial. Otherwise, the opposite of the denial could also be true.[66] Though a person may deny this law, he must live, speak, and think as though it is true.[67]

The law of causality states that everything that has a beginning needs a cause.[68] However, to deny this law is absurd. If the law of causality is not true, then something could be caused to exist by nothing. However, nothing is nothing. Therefore, nothing can do nothing. Hence, nothing can cause nothing. From nothing, nothing comes. If one rejects the law of causality, then there is no basis for modern science. Modern science must assume this law when attempting to discover the relationships that exist between the elements of the universe.[69]

The principle of analogy declares that two effects which are similar often have similar causes.[70] For instance, a watch shows tremendous design and complexity.[71] So does the universe. In fact, a single celled animal has enough genetic information to fill an entire library.[72] Therefore, it seems reasonable to conclude that since it takes an intelligent being to make a watch, it must also have taken an intelligent being to design the universe. It seems rather unlikely that an entire library's worth of information could have evolved by chance. An Intelligent designer is needed.

Finally, the basic reliability of sense perception is accepted by theists and non-theists alike.[73] Though people are sometimes mistaken in the conclusions they draw from what their senses perceive, their sense perceptions can usually be trusted. All people live as though their sense perceptions were reliable. They move when rocks are thrown at them. People stay clear of railroad tracks when they hear the whistle of a coming train. Modern science must assume the basic reliability of sense perception in order to examine nature.

Any strong cosmological argument will be built upon these four presuppositions (the laws of non-contradiction, causality, analogy, and the basic reliability of sense perception). Though the non-theist may deny these four presuppositions for sake of argument, he must presuppose them in everyday life. He must live as if they were true. Any philosophy that cannot be lived, such as is the case with atheism, is not worth believing. Though a person may verbally deny God's existence, he must still live as if the God of the Bible does in fact exist.[74]

## FIVE FINAL POINTS

First, after examining the theistic arguments, it is evident that the strongest philosophical argument for God's existence is some type of cosmological argument. However, this does not mean that the other arguments for God's existence have no place in apologetics. As was shown in this chapter, the moral and teleological arguments can be used very successfully to complete the cosmological argument.[75] Premises from the moral and teleological arguments can be used to unveil some of the attributes of the uncaused Cause.

Secondly, when using the kalaam cosmological argument (as was utilized by Bonaventure) the Christian apologist should not argue against the existence of an actual infinite set. For the Christian believes that God is all-knowing (omniscient). This is usually understood to mean that God knows an actual infinite number of things. Therefore, an actual infinite set does exist (though only in the mind of God). Hence, the Christian apologist is incorrect when he argues against the existence of an actual infinite set. The kalaam argument for God's existence loses no force by merely arguing for the impossibility of traversing an actual infinite set (this is all that Zeno's paradox proves). That would be enough to prove that the universe had a beginning and, therefore, needs a Cause. Or, the apologist may argue for the impossibility of an actual infinite set existing outside the mind of an infinite God.[76]

Third, when doing apologetics, the Christian should adapt his or her argumentation to meet the personal needs of the listener. For some non-theists, psychological arguments for God's existence will be more persuasive. For others, philosophical arguments are more convincing. The goal of apologetics is to lead people to Christ. Therefore one's apologetics should be tailored to meet the needs of the listener.

Fourth, all defenders of the faith must remember that even if their argumentation is effective, the listener may still choose to suppress the truth. It is not easy for people to admit that there exists a God to whom they must answer. The desire for human autonomy (to be one's own master) is very strong. Only the inward persuasion of the

Holy Spirit, working in this case with apologetic argumentation, can convince the human will to accept the existence of the God of the Bible.[77]

Fifth, arguments for God's existence provide strong evidence for the existence of the theistic God. Still, historical evidences are needed to show that Christianity is the true theistic faith (as opposed to Islam and the present-day form of Judaism).[78]

## ENDNOTES

1Craig, 62.

2Ibid., 63.

3J. P. Moreland, *Scaling the Secular City*, 18.

4Craig, 65.

5Aquinas, 12-14.

6Ibid., 12-13.

7Ibid., 13-14.

8Ibid., 12-13.

9Ibid., 25.

10Geisler, *Thomas Aquinas*, 125.

11Aquinas, 60-61.

12Ibid., 23-24.

13Ibid., 20-23.

14Ibid., 19-20.

15Ibid., 39-40.

16Ibid., 13-14.

17Geisler, *Apologetics*, 237-258.

18Winfried Corduan, *Reasonable Faith* (Nashville: Broadman and Holman Publishers, 1993), 102-121.

19Moreland, 18.

20Copleston, *A History of Philosophy* vol. II, 251-252.

21Ibid., 262-265.

22Ibid., 263.

23Ibid., 264.

24Craig, 81, 88.

25Moreland, 34.

26Norman L. Geisler and J. Kirby Anderson, *Origin Science* (Grand Rapids: Baker Book House, 1987), 117.

27Moreland, 35.

28Ibid.

29Ibid.

30Ibid., 38.

31Craig, 81-82.

32Peacock, 83-85.

33Craig, 82.

34Ibid., 82-83.

35Ibid., 83.

36Ibid.

37Ibid.

38Ibid., 84.

39Ibid.

40Ibid., 86.

41Ibid., 90.

42Geisler, *Apologetics*, 246.

43Francis A. Schaeffer, *Trilogy* (Wheaton: Crossway Books, 1990), 283.

44Geisler, *Apologetics*, 247.

45C. S. Lewis, *Mere Christianity*, 19.

46Ibid., 26-29.

47Geisler and Corduan, 112.

48Ibid., 113.

49Ibid.

50Geisler, Apologetics, 249.

51Copleston, *A History of Philosophy*, vol. IV, 324.

52Geisler and Corduan, 164.

53John Hick, *The Existence of God*, 168-169.

54Geisler and Corduan, 164.

55Ibid.

56Copleston, *A History of Philosophy*, vol. IV, 325.

57I disagree with Geisler and Corduan on this point. They consider only the Thomistic cosmological argument using the principle of existential causality as successful. The author of this work finds the arguments put forth by Geisler and Corduan against both the kalaam argument and the use of the principle of sufficient reason unconvincing. See Geisler and Corduan, *Philosophy of Religion*, 172-174.

58Geisler and Feinberg, 129-131.

59Ibid., 87-88.

60Hodge, *Systematic Theology* vol. I, 210.

61Geisler, *Apologetics*, 239.

62Moreland, 245.

63Sproul, Gerstner, and Lindsley, 70-72.

64Ibid.

65Ibid., 72-82.

66Ibid.

67Ibid.

68Craig, 74-75.

69Sproul, Gerstner, and Lindsley, 82.

70Geisler and Anderson, 69, 124.

71Hick, 99-104.

72Geisler and Anderson, 162.

73Sproul, Gerstner, and Lindsley, 71-72.

74Schaeffer, 78-79.

75Geisler, *Apologetics*, 247-249.

76I discussed the rejection of this premise ("the impossibility of an actual infinite set") in a November, 1994 telephone conversation with Dr. J. P. Moreland, professor of philosophy at the Talbot School of Theology. Moreland used this premise in his book *Scaling the Secular City*. Moreland agreed that it is probably best to no longer use this premise in the kalaam cosmological argument, and that the premise "the impossibility of traversing an actual infinite set" would be sufficient in establishing the beginning of the universe. Dr. Moreland also related that the premise of the kalaam argument could be changed to "the impossibility of an actual infinite set in the concrete (outside the mind) realm." This premise could be proven by showing the contradictions that would arise if actual infinite sets existed outside the mind. Some of these contradictions have already been discussed in this chapter. What the Christian should not argue for is the impossibility of an actual infinite set existing in the abstract (inside a mind) realm. For if an actual infinite set cannot exist in a mind, then God cannot know an actual infinite number of things. But, if an actual infinite set exists in a mind, this mind would have to be an infinite Mind (an omniscient Being). Only an infinite Mind can know an infinite number of things. Since it is impossible to traverse an actual infinite set, finite minds will never know everything an infinite Mind knows even if the finite mind continues to learn more and more throughout eternity.

77Craig, 18-27.

78Geisler, *Christian Apologetics*, 263-265.

# CHAPTER 21
# THE PROBLEM OF EVIL

One of the greatest obstacles keeping people from accepting Christ is the problem of evil.[1] This problem can take several different forms. First, the metaphysical problem of evil asks how evil can exist in a world created by an all-good God.[2] Is God the cause of evil, or, is evil itself uncreated and eternal? Maybe evil is not real; it is simply an illusion.[3] The metaphysical problem deals with the origin and reality of evil in God's universe.

Second, the moral problem of evil deals with the evil choices of personal beings.[4] This form of the problem argues that since an all-good God would want to destroy evil, and an all-powerful God is able to destroy evil, the existence of evil proves that no all-good, all-powerful God exists.[5] The Christian apologist defends the existence of an all-good and all-powerful God. Therefore, he will respond to this argument.

The third form of the problem of evil is called the physical problem of evil.[6] The physical problem of evil deals with incidents of natural disasters and innocent human suffering.[7] How could God allow evil to occur that is not directly caused by the abuse of human free will?[8]

The fourth and final form of the problem of evil is not really a philosophical issue. It is the personal problem of evil.[9] The personal problem of evil is not a theoretical question about the existence of evil. Instead, it is a personal struggle with a traumatic experience in one's own life.[10] Examples of this would be the sudden and unexpected death of a loved one, a bitter divorce, the loss of a job, or the like. In these situations, the troubled person does not need philosophical answers. What is needed is encouragement, comfort, and biblical counsel.[11] Since this form of the problem of evil does not deal with philosophical discussion, it will not be dealt with in this chapter. The remainder of this chapter will deal with the first three forms of the problem of evil.

## THE METAPHYSICAL PROBLEM OF EVIL

The metaphysical problem of evil can be stated as follows: 1) God created everything that exists, 2) evil exists, 3) therefore, God created evil.[12] There are several ways people respond to this argument. First, like the Christian Science Cult, some can deny the reality of evil.[13] They view evil as an illusion, but this entails a rejection of Christian Theism which clearly accepts the real existence of evil and offers Christ as its solution.[14] Therefore, viewing evil as an illusion is not an option for the Christian apologist.

A second possible response to the metaphysical problem is dualism. This is the view that God and evil are coeternal.[15] God did not create evil, in this view, since evil is eternal. This view fails in that it makes evil a second ultimate being along with God. God would then no longer be infinite since He and evil would limit each other. However, the cosmological argument has shown that there must be an infinite Being to explain and ground all finite existence. There cannot be two infinite beings, for they would limit each other. If God and evil are both finite, then there would have to be an infinite cause for the existence of both. Dualism would only push the problem of evil further back. It does not offer any ultimate solution to the dilemma. Also, the acceptance of dualism entails a rejection of the existence of the God of the Bible. Therefore, it is not an option for the Christian theist.[16]

The Christian apologist must defend the reality of evil without proposing evil as eternal or as a creation of God.[17] Saint Augustine dealt with this same problem centuries ago. His proposed solution to the metaphysical problem of evil was that all things created by God are good. Nothing in its created nature is evil. Evil, therefore, cannot exist solely on its own. However, evil is real; it does exist. Still, it must exist in something good; it cannot exist on its own. Evil is a privation, a lack or absence of a good that should be there. Evil is a corruption or perversion of God's good creation. Blindness in a man is evil, for God created man to see. But, blindness in a rock is not evil, for God never meant rocks to have sight. Evil, according to Augustine, is a lack of a good that should be there. Augustine stated, "evil has no positive nature; what we call evil is merely the lack of something that is good."[18]

Augustine stated that God did not create evil; He merely created the possibility for evil by giving men and angels free will. When men and angels exercised their free will by disobeying God, they actualized the possibility for evil.[19]

Thomas Aquinas argued against the metaphysical problem of evil along the same lines as did Augustine.[20] This basic response has been the traditional Christian solution to the metaphysical problem of evil. God did not create evil, but, evil exists as a privation or corruption of that which is good. God cannot be blamed for evil. He is only responsible for creating the possibility of evil. When God gave angels and men free will, He created the possibility of evil. Fallen angels and fallen men are responsible for evil through their abuse of free will.[21]

## THE MORAL PROBLEM OF EVIL

The moral problem of evil affirms that an all-good God would want to destroy evil, while an all-powerful God is able to destroy evil. Since evil exists, it is concluded that an all-good, all-powerful God does not exist.[22] Some people respond by denying God's existence (atheism). Others deny that God is all-powerful (finite godism). Rabbi Harold Kushner is an example of the latter. He argues that God is not all-powerful. Kushner declares that mankind needs to forgive God for His failures and help Him to combat evil.[23] Obviously, the options of atheism and finite godism are not viable for Christians. Christians must defend both God's omnipotence (all-powerfulness) and His infinite goodness. Therefore, the moral problem of evil must be answered in another way.

Christian philosophers Geisler and Corduan offer several effective responses to the moral problem of evil. First, there is an unnecessary time limit placed on God.[24] The argument against the existence of the theistic God from moral evil assumes that because evil exists God cannot be both all-good and all-powerful. However, what if an all-good and all-powerful God allowed evil for the purpose of a greater good? What if this God is also in the process of destroying evil and will someday complete the process?[25]

Second, God may have created the possibility of evil for the purpose of a greater good (human and angelic free will). God would not force His love on angels or mankind, for any attempt to force love on another is rape (and not really love at all).[26] Therefore, He gave men and angels the freedom to accept or reject His love and His will. Free will necessitates the possibility of evil coming into the universe.[27] In fact, human and angelic free choices brought evil and human suffering into the world.

Third, God will use evil for good purposes. If evil did not exist, there could be no courage, for there would be nothing to fear. If evil did not exist, man could only love his friends; he could never learn to love even his enemies. Without evil, there would be no enemies.[28] Only an infinite God can know all the good He will bring out of evil (Isaiah 55:8-9).

Fourth, Geisler and Corduan argue that an all-good and all-powerful God is not required to create the best possible world. They reason that all He can be expected to do is create the best possible way to achieve the greatest possible world. Heaven is the greatest possible world.[29]

Several other points could also be made. First, the atheist usually denies the existence of objective evil since he knows that this would admit to the existence of the absolute moral law.[30] The atheist knows that once he acknowledges the absolute moral law, the existence of God (the absolute moral law Giver) surely will follow.[31] For evil to be objectively real, it must exist as a perversion of that which is ultimately good. To escape this conclusion, the atheist usually chooses to deny the existence of evil. Therefore, it is rather ironic that the atheist (who usually denies the existence of evil) attempts to use evil to disprove the existence of the God of the Bible. The presence of evil may be problematic for all other world views (including Christian theism), but it is totally devastating to atheism. If there is no God, then there are also no objective moral values. The most consistent atheists, such as Nietzsche, have readily admitted this.[32]

Second, all world views must deal with the problem of evil, but the God of the Bible is the only guarantee that evil will ultimately be defeated.[33] The God of deism is no longer concerned with the problems of this world (such as evil).[34] In pantheism, evil is an illusion.[35] In atheism, there is no basis to call anything evil.[36] But, the biblical God guarantees that evil will be defeated through Christ's death, resurrection, and return (John 1:29; 1 Peter 2:24; 3:18; Romans 4:25; Isaiah 9:6-7; 11:1-9; Zechariah 9:9-10; Revelation 20;4-6).

Third, non-Christians act as if the existence of evil is an unexpected factor in the Christian world view, but this is not the case. God would not have given mankind the Bible had it not been for the problem of evil. If man had not Fallen in the garden, he would have had no need for salvation (Genesis 3:1-7; Romans 3:10, 23; 5:12; 6:23). The Bible could actually be titled "God's Solution to the Problem of Evil."

In short, the solution to the moral problem of evil (how an all-good, all-powerful God can co-exist with evil) is that God gave humans and angels free will. It is the abuse of this free will by humans and angels that has brought evil and human suffering into existence. God created the possibility for evil (by giving man and angels free will), not evil itself.

Christian philosopher Alvin Plantinga adds an important detail concerning the Christian response to the moral problem of evil. He writes that there are two ways Christians can respond to this dilemma. First, he may develop a free will theodicy. A theodicy is an attempt to explain what was God's reason (or reasons) for allowing evil. On the other hand, according to Plantinga, the Christian does not have to go that far. Instead of presenting a free will theodicy, he may develop a free will defense. In this case, rather than attempting to explain the reason as to why God allows evil and human suffering, the Christian can merely suggest a *possible* reason why God has allowed evil and human suffering.[37] The free will defense, according to Plantinga, is sufficient in itself to show that the existence of evil does not rule out the possible existence of the God of theism.[38]

In other words, since the problem of evil is an attempt to prove God's existence as being impossible, the Christian only needs to provide possible solutions to this problem. Once this is done, God's existence will have been shown to be possible. Further argumentation (such as the cosmological, teleological, moral, and ontological arguments) can then be presented to argue for God's existence with a higher degree of probability.[39]

## THE PHYSICAL PROBLEM OF EVIL

The physical or natural problem of evil deals with evil not directly connected to the abuse of human freedom.[40] All physical or natural evil is at least indirectly related to the abuse of human freedom. Without the Fall of man in history, creation would still be perfect (Genesis 1:31). Still, much physical evil is not directly related to human choices. Natural disasters such as earthquakes, floods, hurricanes, and deaths of innocent infants are examples of physical evil.

Geisler and Corduan list five explanations for physical evil.[41] None of the five are meant to be all-encompassing. Each explains some of the physical evil that occurs. First, some physical evil is necessary for moral perfection.[42] There can be no courage without something evil to fear. Misery is needed for there to be sympathy; tribulation is needed for there to be endurance and patience.[43] For God to build these characteristics in man, He must permit a certain amount of physical evil.

Second, human free choices do cause some physical evil.[44] It would be an obvious error to assume that no physical evil is caused by the abuse of human free will. The choice to drink and drive has caused much physical evil. Many infants have been born with an addiction to cocaine due to their mothers' choice to abuse drugs while pregnant. It is impossible for God to remove all physical evil without tampering with human free will.[45] It is even possible that some major natural disasters are caused by the evil choices of humans. According to the Bible, this was the case with Sodom and Gomorrah (Genesis 18:20-21; 19).

Third, some physical evil is caused by the choices of demons.[46] The Scriptures speak of demons (fallen angels led by Satan) causing suffering to humans (Job 1, 2; Mark 5:1-20). Demons oppose God and His plans, but they will ultimately be defeated by Christ (Revelation 19, 20, 21, 22).

Fourth, God often uses physical evil as a moral warning.[47] Physical pain is often a warning that greater suffering will follow if behavior is not changed. Examples of this would be excessive coughing that is often caused by smoking and heavy breathing caused by over training during a physical workout. Also, God may use pain and suffering to cause a person to focus on him, rather than on worldly pleasures.[48]

Fifth, some physical evils are necessary in the present state of the physical world.[49] To survive, animals often eat other animals. Humans eat animals as well. It appears that, at least in the present state of the creation, lower life forms are subjected to pain and death in order to facilitate the preservation of higher life forms.[50]

Physical evil, therefore, does not present any insurmountable problems for Christian theism. Though man is limited in knowledge and cannot infallibly ascertain why God allows each and every case of physical evil, the five reasons given above should suffice to show that the presence of physical evil in no way rules out the existence of the God of the Bible.

### CONCLUSION

Once the Christian apologist has provided strong evidence for God's existence, he need only give possible reasons why an all-good and all-powerful God would allow evil and human suffering. God has good reasons for allowing evil and human suffering, even though we may not know them fully. Therefore, the existence of evil does not disprove the existence of an all-good and all-powerful God. These two are not mutually exclusive.

## ENDNOTES

1Nash, 177.

2Geisler and Corduan, 318.

3Ibid.

4Ibid., 333.

5Ibid.

6Ibid., 364.

7Ibid.

8Ibid.

9Nash, 179-180.

10Ibid.

11Ibid., 180.

12Geisler and Corduan, 318.

13Mary Baker Eddy, *Science and Health with Key to the Scriptures* (Boston: The First Church of Christ, Scientist, 1971), 293, 447, 472, 480, 482.

14Geisler and Corduan, 318-319.

15Ibid., 319.

16Ibid., 319-320.

17Ibid., 318-320.

18Augustine, *City of God*, 217, 247, 305, 508.

19Geisler and Corduan, 323-324.

20Aquinas, 91-92.

21Geisler and Corduan, 320-330.

22Ibid., 333.

23Kushner, 129,134,145-148.

24Geisler and Corduan, 334.

25Ibid., 348.

26Ibid.

27Ibid.

28Ibid.

29Ibid., 342-343.

30C. S. Lewis, *Mere Christianity*, 34-39.

31Ibid.

32Friedrich Nietzsche, *The Portable Nietzsche*, ed. by Walter Kaufmann, (New York: Penguin Books, 1982), 228.

33Geisler and Watkins, 41.

34Ibid., 148-149.

35Ibid., 99-100.

36Ibid., 59.

37Plantinga, 28.

38Ibid.

39Ibid.

40Geisler and Corduan, 364.

41Ibid., 372-378.

42Ibid., 372-373.

43Ibid., 372.

44Ibid., 373.

45Ibid., 373-374.

46Ibid., 375.

47Ibid., 376.

48Ibid.

49Ibid.

50Ibid., 376-378.

# CHAPTER 22
# MIRACLES

Christianity is a religion based in history. The claims, death, and resurrection of Jesus of Nazareth occurred in history. For this reason, historical apologetics (to be discussed in Part Six) is of great importance. If one can prove that Jesus really did rise from the dead in history, then one will have gone a long way towards establishing Christianity as the true religion. However, before an apologist can engage in presenting historical evidences for the resurrection of Christ, he must first answer the philosophical objections against the possibility of miracles. If miracles are by definition impossible, then it makes no sense to look into history to see if Jesus really rose from the dead.

The strongest philosophical argumentation against miracles came from the pens of Benedict Spinoza (1632-1677) and David Hume (1711-1776). Spinoza was a pantheist.[1] He believed in an impersonal god that was identical to the universe. He reasoned that an impersonal god could not choose to perform miracles. Whatever an impersonal god does, it must do by necessity. Spinoza believed that nature necessarily operates in a uniform manner. Therefore, he argued that the laws of nature cannot be violated. Since miracles would be violations of the laws of nature, they are impossible.[2]

David Hume was a deist. He believed that after God created the universe, He no longer involved Himself with His creation. Hume reasoned that miracles, if they occur, are very rare events. On the other hand, the laws of nature describe repeatable, everyday occurrences. Hume argued that the wise man will always base his beliefs on the highest degree of probability. Since the laws of nature have a high degree of probability while a miracle is improbable, Hume considered the evidence against miracles always greater than the evidence for miracles. Therefore, according to Hume, the wise man will always reject the proposed miracle.[3]

## RESPONSE TO SPINOZA

Spinoza argued that miracles are impossible. Several things should be mentioned in refutation of Spinoza's argument. Though it is true that a pantheistic god cannot choose to perform a miracle (a pantheistic god is impersonal and, therefore, cannot choose anything), there is strong evidence that a pantheistic god does not exist.[4] As the cosmological argument has shown, a theistic God exists.[5] A theistic God is a personal God, and a personal God can choose to perform miracles.

Second, Spinoza's premise that the laws of nature can never be violated is suspect. The laws of nature are descriptive; they are not prescriptive. In other words, the laws of nature describe the way nature usually acts. The laws of nature do not prescribe how nature must act.[6]

Third, Spinoza's definition of a miracle as a violation of the laws of nature is objectionable. It is possible that miracles do not violate the laws of nature; they merely supersede the laws of nature. C. S. Lewis argued along these lines.[7]

Fourth, if God created the universe, then the laws of nature are subject to Him. God can choose to suspend or violate (depending on how one defines a miracle) the laws of nature any time He wishes. In short, Spinoza has failed to show that miracles are impossible.

## RESPONSE TO HUME

Hume, unlike Spinoza, did not argue for the impossibility of miracles. Instead, he argued that miracles were so unlikely that the evidence against them will always be greater than the evidence for them. Hume argued that miracles are improbable, and that the wise man will only believe that which is probable. Hence, the wise man will never accept evidence for a miracle.[8]

The Christian apologist can respond to Hume's reasoning in the following manner. Just because usual events (the laws of nature) occur more often does not mean that the wise man will never believe that an unusual event (a miracle) has occurred.[9] The wise man should not a priori rule out the possibility of miracles. The wise man will examine the evidence for or against a miracle claim, and base his judgment on the evidence. Since there were over 500 witnesses who claimed to have seen Jesus risen from the dead (1 Corinthians 15:3-8), a wise man would not reject the miracle of the resurrection merely because all other men have remained dead. It seems that a wise man would examine a miracle claim if there are reliable eyewitnesses. If there is no good reason to reject the testimony of reliable eyewitnesses, it seems that a wise man would accept their testimony that a miracle has occurred.

## CONCLUSION

Some people will not accept any event unless it has a natural cause. Therefore, they reject miracles because they have a supernatural Cause (God).[10] But, the cosmological argument has shown that the universe itself needs a supernatural Cause (God). Therefore, if there is a God who created the universe, then He would have no problem intervening in His universe by supernaturally working miracles within it. A person cannot rule out miracles simply because his world view does not allow them. If his or world view is weak (such as pantheism and deism), then he has weak reasons for rejecting miracles. If, on the other hand, a person has strong evidence for his world view (such as theism), and that world view is consistent with the reality of miracles, then he has strong reasons for believing that miracles are possible.

This chapter has only shown that miracles are possible. A later section of this work deals with historical apologetics. At that point, evidence will be examined to see whether miracles have occurred or not. Philosophical argumentation can only show that miracles are possible. Historical evidences must be utilized to determine if an alleged miracle (such as the resurrection of Jesus from the dead) has in fact occurred.

## ENDNOTES

1Norman L. Geisler, *Miracles and the Modern Mind* (Grand Rapids: Baker Book House, 1992), 18.

2Ibid., 15.

3David Hume, *An Inquiry Concerning Human Understanding* (New York: The Liberal Arts Press, 1955), 117-141.

4see Chapter 16 of this work.

5see Chapter 20 of this work.

6Terry L. Miethe, ed. *Did Jesus Rise From the Dead?* (San Francisco: Harper and Row, 1987), 18.

7C. S. Lewis, *Miracles*, 59-60.

8Geisler, 23-28.

9Ibid., 27-31.

10Ibid., 50-51.

# CHAPTER 23
# REFUTING MORAL RELATIVISM

Philosophical apologetics often deals with the branch of philosophy called ethics. Ethics deals with issues of morality, that which is right and wrong.[1] The Christian ethical perspective holds to absolute moral values, laws that are universally binding. Often, non-Christian views hold to moral relativism. Moral relativism rejects the idea that there are objective rights and wrongs.[2] What is right for one person is not necessarily right for another person, and vice versa. Each person decides what is right for himself. Many atheists and pantheists are moral relativists.[3]

## AN EXAMINATION OF MORAL RELATIVISM

Friedrich Nietzsche (1844-1900) was a German philosopher. He believed that the advances of human knowledge had proven that belief in God was a mere superstition. Nietzsche therefore reasoned that since "God is dead," all traditional values have died with Him. Nietzsche was angered with his atheistic colleagues who were unwilling to dismiss traditional moral absolutes which had no justification without God's existence.[4]

Nietzsche preached that a group of "supermen" must arise with the courage to create their own values through their "will to power." Nietzsche rejected the "soft" values of Christianity (brotherly love, turning the other cheek, charity, compassion, etc.); he felt they hindered man's creativity and potential. He recommended that the supermen create their own "hard" values that would allow man to realize his creative potential.[5] Nietzsche was very consistent with his atheism. He realized that without God, there are no universal moral values. Man is free to create his own values. It is interesting to note that the Nazis often referred to Nietzsche's writings for the supposed intellectual justification for their acts of cruelty.[6]

Many other atheists agree with Nietzsche concerning moral relativism. British philosopher Bertrand Russell (1872-1970) once wrote, "Outside human desires there is no moral standard."[7] A. J. Ayer believed that moral commands did not result from any objective standard above man. Instead, Ayer stated that moral commands merely express one's subjective feelings. When one says that murder is wrong, one is merely saying that he or she feels that murder is wrong.[8] Jean-Paul Sartre, a French existentialist, believed that there is no objective meaning to life. Therefore, according to Sartre, man must create his own values.[9]

There are many different ways that moral relativists attempt to determine what action should be taken. Hedonism is probably the most extreme. It declares that whatever brings the most pleasure is right. In other words, if it feels good, do it.[10] If this position is true, then there is no basis from which to judge the actions of Adolph Hitler as being evil.[11]

Utilitarianism teaches that man should attempt to bring about the greatest good for the greatest number of people.[12] Utilitarianism is problematic. First, "good" is a meaningless term if moral relativism is true, for then there would be no such thing as good or evil. Second, to say that man "should" do something is to introduce a universal moral command. However, there is no room for universal moral commands in moral relativism.[13]

Joseph Fletcher founded "situation ethics." Situation ethics is the view that ethics are relative to the situation. Fletcher claimed that he was not a moral relativist. He believed that there was only one moral absolute: love. Still, his concept of love was so void of meaning that his view of ethics, for all practical purposes, is synonymous with moral relativism.[14]

The situation never determines what is right. It is God who determines what is right. Still, the situation may aid the Christian in finding which of God's laws should be applied.[15] For when two of God's commands come in conflict due to a situation so that a person cannot obey both, God requires that the person obey the greater command. God then exempts the person from obeying the lesser command. An example of this is the fact that god compliments Rahab the Harlot for lying in order to save two innocent lives (Joshua 2; Hebrews 11:31; James 2:25).[16]

### REFUTING MORAL RELATIVISM

Moral relativists deny absolute moral law. Still, they, like all people, recognize the evil actions of others when they are wronged. When they are wronged, they appeal to an objective and universal law that stands above man. Moral relativists deny absolute moral law in the lecture hall, but they live by it in their everyday lives.[17] Moral relativists reserve the right for themselves to call the actions of Hitler wrong,[18] but, if there is no such thing as right and wrong (as the moral relativists say), they cannot really call any action wrong.

The moral law does not ultimately come from within each individual, for then no one could call the actions of another, such as Hitler, evil.19 The moral law does not ultimately come from each society, for then one society could not call the actions of another society (such as Nazi Germany) wrong.[20] Finally, the moral law does not ultimately come from world consensus,[21] for world consensus is often wrong. World consensus once thought the world was flat. World consensus once considered slavery morally permissible.

Appealing to world or societal consensus as the ultimate source of the moral law is actually just an extension of the view that the individual is the ultimate source. The difference is only quantitative (the number of people increases). However, for there to be a moral law above all men (in order to judge all men), this moral law must be qualitatively above all men. If there is an absolute moral law qualitatively above all men, then there must be an absolute moral law Giver that stands qualitatively above all men. The moral law is not descriptive of what is; it is prescriptive of what should be.[22]

Since the absolute moral law leads directly to the existence of the theistic God (the absolute moral law Giver), many atheists and pantheists may feel compelled to reject it's existence. Also, people who wish to live promiscuous lives often choose to reject God's existence. The apostle John appears to be talking about these people:

And this is the judgment, that the light is come into the world, and men loved the darkness rather than the light; for their deeds were evil. For everyone who does evil hates the light, and does not come to the light, lest his deeds should be exposed (John 3:19-20).

ENDNOTES

1Geisler and Feinberg, 24-26.

2Moreland, *Scaling the Secular City*, 240.

3Geisler and Watkins, 59, 99-100.

4Friedrich Nietzsche, 95-96, 143, 228.

5Ibid., 124-125, 139, 191, 197-198.

6Copleston, *A History of Philosophy* vol. 7, 403.

7Russell, 62.

8Norman L. Geisler, *Christian Ethics* (Grand Rapids: Baker Book House, 1989), 32.

9Geisler and Feinberg, 406.

10Ibid., 400-401.

11Geisler, *Christian Ethics*, 36-37.

12Ibid., 63.

13Ibid., 73-75.

14Ibid., 43-61.

15Geisler and Feinberg, 411.

16Ibid., 424-427.

17Hodge, *Systematic Theology* vol. 1, 210.

18Hick, *The Existence of God*, 183-186.

19Moreland, 246-247.

20Ibid., 243-244.

21Geisler and Feinberg, 355.

22C. S. Lewis, *Mere Christianity*, 27-28.

# PART SIX

# HISTORICAL APOLOGETICS

# CHAPTER 24
# OLD TESTAMENT RELIABILITY

Historical apologetics deals with the providing of historical evidences for the truth of Christianity. Doing historical apologetics entails several lines of argumentation. It attempts to establish the reliability of both the Old and New Testaments. It puts forth evidence for the bodily resurrection of Jesus and the deity of Christ. Finally, historical apologetics presents evidence for the Bible as God's Word.[1]

This chapter will argue that the Old Testament is a compilation of reliable historical writings. The divine authorship of the Old and New Testaments will not be argued for until chapter twenty-eight. The goal of this chapter is to show that the Old Testament is not a book of religious myths. It records historically accurate data; therefore, it should be considered historically reliable.

Since the data concerning Old Testament reliability is so extensive, this chapter will necessarily be selective. Evidence will be provided for only eight (Genesis, Exodus, Leviticus, Numbers, Deuteronomy, Joshua, Isaiah, and Daniel) of the thirty-nine Old Testament books. However, since liberal scholars attack the reliability of these eight books more aggressively than the other Old Testament books, a strong case for the reliability of these eight books will go a long way to proving the reliability of the entire Old Testament. Most of the information in this chapter is derived from Gleason Archer's *A Survey of Old Testament Introduction*.[2]

## THE OLD TESTAMENT MANUSCRIPTS

The Old Testament was written originally in Hebrew and Aramaic.[3] It consists of thirty-nine separate books written at different times and places between 2000BC and 400BC.[4] The three main extant Old Testament manuscripts are the Masoretic Text, the Dead Sea Scrolls, and the Septuagint.[5]

The Masoretic Text is currently considered the standard Hebrew text.[6] It dates back to about 1010AD.[7] It contains the entire Old Testament.[8] Despite its late date, it is considered the purest Hebrew text. No recent manuscript finds have brought suspicion to the Masoretic text.[9] Due to the strict copying techniques of the Masoretes, they have preserved a Hebrew text which essentially duplicates the authoritative texts of Christ's time.[10]

The Dead Sea Scrolls date back to approximately 150-100BC.[11] The Dead Sea Scrolls are the oldest extant Hebrew manuscripts of the Old Testament.[12] These scrolls were found in 1947 in various caves along the northwest coast of the Dead Sea.[13] The Dead Sea Scrolls contain fragments from every Old Testament book except Esther.[14]

The Septuagint is a Greek translation of the Hebrew Old Testament.[15] The Septuagint dates from 250-150BC.[16] When the Masoretic Text, the Dead Sea Scrolls, and the Septuagint are compared, there is essential agreement between them. The few areas of disagreement do not effect the doctrines contained in the Old Testament; the disagreements are mainly copyist errors and variations in spelling.[17]

## LOWER, HIGHER, AND FORM CRITICISM

Lower criticism is the science of discovering the original text on the basis of imperfect copies.[18] This can only be done by comparing the existing copies of the passage in question. Lower criticism is essential in the task of producing accurate translations of the Old (and New) Testaments.

Higher criticism, on the other hand, deals with ascertaining the authorship, date, and integrity of each biblical book.[19] Higher criticism has been abused by liberal scholars who refuse to accept the evidence for the traditional Jewish and Christian view concerning the authorship, date, and integrity of the books of the Bible. This is due, in part, to the common antisupernaturalistic bias held by liberal scholars.[20] This bias rejects the possibility of revelation from God, predictive prophecies, and miracles.

Form criticism seeks to find the oral traditions that supposedly lie behind the written documents.[21] This view is highly subjective; it is often dependent upon the imagination of the scholar.

## THE DOCUMENTARY HYPOTHESIS

The documentary hypothesis is the theory that the Pentateuch (the first five books of the Bible) was a compilation of different written documents composed by different authors at different places and at different times.[22] The traditional view of Moses being the author of the Pentateuch around 1450BC is rejected. The documentary hypothesis holds to much later dates for the writing of the Pentateuch.[23]

Before the eighteenth century, the Mosaic authorship of the Pentateuch was not questioned. However, the rise of deism (the belief in a non-miracle working God) led to a more skeptical approach to the Bible.[24] The process which led to the documentary hypothesis began in 1753 with the speculation of a French physician named Jean Astruc.[25] He was puzzled by the fact that God was called "Elohim" in the first chapter of Genesis, while He was primarily referred to as "Jehovah" (or Yahweh) in the second chapter.[26] He concluded that these different names for God pointed to different written sources. The sources became known as "Elohim" and "Jehovah."[27]

In the 1780's, Johann Gottfried Eichorn applied the distinction between the J (Jehovah) document and the E (Elohim) document throughout most of the Pentateuch.[28] In 1806, Wilhelm M. L. DeWette introduced the view that the entire Pentateuch was written no earlier than the reign of King David (around 1000BC).[29] DeWette also reasoned that the book of Deuteronomy (which later became known as the "D" document) was written at the start of King Josiah's reformation to unify the worship of the Jews in 621BC.[30]

In 1853, Hermann Hupfeld devided the E document into E1 and E2. The E1 document later became known as "P" (the priestly code).[31] In 1869, Abraham Kuener put the four supposed documents in what later became the standard JEDP order.[32]

In 1878, Julius Wellhausen supported this JEDP order with the evolutionary view of religion. This view teaches that man's first religion was animism (the belief that everything in nature has a life force or soul). Animism evolved into polytheism (the belief in many gods). Polytheism led to monalatry (the worshipping one god as supreme over all other gods). Finally, in the evolutionary view of religion, monalatry gave rise to monotheism (the belief in one God).[33]

The gradual development of the documentary hypothesis was completed in Wellhausen's thought. According to Wellhausen, the J document was written in 850BC, while the E document was produced in 750BC. Deuteronomy was composed during King Josiah's reform in 621BC. The Priestly code was considered to be written in various stages between 570BC and 530BC.[34] This was a great departure from the traditional view which, as stated above, held that Moses was the author of all five books (around 1450BC).

## REFUTATION OF THE DOCUMENTARY HYPOTHESIS

The documentary hypothesis is no longer as popular as it once was. Twentieth century scholarship has repudiated this view. Still, rather than returning to the traditional view of Mosaic authorship, twentieth century scholars have tended towards even more speculation. Several more documents have been suggested.[35]

Any evidence for the unity of the Pentateuch is explained away by asserting that a hypothetical editor supposedly put several documents together.[36] It can be said of liberal scholars that they will not allow any evidence to falsify their subjective reasoning. They speculate that two creation accounts (Genesis 1; 2) must mean two different written sources. By doing this, they reject the abundant evidence showing that ancient semitic writers often utilized a style which made use of repetition in their literature. Somehow, twentieth century liberal scholars assume they can scientifically reconstruct the text thousands of years after it was written. They even believe their speculations should hold more weight than the traditional view of the Jews who were themselves much closer to the original documents.[37]

The modern liberal scholars are guilty of circular reasoning. In their attempt to prove that the Bible is merely a human book, they assume that revelation from God is impossible.[38] In spite of the fact that much of ancient pagan history has been shown to be unreliable, liberal scholars assume that these pagan historical writings are always right when they differ from the biblical account[39] Meanwhile, again and again the Bible has been proven to be historically reliable.[40] Another weak assumption is their view that the Hebrews could use only one name for God. History reveals that ancient empires such as Babylon, Ugarit, Egypt, and Greece all had several names for their primary deity.[41] Therefore, there is no justification for speculating the existence of different authors and multiple documents merely because a different name for God (Elohim or Jehovah) is being used.

The evolutionary assumption that the Hebrew religion had evolved into monotheism is also called into question. Israel, after all, was the only nation among its ancient neighbors to have a true monotheistic faith. Israel is the exception rather than the rule. Even if one could prove that the religions of Israel's neighbors evolved towards monotheism, Israel's history is that of a nation that began with monotheism.[42]

Modern liberal scholars are notorious for taking passages out of context in order to "prove" that the Bible contains contradictions. Whenever a conservative scholar produces a possible reconciliation of the passages in question, the solution is automatically rejected by liberal scholarship.[43] Apparently, because of the common liberal bias against anything supernatural, liberal scholars will accept no argument for the traditional view of the Pentateuch.

In short, the documentary hypothesis and its updated versions do not stand on a solid foundation. They are based upon an unjustified bias against the supernatural; they also resort to fanciful speculation. The concept of the JEDP documents was created by the imaginations of liberal scholars. There is no evidence whatsoever that these documents ever existed. This is not to say that Moses did not draw upon information from written sources which predated him, but, if this was the case, objective evidence must be produced for verification. Uncontrolled subjective speculation is not true scholarship; it is the antithesis of scholarship.

## EVIDENCES FOR THE MOSAIC AUTHORSHIP OF THE PENTATEUCH

Merely pointing out the inadequacies of the documentary hypothesis does not prove that Moses wrote the Pentateuch around 1450BC. Therefore, positive evidences for Mosaic authorship must be presented.

First, the entire Pentateuch displays a unity of arrangement. Even the documentarians concede this point by inventing a hypothetical editor to explain the unity of the Pentateuch.[44] This unity of arrangement strongly implies that the Pentateuch had only one author.

Second, both the Old and New Testaments call Moses the author of the Pentateuch (Joshua 8:31; 1 Kings 2:3; Daniel 9:11; Mark 12:26; Luke 20:28; John 5:46-47; 7:19; Acts 3:22; Romans 10:5). Even the Pentateuch itself declares Moses to be its author (Exodus 17:14; 24:4; 34:27; Numbers 33:1-2; Deuteronomy 31:9).[45]

Third, eyewitness details in the Pentateuch indicate the author was a participant in the events he was describing. The author at times is so precise in his details that he lists the exact number of fountains (twelve) and palm trees (seventy) in Exodus 15:27.[46] The author even describes the appearance and taste of the manna from heaven for future generations (Numbers 11:7-8).[47] These precise details make it unlikely that the author was other than an eyewitness of the events he recorded.

Fourth, the author of the Pentateuch was well acquainted with the geography and language of Egypt. He was familiar with Egyptian names and uses Egyptian figures of speech. There is a greater percentage of Egyptian words in the Pentateuch than in the rest of the Bible. This seems to indicate that the author had lived in Egypt and was most likely educated there as well. Moses was born, raised, and educated in Egypt. It is also interesting to note that the author does not attempt to explain these uniquely Egyptian factors. This probably indicates that his original readers were also familiar with the Egyptian culture, and, this is exactly the case with the Israelites that Moses led out of Egypt.[48]

Fifth, the author of the Pentateuch, although familiar with Egypt, shows himself to be unfamiliar with the land of Canaan.[49] This is consistent with Moses. After leaving Egypt, he wandered through the wilderness of Sinai, but did not enter Canaan (the promised land). The author of the Pentateuch, though he describes with great detail the geography and vegetation of Egypt and Sinai, treats the land of Canaan as a place virtually uknown to him or his people.[50] Therefore, the traditional view of Mosaic authorship is much more plausible than the documentary hypothesis.

Sixth, the setting of Exodus through Numbers is that of a desert atmosphere point of view.[51] Even the laws concerning sanitation apply to a desert lifestyle (Deuteronomy 23:12-13).[52] This would not be the case if the author or authors lived an agricultural lifestyle in their own land for nearly a thousand years (which is what the documentary hypothesis teaches).[53] Even the tabernacle (a portable tent that was the Jewish place of worship) implies a nomadic lifestyle of the worshipers.[54]

Seventh, Moses was qualified to be the author of the Pentateuch. He was educated in Egypt, grew up there, and spent much of his later life in the Sinai desert (Acts 7:22).[55]

Eighth, the customs recorded in the Pentateuch were genuine second millennium BC customs.[56] This would not be expected if the Pentateuch was written much later. This point is even stronger when it is realized that many of these customs were not continued on into the first millennium BC. Some of these ancient customs were the legal bearing of children through maidservants, the legality of oral deathbed wills, the possessing of household idols in order to claim inheritence rights, and the way real estate transactions were practiced.[57]

Ninth, the Ras Shamra literature dates back to approximately 1400BC.[58] Therefore, writing existed during Moses' time. Hence, it cannot be argued that written languages had not developed to the degree of the Pentateuch at such an early date, which is what the documentary hypothesis teaches.

Tenth, archaeological finds have confirmed much of the history and customs reported in the Pentateuch, whereas no archaeological find has refuted the history recorded in the Bible.[59] Examples of this are the excavations of the cities of Bethel, Schechem, and Ur.[60] Archaeology has shown that these cities were inhabited as early as 2,000BC (the time of Abraham).[61] This had been denied by liberal scholars until archaeology proved them wrong and the Pentateuch right. The Hittite Legal Code, which dates back to about 1300BC, is another example. It was discovered by archaeologists between 1906 and 1912. It confirms the ancient procedure used by Abraham and several Hittites while engaging in a real estate transaction in Genesis 23.[62] Another example of archaeological confirmation of the historical reliability of the Pentateuch deals with the use of camels.

Genesis records that Abraham owned camels. However, since no nonbiblical references to domesticated camels had been found, liberal scholars assumed the Pentateuch had to have been written at a much later date. However, since 1950, several archaeological findings have shown that the domestication of camels in the middle east occurred as early as 2,000BC.[63]

Eleventh, all the biblical evidence shows that the Jewish Faith was originally monotheistic, and that it later became idolatrous and polytheistic.[64] This runs counter to the evolutionary view of religion. In fact, there is no historical evidence that any nation's religion ever "evolved" into a genuine monotheistic faith. A true monotheistic faith is unique to the Jewish religion and its offshoots (Christianity, Islam, and their offshoots).[65]

Twelfth, liberal objections that the religious customs, writings, and legal code of the Jews were too advanced for the traditional fifteenth century BC date of composition have been shown to be unwarranted. Recent studies of ancient religions show that "primitive" peoples had technical sacrificial language.[66] Also, the Code of Hammurabi (1800BC) is a legal code which is very similar in its sophistication to the Law of Moses.[67] The census lists found in the ancient Semitic world (Mari, Ugarit, and Alalakh) between 2000 and 1500BC have much in common with the census lists found in the Book of Numbers.[68] Finally, Deuteronomy follows the same basic format as the Hittite suzerainty treaties (latter half of the second millennium BC), a treaty agreed upon by a king and his people.[69] Therefore, the Pentateuch appears to be a fifteenth century BC document, and not a much later writing.

Thirteenth, ancient legends of creation and the worldwide flood are universal among primitive peoples. These legends appear to perversions of the true biblical account.[70] An example of this would be a comparison of the ancient Babylonian flood account (the Gilgames Epic) and the Genesis flood account. Whereas the boat in the Babylonian account would never float due to its dimensions, the ark's dimensions as listed in Genesis describe a vessel that would be virtually impossible to capsize.[71]

Fourteenth, the Jews accepted the Law as Mosaic during King Josiah's reform in 621BC. It is therefore hard to believe that a large portion of the Pentateuch had just been written. The Jews of that day could not have been so naive. It seems more likely that they had good reasons to believe the documents they had were copies of the ancient writings of Moses and not recent creations.[72]

Fifteenth, Moses had a good reason for using different names for the one true God. He used different names for God when dealing with different contexts. He referred to God as "Elohim" when discussing His act of creation or His infinite power. Moses seems to have called God "Jehovah" (Yahweh) when speaking of God in terms of His covenant relationship with His elect.[73] It is therefore unreasonable to assume that the utilization of various names for God requires more than one author. In fact, compound names such as Yahweh-Elohim are often used to refer to God. Yahweh-Elohim occurs eleven times in the second chapter of Genesis. It is ludicrous to assume that one compound name for God is the work of two authors writing at different times.[74]

Finally, Moses also had good reasons for varying his diction and style. Good authors commonly vary their text to prevent monotony; Moses would have done the same.[75] Moses would also have to vary his style due to the wide range of his subject material (genealogies, biographies, historical accounts, religious instruction, moral legislation, etc.).[76] The varying of the diction and style of the Pentateuch is therefore no evidence for multiple authors. Even parallel accounts (such as the two creation accounts of Genesis 1 and 2) were common by one author in ancient Semetic literature; it was often used as a type of poetic style.[77]

When all the above factors are taken together, the conclusion becomes obvious. There are extremely good reasons for accepting the traditional view that Moses wrote the Pentateuch between 1450 and 1410BC. There is absolutely no evidence for multiple authors of the Pentateuch (other than the case of Moses' obituary in Deuteronomy 34 which was probably penned by Joshua). Though Moses did apparently refer to written documents which predate him (especially while compiling Genesis), all the evidence favors the early traditional date for the Pentateuch, and not the later dates given by liberal scholars. The evidence points to Mosaic authorship. The liberal view is therefore based upon a bias against the supernatural; it is not based upon a scholarly consideration of the evidence.

## JOSHUA AND THE CONQUEST OF THE PROMISED LAND

Liberal scholars of the twentieth century have denied the reliability of the biblical account of the conquest of the promised land found in the Book of Joshua. However, in 1887AD the Tell el-Amarna tablets were found. They consisted of ancient writings on clay tablets.[78] These tablets contain correspondence between Canaanite kings and the Egyptian Pharoah during a troublesome time. The Canaanite kings were requesting assistance from the Pharoah due to constant invasions by nomadic peoples called the "Habiru." Many scholars believe that the Habiru invaders, or at least many of them, were in fact the Hebrews of Joshua's army.[79] Many of the reports in the Tell el-Amarna tablets confirm specific details as related in Joshua's account of the conquest.[80]

Any descrepencies between the tablets and Joshua's account can be explained by the fact that though all Jews were Hebrews (referred to as Habiru in the tablets), not all Hebrews were Jews. For Abraham, the father of the Jewish nation, was himself a Hebrew (Genesis 14:13). Therefore, the Jews were probably not the only Hebrews invading the land of Canaan during the life of Joshua.[81]

In short, the evidence seems to indicate that there is enough agreement between the Tell el-Amarna tablets and the Book of Joshua to conclude that these tablets provide ancient secular confirmation for the Israelite conquest of the promised land (Canaan).[82] The strength of this conclusion is in no way lessened by the fact that the Habiru invaders of the tablets cannot in every case be equated with Joshua's army.

### THE BOOK OF ISAIAH

Liberal scholars have rejected the traditional view that Isaiah wrote the Book of Isaiah between 740 and 680BC. In an attempt to explain away the supernatural fulfillment of predictive prophecies, these scholars have concluded that there were actually two authors who wrote Isaiah. This is called the "Deutero-Isaiah Theory."[83] They argue that one author wrote the first thirty-nine chapters, while a different author wrote the last twenty-seven chapters.[84] The second author is assumed to have lived in Babylon after the Babylonian Empire had taken the Jews captive in 586BC. If the book is merely a human book (as liberal scholars claim), then, since the last twenty-seven chapters speak of the Babylonian captivity, it must be dated after that event occurred.

Several things can be noted to refute the Deutero-Isaiah theory. First, the entire book of Isaiah exhibits a similar writing style. In fact, conservative scholars have located over forty sentences or phrases that exist in both halves of Isaiah.[85] One would not expect this if there were more than one author. Second, the author is familiar with the Palestine area; he is not familiar with Babylon.[86] However, if the second half of Isaiah was written by a Jew living in Babylon, this would not be the case. Third, Jesus apparently believed that Isaiah wrote both halves of the Book of Isaiah. In one New Testament passage, He quoted from both Isaiah 53 and Isaiah 6 and referred to Isaiah as the author of both (John 12:37-41).[87] Fourth, a prediction of the Medo-Persian overthrow of the Babylonian Empire is mentioned in the first half of Isaiah (Isaiah 13:17-19). This Medo-Persian conquest occurred in 538BC. Even liberal scholars admit that this section of Isaiah was written before the Babylonian captivity (586BC).[88] If the author could predict the future in the first thirty-nine chapters, he could certainly do the same in the last twenty-seven chapters.

There is no good reason to reject the traditional date and authorship of Isaiah; only a bias against the supernatural will cause a scholar to reject the traditional view despite the evidence in its favor. Isaiah chapter 53 is a case in point. It is probably Isaiah's most famous prophecy. In this chapter, Isaiah predicts that the Jewish Messiah would suffer for the iniquities of His people. Since this did not occur until 30AD, there is no way for scholars to date any portion of the Book of Isaiah this late.[89] Therefore, no matter how late Isaiah is dated, the fulfillment of predictive prohecies must be admitted. Hence, the liberal bias against the supernatural is without justification.

## THE BOOK OF DANIEL

Thr traditional view concerning the Book of Daniel is that Daniel wrote it between 590 and 530BC.[90] Daniel lived under both the Babylonian and the Medo-Persian rule over Judah.

The liberal view teaches that the Book of Daniel was written around 165BC to encourage the Jews in Palestine to resist the evil ruler Antiochus Epiphanes.[91] This is due to the fact that Daniel predicts the reign of this vile man. And, as mentioned throughout this chapter, liberal scholars reject the fulfillment of predictive prphecies. Their world view forces them to date the Book of Daniel after the events occurred. Hence, they assume the late date.[92]

There is much evidence for the traditional date of Daniel. First, Daniel uses early Aramaic which is consistent with the sixth century BC date of composition, rather than a second century BC date.[93] Second, the three Greek words found in Daniel do not prove a late date (the Greeks did not takeover the Palestine area until 330BC). The three Greek words are names of musical instruments, which could easily have been known and used in Palestine and Babylon long before the Greeks conquered those regions.[94]

Third, Daniel's theology, contrary to liberal speculation, was not too advanced for such an early date as the sixth century BC. His teaching concerning angels, the end-time resurrection, and the Kingdom of God can also be found in other Old Testament books which predate the sixth century BC.[95]

Fourth, there is strong archaeological confirmation of some of the historical characters found in the Book of Daniel. King Belshazzar was thought to be unhistorical by liberal critics. Secular history records Nabonidus as the last king of the Babylonian Empire. However, later discoveries of cuneiform tablets revealed that Nabonidus shared his reign with his son Belshazzar.[96] Liberal scholars also rejected the historicity of Darius the Mede, but recent scholarship has identified Darius the Mede with an ancient govenor of Babylon named Gubaru. It has also been shown that Darius was probably not a personal name; rather, it was a title of royalty (such as Caesar was for the Romans).[97]

Fifth, several of Daniel's predictions were fulfilled after 165BC.[98] Therefore, there is no reason to date the Book of Daniel around that time. Daniel's prophecies of the four world kingdoms (Daniel 2, 7) predicted that the Medo-Persians would overthrow the Babylonians (this occurred in 538BC). Daniel foretold the Greek conquest of the Medo-Persian Empire (330BC). But, Daniel also prophesied the Roman conquest of Palestine, which occurred in 63BC. This is obviously much later than even the most liberal dating of Daniel (165BC). Hence, there is no way to avoid the conclusion that Daniel contains predictive prophecies that have been fulfilled.[99]

Some of Daniel's most amazing prophecies are Messianic. Daniel predicted that the Messiah would be executed 483 years after the order to rebuild the walls of Jerusalem was issued (Daniel 9:24-27). This would place the death of the Jewish Messiah at about 30AD.[100] Daniel also stated that the death of the Messiah would be followed by the destruction of the temple in Jerusalem (which occurred in 70AD).[101]

No matter how one tries, there is no way to remove the supernatural elements from the Book of Daniel. Even if a person accepts the liberal dating of the book of Daniel (165BC), it is still evident that Daniel predicted the future. He predicted future events that did not occur until after 165BC. Therefore, there is no reason to attempt to date Daniel after the events he predicts, for even the late date for the composition of Daniel must admit the fulfillment of predictive prophecies. Since even the liberal 165BC date would have to admit major fulfillments of prophecies, the evidence supports the traditional date (530BC) for the Book of Daniel.

### CONCLUSION

The Old Testament has been shown to be historically reliable. Many times archaeology has confirmed the Old Testament account. Not once has an archaeological find refuted the history recorded in the Bible.[102] The only reason to reject the historical reliability of the Old Testament is an a priori bias against the possibility of God revealing Himself through propositional form, and, as has been shown, this bias is unwarranted.

### ENDNOTES

1Geisler, *Apologetics*, 285-377.

2Gleason L. Archer, Jr., *A Survey of Old Testament Introduction* (Chicago: Moody Press, 1974), entire book.

3Ibid., 15.

4Ibid., 19.

5Ibid., 37-45.

6Ibid., 44.

7Ibid.

8Ibid.

9Ibid., 42.

10ibid., 66.

11Ibid., 38.

12McDowell, 57-58.

13Archer, 37.

14Tenney, ed., *The Zondervan Pictorial Bible Dictionary*, 206.

15Archer, 45.

16Ibid.

17McDowell, 58.

18Archer, 55.

19Ibid.

20Ibid., 109-110.

21Ibid., 97-98.

22Ibid., 83-84.

23Ibid.

24Ibid., 83.

25Ibid., 84.

26Ibid.

27Ibid.

28Ibid.

29Ibid.

30Ibid., 85.

31Ibid., 87-88.

32Ibid., 89.

33Ibid., 89-90, 148-150.

34Ibid., 91-92.

35Ibid., 94.

36Ibid., 110.

37Ibid., 112.

38Ibid., 109.

39Ibid., 110-111.

40Ibid., 111.

41Ibid., 110.

42Ibid., 111.

43Ibid., 111-112.

44Ibid., 121-122.

45Ibid., 113-114.

46Ibid., 115.

47Ibid.

48Ibid., 115-119.

49Ibid., 119-120.

50Ibid.

51Ibid., 120.

52Ibid.

53Ibid.

54Ibid.

55Ibid., 114-115, 122-123.

56Ibid., 120.

57Ibid., 164.

58Ibid., 170, 172.

59Ibid., 170-182.

60Ibid., 173-174.

61Ibid.

62Ibid., 176-177.

63Ibid., 177.

64Ibid., 147-169.

65Ibid., 149.

66Ibid., 179.

67Ibid., 177.

68Charles F. Pfeiffer and Everett F. Harrison, eds., *The Wycliffe Bible Commentary* (Nashville: The Southwestern Company, 1962), 115.

69Archer, 259-260.

70John J. Davis, *Paradise to Prison* (Grand Rapids: Baker Book House, 1975), 129-133.

71Henry M. Morris, *The Genesis Record* (Grand Rapids: Baker Book House, 1976), 181.

72Archer, 259-268.

73Ibid., 124-129.

74Ibid., 126.

75Ibid., 130.

76Ibid., 129.

77Ibid., 132-135, 138.

78Ibid., 271.

79Ibid., 276.

80Ibid.

81Ibid., 277.

82Ibid.

83Ibid., 336-338.

84Ibid.

85Ibid., 352.

86Ibid., 357.

87Ibid., 356.

88Ibid., 357.

89Ibid., 355.

90Ibid., 387.

91Ibid., 388.

92Ibid.

93Ibid., 398-401.

94Ibid., 395.

95Ibid., 403.

96Ibid., 390-392.

97Ibid., 393-394.

98Ibid., 403-408.

99Ibid., 407.

100Ibid., 409.

101Ibid.

102Ibid., 171.

# CHAPTER 25
# NEW TESTAMENT RELIABILITY

Establishing the reliability of the New Testament is vital to Christian apologetics. Christianity is a religion with deep historical roots. For example, if Jesus did not rise from the dead (an historical event), then the Christian Faith cannot save (1 Corinthians 15:14, 17). If He did not die on the cross for the sins of mankind (an historical event), then Christianity offers no hope (1 Peter 2:24; 3:18). Proving the New Testament can be trusted will go a long way to establishing Christianity as the one true faith.

This chapter will attempt to show that the New Testament accounts were written by eyewitnesses who knew Christ, or persons who knew the eyewitnesses. Evidence will be provided to show that the accounts of Christ's bodily resurrection and His claims to deity were not legends invented decades after Christ's death; rather, they were eyewitness accounts. This chapter will not deal with defending the Bible as the inspired and inerrant Word of God; that topic will be examined in chapter twenty-eight. The purpose of this chapter is to merely show that the New Testament documents are historically reliable.

## MANUSCRIPT EVIDENCE OF THE NEW TESTAMENT
Many historical scholars believe that one cannot know the true Jesus of history since no one no has the original writings of those who knew Him. Only copies of the originals are in existence today. Ironically, these historical scholars will often quote from Plato, as well

as other ancient writers, as if they can know with certainty what Plato originally wrote. This clearly unveils a double standard. Ancient secular writings can be trusted based on late copies, but the New Testament cannot be trusted since the original manuscripts are missing.

The New Testament is by far the most reliable ancient writing in existence today. There exist today over 24,000 copies (5,000 of them in the original Greek language) of the New Testament (either in whole or in part).[1] This should be compared with the fact that only 7 copies presently exist of Plato's Tetralogies.[2] Homer's Iliad is in second place behind the New Testament among ancient writings with just 643 copies.[3]

The earliest copy of Plato's Tetralogies is dated about 1,200 years after Plato supposedly wrote the original.[4] Compare this with the earliest extant copy of the New Testament: the John Ryland's Papyri. It contains a portion of John 18. This fragment is dated at about 125AD, only 25 years after the original is thought to have been written.[5] In fact, there is possibly an even earlier New Testament fragment that was found among the Dead Sea Scrolls. The fragment is called 7Q5; it is dated earlier than 70AD. Though there is heated debate about this manuscript, it has been argued that it is a part of Mark 6:52-53.[6] Again, Homer's Iliad takes second place among ancient writings, second only to the New Testament. The earliest copy of any portion of Homer's Iliad is dated about 500 years after the original writing.[7]

When the contents of the extant manuscripts of the New Testament are compared, there appears to be 99.5% agreement. There is total agreement in the doctrines taught; the corruptions are mainly grammatical.[8] Homer's Iliad once again takes second place behind the New Testament among ancient documents. Homer's Iliad has a 95% accuracy when its copies are compared.[9] Since there are so few remaining copies of Plato's writings, agreement between these copies is not considered a factor (they are probably all copies of the same copy).[10]

TABLE SIX

**Comparison of Three Ancient Writings**

| Ancient Writing | Extant Copies | Earliest Extant Copy | Agreement Between Copies |
|---|---|---|---|
| Homer's Iliad | 643 | 500 years after original | 95% |
| Plato's Tetralogies | 7 | 1,200 years after original | --- |
| New Testament | 24,000 | 25 years after original | 99.5% |

In short, historical scholars can consider the extant New Testament manuscripts to be reliable and accurate representations of what the authors originally wrote. Since the New Testament is by far the most accurately copied ancient writing, to question its authenticity is to call into question all of ancient literature.

## ANCIENT NEW TESTAMENT COPIES

The following manuscripts are some of the better known copies of the New Testament. The John Rylands Papyri is the oldest undisputed fragment of the New Testament still in existence. It is dated between 125 and 130AD. It contains a portion of John 18.[11] The Bodmer Papyrus II contains most of John's Gospel and dates between 150 and 200AD.[12] The Chester Beatty Papyri includes major portions of the New Testament; it is dated around 200AD.[13]

Codex Vaticanus contains nearly the entire Bible and is dated between 325 and 350AD.[14] Codex Sinaiticus contains nearly all of the New Testament and approximately half of the Old Testament. It is dated at about 350AD.[15] Codex Alexandrinus encompasses almost the entire Bible and was copied around 400AD.[16] Codex Ephraemi represents every New Testament book except for 2 John and 2 Thessalonians. Ephraemi is dated in the 400's AD.[17] Codex Bezae has the Gospels and Acts as its contents and is dated after 450AD.[18]

The very early dates of these manuscripts provide strong evidence that the current New Testament is one and the same with the original writings of the apostles. There is no logical reason to doubt the reliability of these manuscripts.

TABLE SEVEN

### Ancient New Testament Copies

| Manuscript | Content | Date |
|---|---|---|
| John Rylands Papyri | Portion of John 18 | 125-130 ad |
| Bodmer Papyrus II | Most of John's Gospel | 150-200 ad |
| Chester Beatty Papyri | Major portions of N.T. | 200 ad |
| Codex Vaticanus | Almost entire Bible | 325-350 ad |
| Codex Sinaiticus | All of N.T. & half of O.T. | 350 ad |
| Codex Alexandrinus | Almost entire Bible | 400 ad |
| Codex Ephraemi | Most of N.T. | 400's ad |
| Codex Bezae | The Gospels & Acts | 450 ad |

## THE APOSTOLIC FATHERS: ANOTHER SOURCE OF N. T. RELABILITY

The New Testament manuscripts are not the only evidence for the reliability of the New Testament. Another source of evidence is found in the writings of the apostolic fathers. The apostolic fathers were leaders in the early church who knew the apostles and their doctrine.[19] Most of their writings were produced between 95 and 150AD.[20]

Liberal scholars have attempted to find the so-called true Jesus of history. It was their goal to find a non-supernatural Jesus who never claimed to be God. These scholars believe that Christ's claim to be God and Savior, and His miraculous life (especially His bodily resurrection from the dead) are merely legends. The true Jesus of history was a great teacher; still, He was merely a man.[21] Therefore, if it can be shown that early church leaders, who personally knew the apostles, taught that the miraculous aspects of Christ's life actually occurred and that Jesus did in fact make the bold claims recorded in the New Testament, then the legend hypothesis fails. Historians recognize that legends take centuries to develop.[22] A legend is a fictitious story that, through the passage of time, many people come to accept as historically accurate. A legend can begin to develop only if the eyewitnesses and those who knew the eyewitnesses are already dead. Otherwise, the eyewitnesses or those who knew them would refute the legend. Therefore, a legend has its beginning a generation or two after the event or person in question has passed. However, before a legend receives wide acceptance, several centuries are needed, for there is still a remembrance of the person or event due to information passed on orally from generation to generation. After several centuries, new generations arise without the sufficient knowledge of the person or event necessary to refute the legend. If a written record compiled by eyewitnesses is passed on to future generations, legends can be easily refuted.

One apostolic father, Clement, was the Bishop of Rome. He wrote his letter to the Corinthians in 95AD. The following is a brief quote from this letter:

> Let us fear the Lord Jesus (Christ), whose blood was given for us.[23] The Apostles received the Gospel for us from the Lord Jesus Christ; Jesus Christ was sent from God.[24] He made the Lord Jesus Christ the firstfruit, when He raised Him from the dead.[25]

It is important to note that Clement of Rome referred to Jesus as "the Lord." This is an obvious reference to Christ's deity, for he uses the Greek word "Kurios" with the definite article[26] (Christ was *the* Lord, not *a* Lord). Clement also spoke of Christ's blood as being shed for us, indicating a belief in Christ's saving work. He declared that the apostles received the Gospel directly from Jesus. Clement also spoke of God raising Jesus from the dead. If any of these statements were opposed to the doctrines of the apostles, the Apostle John, who was still alive at the time, would have openly confronted this first century bishop. However, he did not. Therefore, the writings of Clement of Rome provide strong confirmation of the original message of the Apostles. Contrary to the wishful thinking of skeptics, the teachings of the first century church are exactly what one finds in the New Testament.

The apostolic father, Ignatius, bishop of Antioch, wrote his letters between 110 and 115AD. During that time, he was traveling from Antioch to Rome to be martyred.[27] Ignatius openly wrote about the deity of Christ. He referred to Jesus as "Jesus Christ our God," "God in man," and "Jesus Christ the God."[28] Ignatius stated that "there is one God who manifested Himself through Jesus Christ His Son."[29] Besides ascribing deity to Christ, Ignatius also wrote of salvation in Christ and expressed belief in Christ's virgin birth, crucifixion, and resurrection:

> Christ Jesus our Savior...[30]
>
> Jesus Christ, who dies for us, that believing on His death ye might escape death.[31]
>
> He is truly of the race of David according to the flesh, but Son of God by the Divine will and power, truly born of a virgin.[32]
>
> Be ye deaf therefore, when any man speaketh to you apart from Jesus Christ, who was born of the race of David, who was the Son of Mary, who was truly born and ate and drank, was truly persecuted under Pontius Pilate, was truly crucified and died in the sight of those in heaven and those on earth and those under the earth; who moreover was truly raised from the dead, His Father having raised Him...[33]

The writings of Ignatius show that only fifteen years after the death of the Apostle John, the central doctrines of the New Testament were already being taught. It is highly unlikely that the New Testament manuscripts, referenced by Ignatius, could have been corrupted in such a short amount of time. It is also important to remember that Clement of Rome taught the same doctrines while the Apostle John was still alive.

Another apostolic father Polycarp (70-156AD) was the Bishop of Smyrna. He was a personal pupil of the Apostle John.[34] Had any of the other apostolic fathers perverted the teachings of the apostles, Polycarp would have set the record straight. However, Polycarp's teachings are essentially the same as that of Clement of Rome and Ignatius. Of all the apostolic fathers, Polycarp knew better than any the content of the original apostles' message. Liberal scholars display tremendous arrogance when thay assume that they have more insight into the original apostolic message than Polycarp. Polycarp studied under the Apostle John (85-95AD?); contemporary scholars live nearly 2,000 years later. In his letter to the Philippians, Polycarp wrote:

...Jesus Christ who took our sins in His own body upon the tree, who did no sin, neither was guile found in His mouth, but for our sakes He endured all things, that we might live in Him.[35]

For they loved not the present world, but Him that died for our sakes and was raised by God for us.[36]

...who shall believe on our Lord and God Jesus Christ and on His Father that raised Him from the dead.[37]

Another student of the Apostle John was Papias, the Bishop of Hierapolis. Papias was born between 60 and 70AD and died between 130 and 140AD.[38] Papias wrote that he did not accept the words of any self-proclaimed teacher. Instead, he would talk to others who, like himself, had known at least one of the original apostles. In this way, Papias could discover the teachings of Christ from the sources closest to Christ Himself, rather than rely on hearsay testimony.[39]

Papias wrote of his discussions with persons who spoke with with apostles such as Andrew, Peter, Philip, Thomas, James, John, or Matthew.[40] Papias stated that Mark received the information for his Gospel from the Apostle Peter himself. Papias also related that Matthew originally recorded his gospel in Hebrew, but that it was later translated into Greek to reach a wider audience.[41]

The testimony of the first century and early second century church should be considered extremely reliable. For their teachings many of them were martyred. Since people will only die for what they truly believe, it is reasonable to conclude that the early church sincerely believed they were protecting the true apostolic faith from possible perversions. If they had tampered with the teachings of the apostles, they certainly would not have died for their counterfeit views.

The following conclusions can now be drawn: First, the apostolic fathers form an unbroken chain from the apostles to their day. Second, people who personally knew the apostles accepted the leadership of the apostolic fathers. Third, the apostolic fathers taught essentially the same thing as the New Testament. Fourth, the apostolic fathers and their followers were willing to die for the teachings passed down to them from the apostles themselves. Therefore, our New Testament accurately represents the teachings of the apostles. This includes such key doctrines as the deity of Christ,

His substitutionary death, virgin birth, bodily resurrection, and salvation through Him alone.

## ANCIENT SECULAR WRITINGS: ANOTHER WITNESS

Besides references to Christ in Christian literature which dates back to the first and second centuries AD, there are also ancient secular writings which refer to Christ from that same time period. The significance of these non-Christian writings is that, though the secular authors themselves did not believe the early church's message, they stated the content of what the early church actually taught.

In 52AD, Thallus recorded a history of the Eastern Mediterranean world. In this work, he covered the time period from the Trojan War (mid 1200's BC) to his day (52AD). Though no manuscripts of Thallus' work are known to currently exist, Julius Africanus (writing in 221AD) referred to Thallus' work. Africanus stated that Thallus attempted to explain away the darkness that covered the land when Christ was crucified. Thallus attributed this darkness to an eclipse of the sun.[42] This reveals that about twenty years after the death of Christ, non-believers were still trying to give explanations for the miraculous events of Christ's life.

In 115AD, a Roman historian named Cornelius Tacitus wrote about the great fire of Rome which occurred during Nero's reign. Tacitus reported that Nero blamed the fire on a group of people called Christians, and he tortured them for it. Tacitus stated that the Christians had been named after their founder "Christus." Tacitus said that Christus had been executed by Pontius Pilate during the reign of Tiberius (14-37AD). Tacitus related that the "superstition" of the Christians had been stopped for a short time, but then once again broke out, spreading from Judaea all the way to Rome. He said that multitudes of Christians (based on their own confessions to be followers of Christ) were thrown to wild dogs, crucified, or burned to death. Tacitus added that their persecutions were not really for the good of the public; their deaths merely satisfied the cruelty of Nero himself.[43]

These statements by Tacitus are consistent with the New Testament records. Even Tacitus' report of the stopping of the "superstition" and then its breaking out again appears to be his attempt to explain how the death of Christ stifled the spreading of the gospel, but then the Christian message was once again preached, this time spreading more rapidly. This is perfectly consistent with the New Testament record. The New Testament reports that Christ's disciples went into hiding during His arrest and death. After Jesus rose from the dead (three days after the crucifixion), He filled His disciples with the Holy Spirit (about fifty days after the crucifixion), and they fearlessly proclaimed the gospel throughout the Roman Empire (Acts 1 and 2).

Suetonius was the chief secretary of Emperor Hadrian who reigned over Rome from 117 to 138AD. Suetonius refers to the riots that occurred in the Jewish community in Rome in 49AD due to the instigation of "Chrestus." Chrestus is apparently a variant spelling of Christ. Suetonius refers to these Jews being expelled from the city.[44] Seutonius also reports that following the great fire of Rome, Christians were punished. He refers to their religious beliefs as "new and mischievous."[45]

Pliny the Younger, another ancient secular writer, provides evidence for early Christianity. He was a Roman governor in Asia Minor. His work dates back to 112AD. He states that Christians assembled on a set day, sang hymns to Christ as to a god, vowed not to partake in wicked deeds, and shared "ordinary" food.[46] This shows that by 112AD, it was already common knowledge that Christians worshipped Christ, sang hymns to Him, lived moral lives, assembled regularly, and partook of common food (probably a reference to the celebration of the Lord's Supper).

The Roman Emperor Trajan also wrote in 112AD. He gave guidelines for the persecution of Christians. He stated that if a person denies he is a Christian and proves it by worshipping the Roman gods, he must be pardoned for his repentance.[47]

The Roman Emperor Hadrian reigned from 117 to 138AD. He wrote that Christians should only be punished if there was clear evidence against them. Mere accusations were not enough to condemn a supposed Christian.[48] The significance of these passages found in the writings of Trajan and Hadrian is that it confirms the fact that early Christians were sincere enough about their beliefs to die for them.

The Talmud is the written form of the oral traditions of the ancient Jewish Rabbis. A Talmud passage dating back to between 70 and 200AD refers to Jesus as one who "practiced sorcery" and led Israel astray. This passage states that Jesus (spelled Yeshu) was hanged (the common Jewish term for crucifixion) on the night before the Passover feast.[49] This is a very significant passage, for it reveals that even the enemies of Christ admitted there were supernatural aspects of Christ's life by describing Him as one who "practiced sorcery." This source also confirms that Jesus was crucified around the time of the Passover feast.

Another anti-Christian document was the Toledoth Jesu, which dates back to the fifth century AD, but reflects a much earlier Jewish tradition. In this document, the Jewish leaders are said to have paraded the rotting corpse of Christ through the streets of Jerusalem.[50] This obviously did not occur. The earliest preaching of the gospel took place in Jerusalem. Therefore, parading the rotting corpse of Christ through the streets of Jerusalem would have crushed the Christian faith in its embryonic stage. However, some of the other non-Christian authors mentioned above stated that Christianity spread rapidly during the first few decades after Christ's death. The preaching of Christ's resurrection would not have been persuasive if His rotting corpse had been publicly displayed.

It is also interesting to note that the Jewish religious leaders waited quite a long before putting a refutation of the resurrection into print. Certainly, it would have served their best interests to disprove Christ's resurrection. But as far as written documents are concerned, the first century Jewish authorities were silent regarding the resurrection of Jesus.

Lucian was a Greek satirist of the second century. He wrote that Christians worshipped a wise man who had been crucified, lived by His laws, and believed themselves to be immortal.[51] Thus, this ancient secular source confirms the New Testament message by reporting the fact that Jesus was worshipped by His earliest followers.

Probably the most interesting of all ancient non-Christian references to the life of Christ is found in the writings of the Jewish historian named Josephus. Josephus was born in 37 or 38AD and died in 97AD. At nineteen, he became a Pharisee (a Jewish religious leader and teacher).[52] The following passage is found in his writings:

Now there was about this time Jesus, a wise man, if it be lawful to call him a man; for he was a doer of wonderful works, a teacher of such men as receive the truth with pleasure. He drew over to him both many of the Jews and many of the Gentiles. He was (the) Christ. And when Pilate, at the suggestion of the principal men amongst us, had condemned him to the cross, those that loved him at the first did not forsake him; for he appeared to them alive again the third day; as the divine prophets had foretold these and ten thousand other wonderful things concerning him. And the tribe of Christians, so named after him, are not extinct at this day.[53]

Since Josephus was a Jew and not a Christian, many scholars deny that this passage was originally written by him. These scholars believe this text was corrupted by Christians. Gary Habermas, chairman of the philosophy department at Liberty University, dealt with this problem in the following manner:

There are good indications that the majority of the text is genuine. There is no textual evidence against it, and, conversely, there is very good manuscript evidence for this statement about Jesus, thus making it difficult to ignore. Additionally, leading scholars on the works of Josephus have testified that this portion is written in the style of this Jewish historian. Thus we conclude that there are good reasons for accepting this version of Josephus' statement about Jesus, with modifications of questionable words. In fact, it is possible that these modifications can even be accurately ascertained. In 1972 Professor Schlomo Pines of the Hebrew University in Jerusalem released the results of a study on an Arabic manuscript containing Josephus' statement about Jesus. It includes a different and briefer rendering of the entire passage, including changes in the key words listed above...[54]

Habermas goes on to relate the Arabic version of this debated passage. In this version, Jesus is described as being a wise and virtuous man who had many followers from different nations. He was crucified under Pontius Pilate, but his disciples reported that, three days later, He appeared to them alive. Josephus added that Jesus may have been the Messiah whom the prophets had predicted would come.[55]

It is highly unlikely that both readings of this controversial passage are corrupt. One of these two readings probably represents the original text. The other reading would then be a copy that was tampered with by either a Christian or a non-Christian. Whatever the case may be, even the skeptic should have no problem accepting the Arabic reading. Still, even if only this reading is accepted, it is enough. For it is a first century testimony from a non-Christian historian that declares that those who knew Jesus personally claimed that He had appeared to them alive three days after His death by crucifixion under Pilate.

Several things can be learned from this brief survey of ancient non-Christian writings concerning the life of Christ. First, His earliest followers worshipped Him as God. The doctrine of Christ's deity is therefore not a legend or myth developed many years after Christ's death (as was the case with Buddha). Second, they claimed to have seen Him alive three days after His death. Third, Christ's earliest followers faced persecution and martyrdom for their refusal to deny His deity and resurrection. Therefore, the deity and resurrection of Christ were not legends added to the text centuries after its original composition. Instead, these teachings were the focus of the teaching of Christ's earliest followers. They claimed to be eyewitnesses of Christ's miraculous life and were willing to die horrible deaths for their testimonies. Therefore, they were reliable witnesses of who the true Jesus of history was and what He taught.

## ANCIENT CREEDS FOUND IN THE NEW TESTAMENT

The writings of both the apostolic fathers and ancient non-Christian authors declare that the earliest Christians did in fact teach that Jesus is God and that He rose from the dead. The manuscript evidence for the New Testament is stronger than that of any other ancient writing. Another piece of evidence for the authenticity and reliability of the New Testament manuscripts is the ancient creeds found in the New Testament itself.

Most scholars, whether liberal or conservative, date Paul's epistles before the Gospels were put into written form.[56] Just as the teachings of the Jewish Rabbis had originally been passed on orally, it appears that the Gospel was first spread in the form of oral creeds and hymns.[57] J. P. Moreland states that Paul's epistles contain many of these pre-Pauline creeds and hymns, that they were originally spoken in the Aramaic tongue (the Hebrew language of Christ's day), and that most scholars date these creeds and hymns between 33AD and 48AD.[58] Since Paul's writings are dated in the 50's AD or 60's AD by most scholars, the creeds he recorded in his letters point to an oral tradition which predates his writings. Most scholars will at least admit that these ancient creeds originated before 50AD.[59]

Excerpts from some of these ancient creeds found in the letters of Paul are as follows:

...that if you confess with your mouth Jesus as Lord, and believe in your heart that God raised Him from the dead, you shall be saved (Romans 10:9).

For I delivered to you as of first importance what I also received, that Christ died for our sins according to the Scriptures, and that He was buried, and that He was raised on the third day according to the Scriptures, and that He appeared to Cephas, then to the twelve. After that He appeared to more than five hundred brethren at one time, most of whom remain until now, but some have fallen asleep; then He appeared to James, then to all the apostles; and last of all, as it were to one untimely born, He appeared to me also (1 Corinthians 15:3-8).

Have this attitude in yourselves which was also in Christ Jesus, who, although He existed in the form of God, did not regard equality with God a thing to be grasped, but emptied Himself, taking the form of a bondservant, and being made in the likeness of men. And being found in appearance as a man, He humbled Himself by becoming obedient to the point of death, even death on a cross. Therefore also God highly exalted Him, and bestowed on Him the name which is above every name, that at the name of Jesus every knee should bow, of those who are in heaven, and on earth, and under the earth, and that every tongue should confess that Jesus Christ is Lord, to the glory of God the Father (Philippians 2:5-11).

And He [Christ] is the image of the invisible God, the first-born of all creation. For by Him all things were created, both in the heavens and on earth, visible and invisible, whether thrones or dominions or rulers or authorities-all things have been created by Him and for Him. And He is before all things, and in Him all things hold together (Colossians 1:15-17).

These ancient creeds clearly prove that the first generation Christians believed that Jesus had risen bodily from the dead, that He is God, and that salvation comes through Him.[60] The followers of Buddha attributed deity to the founder of their religion centuries after his death.[61] However, the earliest followers of Christ, those who knew Him personally, considered Him to be God.[62] It is almost universally recognized that these creeds were formulated before 50AD. Therefore, they represent the Gospel in its original form.

The belief in Christ's deity and resurrection is not based on later corruptions of the New Testament text as liberal scholars believe. The doctrines of Christ's deity and resurrection are not legends that took centuries to develop. These doctrines were held by the first generation church, those who knew Jesus personally. The gospel message found in the New Testament is the same message proclaimed by the apostles themselves.

Less than twenty years after Christ's death, hymns were already being sung in Christian churches attributing deity to Christ. The apostles were still alive and had the authority to suppress the idea of Christ's deity if it was a heresy, but, they did not. All the available evidence indicates that they not only condoned it, but that it was their own teaching. Therefore, liberal scholars such as John Hick have no justification for their claims that the deity of Christ was a legend that developed near the end of the first century AD.[63] The historical evidence indicates that the Christian church always believed in Christ's deity. Therefore, to deny that Christ claimed to be God is to call the apostles liars.

Nearly 2,000 years after the death of Christ a forum of liberal scholars called the "Jesus Seminar" has been meeting since 1985. These scholars vote to decide which biblical passages they believe Jesus actually said.[64] This is ironic since the evidence shows that Christianity proclaimed Christ's deity and resurrection from its inception. The early church accepted the deity of Christ. The early church was willing to suffer horrible persecution for this belief. Sincere eyewitness testimony should not be ignored.

## THE OPINIONS OF THE EXPERTS

The testimonies of some of the world's leading experts can be called upon to further verify the authenticity and reliability of the New Testament manuscripts. Dr. John A. T. Robinson, one of England's leading New Testament critics, came to the conclusion that the entire New Testament was written before the fall of Jerusalem in 70AD.[65]

Sir William Ramsey was one of the world's greatest archaeologists. His thorough investigation into Luke's Book of Acts led him to the conclusion that Acts was a mid-first century document that was historically reliable.[66]

William F. Albright is one of the world's foremost biblical archaeologists. He states that there is no evidential basis for dating any New Testament book after 80AD.[67]

Sir Frederic Kenyon was one of the world's leading experts on ancient manuscripts. His research led him to conclude that the New Testament is essentially the same as when it was originally written.[68]

Millar Burrows, the great archaeologist from Yale, stated that there is no doubt that archaeological research has strengthened confidence in the historical reliability of the Bible. Burrows also stated that the skepticism of liberal scholars is based on their prejudice against the supernatural, rather than on the evidence itself.[69]

F. F. Bruce, New Testament scholar from Manchester University in England, stated that if the New Testament writings had been secular works, no scholar would question their authenticity. Bruce believes that the evidence for the New Testament outweighs the evidence for many classical works which have never been doubted.[70]

Bruce Metzger is a famous textual critic from Princeton. He has stated that the New Testament has more evidence in its favor than any other writings from ancient Greek or Latin literature.[71]

It is clear that the evidence favors the authenticity and reliability of the New Testament. Scholars who do not allow their bias against the supernatural to influence their conclusions have recognized this fact. Scholars who reject the reliability of the New Testament manuscripts do so because they chose to go against the overwhelming evidence. However, such a rejection is not true scholarship; it is an a priori assumption.

CONCLUSION

Evidence from the existing New Testament manuscripts, from the writings of the apostolic fathers, from the works of ancient secular authors, from the ancient creeds and hymns found in the New Testament, and from the opinions of the world's leading experts have been examined. All this evidence leads to the conclusion that the existing New Testament manuscripts are reliable and authentic testimony of what the apostles wrote. A person is free to deny this conclusion, but to do so is to go against all the available evidence.

The key point is that the original apostles taught that Jesus rose from the dead, and that He claimed to be God incarnate and the Savior of the world.

ENDNOTES

1McDowell, 42-43.

2Ibid.

3Ibid., 43.

4Ibid.

5Ibid.

6Corduan, 192.

7McDowell, 43.

8Ibid.

9Ibid.

10Ibid.

11Ibid., 46.

12Ibid., 46-47.

13Ibid., 47.

14Ibid.

15Ibid., 47-48.

16Ibid., 48.

17Ibid.

18Ibid.

19Cairns, 73.

20Ibid.

21Gary R. Habermas, *Ancient Evidence for the Life of Jesus* (Nashville: Thomas Nelson Publishers, 1984), 42.

22Josh McDowell and Bill Wilson, *He Walked Among Us* (San Bernardino: Here's Life Publishers, 1988), 130.

23Lightfoot and Harmer, 67.

24Ibid., 75.

25Ibid., 68.

26Ibid., 17.

27Ibid., 97.

28Ibid., 137, 139, 149, 150, 156.

29Ibid., 144.

30Ibid., 137.

31Ibid., 147.

32Ibid., 156.

33Ibid., 148.

34Cairns, 74.

35Lightfoot and Harmer, 180

36Ibid.

37Ibid., 181.

38Ibid., 514.

39Ibid., 527-528.

40Ibid., 528.

41Ibid., 529.

42Habermas, 93.

43Ibid., 87-88.

44Ibid., 90.

45Ibid.

46Ibid., 94.

47Ibid., 96.

48Ibid., 97.

49Ibid., 98.

50Ibid., 99-100.

51Ibid., 100.

52Ibid., 90.

53Flavius Josephus, *The Works of Josephus* William Whiston, trans. (Peabody: Hendrickson Publishers, 1987), 480.

54Habermas, 91.

55Ibid., 91-92.

56McDowell and Wilson, 168-170.

57Ibid., 170.

58Moreland, *Scaling the Secular City*, 148-149.

59Ibid.
60Ibid., 149.

61Josh McDowell and Don Stewart, *Handbook of Today's Religions* (San Bernardino: Here's Life Publishers, 1983), 307-308.

62Moreland, 149.

63John Hick, *The Center of Christianity* (New York: Harper and Row, Publishers, 1978), 27-29.

64J. P. Moreland and Michael J. Wilkins, *Jesus Under Fire* (Grand Rapids: Zondervan Publishing House, 1995), 2-3.

65McDowell, *Evidence*, 63.

66Roy Abraham Varghese, ed. *The Intellectuals Speak Out About God* (Dallas: Lewis and Stanley Publishers, 1984), 267-268.

67Ibid., 267.

68Ibid., 274.

69McDowell, *Evidence*, 66.

70Varghese, 274.

71Ibid., 205.

# CHAPTER 26
# DID JESUS RISE FROM THE DEAD?

Chapter twenty-two of this work revealed that one should not a priori rule out the possibility of miracles. A person should not reject a miracle claim simply because it does not fit into his world view. The evidence for and against a particular miracle claim must be weighed. This chapter will examine the historical evidence for the bodily resurrection of Jesus from the dead.

The importance of Christ's resurrection should not be overlooked. The apostle Paul considered belief in Christ's resurrection to be necessary for salvation (Romans 10:9). Paul also stated: ...and if Christ has not been raised, then our preaching is vain, your faith also is vain...and if Christ has not been raised, your faith is worthless; you are still in your sins (1 Corinthians 15:14, 17).

Paul was quick to point out that if Christ could not raise Himself from the dead, then faith in Him would be worthless. Therefore, Christianity stands or falls on the resurrection of Christ. If the resurrection really happened, then Christianity is true and Jesus is the only Savior. However, if the resurrection never occurred, then Christianity is just another false religion, promoting a false messiah.

CHRIST'S RESURRECTION WAS BODILY

Before examining the evidence for Christ's resurrection, the nature of that resurrection must be discussed. Throughout the centuries the Christian Church has recognized that Christ's resurrection was bodily.[1] Despite this fact, many today deny that

Jesus rose bodily from the dead. The Jehovah's Witnesses are a non-Christian cult which denies Christ's bodily resurrection. Their literature states:

> On the third day of his being dead in the grave his immortal Father Jehovah God raised him from the dead, not as a human Son, but as a mighty immortal spirit Son, with all power in heaven and earth under the Most High God.[2]

> Jesus was the first one to rise from the dead...This firstborn one from the dead was not raised out of the grave a human creature, but was raised a spirit.[3]

Unfortunately, the denial of the bodily resurrection of Christ is no longer limited solely to non-Christian cults. Even evangelical scholar Murray Harris has denied that Jesus rose in the body which was crucified.[4] To make matters worse, many evangelical scholars, rather than refuting his heresy, have come to Harris' defense when he was confronted by Christian apologist Norman Geisler.[5]

If Christ did not rise bodily, then there would be no way to verify the truth of the resurrection. Presumably, His corpse would have been rotting in the tomb when the apostles were proclaiming Him as the risen Savior. Although those who hold to a spiritual resurrection of Christ usually invent an additional miracle through which Christ's corpse disappears, it seems more reasonable to conclude that either Jesus rose bodily or His corpse remained in the tomb. Since the New Testament records that the tomb was empty, it implies that the resurrection was bodily. A few passages of Scripture will suffice to show that Christ's resurrection, according to the apostles, was bodily:

> He is not here, for He has risen, just as He said. Come, see the place where He was lying (Matthew 28:6).

> Jesus answered and said to them, "Destroy this temple, and in three days I will raise it up."...But He was speaking of the temple of His body (John 2:19, 21).

> And after eight days again His disciples were inside, and Thomas with them. Jesus came, the doors having been shut, and stood in their midst, and said, "Peace be with you." Then He said to Thomas, "Reach here your finger, and see My hands; and reach here your hand, and put it into My side; and be not unbelieving, but believing" (John 20:26-27).

> And while they were telling these things, He Himself stood in their midst. But they were startled and frightened and thought that they were seeing a spirit. And He said to them, "Why are you troubled, and why do doubts arise in your hearts? See My hands and My feet, that it is I Myself; touch Me and see, for a spirit does not have flesh and bones as you see that I have." And when He had said this, He showed them His hands and His feet. And while they still could not believe it for joy and were marveling, He said to them, "Have you anything here to eat?" And they gave Him a piece of broiled fish; and He took it and ate it before them (Luke 24:36-43).

The apostles were eyewitnesses of Christ's post-resurrection appearances. Their testimony revealed several important points. First, the tomb was empty. Second, Christ appeared to them on several occasions. Third, they *thought* He was a spirit. Fourth, Jesus proved to them that He was physical by inviting them to touch His body and by eating with them. Fifth, His pierced side, hands, and feet showed that His resurrection body was the body which was crucified. Therefore, it is clear that the apostles taught that Christ rose bodily. The debate about whether Christ's resurrection was bodily is usually based upon this passage:

> So also is the resurrection of the dead. It is sown a perishable body, it is raised an imperishable body; it is sown in dishonor, it is raised in glory; it is sown in weakness, it is raised in power; it is sown a natural body, it is raised a spiritual body...(1 Corinthians 15:42-44).

### THE SPIRITUAL BODY

Many people misunderstand the phrase "spiritual body." They mistake this phrase for signifying some type of immaterial spirit. However, this is not the case. In the Greek, the phrase is *"soma pneumatikon."* The word *soma* almost always refers to a physical body. Still, in this passage this physical body is somehow described as being "spiritual" (*pneumatikon*). But, the spiritual body is contrasted with the natural body. The natural body refers to the physical body before physical death. The Greek words for natural body are *"soma psuchikon."* Literally, this phrase means a "soulish body." The word soul usually carries with it the idea of immateriality, but, in this passage, it cannot. It is referring to the human body before death, and, the human body is of course physical, despite the adjective "soulish." Therefore, if the "soulish body" is physical, then there should be no difficulty viewing the "spiritual body" as also being physical. The soulish *body* is sown (buried) at death, but, this same body is raised as a spiritual *body*; it receives new powers. It is no longer a natural body; it is a supernatural body. The body is changed, but it is still the same body. For, the body that was sown (buried) is the same body that will be raised. Gary Habermas discussed Christ's spiritual body in the following words:

> ...the Gospels and Paul agree on an important fact: the resurrected Jesus had a new spiritual body. The Gospels never present Jesus walking out of the tomb...when the stone is rolled away, Jesus does not walk out the way He does in apocryphal literature. He's already gone, so He presumably exited through the rock. Later He appears in buildings and then disappears at will. The Gospels clearly say that Jesus was raised in a spiritual body. It was His real body, but it was changed, including new, spiritual qualities.[6]

Paul is using the term spiritual body to contrast it with the natural body. He is making the point that Christ's body after the Resurrection (and ours too) has different characteristics to it than it did before...But the point is made very clearly that what is being talked about is the same body, the contrast here is not between physical body and spiritual body, but rather between the same body in different states or with different characteristics.[7]

Walter Martin, the foremost authority on non-Christian cults during his lifetime, also discussed Christ's spiritual body in his greatest work, *Kingdom of the Cults*:

> However, Christ had a "spiritual body" (1 Corinthians 15:50, 53) in His glorified state, identical in form to His earthly body, but immortal, and thus capable of entering the dimension of earth or heaven with no violation to the laws of either one.[8]

Therefore, Christ rose in the same body in which He lived and died. However, His body had been changed in the "twinkling of an eye" (1 Corinthians 15:50-53) so that His mortal body (a body capable of death) was glorified and became immortal (incapable of death). In

His spiritual body, He can apparently travel at the speed of thought, unhindered by distance. The Bible teaches that in the first resurrection all believers will receive glorified bodies. Believers' bodies will be changed into glorified and immortal bodies. The presence of sin will be totally removed from them (1 Corinthians 15:50-53).

Therefore, the apostles claimed that Jesus rose bodily from the dead. Since the resurrection occurred in the physical realm it could be verified; it could be proven true or false. In reference to Christ's resurrection, only four options exist: 1) the resurrection accounts may be legends, 2) the accounts may be lies, 3) the apostles may have been sincere but deceived, or 4) the apostles were telling the truth. The remainder of this chapter will determine, by process of elimination, which of these four options best explains the available evidence.

## THE RESURRECTION ACCOUNTS WERE NOT LEGENDS

The resurrection accounts were not legends. The evidence presented in the last chapter clearly shows that the resurrection accounts predate even the New Testament itself. Legends usually take centuries to evolve.[9] But, as chapter twenty-five has shown, the earliest known written resurrection accounts date back to less than twenty years after Christ's death. These accounts were ancient creeds and hymns of the first generation church (1 Corinthians 15:3-8; Romans 10:9; etc.). There is simply no way that a *resurrection legend* could receive universal acceptance (in order to become a hymn or creed) in the church while the apostles themselves led the church. If the resurrection account was merely a legend, the apostles would have refuted it. If the apostles chose not to refute a fictitious resurrection story, then they would have purposely perpetrated a falsehood. In that case, however, the resurrection accounts would not be legends; instead, the apostles would be liars.

The apostles knew Jesus personally. They were eyewitnesses of the events of His life and the things He taught. The apostles also led the early church. They were the authoritative witnesses to the facts concerning Christian doctrine, history, and practice. No legend could gain wide acceptance in the first generation church with the apostles in positions of authority. Since it can be shown that the resurrection accounts were not legends, some have concluded that the apostles were liars.

## THE APOSTLES WERE NOT LIARS

Skeptics sometimes accuse the apostles of fabricating the resurrection accounts. One theory suggests that the apostles stole the body of Jesus from the tomb.[10] In fact, this was the first attempted refutation of Christ's resurrection (Matthew 28:11-15).

Though it would be ludicrous to suggest that the apostles overpowered the Roman soldiers who guarded Jesus' tomb, this point will not be argued here. For many skeptics reject the apostolic witness concerning the guards at the tomb. Apart from the debate over whether or not the tomb was guarded, it can still be shown that the apostles were not liars. The apostles claimed that they saw Jesus risen from the dead, and, they were willing to suffer and die for their testimony. It is clearly against human nature for men to die for what they know to be a hoax.

Death by martyrdom is probably a more accurate way to determine if someone is telling the truth than even modern lie-detector tests. William Lane Craig describes the horrible sufferings that the first generation Christians endured for their faith:

> One of the most popular arguments against this theory is the obvious sincerity of the disciples as attested by their suffering and death...Writing seventy years after Jesus' death, Tacitus narrates Nero's persecution about thirty years after Christ, how the Christians were clothed with the skins of wild beasts and thrown to the dogs, how others were smeared with pitch and used as human torches to illuminate the night while Nero rode about Rome in the dress of a charioteer, viewing the spectacle. The testimonies of Suetonius and Juvenal confirm the fact that within thirty-one years after Jesus' death, Christians were dying for their faith. From the writings of Pliny the Younger, Martial, Epictetus, and Marcus Aurelius, it is clear that believers were voluntarily submitting to torture and death rather than renounce their religion. This suffering is abundantly attested in Christian writings as well.[11]

*Fox's Book of Martyrs* lists the deaths of eight of the twelve original apostles. James (John's brother) was put to death with the sword by order of Herod Agrippa I. The apostle Philip was crucified. Matthew (who wrote one of the Gospels) was beaten to death with an axe-shaped weapon. Andrew (Peter's brother) was crucified on an X—shaped cross. Peter (author of two epistles) was crucified upside down by order of Nero. Bartholomew was crucified. Thomas was killed when a spear was thrust through him. Simon the Zealot was crucified.[12]

*Fox's Book of Martyrs* also discusses the deaths of other New Testament authors. James (a half-brother of Christ and author of the epistle bearing his name) was beaten and stoned to death. Jude (another half-brother of Jesus and author of the epistle bearing his name) was crucified. Mark (author of the Gospel bearing his name) was dragged to pieces in Alexandria. Paul (who wrote thirteen epistles) was beheaded in Rome. Luke (who wrote the Gospel named after him and Acts) was hanged on an olive tree.[13]

The apostles claimed to have seen Christ risen from the dead. They were willing to suffer and die for this claim. It is against human nature for one to die for what one knows to be a lie. Therefore, the apostles did not steal the body. They were not lying. They were sincere. They believed that they had really seen the resurrected Lord. Hence, they were either sincere but deceived, or they were telling the truth.

### THE APOSTLES WERE NOT DECEIVED

Most of today's New Testament scholars recognize that the apostles were sincere in their belief that they had seen Jesus risen from the dead. Therefore, in an attempt to explain away the resurrection, some of these scholars accept one of several theories devised to explain how the apostles were deceived into thinking they had seen the risen Lord. It is interesting to note that these theories have all been refuted by other skeptics.[14]

*The swoon theory* suggests that Christ never actually died on the cross. Instead, He only passed out but was mistaken for dead. Christ then, according to this view, revived in the tomb. When He visited the apostles, they mistakenly proclaimed Him as risen from the dead.[15] The swoon theory is easily refuted. The apostle John recorded in his Gospel strong evidence for Christ's death on the cross:

The Jews therefore, because it was the day of preparation, so that the bodies should not remain on the cross on the Sabbath (for the Sabbath was a high day), asked Pilate that their legs might be broken, and that they might be taken away. The soldiers therefore came, and broke the legs of the first man, and of the other man who was crucified with Him; but coming to Jesus, when they saw that He was already dead, they did not break His legs; but one of the soldiers pierced His side with a spear, and immediately there came out blood and water (John 19:31-34).

Death by crucifixion was a horrible ordeal. To prolong the sufferings of the crucified person, a wooden block was placed under the feet to give him leverage to straighten up in order to breathe. When the Jewish authorities wanted to quicken the deaths of the victims so that they would not be on the cross during their feast days, they would have the Roman soldiers break the legs of the crucified victims. Being unable to straighten up in order to breathe, the victim would quickly die.[16]

In Christ's case, the Roman soldier saw that He was already dead. Still, being a good soldier who was conscientious about his job, he confirmed his view that Christ was dead by thrusting his spear into Christ's side. In this way, if the soldier was mistaken and Christ was actually alive, the spear wound would be fatal. The soldier, an expert in mortal combat, was surely trained in how to deliver a death blow to an enemy. Therefore, if Christ had been alive, the piercing of His side would have certainly killed Him.

Another detail in this passage provides evidence that Christ did in fact die. The apostle John reported a flow of "blood and water" coming from Christ's side as a result of the spear wound. Today, medical science has shown that this phenomenon proves that Christ was dead prior to the spear wound.[17] The flow of "blood and water" could only occur if the wound was inflicted upon a corpse. It should also be noted that this medical knowledge was unknown in John's day. Therefore, he had no knowledge that his reporting of this detail was irrefutable proof of death. Hence, he could not have fabricated this event in an attempt to prove Christ's death.[18]

The evidence, therefore, clearly indicates that Jesus died on the cross. Still, even if He did survive the cross, imminent death would follow due to His injuries from the scourging and crucifixion. Furthermore, even if He survived these injuries, there is no way in His battered condition He would have been able to convince His disciples that He had conquered death for all mankind.[19] The evidence declares that Jesus did die.

Some skeptics have proposed the *wrong tomb theory*. This view holds that everyone went to the wrong tomb and thus proclaimed Christ as risen.[20] However, this theory also has many problems. It offers no explanation for the apostles' claim to have seen the risen Christ on several occasions, and the apostles' willingness to die for their testimony. Also, the Jewish religious authorities would have searched every tomb in the Jerusalem area in an attempt to produce the rotting corpse of Christ. They had both the means and the desire to do so. Had they produced the corpse, Christianity would have been dealt a death blow while still in its infancy. The fact that the Jews did not produce the corpse of Christ is itself evidence of the empty tomb.[21] Again, any claim that the disciples stole the body offers no explanation as to how they could have been willing to die for what they knew to be a hoax.

Other skeptics have proposed the *hallucination theory*. This theory states that the apostles did not really see the resurrected Christ; instead, they only hallucinated and thought they saw the risen Lord.[22] However, psychologists say that hallucinations occur inside a person's mind. It is therefore impossible for two people—not to mention 500—to have had the same hallucination at the same time. Since many of the reported appearances of the risen Christ were to groups of people, the hallucination theory fails to explain the resurrection accounts.[23]

Another attempt to explain away the resurrection is the *hypnotic theory*. This highly speculative view suggests that the witnesses of Christ's post-resurrection appearances were all hypnotized. They did not actually see the risen Lord. Today, modern hypnotists deny this possibility.[24] Christian scholar Gary Habermas sums up the failure of skeptics to explain away the resurrection of Christ:

> One interesting illustration of this failure of the naturalistic theories is that they were disproven by the nineteenth-century older liberals themselves, by whom these views were popularized. These scholars refuted each other's theories, leaving no viable naturalistic hypotheses.

For instance, Albert Schweitzer dismissed Reimaru's fraud theory and listed no proponents of this view since 1768. David Strauss delivered the historical death blow to the swoon theory held by Karl Venturini, Heinrich Paulus, and others. On the other hand, Friedrich Schleiermacher and Paulus pointed out errors in Strauss's hallucination theory. The major decimation of the hallucination theory, however, came at the hands of Theodor Keim. Otto Pfleiderer was critical of the legendary or mythological theory, even admitting that it did not explain Jesus' resurrection. By these critiques such scholars pointed out that each of these theories was disproven by the historical facts.[25]

## CONCLUSION: THE APOSTLES WERE TELLING THE TRUTH

The failure of these theories shows that the apostles told the truth. Jesus did rise from the dead. Four facts of history add further support to the case for the resurrection of Christ from the dead. First, the apostles, who were devout Jews, changed the Sabbath day from Saturday to Sunday in honor of the Lord's resurrection. Only a miracle such as the resurrection (which occurred on a Sunday) would lead them to change their sacred day of rest (a fifteen-hundred-year-old religious tradition).[26] Second, the Jewish religious leaders during the time of Christ remained silent as far as written records are concerned. Accusing the apostles of stealing the body was a failure. The punishment for Roman guards sleeping on post was death.[27] Thus, it is unlikely that well-trained Roman guards would allow a small group of Galilean fishermen to overpower them. The Jewish religious leaders, seeing the failure of their alternative explanation of the resurrection, chose not to record it in writing. The silence of the Jews provides strong evidence for the fact of the empty tomb. The Jewish religious leaders had every reason to refute the resurrection. They did not; therefore, it is safe to conclude that they could not. Third, despite the fact that the resurrection was being proclaimed right in Jerusalem (near the tomb of Christ), the new church grew rapidly. All that had to be done to disprove Christianity (which was the intention of the Jewish religious leaders) was to produce the rotting corpse of Christ. Yet, the church grew rapidly. The only explanation for this is that no one could refute the apostolic testimony to the resurrection of Christ.[28] Last, the conversion of both James and the apostle Paul can only be adequately understood as a direct consequence of the resurrection.[29] James was one of the half-brothers of Jesus. He was very skeptical about His brother's claim to be the Jewish Messiah (John 7:1-5). Anything short of seeing His brother risen from the dead would fail to explain his dramatic conversion and subsequent rise to leadership in the early church (1 Corinthians 15:7; Acts 15:13-21; Galatians 1:18-19; 2:9). Paul was originally a Pharisee and apparently the leading enemy of the church (Philippians 3:4-6; Acts 8:1-3). If one rejects the post-resurrection appearance of Christ to him on the road to Damascus, then the reason for his conversion is a mystery (Acts 9:1-9).

The evidence for Christ's resurrection is overwhelming. The empty tomb stands as a monument to Christ's victory over death, a monument that, though attacked throughout the ages, remains standing and unmoved. The empty tomb is not a silent witness: the echoing of the angel's voice can still be heard coming from it, "He is not here, for He has risen, just as He said. Come, see the place where He was lying" (Matthew 28:6).

ENDNOTES

1Geisler, *The Battle for the Resurrection*, 51.

2*Let God Be True* (Brooklyn: Watchtower Bible and Tract Society, 1946), 43.

3Ibid., 272.

4Murray Harris, *Raised Immortal: Resurrection and Immortality in the New Testament* (Grand Rapids: William B. Eerdmanns, 1985), 126.

5Norman L. Geisler, *In Defense of the Resurrection* (Charlotte: Quest Publications, 1991), 8-13.

6Gary Habermas and Anthony Flew, *Did Jesus Rise From the Dead?* (San Francisco: Harper and Row Publishers, 1987), 58.

7Ibid., 95.

8Martin *Kingdom of the Cults*, 86.

9Craig, 197.

10Ibid., 179-180.

11Ibid., 175-176.

12John Foxe, *Foxe's Book of Martyrs* (Springdale: Whitaker House, 1981), 6-13.

13Ibid.

14Habermas and Flew, 20-21.

15Habermas, *Ancient Evidence for the Life of Jesus*, 54-58.

16Kenneth E. Stevenson and Gary R. Habermas, *Verdict on the Shroud* (Wayne: Banbury Books, 1981), 178-179.

17Ibid., 184.

18Ibid.

19Ibid.

20McDowell, 255.

21Ibid.

22Habermas, *The Resurrection of Jesus*, 26-28.

23McDowell, 249.

24Morris, *Many Infallible Proofs*, 94.

25Habermas and Flew, 20-21.

26Ibid., 22.

27McDowell, 242.

28Craig,178, 190.

29Ibid., 195-196.

# CHAPTER 27
# IS JESUS GOD?

The deity of Christ is hard to accept for many people. For one to admit that Jesus is God in the flesh is to admit that he owes Him complete allegiance. Recognition of Jesus' Godhood calls for the abandonment of one's autonomy. Therefore, many people refuse to worship Jesus as God and consider Him to be merely a great human teacher. Mohandas K. Gandhi said of Christ:

> It was more than I could believe that Jesus was the only incarnate son of God. And that only he who believed in Him would have everlasting life. If God could have sons, all of us were His sons. If Jesus was like God...then all men were like God and could be God Himself.[1]

The internationally respected theologian, John Hick, also denies Christ's deity:

> Now it used to be assumed—and in some Christian circles is still assumed—that this Jesus, who lived in Palestine in the first third of the first century AD, was conscious of being God incarnate, so that you must either believe him or reject him as a deceiver or a megalomaniac. "Mad, bad, or God" went the argument. And of course if Jesus did indeed claim to be God incarnate, then this dilemma, or trilemma, does arise. But did he claim this? The assumption that he did is largely based on the Fourth Gospel, for it is here that Jesus makes precisely such claims. He says "I and the Father are one," "No one comes to the Father, but by me" and "He who

293

has seen me has seen the Father." But it is no secret today, after more than a hundred years of scholarly study of the scriptures, that very few New Testament experts now hold that the Jesus who actually lived ever spoke those words, or their Aramaic equivalents. They are much more probably words put into his mouth by a Christian writer who is expressing the view of Christ which had been arrived at in his part of the church, probably two or three generations after Jesus' death. And it is likewise doubted whether the few sayings of the same kind in the other gospels are authentic words of Jesus. How, then, did this Christian deification of Jesus—which began within the first decades after his death and was essentially completed by the end of the first century—take place? Such a development is not as hard to understand in the ancient world as it would be today...[2]

It is interesting that Hick admits that the New Testament, quotes Jesus as claiming to be God. Second, he acknowledges that the deity of Christ was being taught within a few decades of Christ's death (which is what the creeds prove). And, third, Hick recognizes that the deity of Christ was completely established as church doctrine by the end of the first century AD. However, by admitting these three facts, Hick is inadvertently conceding that all the available evidence points to the authenticity of Christ's claims to be God. Surely the apostles would have stopped this heresy (if indeed it was a heresy) when it started just decades after Christ's death. The Apostle John would also have opposed this teaching as it was being established as church dogma at the end of the first century AD.

Contrary to what John Hick believes, true scholarship bases its decisions on the evidence, not on mere speculation. All the available evidence points to the fact that Christ did claim to be God. The eyewitnesses who heard these claims died horrible deaths refusing to deny their validity. No liberal scholar has ever proposed an adequate explanation as to how a legend that Jesus claimed to be God could develop while the original apostles (those who personally knew Christ) were still alive and leading the new church. Legends take centuries to develop into dogma.[3] Any attempted origination of legends cannot get started while honest eyewitnesses are still alive (especially if these honest eyewitnesses hold positions of authority in the church). Therefore, liberal scholars like Hick can believe what they wish. However, to deny that Christ claimed to be God is to simply ignore all the available evidence. Liberal scholars throw out any passages of the Bible that do not agree with their antisupernaturalistic biases, but this is not true scholarship. True scholarship examines the evidence; it does not speculate as to how the evidence can be explained away. *The World Book Encyclopedia* is an example of the high regard in which many people esteem Jesus, while stopping short of calling Him God:

> Jesus Christ was the founder of the Christian religion. Christians believe that He is the Son of God who was sent to earth to save mankind. Even many persons who are not Christians believe that He was a great and wise teacher. He has probably influenced humanity more than anyone else who ever lived.[4]

It is not wise to call Jesus merely a great man and teacher since He claimed to be God. For no merely great man or wise teacher would claim to be God. If Jesus claimed to be God, then we must view Him as either a liar, insane, or God. There are no other alternatives, and no ignoring of the evidence will help.

## JESUS CLAIMED TO BE GOD

In chapter twenty-five it was shown that the message found in the New Testament is one and the same as the message of the first generation church. The ancient creeds found in the New Testament predate the New Testament and represent the teachings of the apostles themselves.[5] Several of these ancient creeds teach the deity of Christ (Philippians 2:5-11; Romans 10:9-10; 1 Timothy 3:16). Therefore, there is no reason to doubt that Jesus claimed to be God. The leaders of the first generation church taught that Jesus is God, and they were willing to die for their testimony. Hence, there is no reason (apart from an a priori bias) to reject the claims of deity made by Christ in the New Testament. The Jews understood that Jesus was claiming to be God:

> But He answered them, "My Father is working until now, and I myself am working." For this cause therefore the Jews were seeking all the more to kill Him, because He not only

was breaking the Sabbath, but also was calling God His own
Father, making Himself equal with God (John 5:17-18).

Whenever Jesus spoke of a unique Father-Son relationship
between God the Father and Himself, the Jews understood Him to be
claiming equality with God the Father. Jesus spoke to the Jews in their
language. He communicated to them on their terms. They
understood Jesus to be claiming to be deity. If Jesus never meant to
claim to be God, then He was one of the poorest communicators who
ever lived. If Jesus was misunderstood by His listeners, He should
have clarified His words. A clear and articulate representation of His
words would have been in His best interest; He was executed for
blasphemy (Mark 14:60-64).

Jesus taught that He deserved the same honor that the Father
deserved:

> For not even the Father judges anyone, But He has given
> all judgment to the Son, in order that all may honor the Son,
> even as they honor the Father. He who does not honor the
> Son does not honor the Father who sent Him (John 5:22-23).

Since the Father is God, the honor due Him is worship. Therefore,
Jesus taught that He also deserved to be worshipped. Despite the fact
that the Old Testament Law forbid the worship of any being other
than God (Exodus 20:1-6), Jesus accepted worship on numerous
occasions (Matthew 2:11; 14:33; 28:9; John 9:38; 20:28-29). Jesus also
stated:

> You are from below, I am from above; you are of this
> world, I am not of this world. I said therefore to you, that you
> shall die in your sins; for unless you believe that I am He, you
> shall die in your sins.... Truly, truly, I say to you, before
> Abraham was born, I am (John 8:23-24; 58).

The Jewish religious leaders understood Jesus' claim to deity in this
passage: "they picked up stones to throw at Him" (John 8:59). The
comments of J. Dwight Pentecost are helpful:

> Christ affirmed, "Before Abraham was born, I am!" (v.
> 58). "I AM" was the name of the Self-existing God who had
> revealed Himself to Moses at the burning bush (Exod. 3:14).
> Jesus Christ was claiming to be "I AM", the Self-existent
> God. He was claiming eternity. To the Jews this was
> blasphemy.[6]

Merrill C. Tenney also elaborates on this specific claim of Christ:

In actuality the phrase "I am" is an assertion of absolute, timeless existence, not merely of a personal identity as the English equivalent would suggest. A comparison of the use of the phrase, "I am" with self-revelation of Jehovah in the Old Testament shows that much the same terminology was employed. God, in commissioning Moses (Ex. 3:14), said: "Thus shalt thou say to unto the children of Israel, I AM hath sent me unto you." When the Jews heard Jesus say, "Before Abraham was born, I am," they took the statement to mean not priority to Abraham, but an assertion of deity. To them it was blasphemy, and they picked up stones to cast at Him.[7]

It is important to note two things about this passage. First, Jesus did not say, "Before Abraham was, I was." This would have been merely a claim to have preexisted Abraham. Though this would be a bold claim in itself, Christ actually said far more than that. Jesus was claiming that His existence is always in the present tense. In other words, He was claiming eternal existence for Himself. He was declaring himself to have absolutely no beginning. He was claiming that He was not bound by time. He was declaring Himself to be the eternal God. Second, Christ probably spoke these words in Aramaic (the common language of the Hebrews of his day). Therefore, He probably did not use the Greek words *"ego eimi"* for "I AM." Rather, He would have used the Hebrew "YHWH." This was the title for the eternal God. Out of reverence for God, the Jews never spoke this word. So here, Christ was not only speaking the unspeakable title of God (YHWH), but He was using it to refer to Himself. Properly understood, this was probably Christ's most unambiguous claim to deity. The Jews clearly understood this, and for this reason they attempted to stone him. Another clear claim to deity made by Christ is the following passage:

"I and the Father are one." The Jews took up stones again to stone Him. Jesus answered them, "I showed you many good works from the Father; for which of them are you stoning Me?" The Jews answered Him, "For a good work we do not stone You, but for blasphemy; and because You, being a man, make yourself out to be God" (John 10:30-33).

Concerning this passage, Merrill F. Unger wrote, "Jesus asserted His unity of essence with the Father, hence His unequivocal deity...and the Jews understood Him."[8] In this passage, Jesus clearly claimed to be equal with God the Father. Christ said that His nature is identical to that of the Father. The Jews understood Him to be calling Himself God. They later sentenced Him to death for these claims to deity.

Jesus also made other claims to deity. He said that, "He who has seen Me has seen the Father" (John 14:9). When He prayed to the Father, He asked the Father to return to Him the glory which He and the Father shared before the universe was created (John 17:5).

The apostles were Jesus' closest associates. They were more familiar with the teachings of Christ than anyone else and they called Jesus God (Matthew 1:23; John 1:1; John 20:28; Philippians 2:6; Colossians 2:9; Titus 2:13; 2 Peter 1:1). This is further confirmation that Jesus did in fact claim to be God.

Considering the strong evidence for the reliability of the New Testament, Christ's claims to deity cannot be considered as legends. The teaching that Jesus is God predates the New Testament (as shown in the ancient creeds), and is best explained by attributing the source of this doctrine to Jesus Himself. It must be remembered that the apostles were not liars. They were sincere enough about their beliefs to die for them, and they recorded unambiguous statements made by Christ attributing deity to Himself.

The deity of Christ is not a legend. Jesus claimed to be God incarnate. Hence, one cannot consider Him to be simply a great man; for no mere man claims to be God. If Jesus is not God, then He was either a liar or insane. There are no other options.

JESUS WAS NOT A LIAR
The absurd idea that Jesus was a liar who claimed to be God can be easily refuted. For Christ is considered, even by many who reject His claim to deity, to have taught the highest standard of morality known to man. His teachings have motivated such actions as the abolition of slavery, government by the consent of the people, the modern hospital system, education for all children, and charitable programs for the needy. A liar could not have possibly encouraged these movements.

Christ has had a positive impact on mankind like no other person. It is extremely unlikely that so much good could come from a deceiver who led people astray by claiming to be God. The eyewitness accounts of the apostles display the tremendous love Christ had for people. It is not possible that a self-centered and egotistical liar could express genuine affection for his fellow man like that expressed by Christ. The question can also be asked, "Would a liar die for his lie?" It is doubtful that Jesus would lie and then suffer death by crucifixion as a consequence.

It has already been shown that the resurrection of Jesus was a historical event and not a hoax. But, why would God raise a blaspheming liar from the dead? Christ offered His resurrection as proof for His claims to deity (John 2:18-21; Matthew 12:38-40). Therefore, His resurrection proves the validity of His claims to be God. He claimed to be God and then proved it by doing what no mere man could do—He rose from the dead.

## JESUS WAS NOT INSANE

Christ's claims to deity have been shown not to be legends or lies, but the possibility remains that Jesus may have been insane. Could it be that Jesus claimed to be God because He was mentally disturbed?

Often, people compare Jesus of Nazareth with other respected religious leaders. However, very few of these leaders (if any) claimed to be God in a unique sense. Some have claimed to be God, but then teach that we are all God. Jesus claimed to be God in a sense that no other man could claim to be God. Usually, when a religious leader makes a claim as bold as this, it is evidence that he is unbalanced. Charles Manson and David Koresh are two examples of this type of religious leader. The evidence for their instability is obvious. However, this is not so in the case of Jesus. He made bold claims to deity, but also backed these claims by the life He lived and the things He did.

Declaring Christ to be insane is not a common view. Nearly everyone admits that He was a great teacher, even if they reject His deity. However, insane people make lousy teachers. The teachings of Christ are not the teachings of a mad man. They are the greatest teachings ever taught by a man, and this man claimed to be God incarnate.

The miraculous life of Christ is also evidence that He was not insane. Christ gave evidence for His bold claims through His supernatural works. The apostles were eyewitnesses of these miracles. Even the enemies of Christ, the Jewish religious leaders of His day, did not deny His miracles. Instead, they stated in their Talmud that Jesus "practiced sorcery."[9] Though they rejected Jesus' message, they were forced to admit that He did supernatural works. However, the powerful influence for good that Christ has had upon mankind declares His miracles to be from God and not from Satan. Therefore, Jesus' miracles show that He was not insane. They provide strong evidence to support His claim to be God.

Another piece of evidence that shows Christ was not insane is the fact that His life and works were prophesied hundreds of years before His birth. A small fraction of the prophecies He fulfilled are listed below:

1) He was a descendant of Abraham (Genesis 12:1-3; fulfilled in Matthew 1:1-2 and Luke 3:34)

2) He was from the tribe of Judah (Genesis 49:10; fulfilled in Matthew 1:3 and Luke 3:33)

3) He was a descendant of Jesse (Isaiah 11:1; fulfilled in Matthew 1:5-6 and Luke 3:32)

4) He was a descendant of David (Jeremiah 23:5; fulfilled in Matthew 1:1, 6 and Luke 3:31)

5) He was born to a virgin (Isaiah 7:14; fulfilled in Matthew 1:18-25 and Luke 1:34-35)

6) He was born in Bethlehem (Micah 5:2; fulfilled in Matthew 2:1 and Luke 2:1-7)

7) His birth announced by a star (Numbers 24:7; fulfilled in Matthew 2:1-2)

8) His forerunner (Isaiah 40:3; fulfilled in Matthew 3:1-3 and Mark 1:2-4)

9) The specific time of His first coming (Daniel 9:24-27 predicts that the Messiah would be executed before the temple would be destroyed. The destruction of the temple occurred in 70AD. Matthew 27:1-2, 26 states that Jesus was crucified when Pilate was governor of Judea. Pilate reigned as governor in Judea from 26AD to 36AD.)

10) His miracles (Isaiah 35:4-6; fulfilled in Matthew 11:1-6)

11) His parables (Psalm 78:2; fulfilled in Matthew 13:3)

12) He was rejected by the Jews (Isaiah 53; fulfilled in Matthew 23:37; 27:22-25; Romans 10:1-3; 11:25)

13) He received a wide Gentile following (Isaiah 42:1-4; fulfilled in Romans 9:30-33; 11:11 and confirmed in the history of the church)

14) He was betrayed for 30 pieces of silver (Zechariah 11:12-13; fulfilled in Matthew 26:14-16)

15)He was forsaken by His disciples (Zechariah 13:7; fulfilled in Matthew 26:56)

16) He entered Jerusalem on a donkey while receiving a king's welcome (Zechariah 9:9; fulfilled in Matthew 21:1-11)

17) He was silent before His accusers (Isaiah 53:7; fulfilled in Matthew 26:63; 27:14)

18) He was crucified (Psalm 22:16; fulfilled in Matthew 27:35)

19) Soldiers cast lots for His garments (Psalm 22:18; fulfilled in Matthew 27:35)

20) His bones were not broken (Psalm 34:20; fulfilled in John 19:31-34)

21) His side was pierced (Zechariah 12:10; fulfilled in John 19:34)

22) He was buried in a rich man's tomb (Isaiah 53:9; fulfilled in Matthew 27:57-60)

23) His resurrection from the dead (Psalm 16:10; fulfilled in Matthew 28:1-9)

24) His ascension (Psalm 68:18; fulfilled in Acts 1:9-11)

25) His position at the Father's right hand (Psalm 110:1; fulfilled in Hebrews 1:3)

As was noted earlier, these are just a few of the many prophecies that were fulfilled by Christ.[10] Even liberal scholars admit that these prophecies were recorded hundreds of years before Christ's birth. Although they deny the traditional early dates of the Old Testament books, it is almost universally accepted that the Septuagint (the Greek translation of the Hebrew Old Testament) was completed two hundred years before Christ was born.[11]

Most liberals do not consider some of the prophecies listed above as having been fulfilled by Christ. This is because these liberals a priori deny the possibility of miracles. Since they deny Christ's resurrection, they also deny that Christ fulfilled the Old Testament prophecy of the resurrection. Even if one removes the Old Testament predictions concerning the supernatural aspects of Christ's life, one is still left with the evidence from the fulfillment of prophecies of the non-supernatural aspects of Christ's life. Norman Geisler has noted that the chances of Christ fulfilling just sixteen of these prophecies by mere coincidence are 1 in $10^{45}$ (a one with forty-five zeroes after it).[12]

In fact, three of these Old Testament predictions concerning the Messiah—Daniel 9:26; Isaiah 42:4; Isaiah 53—are enough to prove that only Jesus of Nazareth meets the messianic qualifications. Daniel 9:26 stated that the Messiah would be executed before the destruction of the temple (which occurred in 70AD). Isaiah 42:4

teaches that the Gentile nations would expectantly await Christ's law. Isaiah 53 declares that the Jews would reject their Messiah. Jesus of Nazareth is the only person in history who has fulfilled all three of these prophecies. He claimed to be the Jewish Messiah and was crucified around 30AD (forty years before the temple was destroyed), the Jews rejected Him, and He received a wide Gentile following.

The life of an insane man would not be prophesied. It is also unlikely that these predictions would refer to an insane man as the Messiah (God's anointed one) and "the mighty God" (Isaiah 9:6). More than 200 years before Jesus' birth, His life and works were predicted. He fulfilled these prophecies and performed many miracles. It is absurd for someone to call Jesus insane. To accept His claims is the only reasonable response.

The historical evidence shows that Jesus claimed to be God and proved it by raising Himself from the dead. History shows these claims are not legends, and that He was not a liar, insane, or merely a great man. Therefore, Jesus of Nazareth is God.

THEREFORE, JESUS IS GOD

The following ancient creed was formulated and proclaimed by the first generation church. It declares Jesus to be God and Savior, and instructs all creation to surrender to His Lordship:

> Have this attitude in yourselves which was also in Christ Jesus, who, although He existed in the form of God, did not regard equality with God a thing to be grasped, but emptied Himself, taking the form of a bond-servant, and being made in the likeness of men. And being found in appearance as a man, He humbled Himself by becoming obedient to the point of death, even death on a cross. Therefore also God highly exalted Him, and bestowed on Him the name which is above every name, that at the name of Jesus every knee should bow, of those who are in heaven, and on earth, and under the earth, and that every tongue should confess that Jesus Christ is Lord, to the glory of God the Father (Philippians 2:5-11).

This ancient creed states that the day will come when all creation will bow down before Christ and confess that He is Lord. One can bow to Jesus now, or one can bow to Jesus later, but, the fact remains, that the day will come when all will bow before Christ, both the saved and the unsaved. The saved will bow before Jesus to worship Him as their Savior and King. The lost will bow before Him, due to their fear of His power and authority.

## ENDNOTES

1Mohandas K. Gandhi, *Mahatma Gandhi Autobiography* (Washington, D. C.: Public Affairs Press, 1948), 170.

2John Hick, *The Center of Christianity* (San Francisco: Harper and Row, 1968), 27-28.

3Michael J. Wilkins and J. P. Moreland, eds., *Jesus Under Fire* (Grand Rapids: Zondervan Publishing House, 1995), 154.

4*The World Book Encyclopedia* vol. 11, (Chicago: World Book, Inc., 1985), 82.

5Moreland, *Scaling the Secular City*, 148-149.

6J. Dwight Pentecost, *The Words and Works of Jesus Christ* (Grand Rapids: Academie Books, 1981), 288.

7Merrill C. Tenney, *John, the Gospel of Belief* (Grand Rapids: William B. Eerdmans Publishing Company, 1948), 150.

8Merrill F. Unger, *Unger's Bible Handbook* (Chicago: Moody Press, 1966), 555.

9Habermas, *Ancient Evidence for the Life of Jesus*, 98.

10For a fuller treatment of Old Testament prophecies fulfilled by Christ, see: Josh McDowell, 141-177.

11Ibid.,144.

12Geisler, *Apologetics*, 343.

# CHAPTER 28
# IS THE BIBLE GOD'S WORD?

The preceding chapters have provided strong evidence for the historical reliability of the Bible, as well as for the resurrection and deity of Christ. In this chapter, evidence showing the Bible to be God's Word will be examined. The case for the inspiration of the Scriptures builds upon the evidence produced in the last four chapters.

CHRIST'S TEACHINGS CONCERNING THE OLD TESTA-MENT

This work has shown that the evidence demonstrates that Jesus is God. Therefore, whatever Jesus taught should be accepted as true and authoritative. John W. Wenham discussed Christ's view of the Old Testament:

> Our Lord not only believed the truth of the Old Testament history and used the Scriptures as final authority in matters of faith and conduct, he also regarded the writings themselves as inspired. To Him, Moses, the prophets, David, and the other Scripture writers were given their messages by the Spirit of God.[1]

Some of Christ's teachings concerning the Old Testament are as follows:

> Do not think that I came to abolish the Law or the Prophets; I did not come to abolish, but to fulfill. For truly

I say to you, until heaven and earth pass away, not the smallest letter or stroke shall pass away from the Law, until all has been accomplished (Matthew 5:17-18).

And He answered and said to them, "And why do you yourselves transgress the commandment of God for the sake of your tradition? For God said, 'Honor your father and mother,' and, 'He who speaks evil of father or mother, let him be put to death.' " (Matthew 15:3-4)

But regarding the resurrection of the dead, have you not read that which was spoken to you by God, saying, "I am the God of Abraham, and the God of Isaac, and the God of Jacob"? (Matthew 22:31-32)

He was also saying to them, "You nicely set aside the commandment of God in order to keep your tradition. For Moses said, 'Honor your father and your mother'; and, 'He who speaks evil of father or mother, let him be put to death'; but you say, 'If a man says to his father or mother, anything of mine you might have been helped by is Corban (that is to say, given to God),' you no longer permit him to do anything for his father or his mother; thus invalidating the word of God by your tradition which you have handed down..." (Mark 7:9-13).

David himself said in the Holy Spirit, "The Lord said to my Lord, 'Sit at My right hand, until I put Thine enemies beneath Thy feet.'" (Mark 12:36)

It is abundantly clear that Jesus considered the entire Old Testament (what the Jews of His day called "the Law and the Prophets") to be the inspired Word of God. He referred to the Old Testament authors as prophets (Matthew 11:13; 12:39; 22:40; 23:31-35; 24:15; 26:56; Luke 16:16-17, 31; 18:31; 24:44; John 6:45), meaning proclaimers of God's truth. In fact, Jesus spoke of the prophets as beginning with Abel and ending with Zechariah (Luke 11:49-51). This covers the exact time period of the Old Testament, from creation to about 400BC. Since Christ is God Himself, his view of the Old Testament must be correct. Therefore, the Old Testament is the written Word of God.

## CHRIST'S VIEW OF THE NEW TESTAMENT

Christ ascended to heaven before the New Testament was recorded. However, the promises He made to his apostles guaranteed that the New Testament would be the inspired Word of God:

> Go therefore and make disciples of all nations, baptizing them in the name of the Father and the Son and the Holy Spirit, teaching them to observe all that I commanded you; and lo, I am with you always, even to the end of the age (Matthew 28:19-20).

> Heaven and earth will pass away, but My words will not pass away (Mark 13:31).

> But the Helper, the Holy Spirit, whom the Father will send in My name, He will teach you all things, and bring to your remembrance all that I said to you (John 14:26).

> When the Helper comes, whom I will send to you from the Father, that is the Spirit of truth, who proceeds from the Father, He will bear witness of Me, and you will bear witness also, because you have been with Me from the beginning (John 15:26-27).

> But when He, the Spirit of truth, comes, He will guide you into all the truth; for He will not speak on His own initiative, but whatever He hears, He will speak; and He will disclose to you what is to come (John 16:13).

> But you shall receive power when the Holy Spirit has come upon you; and you shall be My witnesses both in Jerusalem, and in all Judea and Samaria, and even to the remotest part of the earth (Acts 1:8).

From these quotes of Christ, five conclusions can be drawn. First, Jesus promised that His teachings would be preserved. Second, He said that the Holy Spirit would remind the apostles of all that He told them. Third, the Holy Spirit would reveal future events to the apostles. Fourth, the Holy Spirit would guide the apostles into the truth (prevent them from promoting doctrinal errors). Fifth, the Holy Spirit would empower the apostles to be Christ's authoritative representatives to the world.

From the above conclusions it is clear that Christ promised to preserve His teachings through the apostles' writings. Obviously, these writings make up the New Testament. Since Jesus is almighty

God, His plan cannot be thwarted. Therefore, since He promised to preserve His words through the teachings of the apostles, then their teachings (which have been passed on to future generations) are the teachings of Christ. Hence, they are the Word of God.

It should also be noted that Jesus taught that only the Old Testament and the teachings of His apostles (the New Testament) were the Word of God. The evidence declares Jesus to be God. Jesus taught that both the Old and New Testaments are the Word of God. Therefore, the Old and New Testaments are the Word of God.

## THE SUPERNATURAL WISDOM OF THE BIBLE

The evidence presented above is sufficient to demonstrate that the Bible is God's Word. Still, there are other factors which help corroborate this evidence. The supernatural wisdom and the fulfilled prophecies of the Bible verify that the Bible is God's Word.

Christian thinkers such as Blaise Pascal (1623-1662)[2] and Francis Schaeffer (1912-1984)[3] have noted that only the Bible offers an adequate explanation for both man's greatness and man's wretchedness. Modern man, even with all his accumulated knowledge, cannot sufficiently account for both aspects in man. Atheistic evolutionists may be able to explain the wretchedness of man, for they see man as merely an animal, but they cannot satisfactorily account for man's greatness. New Age Pantheists recognize man's greatness by attributing godhood to him, but, they offer no convincing reason why man is so wretched. The Bible alone offers an adequate explanation for both aspects of man. Man is great because he was created in God's image; he is wretched because he is in a fallen state.[4] This indicates that the wisdom found in the Bible supersedes the wisdom of man.

Evidence for the supernatural wisdom of the Bible can also be seen in the realm of science. At a time when men thought the earth was flat, the Bible taught that it was a sphere (Isaiah 40:22, 700BC). At a time when men thought the earth rested on the back of a giant turtle, the Bible taught that is was suspended in space (Job 26:7, 2000BC). At about 1500BC the Bible taught that the stars could not be counted (Genesis 15:5); yet, in 150AD an astronomer named Ptolemy taught that there were exactly 1056 stars.[5] Today, modern science confirms that the stars are innumerable.

In about 1850AD, the first and second laws of thermodynamics were discovered by modern science. The first law teaches that no new energy is being created or destroyed. The second law teaches that, though the amount of energy in the universe remains constant, the amount of usable energy is running down. Therefore, the universe is winding down. The Bible taught both of these laws thousands of years ago. The Bible states that God is resting from His creation work (Genesis 2:1-3), and that the universe will someday pass away (Mark 13:31; Isaiah 40:31). The Bible does teach, however, that God will make a new heaven and a new earth when the old ones pass away (Revelation 21:1).

There was no such thing as modern science in biblical times. Hence, the information mentioned above demands a source which transcends that of man, a supernatural source.[6]

FULFILLED PROPHECIES

The Bible claims repeatedly to be the Word of God. One of the most powerful witnesses to the truth of this claim is the many fulfilled prophecies proclaimed in the Bible. This work has already examined a sample of prophecies fulfilled by Christ. Here, a few more of the many biblical prophecies that have already come to pass will be discussed.

The Bible has made many predictions concerning the future of great nations and cities. The following is a brief discussion of a few of the prophecies fulfilled concerning these cities and nations.

Around 590—570BC, the prophet Ezekiel predicted that the city of Tyre would be destroyed and never be rebuilt, and that it would become a barren rock which fishermen would use to mend their nets (Ezekiel 26:4, 5, 14). Though Tyre was destroyed and rebuilt many times throughout history, it was ultimately devastated in 1291AD by Muslim invaders. Today, all that is left of the ancient site of Tyre is a small fishing community which uses the barren ground to dry their nets.[7]

In the sixth century BC, Ezekiel also predicted that the city of Sidon would suffer much violence and bloodshed throughout her history, yet remain in existence (Ezekiel 28:23). Though Sidon has been invaded and defeated numerous times throughout her history, the city still exists today.[8]

In 625BC, the prophet Zephaniah predicted that the city of Ashkelon would someday be destroyed, but that it would eventually be inhabited by the Jews (Zephaniah 2:4, 6). Ashkelon was destroyed in 1270AD by Sultan Bibars. The city remained uninhabited for centuries until the nation of Israel was reestablished in 1948. Now, the Jews have rebuilt and re-inhabited Ashkelon.[9]

Zephaniah also predicted that the Philistines—a powerful enemy of the Jews throughout much of the Old Testament—would be totally wiped out. Though they continued to prosper for many centuries, they eventually became extinct in 1200AD (Zephaniah 2:5).[10]

The prophet Obadiah, writing in either 841BC or 586BC, prophesied the extinction of the Edomites, who were the descendants of Esau and enemies of the Jews (Obadiah 18). When the Romans devastated the city of Jerusalem in 70AD, they also defeated the remnants of Edom (called the Idumeans at that time). At that time, all traces of the Edomites disappear.[11]

In 740—680BC, the prophet Isaiah predicted that Egypt would still be a nation in the last days (Isaiah 19:21-22). In spite of the many wars Egypt has encountered throughout her four-thousand year history, this ancient nation remains in existence to this day.[12]

In 1410BC, Moses predicted that Israel would be scattered among the nations of the world (Deuteronomy 28:64). The prophet Hosea, in 710BC, predicted this dispersion of Israel as well (Hosea 9:17). History records that after the Romans destroyed Jerusalem, the Jews were scattered throughout the world.[13]

Both Isaiah and Ezekiel prophesied that Israel would be regathered in her land in the last days (Isaiah 11:11-12; Ezekiel 37:21). This happened in 1948AD when the nation of Israel was reestablished. The Jews continue to return to their land to this day.[14]

God told Abraham that those who cursed Israel would be cursed by God (Genesis 12:3). This prophecy has been fulfilled many times. Babylon, Assyria, Philistia, the Roman Empire, and Nazi Germany are a few examples of nations or empires that persecuted and oppressed Israel. While the tiny nation of Israel still exists today, Babylon, Assyria, Philistia, the Roman Empire, the Soviet Union, and Nazi Germany have collapsed and are no longer in existence. During the 1930's and 1940's, Nazi Germany had slaughtered six-million Jews and its war machine was devastating Europe. By 1948, Nazi

Germany was nonexistent and the Jews had control of their homeland—the nation of Israel— for the first time since 586BC.[15]

Each of these prophecies has been fulfilled to the detail. Many other biblical prophecies have also been fulfilled. It should also be noted that no futuristic prophecy of Scripture has ever been shown to be false. This separates the Bible from false prophets such as Edgar Cayce and Jean Dixon. Their success rate is much lower than the perfect accuracy of the predictions made by the Bible.[16] Henry Morris made the following comment:

> It seems reasonable to conclude that the phenomenon of fulfilled prophecy constitutes a unique and powerful evidence of the divine inspiration of the Bible.[17]

The evidence provided above for the Bible being God's Word is threefold. First, Jesus (who is God) taught that the Bible is God's Word. Second, the Bible contains insights that go beyond mere human wisdom. Third, the Bible made numerous predictions, many of which have been fulfilled. None of these predictions have proven false (though some prophecies have yet to be fulfilled). In short, there are good reasons for believing the Bible is God's Word. Those who reject the divine inspiration of the Bible have failed to explain the three factors above.

## IMPLICATIONS OF THE DIVINE INSPIRATION OF THE BIBLE

Since the Bible can be shown to be God's Word, several implications follow. First, since the cosmological argument has shown God to be infinite and perfect, there can be no error in His Word as originally recorded. God can only proclaim truth; otherwise, He would be less than perfect. Therefore, the Bible is wholly true (inerrant). Second, since the Bible is God's inerrant Word, it is authoritative. God has spoken, and everything must be tested by the truth He has given. Third, whatever is taught in God's inerrant and authoritative Word should be adhered to by all.

This work has already presented evidence for some of the major tenets of orthodox Christianity (the existence of one God, creation by God, the resurrection of Jesus, and Christ's deity). Since the evidence indicates the Bible is God's Word, whatever it teaches must be true. Therefore, other important Christian doctrines (e.g., salvation by grace through faith in Christ, the substitutionary death of Christ, the

Trinity, and Christ's future return to earth) can be defended by showing that they are taught in the Bible.

Concerning salvation, the Bible teaches that all people are sinners who cannot save themselves (Romans 3:10, 23; 6:23; Matthew 19:25-26). Scripture teaches that man cannot earn his salvation; salvation is a free gift given by God's grace (unmerited favor) to those who trust (believe) in Jesus for salvation (Ephesians 2:8-9; John 3:16-18; 6:35, 47; Romans 6:23). Only through Jesus can man be saved (John 14:6; Acts 4:12).

The Bible teaches that Jesus took mankind's punishment upon Himself by dying on the cross for their sins (Isaiah 53:5-6, 12; Matthew 1:21; Mark 10:45; John 1:29; Romans 5:8-10; Ephesians 1:7; 2 Corinthians 5:15, 21; 1 Timothy 2:4-6; Hebrews 10:10, 14; 1 Peter 2:24; 3:18; 1 John 1:7; 2:1-2; Revelation 5:9). The God of the Bible is holy and just; He cannot forgive sin unless it has been paid for in full. The good news is that Jesus (who is fully man and fully God) is the ultimately worthy sacrifice who has paid for the sins of the world through His death on the cross (Revelation 5:1-14). He died as a substitute for all of mankind. Those who accept Jesus as their Savior receive the salvation and forgiveness that He has purchased for them.

One of the most controversial teachings of Christianity is the doctrine of the Trinity, for this teaching transcends human understanding. This doctrine declares that the one true God eternally exists as three equal Persons (the Father, Son, and Holy Spirit). God is one in essence or nature (Mark 12:29; John 10:30), but three in Personhood (Matthew 3:16-17; John 14:16, 26; 15:26).

The Bible teaches that the Father is God (Galatians 1:1; 1 Peter 1:2). However, Jesus (the Son) is also called God and is described in ways that could only apply to God (Isaiah 9:6; Zechariah 14:5; John 1:1, 14; 5:17-18, 22-23; 8:58-59; 10:30-33; 17:5, 24; 20:28; Romans 9:5; Colossians 2:9; Titus 2:13; Hebrews 1:8; 2 Peter 1:1; 1 John 5:20; Revelation 1:17-18). Jesus is worshipped as God (Matthew 2:11; 28:9; John 9:38). The Holy Spirit is also called God (Acts 5:3-4; 1 Corinthians 3:16).

Some have speculated that the Father, Son, and Holy Spirit, since they are one God, must also be one Person, but, this is not what the Bible teaches. The Bible teaches that the Father, Son, and Holy Spirit are three distinct Persons (Isaiah 48:12-16; Psalm 110:1; Matthew

3:16-17; 28:19; John 14:16, 26; 15:26). Before anything was created, the three Persons of the Trinity communicated with each other (Genesis 1:26; 11:7), shared the glory of God (John 17:5), and loved each other (John 17:24). Even while Christ was on earth, He and the Father spoke to one another, thus proving they were not the same Person (Matthew 3:16-17; 26:39; Luke 23:46; John 17:1). When all the data is considered, it is clear that the Bible teaches that there is only one true God, but this God eternally exists as three equal Persons. Hence, the Bible teaches the doctrine of the Trinity.

The Bible also teaches that Jesus Christ will someday return to earth in power and glory. After His return, He will rule over the nations for one-thousand years (Matthew 24:29-31; Revelation 11:15; 19:11-16; 20:4-6).

Since the available evidence declares the Bible to be God's Word, whatever it teaches must be true. Therefore, the biblical teachings concerning salvation, Christ's substitutionary death, the Trinity, and Christ's return should be accepted. It is also important to note that since whatever the Bible teaches is true, the morality taught in the Bible is authoritative. If God calls a practice wrong, then it is wrong, regardless of common political sentiment. Though the Bible student must differentiate between absolute moral laws which are universally binding on all men and temporary cultural laws prescribed for a specific people at a specific time, absolute moral laws taught in the Bible should be adhered to by all. The day will come when all must answer to God, at the judgment (2 Corinthians 5:10; Revelation 20:11-15).

CONCLUSION

The argument of this chapter is threefold. First, Jesus of Nazareth, who is God incarnate, taught that the Bible is God's Word. Therefore, the Bible is the Word of God. Second, this is confirmed by the supernatural wisdom of the Bible, as well as the many fulfilled prophecies of the Bible. Third, since God has been shown to be infinitely perfect, His Word is totally trustworthy. Therefore, whatever the Bible teaches is true.

Since the Bible teaches that salvation comes only through trusting in Jesus as one's Savior, then Christianity is the one true faith. All religions which deny salvation only through Christ alone are false religions. One's eternal destiny depends on his response to Christ. It is Jesus who calls out to all mankind, "Come to Me, all who are weary and heavy-laden, and I will give you rest" (Matthew 11:28).

## ENDNOTES

1Norman L. Geisler, ed., *Inerrancy* (Grand Rapids: Academie Books, 1980), 16-17.

2Pascal, 56-61.

3Schaeffer, *Complete Works* vol. 1, 293-304.

4Pascal, 56-61.

5H. L. Willmington, *That Manuscript From Outer Space* (Nashville: Thomas Nelson Publishers, 1974), 99.

6Ibid.

7McDowell, 270-280.

8Ibid., 280-281.

9Ibid., 283-285,

10Morris, *Many Infallible Proofs*, 183.

11Tenney, *The Zondervan Pictorial Bible Dictionary*, 233-234.

12Morris, *Many Infallible Proofs*, 182.

13Ibid., 186-187.

14Ibid.,   187-188.

15Ibid.,   186.

16The predictions of Scripture are always clear in their meaning and no prophecy of Scripture has ever been shown to be inaccurate. On the other hand, the prophecies of Edgar Cayce and Jeane Dixon have been shown to be extremely vague and often inaccurate. Specific cases of false prophecies uttered by Cayce and Dixon are documented in Josh McDowell and Don Stewart, *Handbook of Today's Religions*, 169-174, 181-185. According to Deuteronomy 18:22, one failed prophecy is enough to identify a person as a false prophet. Hence, both Cayce and Dixon are false prophets while, as mentioned above, no prediction of the Bible has been shown to be false.

17Morris, *Many Infallible Proofs*, 198-199.

# PART SEVEN

# SCIENTIFIC APOLOGETICS

# CHAPTER 29
# THE SCIENTIFIC CASE FOR CREATION

Today, many people believe that evolution is a biological fact. However, this is not the case. Science, by definition, deals with probabilities, not certainties. The next two chapters will explore the creation-evolution debate. This chapter will draw heavily upon the information found in the book *Origin Science* by Norman L. Geisler and J. Kirby Anderson.[1]

## HISTORY OF THE CREATION-EVOLUTION DEBATE
The creation model is the view that God created the universe without using evolution. The creation model dominated modern science before 1860.[2] Modern science was started by men who believed in the existence of the God of the Bible. Galileo, Isaac Newton, Francis Bacon, Johannes Kepler, and Blaise Pascal are just a few who fit into this category.[3] Their belief in God's existence formed the foundation for modern science. They believed that a reasonable God created the universe in a reasonable way, so that through reason man could find out about the universe in which he lives.[4] In other words, the universe makes sense only because God designed it to make sense. Today, however, atheistic evolutionists have rejected this base for modern science.[5] They have rejected the existence of a reasonable God. But the question that they must face is this: "Without a reasonable God, can a person really expect the universe to make sense?"

The evolution model is the view that life spontaneously evolved from non-life without intelligent intervention.[6] The evolution model dominated modern science after 1860.[7] Charles Darwin published his book *The Origin of Species* around that time.[8] Darwin proposed a naturalistic explanation for the origin of the universe, first life, and new life forms.[9] He taught that nature can be explained without appealing to a supernatural origin. Darwin's proposal quickly became the predominant "scientific" view.

THE SCIENTIFIC METHOD

Evolution is not a scientific fact. The scientific method consists of six steps: 1) observation, 2) proposal of a question or problem, 3) hypothesis (an educated guess), 4) experimentation, 5) theory (a hypothesis with a high degree of probability), and 6) natural law (a theory shown to be valid on a universal scale).[10] Evolution is not a scientific law or theory, let alone a scientific fact. The supposed evolutionary changes from one species to another cannot be observed.[11] They supposedly occurred in the past. Therefore, since observation is the initial step in the scientific method, evolution cannot be proven through the scientific method.

The creation view is in the same category as evolution. Creation, scientifically speaking, is not a fact, law, or theory. Like evolution, the supposed creation is a singular event in the past. It cannot be observed. Therefore, both creation and evolution are only scientific models; they represent different ways to interpret the same evidence.[12]

This does not mean that creation and evolution cannot claim to be scientific. Contrary to popular belief, the scientific method is not the only way to search for truth in the field of science. Forensic science (crime scene investigation) does not use the scientific method, for the crime can no longer be observed. Still, forensic science is a legitimate science.[13] Science can be separated into two main divisions: operation science and origin science. Operation science deals with the repeatable; it is science of the observable present. It uses the scientific method. Forensic science, creation, and evolution do not fall into this category.[14] Origin science, on the other hand, deals with the non-repeatable; it deals with the singular events of the past. Origin science does not utilize the scientific method since singular events of the past can no longer be observed.[15] Forensic science, creation science, and evolutionary science fall into this category.

ORIGIN SCIENCE

Since the non-repeatable events of the past cannot be observed, origin science does not make use of the scientific method. Instead, origin science uses the principles of analogy (also called uniformity) and causality to determine whether or not a model is plausible.[16] The principle of analogy states that when a scientist observes a cause bringing about a certain effect in the present, he should posit the same kind of cause for a similar effect in the past.[17] In other words, similar effects usually have similar causes. The principle of causality states that every event must have an adequate cause.[18] A scientist should use these two principles to determine the plausibility (or lack of plausibility) of a particular model.

Since the creation model and the evolution model fall under the heading of origin science, the principles of analogy and uniformity must be applied to them to determine which model is more plausible. It must be understood that the creation model and the evolution model both deal with the same evidence. An example of this is common anatomy. Common anatomy deals with the similarities in the body parts of different species. Examples of common anatomy are the similarities that exist concerning the arm of a man, the arm of an ape, the wing of a bird, and the fin of a shark. Both creationists and evolutionists agree to the common anatomy between different species of animal life. However, the two models interpret the evidence differently. The evolution model teaches that common anatomy proves common ancestry.[19] Common ancestry is the view that all species are related since one species has evolved into another. The creation model teaches that the same data (common anatomy) proves the existence of a common Designer. Animals often share common anatomy due to their being created and designed by the same God.[20]

Which model is more plausible? In order to answer this question, the principles of analogy and causality must be applied to the origin of the universe, the origin of first life, and the origin of new life forms. Both the creation model and the evolution model must be tested in these three areas to ascertain which model is more plausible.

## THE ORIGIN OF THE UNIVERSE

Did the universe have a beginning, or did it always exist? This is a very important question. For if the universe had a beginning, it would need a cause. It could not have evolved into existence from nothing. If the universe is eternal then it may not need a cause. Fortunately, science is not silent on this question. The second law of thermodynamics is called energy deterioration. This law says that the amount of usable energy in the universe is running down.[21] Eventually, all the energy in the universe will be used up. This means that the universe is winding down. If it is winding down, it had to have been "wound up." If the universe is going to have an end, it had to have a beginning. There had to be a time when all the energy in the universe was usable; this marks the beginning of the universe.

The expansion of the universe and the big bang model also confirm the beginning of the universe.[22] In 1929, astronomer Edwin Hubble discovered that the universe is expanding at the same rate in all directions.[23] As time moves forward the universe is growing apart. This means that if one went back in time the universe would get denser. If one goes back in time far enough, the entire universe would be contained in what scientists have called "a point of infinite density."[24] But, a point can only be finitely dense. For a point to be infinitely dense it would have to be non-existent. Therefore, the universe came into existence from nothing a finite time ago.

There have been two main attempts to refute the beginning of the universe. The first is the steady-state model. This view holds that the universe had no beginning. Instead, it always existed in the same state. However, because of the mounting evidence for the big bang model, this view has been abandoned by most of its adherents.[25]

The second attempt to evade the beginning of the universe is called the oscillating model. This model teaches that, at some point during the universe's expansion, gravity will halt the expansion and pull everything back together again. From that point there will be another big bang. This process will be repeated over and over again throughout all eternity. However, the oscillating model fails for three reasons. First, there is no known principle of physics that would reverse the expansion of the universe into another big bang. Second, current scientific research has shown that the universe is not dense enough for gravity to pull it back together again. Third, even if one could prove that several big bangs have occurred, the second law of thermodynamics would still require that there was a first big bang.[26]

Therefore, science has shown that the universe had a beginning, but, since from nothing, nothing comes, something must have caused the universe to come into existence. Everything that has a beginning needs a cause. Since the universe needs a cause, the creation model is more plausible than the evolution model. If the universe were eternal, then the evolution model could claim some type of plausibility. But, for the above reasons, this is not the case. The universe is not eternal; it had a beginning. Something separate from the universe had to cause it to come into existence.

### THE ORIGIN OF FIRST LIFE

Evolution teaches spontaneous generation—that life came from non-life without intelligent intervention.[27] However, spontaneous generation violates the law of biogenesis and the cell theory. The law of biogenesis states that "all living things arise only from other living things."[28] The cell theory defines the cell as the most basic unit of life, and declares that "new cells arise only from pre-existing cells."[29] Both the law of biogenesis and the cell theory are accepted by evolutionists; the evolutionists merely assume that first life is the exception to these principles. But, a model that violates scientific theories and laws should be abandoned. This is especially true when there is a rival model that does not violate scientific theories and laws.

The creation model posits the existence of an intelligent Being in order to bridge the gap from non-life to life. The creation model recognizes that the specified complexity (highly complex information) found in a single-celled animal could not be produced by chance. A single-celled animal has enough genetic information to fill one volume of an encyclopedia.[30] Just as an explosion in a print shop cannot randomly produce one volume of an encyclopedia, there is no way that a single-celled animal could have been produced by mere chance. Intelligent intervention was needed.[31]

Natural laws by themselves do not produce specified complexity. Geisler illustrates this point by stating that though natural laws can explain the Grand Canyon, they cannot explain the faces on Mount Rushmore.[32] The faces on Mount Rushmore reveal evidence of intelligent design.

Evolutionists often offer the Miller and Urey experiments as evidence that life has been produced from non-life in the laboratory. In response, several things should be noted. First, Chandra Wickramasinghe, one of Britain's most eminent scientists, calls these experiments "cheating." Miller and Urey start with amino acids, break them down, and then recover them. They do not produce something that wasn't there to begin with.[33] Second, Geisler states that the Miller and Urey experiments do not produce life. They only produce amino acids, which are the building blocks of life. Amino acids are to life what a single sentence is to one volume of encyclopedia.[34] Third, Geisler points out that even if these experiments did produce life from non-life in the laboratory (which they don't), it would support the creation model, not the evolution model. The reason for this is clear. The experiments would merely prove that to get life from non-life intelligent intervention (i.e., the scientists) is needed. The experiments would not prove that life spontaneously arose from non-life.[35]

Therefore, the creation model is more plausible than the evolution model when explaining the origin of first life. Intelligent intervention is necessary to produce life from non-life. It could not have happened by accident.

THE ORIGIN OF NEW LIFE FORMS

Many people believe that the fossil record proves evolution, but, this is not the case. In the fossil record, new life forms appear suddenly and fully developed.[36] There is no evidence of transitional forms (missing links). There are no fins or wings becoming arms. There are no intermediate forms. The gaps between forms in the fossil record are evidence against evolution, not for evolution.

Evolution teaches that single-celled animals eventually evolved into human beings. Of course, evolutionists claim this took large quantities of time to be accomplished. A single-celled animal contains enough information to fill one volume of encyclopedia,[37] but, the human brain contains enough information to fill twenty million volumes of encyclopedia.[38] Natural law, no matter how much time is involved, can never produce twenty million volumes of encyclopedia from one volume. Intelligent intervention is needed to produce more complex information.[39]

Evolutionists often point to mutations as the process by which evolution takes place.[40] However, mutations do not add more complex information to the genetic code. Instead, they merely garble the already existing genetic code.[41] For evolution to take place, new genetic information is needed. For example, single-celled animals would need new genes for the development of teeth, yet mutations produce no new genetic information.[42]

Simple life forms do not go to complex life forms through natural law alone.[43] Time plus chance plus natural laws can never produce more complex information.[44] Something must impart more information. Therefore, the creation model is more plausible than the evolution model concerning the origin of new life forms.

## CONCLUSION

The scientific case for creation is very strong. Though it is true that creationists have never seen the invisible Creator, evolutionists also have never seen the supposed evolutionary changes of the past. The principles of analogy and causality support creationism as a superior model to evolution. Blind chance and natural laws are inadequate causes for the origin of the universe, first life, and new life forms. An intelligent Cause is needed in each case. The cause of the beginning of nature cannot be nature itself. No being can preexist its own existence in order to cause its own existence. Therefore, nature needs a supernatural Cause. This supernatural Cause must be an intelligent Being to bring life from non-life and complex life forms from simple life forms. Hence, the creation model is more plausible than the evolution model.

## ENDNOTES

1Norman L. Geisler and J. Kirby Anderson, *Origin Science* (Grand Rapids: Baker Book House, 1987), entire book.

2Ibid., 37-52.

3Ibid.

4Ibid., 37-40, 51.

5Ibid., 52.

6Ibid., 82-86.

7Ibid.

8Ibid.

9Ibid.

10Tom M. Graham, *Biology, the Essential Principles* (Philadelphia: Saunders College Publishing, 1982), 6.

11Geisler and Anderson, 15.

12Ibid.

13Ibid., 25.

14Ibid., 36.

15Ibid., 127-132.

16Ibid.

17Ibid., 131-132.

18Ibid., 130-131.

19Morris, *Many Infallible Proofs*, 252-255.

20Ibid.

21Graham,  75.

22Craig,  81-83.

23Ibid.,  82.

24Ibid.

25Ibid.,  83.

26Ibid.,  83-88.

27Morris,  260.

28Graham,  18.

29Ibid.,  12.

30Geisler and Anderson, 162.

31Ibid.,  162-163.

32Ibid.,  141.

33Varghese,  34.

34Geisler and  Corduan,  105-106.

35Geisler and  Anderson,  138-139.

36Ibid.,  150-152

37Ibid.,  162.

38Ibid.

39Ibid.,  163.

40Morris, 256.

41Ibid.

42Charles Caldwell Ryrie, *You Mean the Bible Teaches That...*(Chicago: Moody Press, 1974), 111.

43Geisler and Anderson, 150.

44Scott M. Huse, *The Collapse of Evolution* (Grand Rapids: Baker Book House, 1983), 94.

# CHAPTER 30
# THE SCIENTIFIC CASE
# AGAINST EVOLUTION

The last chapter examined and defended the scientific case for creation. In this chapter, the scientific case against evolution will be discussed. There are major problems with the evolution model that render it obsolete as an explanation of the available scientific data. This chapter will comment briefly on these problem areas.

## THERMODYNAMICS

Thermodynamics deals with the relationship between heat, energy, and work.[1] The first and second laws of thermodynamics pose serious problems for evolution. The first law of thermodynamics is called energy conservation. It states that the amount of energy in the universe remains constant; no energy is now being created or destroyed.[2] This means that if the universe had a beginning, whatever process or act that brought the universe into existence is no longer in operation today. In other words, the "creation process" is no longer operating today. Therefore, either the universe is eternal or the universe was created in the past; no continuing creative process is occurring.

The second law of thermodynamics is called entropy. Though the amount of energy in the universe remains constant, it changes form. The second law states that when energy changes form it becomes less usable.[3] Therefore, the amount of usable energy in the universe is running out. This means that the day will come when all the energy in the universe will have been used up. This will be the death of the universe. There must have been a time when all the energy of the universe was usable; this would be the beginning of the universe. In other words, since the universe is going to have an end, it is not eternal. If it is not eternal, then it must have had a beginning. The big bang model and the expansion of the universe also confirm the beginning of the universe.[4]

The evolutionist faces a dilemma. The first and second laws of thermodynamics together declare that the universe had a beginning. The evolutionists cannot deny these laws, for they are considered to be the most firmly established laws of modern science.[5] But, evolution runs counter to these two laws. When a scientific model contradicts a scientific law, the model should be abandoned. Since the first and second laws of thermodynamics teach that the universe had a beginning, then something outside the universe must have caused the universe to come into existence. For, from nothing nothing comes. Therefore, the universe could not have evolved into existence out of nothing.

### EVOLUTIONARY DATING METHODS

The evolutionary dating methods are inconsistent and unreliable. All evolutionary dating methods are based upon uniformitarianism.[6] Uniformitarianism assumes that there were no world-wide catastrophes; therefore, the rate of decay has remained constant. Uniformitarianism assumes that today's processes have continued at the same rate throughout all time. However, if there were a world-wide flood and a special creation by God, then this uniformitarian assumption would be unwarrented.[7]

Evolutionary dating methods have been shown to be unreliable. Rocks known to have been only a few hundred years old have been dated to be hundreds of millions of years old.[8] Henry Morris has stated that there are many different ways to date the earth's age, but evolutionists only use those methods which give astronomically old dates since evolution needs millions of years to seem even slightly possible.[9] Two methods which point to a young earth are population statistics and the earth's magnetic field.[10] If one assumes the principle of uniformitarianism, then due to the present rate at which the population of mankind increases, the start of the present population would take one back 4,300 years to the traditional date for the flood.[11] Concerning the strength of the earth's magnetic field, if one assumes that the present rate of decay remains the same going back indefinitely into the past, then about 7,000 years ago it would have been too strong to sustain life.[12]

The most convincing argument for an old earth is probably that of the speed of light.[13] The speed of light is assumed by scientists to be constant. The light of distant stars and galaxies can be seen on earth. Since it would have taken billions of years for the light of some of these celestial bodies to reach earth (assuming the speed of light has remained the same throughout all time), the universe must be billions of years old.[14] However, Barry Setterfield of Australia studied every measurement of the speed of light and found that the speed of light has not been constant throughout all time; it had been faster in the past.[15] Setterfield's research, if reliable, reveals the age of the universe to be only 6,000 years old.[16]

Even if the universe is old, this would not refute the creation model. Many creationists believe in an old universe.[17] However, if the universe is young, the evolution model is destroyed. One thing is clear: the principle of uniformitarianism is an assumption that appears to go against the evidence. If uniformitarianism is true, then all the dating methods would reveal the same approximate dates. These dates would be old or young; they would not be old and young. Since some dating methods point to an old earth and others point to a young earth, the evolutionary dating methods are unreliable. Since uniformitarianism is not a given, the date of the universe is an open question.

THE FOSSIL RECORD

The fossil record is assumed to prove evolution, but, this is not the case. The fossil record shows no evidence of transitional forms (missing links). New life forms appear suddenly and fully developed.[18] There are no animals with half-fins or half-wings in the fossil record. If there were transitional forms, why have none been found? This is a serious problem for evolutionists. Harvard paleontologists Stephen Jay Gould and Louis Agassiz have admitted this lack of evidence for evolution in the fossil record.[19] Aggassiz, a nineteenth-century creationist, stated:

> Species appear suddenly and disappear suddenly in the progressive strata.... the supposed intermediate forms between the species of different geological periods are imaginary beings, called up merely in support of a fanciful theory.[20]

Gould, a twentieth century evolutionist, stated:

> In any local area, a species does not arise gradually by the steady transformation of its ancestors; it appears all at once and "fully formed."[21]

It is interesting to note that the first geologists believed that the fossil record was evidence for the world-wide flood recorded in the Bible.[22] This view is strengthened by the fact that fossilization is extremely rare today. Even if the earth existed for millions of years, that would not be enough time for the present fossil record to have been produced without any world-wide catastrophes.[23] Fossilization is world-wide and caused by the rapid burial of animals, which is something a world-wide flood would do.[24]

Another problem for evolution concerning the fossil record is polystrate fossils. These are fossils that extend through two or more layers of sedimentary rock.[25] These fossils are usually trees. In order for a standing tree to be fossilized, it would have to be quickly buried before it decayed. However, in these polystrate fossils, the several layers of earth through which the tree extends supposedly took millions of years to form.[26] This reveals that evolutionists are mistaken when they assume that layers of sedimentary rock must take millions of years to form and therefore indicate large quantities of time. No tree can live for millions of years. Therefore, these layers of sedimentary rock are not evidence for an old earth. They could have been formed rapidly.[27]

Another problem for evolution is the fact that the fossil record often appears out of sequence.[28] Sometimes "old" fossils appear resting on rock layers containing "younger" fossils.[29] The geologic column is "an imagined chronological arrangement of rock units in columnar form with the presumed oldest units at the bottom and presumed youngest at the top."[30] However, the world is full of strata appearing in the wrong order.[31] If these layers took millions of years to be formed as evolutionists say, then this would not be the case.

If one assumes the possibility that the fossil record was formed rapidly, the world-wide flood offers the a better explanation. The flood would tend to bury fossils in this order. First, deep oceans creatures would be fossilized. Then, creatures in shallower water, followed by amphibians and land-bordering creatures. Next would be swamp, marsh, and low river-flat creatures (especially reptiles). After that, higher mammals who retreated to higher ground in their attempt to escape the flood would be fossilized. Finally, humans would be overtaken.[32] This would be the "standard" order; still, there would be many exceptions due to upheavals in the earth's crust during and after the world-wide flood.[33] A world-wide catastrophe such as the flood offers a much more plausible explanation for these exceptions than evolution does.[34]

Other interesting aspects of flood geology are the canopy theory and the global ice age. The canopy theory refers to Genesis 1:6-8.[35] In that passage, the Bible teaches that God surrounded the earth's atmosphere with a huge canopy of water. This would have worked liked the ozone layer does today. It would have filtered out poisonous rays from the sun, thus increasing longevity. This may explain why the Bible records pre-flood men living more than nine-hundred years (Genesis 5). After the flood, man's life-span would drastically decrease. The water contained in the canopy descended in the great flood (Genesis 6:11-12) and covered the entire earth (Genesis 7:19). This would explain why three-fourths of the earth's surface is covered with water. In fact, if the earth were a completely smooth sphere, it would be covered by water 1.5 miles in depth.[36] After the flood, tremendous upheavals in the earth's crust due to the catastrophe would cause valleys to sink and mountains to rise (Psalm 104:5-9). The mountains that rose would become the dry land man now inhabits. The upheavals in the earth's crust could also explain much of the continental shifts that scientists have shown to have occurred.

A global flood would cause a global ice age.[37] Today, evolutionists accept the global ice age, but they reject a universal flood which could have caused it. Because of this, glacial geologists have failed to determine what caused the ice age. Also the lack of vegetation due to the ice age would have killed off most of the dinosaurs, though some recent dinosaur sightings are well-documented.[38]

## LACK OF TRANSITIONAL FORMS

A devastating problem for the evolution model is the lack of transitional forms. No one possesses an undisputed missing link. All the supposed missing links between apes and men have been dismissed. Neanderthal Man and Cro-Magnon Man both have the features of modern man.[39] Colorado Man turned out to be a member of the horse family.[40] Java Man (also known as Pithecanthropus) was shown to be the remains of a large gibbon.[41] Heidelberg Man consisted of only a lower jaw.[42] Obviously, a lower jaw is insufficient evidence for a missing link. One can only speculate as to the makeup of the rest of the skull and skeleton. The Piltdown Man was revealed to be a clever hoax.[43] The Peking Man is now thought to be a large monkey or baboon.[44] The Southern Ape (also called Australopithecus), Dryopithecus, and Ramapithecus were extinct apes.[45] The East African Man (Zinjanthropus) was shown to be an ape.[46] Finally, the Nebraska Man, which consisted of only one tooth, was proven to be the tooth of an extinct pig.[47] This is rather interesting since this tooth had been presented as evidence in the 1925 "monkey trial" as "evidence" for the evolutionary model.[48] When the tooth of an extinct pig is mistaken for the tooth of the missing link between apes and men, it shows how subjective modern science has become. Though high school and college textbooks show drawings of the missing links from apes to men, the fact is that this art merely depicts the vivid imagination of scientists. No undisputed missing link between apes and men has been discovered.

Archaeopteryx was once thought to be a transitional form between reptiles and birds.[49] It had features resembling that of a reptile (teeth, lizard-like tail, and claws). But, archaeopteryx also had wings and feathers similar to a bird. Still, the archaeopteryx was fully developed. It did not have half-wings or the like. Archaeopteryx has now been classified as a bird. This is due to the fact that every characteristic of archaeopteryx can be found in some genuine bird, though some of its features are not found in reptiles.[50] It should also be noted that the supposed evolution of reptiles into birds is highly improbable. The lungs of a reptile have millions of tiny air sacs, while the lungs of birds have tubes. In order for a transitional form to exist between a reptile and a bird it would have to breathe without having fully-developed lungs.[51]

An extinct, small three-toed animal called Eohippus was once thought to be the ancestor of the modern, large, one-toed horse.[52] It is now doubtful that Eohippus should have ever been classified in the horse family. Eohippus is probably an extinct type of hyrax.[53] Evolutionists believe that invertebrates (animals without backbones) have evolved into vertebrates (animals with backbones). However, no transitional form between the two has ever been found.[54]

This lack of transitional forms is very problematic for the evolution model. It has been over 130 years since Darwin wrote *The Origin of Species*. Still, no missing links have been found. Due to this absence of evidence for evolution, modern evolutionists like Stephen Jay Gould have proposed a new model called "Punctuated Equilibrium."[55] Whereas evolution means "gradual change," Punctuated Equilibrium teaches that the changes occurred so suddenly that transitional forms did not survive long enough to be fossilized. It appears that Punctuated Equilibrium is an attempt to explain away the absence of evidence for evolution—but it fails as well.

Since there is no evidence of missing links in the fossil record, evolution should be rejected. The lack of transitional forms in the fossil record is evidence against evolution and in favor of the creation model, which teaches that there are no missing links.[56]

## MUTATIONS

Evolutionists need a mechanism that explains how evolution has supposedly occurred. Many evolutionists believe that mutation is this mechanism.[57] However, as was mentioned in the last chapter, mutations merely scramble the already existing genetic code. No new genetic information is added.[58] Yet, for evolution to have occurred, a mechanism is needed through which new genes are produced. Therefore, mutations fail to explain evolution. Evolutionists claim that they believe the present interprets the past. However, there is no mechanism in the present that spontaneously produces new genetic information. Until such a mechanism is found, evolution can only be accepted by "blind faith."

## HEISENBERG'S PRINCIPLE OF INDETERMINACY

Heisenberg's principle of indeterminacy is a theory in quantum physics. Quantum physics deals with the atom and the motion of subatomic particles.[59] The principle of indeterminacy states that it is impossible to determine both the position in space of a subatomic particle and that particle's motion at the same time.[60] Therefore, subatomic particle movement is currently unpredictable for man. This simply means that scientists aren't yet able to accurately predict where a specific particle will be at a given moment. Some scientists have wrongly concluded from this that things can occur on the subatomic level without a cause. If this were true, then it would be possible that the universe just popped into existence without a cause. If this were the case, it would not favor either evolution or creation. If things can come into existence without a cause, then the basis for modern science crumbles. All experiments would be a waste of time, for any given phenomena could have come into existence without a cause. Therefore, there would be no need to study the elements of the universe any longer. Modern science would die.

Albert Einstein believed that Heisenberg's principle did not prove that things can occur without a cause. Einstein held that the causes actually do exist, though man may not be able to find them.[61] Man is limited in knowledge, and there may be some causes he is unable to find.[62] Heisenberg's principle, therefore, cannot come to the aid of evolution; the universe (since it had a beginning) needs a cause.

## CONCLUSION

In conclusion, evolution is not a proven fact. It is assumed to be true by many scientists, but they have offered no convincing proofs. There is no evidence for the evolution model. This can be seen in the many unproven assumptions held by evolutionists.

First, there is no evidence for spontaneous generation. The belief that life evolved from non-life contradicts both the cell theory and the law of biogenesis. The Miller-Urey experiments have failed to produce life in the lab (if they were successful, it would be evidence for the creation model not the evolution model).

Second, there is no evidence for the evolutionary assumption that the universe is eternal. Evolutionists must accept this by faith. Evolutionists may assume that the universe evolved into existence from nothing, but this assumption goes against all available scientific evidence.

Third, there is no evidence that intelligence could come from non-intelligence. Intelligence shows evidence of design; it could not have been produced by chance.

Fourth, no evidence has been found proving that multi-celled animals came from single-celled animals. (Even the human embryo does not evolve into a human; it has its full human genetic code at conception.63)

Fifth, there is no evidence for the evolution of animals with backbones from animals without backbones.64 Though there should be multitudes of transitional forms between the two groups, none have been found.

Sixth, there is no evidence for the common ancestry of fish, reptiles, birds, and mammals.[65] Common anatomy could point to a common Designer; it does not necessarily point to common ancestry.

All the major gaps that evolution must cross are assumed to have occurred; they have not been proven to have occurred. Therefore, evolution itself is an unproven assumption. Those who dogmatically proclaim it as truth spend more time explaining away the scientific evidence against their view than they do providing evidence for their view. Any scientific model which lacks plausibility should be abandoned. Such is the case with evolution.

Evolution needs God, but God does not need evolution. If evolution is true, then God is needed to bring the universe into existence from nothing, to bring life from non-life, and complex life forms from simple life forms. In each case, a miraculous superseding of natural laws is needed. However, if God exists, He doesn't need evolution. He could have either started the long evolutionary process or He could have created the universe in six literal days. God could have used evolution, but if He did, He covered His tracks. He left no evidence. Since God is not the author of deception, it is reasonable to conclude that evolution is a myth, devoid of any scientific evidence.

## ENDNOTES

1Tom M. Graham, *Biology, the Essential Principles* (Philadelphia: Saunders College Publishing, 1982), 75.

2Ibid.

3Ibid.

4Hugh Ross, *The Fingerprint of God* (Orange: Promise Publishing Company, 1991), 53-105.

5Henry M. Morris, *Science and the Bible* (Chicago: Moody Press, 1986), 17.

6Ibid., 66.

7Ibid.

8Morris, *Many Infallible Proofs*, 292-293.

9Ibid., 294.

10Ibid., 295-296.

11Ibid., 296.

12Ibid., 295.

13Paul D. Ackerman, *It's A Young World After All* (Grand Rapids: Baker Book House, 1986), 72.

14Ibid., 73.

15Ibid., 74.

16Ibid., 75.

17see Hugh Ross, *Creation and Time* (Colorado Springs: NavPress, 1994), entire book.

18Geisler and Anderson, *Origin Science,* 150-153.

19Ibid., 150-152.

20Louis Agassiz, "Contribution to the Natural History of the United States," *American Journal of Science,* (1860): 144-145.

21Stephen Jay Gould, "Evolution's Erratic Pace," *Natural History,* (May 1977): 14.

22Morris, *Science and the Bible,* 67.

23Huse, 46.

24Ackerman, 83.

25Ibid., 84.

26Ibid.

27Ibid.

28Morris, *Science and the Bible,* 68-69.

29Ibid.

30Huse, 147.

31Morris, *Science and the Bible,* 70.

32Ibid., 73.

33Ibid., 74.

34Ibid., 75.

35Ibid., 82-85.

36Ibid., 83.

37Ibid., 81.

38Henry M. Morris, *The Biblical Basis for Modern Science* (Grand Rapids: Baker Book House, 1984), 350-359. Some of the recent dinosaur sightings noted by Morris include: smaller brontosaurus in the rain forests of the Congo, living plesiosaurs in the Loch Ness and numerous other waterways, and what appears to be a freshly decayed plesiosaur captured and photographed by Japanese fishermen off the coast of New Zealand.

39Morris, *Science and the Bible*, 58.

40Huse, 98.

41Morris, *Science and the Bible*, 56.

42Marvin Lubenow, *Bones of Contention* (Grand Rapids: Baker Book House, 1992), 79.

43Morris, *Science and the Bible*, 56.

44Ibid.

45Ibid., 57-58.

46Lubenow, 167.

47Morris, *Science and the Bible*, 58.

48Ibid.

49Huse, 110.

50Morris, *Science and the Bible*, 267-268. see also Huse, 110-112.

51Huse, 112.

52Morris, *Science and the Bible*, 54-55.

53Ibid.

54Huse, 44.

55Geisler and Anderson, 150-153.

56Ibid.

57Morris, *Science and the Bible*, 46-47.

58Ibid.

59*The World Book Encyclopedia* (Chicago: World Book, Inc., 1985), vol. 16, 4.

60Roy E. Peacock, *A Brief History of Eternity* (Wheaton: Crossway Books, 1990), 56-59.

61Ibid., 59.

62Moreland, *Scaling the Secular City*, 38-39.

63Huse, 120.

64Ibid., 44.

65Ibid.

# PART EIGHT

# COMPARATIVE RELIGIOUS APOLOGETICS

# CHAPTER 31
# WORLD RELIGIONS

The eighth methodology for defending the Christian faith is comparative religious apologetics. This area of apologetics deals with the refutation of non-Christian world religions, non-Christian cults, the occult, and the New Age movement. This chapter will discuss and evaluate Judaism, Islam, Hunduism, Buddhism, and several lesser-known religions in light of the Christian faith.

## JUDAISM

True Judaism is the root of Christianity; Christianity is the fulfillment of Judaism. The Old Testament is Jewish. The apostles, who wrote the New Testament, are Jewish. Jesus, who is worshipped by Christians as the incarnate God, is Jewish. Therefore, true Judaism accepts the essential truths of Christianity. The God of Israel is the God of Christianity. Unfortunately, modern Judaism has rejected Jesus as the Jewish Messiah. Therefore, modern Judaism has apostatized from the one true faith-salvation in Jesus alone.[1]

There are three main branches of modern Judaism. Orthodox Judaism continues to observe most of the ceremonial laws with the exception of temple practices—there is currently no temple. Orthodox Jews accept the Old Testament as God's inspired word. They express a special reverence for the Torah (the first five books of the Bible).[2]

The Reform branch of Judaism is theologically liberal. Reform Jews reject the divine inspiration of the Old Testament. The Torah is viewed merely as an ethical guidebook. The Jewish Messiah is considered to be a mere symbol for the emancipation of the Jewish people. Still, Reform Jews are very proud of their national heritage.[3]

The Conservative branch of modern Judaism stands between the other two branches. Much emphasis is placed upon the God of Israel as the one true God. Still, Conservative Jews are more likely to reject traditional Jewish beliefs than are the orthodox Jews.[4]

Because of this diversity within contemporary Judaism, it is impossible to utilize one apologetic approach for all Jews. Reform Jews can usually be evangelized in the same fashion as one would an agnostic or a non-Christian theist (depending on the personal beliefs of the individual). However, the Conservative and Orthodox Jews have great respect for the Old Testament. It is often possible to discuss Old Testament messianic prophecies with Conservative and Orthodox Jews. The goal in these dialogues would be to lead the Jewish person to accept Jesus as the Jewish Messiah and the Savior of mankind. This is the same approach that Paul used in the synagogues as he witnessed to Jews (Acts 17:1-2).

Christ's fulfillment of Old Testament predictions should be presented. A few examples should be noted. Micah 5:2 predicts that the Messiah would be born in Bethlehem. Zechariah 9:9 states that the Messiah would receive a king's welcome while entering Jerusalem on a donkey. Isaiah 53 prophesies that the Jews would reject their Messiah when He comes, while Isaiah 42:4 states that the Jewish Messiah would receive a large Gentile following. Daniel 9:24-27 relates that the Messiah would be executed before the destruction of the temple (which occurred in 70AD). Psalm 22 identifies the type of death the Messiah would suffer as crucifixion. Only Jesus of Nazareth fulfilled all of these prophecies.

Christian apologists must attempt to persuade Orthodox and Conservative Jews to accept Christ's death on Calvary as the fulfillment of all the Old Testament sacrifices. The Jewish person must see that Christ offered His body as a sacrifice for the sins of mankind (1 Corinthians 5:21; 1 Peter 2:24; 3:18). Many Jews believe in salvation by works. Therefore, they must be told that salvation is solely by God's grace and that it is given to all who trust in Jesus, the Jewish Messiah, for salvation (Ephesians 2:8-9; John 3:16-18; 14:6; Romans 6:23).

Christian apologists must clearly display their love for Jewish people. It is an unfortunate fact that the Christian church has not always been free from the sin of anti-Semitism. Therefore, it is only natural for Jewish people to be wary of dialogue with Christians. The Christian would do well to establish a genuine friendship with Jewish people before attempting to lead them to Christ.

## ISLAM

The Islamic faith is the fastest growing religion in the world.[5] Islam was founded by a shepherd and trader named Muhammad (570-632AD).[6] While residing in Arabia, he rebelled against the polytheism and the superstitions of his homeland.[7] He was familiar with Judaism and Christianity, and these religions influenced him to believe in the existence of only one God.[8] Muhammad called this one God, "Allah." He supposedly received several visions and recorded them into what later became the Muslim holy book, the Koran.[9]

It was Muhammad's goal to unite the Arab tribes under Allah's rule.[10] To accomplish this goal, he often used militaristic acts to "convert" cities to Islam.[11] Since Muhammad died without choosing his successor, divisions arose within Islam.[12]

Today, Islam is split into three main groups: the Sunnis, the Shi'ites, and the Sufis.[13] Most Muslims are Sunnis. They follow the Koran as their highest authority and consider themselves the true followers of their prophet Muhammad's teachings.[14] Shi'ite Muslims believe their leader (called the "Ayatollah") speaks for God. Shi'ite Muslims believe that the Ayatollah can infallibly call for a holy war.[15] The Sufis are Islamic mystics who seek personal experiences of God.[16] It should be added that the Black Muslim movement in America is considered by traditional Muslims to be a heretical offshoot of historical Islam.[17]

Muslims believe that there is only one God and that He is called Allah. They accept the Torah of Moses, the Psalms of David, the Gospels of Christ, and the Koran as inspired works of God.[18] Still, Muslims believe that the Koran is the final and most authoritative word God has given to man.[19] Hence, if there is any disagreement between a sacred book and the Koran concerning any teaching, the Muslim will accept the teaching found in the Koran. The Old or New Testament teaching called into question is usually attributed to copyist errors. The six greatest prophets are listed as Adam, Noah, Abraham, Moses, Jesus, and Muhammad. However, Muhammad is considered to be the greatest of these prophets.[20] Islam teaches that there will be a resurrection and time of judgment in the last days. Hell will be the final destiny of all those who have opposed the work of Muhammad and Allah. Heaven will be populated by those who obeyed Allah and His prophet.[21] To become a Muslim, a person must publicly recite, "There is no God but Allah, and Muhammad is the prophet of Allah."[22] Muslims must pray five times a day facing Mecca, one of their holy cities.[23] Muslims are required to give alms and to follow prescribed fasts.[24] Each Muslim must make a pilgrimage to the city of Mecca at least once.[25]

Muslims deny the doctrine of the Trinity; they believe that God is only one Person.[26] Muslims deny the deity of Christ, lowering His status to that of a mere man, though a great prophet.[27] Muslims deny that Jesus died for the sins of mankind and that salvation comes through Him. In fact, they deny even that He died on the cross.[28] Muslims also reject that Jesus rose from the dead.[29] They teach that Jesus was a sinless prophet, but that He was not as great as Muhammad.[30] Muslims believe that man can be saved through human effort-obedience to the commands of Allah (as given through His prophet Muhammad).[31]

To refute Islam, the Christian apologist should focus on the contradictions in the Koran. The Koran[32] teaches that Jesus ascended to heaven without dying (Surah 4:157-158), but it also teaches that Jesus predicted His own death and resurrection (Surah 19:33). In Surah 2:256, Muhammad proclaims religious tolerance, but, in Surah 9:5, he commands Muslims to slay all who refuse to worship Allah alone. One passage in the Koran states that Allah created the universe in six days (Surah7:54), while another passage speaks of eight days of creation (Surah 4:8-15). It appears that Muhammad learned about the Bible through secondary sources that were unreliable, for he mistakenly credits Haman, who lived around 500BC, with building the Tower of Babel, which was built around 2300BC (Surah 28:37-38). Muhammad also wrongly considered Haman to be a contemporary of Moses, who lived from about 1525BC to 1400BC (Surah 29:39). Many other contradictions found in the Koran could be identified by the Christian apologist in order to show that the Koran could not possibly be the infallible word of God.

Besides critiquing the Koran, the Christian apologist should also defend the historicity of the Gospel accounts of Christ. The Christian apologist should present historical evidences for the death, resurrection, and deity of Christ. For example, ancient evidence for Christ's death by crucifixion abounds. There is solid manuscript evidence for Christ's death found in the Bodmer Papyrus II (150-200AD-contains most of John's Gospel), the Chester Beatty Papyri (200AD-contains most of the New Testament), and the Vaticanus and Sinaiticus (350AD-each contains most of the New Testament).[33] There are even ancient non-Christian sources dated between 52AD and 200AD which speak of Christ's death by crucifixion (Thallus, Josephus, Tacitus, and the Jewish Talmud).[34] There is much historical evidence for the Jesus of the Bible. This should be utilized to persuade Muslims that their Jesus is not the Jesus of the Bible, and that only the true Jesus of the Bible can save mankind from its sins.

## HINDUISM

Hinduism is one of the oldest religions in the world. It is also one of the most complex religious systems. It is actually a family of religions since it has many diverse sects. A Hindu can be a pantheist, a polytheist, a monotheist, an agnostic, or even an atheist. Hinduism claims to be tolerant of all faiths. It believes there are many paths to God.[35]

The Hindus have a variety of sacred writings written between 1400BC and 500AD. Among these are the Vedas, the Upanishads, Ramayana, Mahabharata, and the Puranas.[36] The most sacred of all Hindu writings is the Bhagavad Gita. The Bhagavad Gita dates to the first century AD; it is found in the Mahabharata. This work teaches that devotion to the god of one's choice brings salvation. This writing also speaks of Krishna, a supposed manifestation of the god called Vishnu.[37]

There is a common core of Hindu beliefs despite the diversity within Hinduism. Brahman is the ultimate reality for the Hindu. God is everything (pantheism). The Hindu god is a three-in-one god; Brahman is the creator, Vishnu the preserver, and Shiva the destroyer. (This three-in-oneness is not to be mistaken with the

Christian doctrine of the Trinity, for the three are only manifestations of the Hindu god; they are not three eternal persons.) The soul of each human is part of Brahman (god), and the physical world is thought to be an illusion (called Maya).[38]

Karma is the Hindu belief that the consequences from a person's actions of a previous life determine his present state of existence. Negative karma must be worked off through suffering and multiple reincarnations before Nirvana (eternal bliss) can be achieved. Nirvana is when a person is freed from the long cycle of reincarnation and becomes one with Brahman.[39]

Hindus believe that salvation (freedom from the cycle of reincarnations) can be achieved in one of three ways. The first way is through works and rituals. The second way is through the attaining of knowledge. The third way is through devotion to a deity of one's choice. Usually, Hindu meditation is an essential aspect of this third way.[40]

Christianity and Hinduism are not compatible. The god of Hinduism is usually considered to be an impersonal god.[41] Brahman is an indefinable concept; it is not the personal, loving God of the Bible (John 3:16). Negative karma is not to be equated with the Christian concept of sin, for, in Hinduism, ultimate reality is beyond the concepts of right and wrong.[42] As Francis Schaeffer pointed out, if the universe had an impersonal beginning, then the universe is "totally silent" concerning moral values.[43] Hinduism also rejects Christ's unique claim to deity. At most, Hindus will accept Jesus as one of many manifestations of their god.[44] In, Hinduism salvation is through human effort, not through the grace of God.[45] Hindus believe in reincarnation, not a future resurrection.[46] On each of these vital points, Hinduism is opposed to Christianity. They cannot both be true.

The Christian apologist should be prepared to refute pantheism, as well as polytheism, when evangelizing Hindus. Historical apologetics may be useful in showing the Hindu the uniqueness of Christ. Since Hinduism collapses into moral relativism, the Christian apologist must be prepared to argue for absolute moral laws (moral values that are universally valid). Dialogue between Hindus and Christians is very difficult due to the vast gulf between these two schools of thought. Nevertheless, God has called His followers to preach His Gospel to all people.

BUDDHISM

Buddhism came into existence about 500BC. At that time, many people in India were disillusioned with Hinduism. Because of this disillusionment, many different sects arose from Hinduism. Of these offshoots, Buddhism was the most successful.[47]

Buddhism was founded by Siddhartha Gautama, who later became known as Buddha. Buddha was married and had a son. He was a prince who lived a sheltered and pleasurable life. One day, he left the palace to see life in the outside world. This experience taught him about sickness, old age, death, hunger, and poverty. Eventually, Buddha left the palace and his family to seek "enlightenment." While meditating under a fig tree, he reached nirvana. He decided to proclaim the truth he had learned while meditating under the tree. This truth can be summed up under the four noble truths and the eightfold path.[48]

The four noble truths are 1) the existence of suffering, 2) one's desire for the pleasures of the senses causes suffering, 3) the extinguishing of one's desires will end suffering, and 4) the extinguishing of one's desires through the eightfold path.[49]

The eightfold path is 1) right views, 2) right attitude, 3) right speech, 4) right conduct, 5) right livelihood, 6) right effort, 7) right mindfulness, and 8) right contemplation or meditation.[50] Through the eightfold path, one can attain nirvana, the cessation of all desire.[51]

Although Buddha was himself deified by some of his followers many years after his death, he himself was an agnostic concerning the existence of God and the afterlife.[52] Both pantheists and atheists can be found within Buddhism. Buddhism holds to the teaching of reincarnation, with nirvana as the ultimate escape from the cycle of reincarnation.[53] Evil is merely an illusion caused by ignorance. As in Hinduism, moral values in Buddhism are ultimately relative.[54] Still, in a contradictory fashion, Buddhism forbids certain behavior such as the killing of living things (including insects), adultery, stealing, telling falsehoods, and the drinking of intoxicants.[55]

Buddhism is obviously opposed to the Christian Faith. The Christian believes that God created the universe (Genesis 1:1), while

Buddhists are monists—they believe all reality is one. Buddhists reject the personal, loving God of the Bible (John 3:16; Romans 5:8). Buddhism denies the reality of sin against God (Romans 3:10, 23; 5:12; 6:23) and the need for a Savior (John 3:16-18; 14:6; 1 Peter 2:24; 3:18). Buddhists also deny the unique deity of Christ (John 1:1, 14; Titus 2:13). Therefore, the Christian apologist must present a persuasive case for the truth of Christianity, while also refuting the major premises of Buddhism.

## JAINISM

Jainism (an offshoot of Hinduism) was founded in India by Mahavira, a contemporary of Buddha. Mahavira lived a life of self-denial for twelve years. During that time, he did not speak; he wandered naked and unwashed, meditating daily, throughout India until he found nirvana. At that point, he accepted followers and began to teach his beliefs. Mahavira refused to acknowledge or worship any god. Despite his atheism, however, he (like Buddha) was deified years after his death by his followers. Jainism teaches the equality of all people. It renounces the killing of any living thing, sexual pleasures, and worldly goods. Jainism teaches reincarnation, non-violence, and strict vegetarianism. Jainism encourages its adherents to flee from both hate and love.[56]

When witnessing to Jainists, Christian apologists should provide evidence from nature for God's existence and historical evidences for the deity and resurrection of Christ. Christ's command to love God with all one's being and to love one's neighbor as oneself (Mark 12:30-31) directly contradicts the Jainist belief that man is to renounce both hate and love. The Jainist acceptance of reincarnation is also unbiblical (Hebrews 9:27; Luke 16:19-31). Reincarnation teaches that salvation is attainable through human effort, whereas, the Bible clearly states that man can only be saved by God's grace through faith alone (Ephesians 2:8-9; Romans 3:20-24).

## CONFUCIANISM

Confucianism was founded by Confucius (another contemporary of Buddha) in China. Confucius was a moral reformer and a government official. In its purest form, Confucianism is more of an ethical system than a religion. Its founder is famous for his moral philosophy of life. Confucianism is agnostic about the spiritual realm. Man is viewed as basically good in this system of thought. Confucius (like Buddha and Mahavira) was later worshipped as a god by his followers.[57]

Christian apologists should argue for the biblical view of man as sinful in nature (Romans 3:10, 23; Jeremiah 17:9). Confucius misdiagnosed man, for man is not basically good. Man is sinful and in desperate need of salvation (Matthew 19:25-26). Only through Jesus can man be saved (John 14:6). Christians should also counter Confucius' lack of emphasis on the spiritual realm and the hereafter. If there is no life after death, then life on earth is meaningless, for a million years from now it would not make any difference how one lived their life. Confucius' preoccupation with morality and government issues is inconsistent with his agnosticism concerning the hereafter.

### TAOISM

Taoism is a Chinese religion supposedly founded by Lao-tzu. (Some scholars doubt that he ever existed.) Lao-tzu was thought to have been born around 600BC. Lao-tzu opposed tyranny and the idea of government itself. His philosophy is called the "Tao," which means the way or path of ultimate reality. The Tao is the way of the universe — the way one should order one's life. Man is to live a passive life of inactivity, indifference, and irresponsibility. Avoidance of all stress and violence is emphasized. This will enable men to live in harmony with the universe. Taoism teaches that all things emanate from the Tao, including the Yin and the Yang. The Yin represents the negative side of the universe (the female, evil, darkness, death, winter, passive). The Yang represents the positive side of the universe (the male, good, light, life, summer, active). Taoism's god is an impersonal force.[58]

The Christian, when dealing with a Taoist, should provide evidence from nature for the personality of God. The design and complexity of the universe reveals that God is an intelligent designer, and the moral judgments that people make show that the Cause of the universe is a moral Being. The Christian ethic is opposed to the ethic of the Tao—an ethic of inactivity, indifference, and irresponsibility. Christianity teaches its adherents to stand up for that which is good, to fight the good fight of faith, to press on in service for God, and to oppose that which is evil (Ephesians 6:13; 1 Timothy 6:12; Philippians 3:14; James 4:7). Man's ultimate goal should not be to live at harmony with the universe. Man's ultimate goal should be to live in harmony with the personal God of the Bible, and this harmony with God can only be received through Jesus (Romans 5:1; 2 Corinthians 5:18; 1 Timothy 2:5).

SHINTOISM

Shintoism is purely a Japanese religion. It is one of the world's oldest religions. It is not really a system of beliefs. Shintoism teaches that the Japanese islands were the first divine creation and that Japanese emperors were descendants of the sun-goddess, Amaterasu. Even as late as World War II, Shintoism was still being taught in Japanese schools. Between the two world wars the Japanese Emperor was worshiped. The essential beliefs of Shintoism are 1) Japan is the country of the gods, 2) her people are descendants of the gods, and 3) the Japanese people are superior in intelligence and courage.[59]

The Christian can respond to Shintoism by stating that all people are equal in God's eyes since all bear His image (Genesis 1:26-27; 9:6). All mankind is related since all people are descendants of Adam and Eve (Acts 17:26; Genesis 3:20). The Christian must also attempt to persuade the Shintoist that all people are sinners who can only be saved by Jesus (Romans 3:10, 23; John 3:16-18).

ZOROASTRIANISM

Zoroastrianism was founded by Zoroaster around 650BC in Persia (modern Iran). At that time, the Persians were polytheistic. Zoroaster protested against polytheism. Still, Zoroastrianism teaches dualism, the belief in two gods. Ahura-Mazda is the perfect and all-knowing creator; Angra Mainyu is co-eternal with Ahura-Mazda. Angra Mainyu is the evil spirit of destruction that has been at war with the Ahura Mazda throughout all eternity. Zoroastrianism teaches that good will ultimately triumph over evil. Today, Zoroastrianism has only about 100,000 adherents.[60]

The refutation of the dualistic world view presented in chapter 16 of this work can be effectively utilized against this religion. If two equally powerful gods—one good and one evil—exist, then there is no guarantee that evil will be defeated. All finite existence must depend on infinite existence for its being, but two equal gods cannot be infinite, for they limit each other. Therefore, if the two finite gods of Zoroastrianism exist, there must also exist an infinite God who is the Cause of their existence.

## SIKHISM

Sikhism attempts to harmonize the beliefs of Hinduism and Islam. It was founded by Nanak in India around 1500AD. Sikhism teaches the existence of one impersonal god called "sat nam." Salvation is achieved through knowing this god and being absorbed into him (the merging of the individual soul with the world soul). Hindu polytheism is rejected, while the Islamic belief in one god is affirmed. Sikhism retains the Hindu belief in reincarnation.[61]

Sikhism can be refuted by providing evidence from nature for the personality of God, and by disproving reincarnation. The need for personal salvation through Christ must be proclaimed and defended.

## A GENERAL APOLOGETIC AGAINST ALL NON-CHRISTIAN RELIGIONS

Christian apologists, when dealing with non-Christian religions, must defend the essential Christian beliefs as this work has done, as well as refute the doctrines that are proclaimed by the religion in question. In closing this chapter, three points should be made regarding the superiority of the Christian faith.

First, the God of Christianity is more just than the gods of the world religions, for the God of the Bible cannot forgive sin unless it has been paid for in full. He cannot ignore or overlook sin. The God of Christianity demands the ultimate penalty (the eternal flames of hell) for rebellion against Him. Only an ultimately worthy sacrifice can atone for the sins of mankind. The non-Christian world religions, on the other hand, either attempt to explain away the reality of sin and guilt, or accept the reality of sin, but downplay its severity so that man can atone for his own sins.

Second, the God of Christianity is more loving than the gods of the world religions. His justice demands that He punish all sin, but, His love caused Him to go to the cross to die for the sins of mankind (1 Peter 2:24; 3:18). God became a man (John 1:1, 14; Philippians 2:5-8) and took the punishment for mankind. The ultimately worthy sacrifice (Jesus) was offered as a substitute for the sins of all people. However, God's love cannot be forced upon anyone. Forced love is not love; it is rape. Though Jesus paid the price for the sins of mankind, God gives each person the freedom to accept or reject His forgiveness and salvation by accepting or rejecting Jesus as Savior. God desires to save every person (Matthew 23:37; 1 Timothy 2:1-6; 2 Peter 3:9), but as a God of love, He will not force His will on His creatures.

Third, the Christian salvation message makes more sense than the salvation message in any other world religion. All the major world religions teach that limited and imperfect man can reach the unlimited and perfect God on his own. However, it is impossible for a limited being on its own to reach an unlimited Being. Christianity teaches that if man is to be saved, it must be accomplished by the unlimited God Himself. When the disciples asked Jesus how man could be saved, He responded, "With men this is impossible, but with God all things are possible" (Matthew 19:25-26). Therefore, man must look to God for salvation. Salvation is by God's grace alone (Ephesians 2:8-9); it is not earned through human effort.

Christianity is the one true faith. It differs from all other world religions on essential matters. Therefore, Christianity and the world religions cannot all be true. If Christianity is true, the other religions are false.

ENDNOTES

1McDowell and Stewart, *Handbook of Today's* Religions, 364.

2Ibid., 370-371.

3Ibid., 371-372.

4Ibid., 371.

5Ibid., 377.

6Ibid., 378.

7Ibid., 379.

8Ibid.

9Ibid.

10Ibid., 381.

11Norman L. Geisler and Abdul Saleeb, *Answering Islam* (Grand Rapids: Baker Book House, 1993), 76-79.

12McDowell and Stewart, 381.

13Ibid., 382-384.

14Ibid., 382.

15Ibid., 382-384.

16Ibid., 383-384.

17Robert Morey, *The Islamic Invasion* (Eugene: Harvest House Publishers, 1992), 161.

18McDowell and Stewart, 390.

19Ibid.

20Ibid.

21Ibid.

22Ibid., 391.

23Ibid.

24Ibid.

25Ibid., 391-392.

26Ibid., 393.

27Ibid., 394.

28Ibid.

29Ibid.

30Ibid.

31Ibid., 396-397.

32*The Koran* trans. by N. J. Dawood, (New York: Penguin Books, 1990).

33McDowell, 46-48.

34Habermas, *Ancient Evidence for the Life of Jesus*, 87-98.

35McDowell and Stewart, 283-284.

36Ibid., 284-287.

37Ibid., 286-287.

38Ibid., 287-289.

39Ibid.,  289.

40Ibid.,  290-291.

41Ibid.,  292.

42Ibid.,  292-293.

43Francis A. Schaeffer, *Trilogy* (Wheaton: Crossway Books, 1990),  293.

44McDowell and Stewart, 292-293.

45Ibid.,  293.

46Ibid.,  289.

47Ibid.,  304.

48Ibid.,  305-306.

49Smart,  98-99.

50Ibid.,  101.

51Ibid.,  100.

52McDowell and Stewart, 307-308.

53George A. Mather and Larry A. Nichols, *Dictionary of Cults, Sects, Religions and the Occult* (Grand Rapids: Zondervan Publishing House, 1993), 46.

54Ibid.

55McDowell and Stewart, 311.

56Ibid.,   296-301.

57Ibid.,   325-338.

58Ibid.,   339-348.

59Ibid.,   349-355.

60Ibid.,   356-363.

61Ibid.,   400-405.

# CHAPTER 32
# NON-CHRISTIAN CULTS

The late Dr. Walter Martin was the world's leading authority on non-Christian cults. He defined a cult as "a group of people gathered about a specific person or person's misinterpretation of the Bible."[1] Martin stated that "the cults contain many major deviations from historic Christianity"; yet, they still claim to be Christian.[2]

This chapter will examine and refute several non-Christian cults. Most cults consider the Bible to be God's Word (though they misinterpret its contents). Therefore, many cults can be refuted through the presentation of scriptural passages that contradict their teachings.

## MORMONISM

Mormonism is also known as the Church of Jesus Christ of Latter-Day Saints. Joseph Smith founded this cult in New York state in the 1820's.[3] Smith moved the cult first to Ohio, then to Illinois. After Smith's death in Illinois, he was succeeded by Brigham Young, who moved his followers to Utah in the late 1840's.[4] There the cult grew to what it is today.

Mormonism has several sacred writings. The Bible is considered God's Word, so long as it has been translated correctly.[5] *The Book of Mormon* is supposedly an inspired account of the Hebrews who left the Holy Land for America around 589BC.[6] Smith claimed *The Book of Mormon* was revealed to him by an angel named Moroni.[7] The historical inaccuracies contained in the Book of Mormon are well documented.[8] Evidence has been presented indicating that a retired pastor named Solomon Spalding was the real author of *The Book of Mormon*.[9] Though Spalding intended this work to be a novel, Joseph Smith gained access to it after the death of Spalding and proclaimed it to be divine revelation.[10]

*Doctrine and Covenants* is another sacred Mormon writing. It contains most of the unique Mormon doctrines (priesthood functions, plurality of gods, eternal progression, principles of polygamy).[11]

*The Pearl of Great Price* contains the Book of Moses (which deals with the first six chapters of Genesis), the Book of Abraham (Abraham's writings while in Egypt), and the official history of the Mormon church.[12] Mormons, in addition to their sacred writings, accept the prophecies of their living prophets as authoritative revelation from God.[13] Most of these prophecies are found in *Journal of Discourses*.

Mormon doctrines contradict the Bible in essential areas. Mormon theology denies the Christian doctrine of the Trinity. Though Mormons believe the Father, Son, and Holy Spirit are three separate Persons, they reject the Christian view that they are one God. The Latter-Day Saints teach that the Father, Son, and Holy Spirit are three separate gods.[14] This is consistent with the Mormon doctrine of the plurality of gods, the teaching that there are an infinite number of gods in existence.[15] This contradicts the biblical teaching of only one true God (Exodus 20:1-6; Deuteronomy 6:4; Isaiah 43:10; 44:6; 45:5-7, 14, 22; 1 Corinthians 8:4-6; 10:19-20; 1 Timothy 2:5). In a strange twist of theology the Book of Mormon teaches the doctrine of the Trinity (2 Nephi 31:21; Alma 11:44)! Still, Mormon doctrines contradict both the Bible and their own Book of Mormon by denying the doctrine of the Trinity.

Not only do Mormons teach the plurality of gods, they also believe that male Mormons can someday become gods.[16] This is called the doctrine of eternal progression. Mormon prophets have taught that God was once a man, and that He became a god; likewise, men can become gods.[17] The Bible teaches that there is only one true God, and that there never were nor ever will be any other gods. God proclaims, "Before Me there was no God formed, and there will be none after

Me" (Isaiah 43:10). In fact, it is not God who said that men could become gods; Satan is the originator of that lie (Genesis 3:5).

The Mormon church proclaims a different Jesus than the Jesus of the Bible. Their Jesus is not God the second Person of the Trinity. The Mormon Jesus is one of many gods. He was not always God. In fact, the Jesus of Mormonism is getting better. He is still progressing in His godhood.[18] Again, the Latter-Day Saints are refuted by the Bible which teaches that Jesus was God from the beginning. He never became a god (John 1:1, 14). For, "Jesus Christ is the same yesterday and today, yes and forever" (Hebrews 13:8).

Mormons do not accept the Bible as the final Word of God; they add their own "sacred" books. However, the Bible declares itself to be "the faith which was once for all delivered to the saints" (Jude3). Scriptural warnings against adding to God's Word are ignored by Mormons (Proverbs 30:5-6; Revelation 22:18-19). The fullness of God's revelation to man culminated in the incarnation and ministry of Jesus (Hebrews 1:1-3). Those who knew Jesus personally (the apostles) were His authoritative witnesses (John 15:26-27; Ephesians 2:20). Any future "revelation" must be tested by the authoritative witness of the apostles. When this is done, Mormonism fails the test.

Mormonism proclaims a different salvation than that of the Bible. Salvation in Mormonism is attained by exercising faith in Jesus, plus Mormon baptism, good works, and obedience to Mormon ordinances.[19] This contradicts the Christian doctrine of salvation by God's grace alone through faith in Jesus alone (John 3:16-18; 14:6; Romans 3:10, 23; 6:23; Ephesians 2:8-9). Mormonism teaches that Jesus died so that all men would be resurrected and then judged according to their works.[20] The Bible, however, teaches that Jesus died so that all who trust in Him for salvation would receive the free gift of eternal life (John 1:29; Ephesians 1:7; 1 Peter 2:24; 3:18; 1 John 1:7). The biblical view of salvation is through the work of Christ; the Mormon view of salvation is through human effort.

Mormons believe that their church alone has the true priesthood.[21] Scripture declares that all believers are priests of God (1 Peter 2:4-5; Revelation 1:6). All true believers are called priests because they intercede on behalf of others and they offer their bodies as living sacrifices to the Lord (Romans 12:1-2). The Old Testament priesthood with all its symbols and ceremonies was fulfilled in Christ (Colossians 2:16-17; Hebrews 10:1, 10-14). Jesus is

the only mediator that mankind needs (1 Timothy 2:5). People do not need the Mormon priesthood to find eternal life; people need Jesus, the true Jesus of the Bible.

The Mormon practice called baptism for the dead is unscriptural.[22] The Word of God declares that people do not get a second chance for salvation after death (Luke 16:19-31; Hebrews 9:27). Therefore, one should not be baptized for another person who has died.

Joseph Smith and Brigham Young practiced polygamy despite the fact that it was forbidden in the Bible.[23] Jesus said that, "He who created them from the beginning made them male and female...and the two shall become one flesh" (Matthew 19:4-5). Paul demanded that an elder or deacon must be "the husband of one wife" (1 Timothy 3:2, 12). Joseph Smith and Brigham Young were not qualified to be elders or deacons in a local church, not to mention founders of a new "Christian" religious movement. Even the Book of Mormon admits that the Old Testament saints who practiced polygamy greatly displeased the Lord (Jacob 2:24).

Obviously, Mormonism is a perversion of the Word of God. Mormonism is not the one true faith; it is a non-Christian cult. When it is tested against scripture, it fails miserably.

### JEHOVAH'S WITNESSES

The Jehovah's Witnesses (also known as the Watchtower Bible and Tract Society) trace their roots to Charles Taze Russell. He began to teach Bible studies in the 1870's. Though Russell was raised in a Christian home, he thought that the scriptural teaching of eternal torment was unjust. He also believed that Christ's return would be invisible. He denied Christ's deity and bodily resurrection, as well as salvation by grace. He began to believe that his own interpretation of the Bible was the supreme authority.[24] He predicted that Armageddon would occur in 1914; this prophecy obviously failed.[25]

After Russell's death, Joseph Franklin Rutherford succeeded him as president. Rutherford retained the doctrines of Russell, and added the emphasis on "Jehovah" as the only true name for God.[26]

Rutherford's predictions of Armageddon also failed in 1918 and 1925.[27]

The Jehovah's Witnesses "translated" their own version of the Bible called the *New World Translation* of the Bible. This translation is not supported by any reputable Greek or Hebrew scholar. In John 1:1, all recognized translations refer to Jesus as "God." But, in the Jehovah's Witnesses' translation Jesus is called "a god."[28] Other passages in the *New World Translation* contain questionable readings that strip Christ of His deity.[29]

Jehovah's Witnesses deny Christ's deity. They have become experts in explaining away scriptural passages that attribute deity to Jesus (Isaiah 9:6; Zechariah 14:5; John 1:1; 5:17-18; 8:23-24, 58; 10:30-33; 20:28; Philippians 2:5-7; Colossians 2:9; 2 Peter 1:1; Revelation 1:17-18). However, these passages do in fact teach that Jesus is God. Though Jehovah's Witnesses often sound confident when attacking these verses, their unique interpretations (or translations) of these passages lack scholarship. Downplaying Christ's deity, Jehovah's Witnesses often overemphasize passages which speak of the limitations of Christ's human nature (Matthew 24:36) and His submission to the Father in order to provide salvation for mankind (John 14:28; Philippians 2:5-8). The Watchtower interprets Colossians 1:15 and Revelation 3:14 to mean that Jesus is the first being that God created. However, the former verse actually declares Christ to be the supreme ruler over all creation since He is its Creator (Colossians 1:15-17). Revelation 3:14 declares Christ to be the origin of all creation. In other words, He is the source of all created existence.[30]

Jehovah's Witnesses also deny the Christian doctrine of the Trinity. Though the Bible teaches that there is only one God (Isaiah 43:10; 44:6), the Word of God declares that the Father is God (Galatians 1:1), the Son is God (Titus 2:13), and the Holy Spirit is God (Acts 5:3-4). The Scriptures also maintain that the Father, Son, and Holy Spirit are three distinct Persons (Matthew 3:16-17; 28:19; John 14:16, 26). Therefore, there is only one God, but this one God exists eternally as three equal Persons. This is the Christian doctrine of the Trinity. However, the Jehovah's Witnesses teach that only the Father is God. They consider Jesus to be a lesser god; He was God's first creation.[31] Jehovah's Witnesses believe that the Holy Spirit is nothing more than God's active, impersonal force.[32] However, the Bible clearly identifies the Holy Spirit as a Person. He is called "another Helper" (John 14:16), and He bears witness of Christ (John 15:26). He can be lied to (Acts 5:3-4) and grieved (Ephesians 4:30). He also speaks (Acts 8:29; 10:19; 13:2; 21:11). Though the doctrine that God is a three-Person Being goes beyond human understanding, it is not contradictory. The doctrine of the Trinity is biblical. To deny this doctrine is to oppose the clear teaching of Scripture in this area.

The Watchtower Society denies that Jesus rose bodily from the dead. They teach that He was raised as a spirit being.[33] However, Jesus predicted that He would raise His own body from the dead (John 2:19-21). Jesus also proved He had risen bodily from the dead by showing the apostles His wounds, allowing them to touch His body, and by eating food with them (Luke 24:36-43; John 20:26-27).

Jehovah's Witnesses deny that Christ will visibly and bodily return to earth someday.[34] They believe that Jesus invisibly returned to Brooklyn, New York in 1914.[35] This contradicts the biblical teaching that Jesus' return to earth will be bodily and visible (Revelation 1:7; Matthew 24:23-31; Acts 1:9-12). Christ will return to the nation of Israel (Zechariah 14:3-5), not Brooklyn, New York.

The Watchtower denies salvation by God's grace alone through faith in Jesus alone (John 3:16-18; Romans 3:10, 20-23; Ephesians 2:8-9; 1 Peter 3:18; 2 Corinthians 5:15, 21). They teach that Jesus' death removed the effects of Adam's sin on mankind so that people can now save themselves by living a righteous life until death.[36]

Jehovah's Witnesses deny the existence of the human soul. They believe that after death man ceases to exist until he is resurrected to be judged. This is called soul-sleep.[37] However, the Word of God declares that when a believer dies, he or she immediately goes to be with the Lord (Acts 7:59; Philippians 1:21-24; 2 Corinthians 5:8). The Bible also teaches that nonbelievers who die do not ceases to exist, but go immediately into conscious torment (Luke 16:19-31).

The Jehovah's Witnesses also deny the eternal, conscious torment of the wicked. They teach that annihilation is the final state of the lost.[38] However, the Word of God declares that nonbelievers will be "thrown into the lake of fire" where they will be "tormented day and night forever" (Mark 9:47-48; Revelation 14:9-11; 20:10, 15).

The Watchtower society contradicts the Word of God in many other areas as well. They refuse to salute the United States flag or fight in any war to defend this nation.[39] This disobeys the biblical commands to submit to the governing authorities and render them the honor they are due (Mark 12:17; Romans 13:1-7). Jehovah's Witnesses condemn the usage of any name for God other than "Jehovah."[40] Yet, Jesus instructed His disciples to call God "our Father" (Matthew 6:9). The Watchtower organization claims to be God's prophet,[41] but the Word of God shows their organization to be a false prophet: Their prophecies have failed (Deuteronomy 18:20-22), they have produced the "bad fruit" of heresies (Matthew 7:15-23), and they have proclaimed the return of a hidden, invisible Christ—Jesus taught His return to earth would be visible to all (Matthew 24:23-27; Revelation 1:7). Therefore, their claim to be the "witnesses" of Jehovah is false.

## CHRISTIAN SCIENCE

The Christian Science cult was founded by Mary Baker Eddy in 1866.[42] Christian Science teaches that God is an impersonal force and that sin, death, pain, and sickness are illusions.[43] Christian Scientists also deny the existence of the material realm.[44] They deny that Jesus is the Christ. Instead, they view Jesus as a mere man who exercised His "Christ consciousness" to a greater extent than any other person. All people have the "divine idea" or "Christ consciousness" within them and some exercise it better than others.[45] Salvation in Christian Science is the recognition that sin and death are illusions.[46] Jesus' death on the cross does not cleanse anyone from sin.[47]

In response to Christian Scientists, Christians must declare that God is a personal Being who can communicate with and love His creatures (Exodus 3:14; John 3:16). He is not the impersonal force proclaimed by Mary Baker Eddy. The Bible teaches that sin, death, pain, and sickness are real (1 John 1:8-10; Romans 3:23; Hebrews 9:27; Romans 6:23). Scripture relates that the material universe does exist (Genesis 1:1; Colossians 1:15-16). The Bible identifies Jesus as the Christ (1 John 5:1) and as God in the flesh (John 1:1, 14). The Word of God reveals that man can only be saved through Jesus (John 3:16-

18; 14:6) and that salvation was provided when Jesus died on the cross for man's sin (1 Peter 2:24; 3:18).

## THE UNITY SCHOOL OF CHRISTIANITY

The Unity School of Christianity is an offshoot of Christian Science.[48] Founded by Charles and Myrtle Fillmore, this cult teaches that man is divine; all have the "Christ-consciousness" within them.[49] Unity views Jesus as merely a man who exercised His Christ-consciousness more than any other man.[50] Sin, the devil, and eternal punishment do not exist; they are illusions.[51] Salvation in the Unity cult is through reincarnation, and everyone will eventually be saved.[52] Unlike Christian Science, the Unity School of Christianity does believe in the existence of the physical world.53

The teachings of the Unity cult can be refuted in much the same fashion as those of Christian Science. However, a scriptural refutation of reincarnation should be added when dealing with Unity. The Bible teaches that it is appointed for man to die once, not many times (Hebrews 9:27). The Word of God makes it clear that Jesus alone was punished for our sins (Hebrews 1:3; 1 Peter 2:24; 3:18); man does not need to be purged for his own sins through reincarnation. Jesus clearly taught that a deceased person cannot return to this world for a second chance (Luke 16:19-31).

## THE UNIFICATION CHURCH

The Unification Church was founded in 1954 by the Reverend Sun Myung Moon.54 Moon taught that mankind fell spiritually when Eve had sexual intercourse with Lucifer, and that mankind fell physically when Eve later had sexual intercourse with Adam.55 Moon instructed his disciples that Jesus prematurely died, having only provided for man's spiritual salvation.56 According to Moon, Jesus failed to provide physical salvation for mankind by raising a family who would inherit His sinless nature. He died before He could procure such a family. Now, it is up to Moon to physically save mankind.57 Though he has never openly declared so, Moon strongly implies that He is the Lord of the second advent.58 His cult denies the deity of Christ.59

When witnessing to Moon's followers, it should be pointed out that the Bible teaches that the Fall of mankind was due to disobedience of a clear command of God (Genesis 3:1-6). It had nothing to do with sex. The Scriptures teach that Jesus did not fail, and He accomplished salvation completely for mankind (1 Peter 2:24; 3:18; Hebrews 10:14; Matthew 20:28). Even the physical redemption of believers was accomplished by Christ's death, though it won't be realized until Christ's return (1 Corinthians 15:50-57; Revelation 20:1-6). People do not need Moon to save them. Jesus is the only Savior. Moon is also not the Lord of the second advent, for Jesus taught that He Himself would return to earth (John 14:1-3; Acts 1:9-11; Revelation 22:20).

## THE WAY INTERNATIONAL

The Way International was founded by Victor Paul Wierwille.[60] This cult denies that Jesus is God. According to them, Jesus did not pre-exist His conception in the womb of Mary.[61] Wierwille taught the doctrines of soul-sleep and annihilation of the wicked.[62] Since sins are thought to have no detrimental effect on the human spirit once saved, repentance is seldom stressed in the cult.[63]

When confronting members of this cult, the Christian apologist must defend the deity of Christ (Isaiah 9:6; John 1:1, 14; Titus 2:13; 2 Peter 1:1) and argue for His pre-existence (John 1:1-14; 8:58; 17:5; Colossians 1:15-17). The defender of the Christian faith should refute the concept of soul-sleep (Luke 16:19-31; 2 Corinthians 5:8) and give scriptural support for eternal conscious torment in hell (Revelation 14:9-11; 20:10, 15). Those in the Way International need to be informed that sin does effect the spiritual nature of man. God calls men and women to flee from their sinfulness (John 8:11, 31-36; 1 John 2:1; Romans 3:31; 6:14-18; 1 Corinthians 6:18; Hebrews 10:26-27).

## SCIENTOLOGY

Scientology was founded by L. Ron Hubbard.[64] Scientology teaches that mankind is descended from a race of uncreated, all-powerful gods called thetans. Thetans surrendered their power in order to come to earth. They gradually evolved from non-life to life, and eventually into humans who had forgotten their own deity. Scientologists counsel others to overcome their problems by remembering their own deity.[65] This is often done through past-lives-regression therapy.[66] The deity of Christ, the sinfulness of man, and the eternal flames of hell are all denied.[67] When dealing with scientologists, Christians should show that the belief that man is divine originated with Satan (Genesis 3:1-6). It must be pointed out that all are sinners (Romans 3:10, 23) who need Christ's salvation (John 3:16-18; 14:6). Evidence for Christ's deity and eternal conscious torment should be presented as well as a refutation of reincarnation.

THE UNITARIAN UNIVERSALIST ASSOCIATION

The Unitarian Universalist Association is the result of a merger between two heretical groups.[68] The Unitarian Church denied that Jesus is God and taught that God is only one Person (the Father).[69] The Universalist Church taught that all people will ultimately be saved.[70] These two heretical movements merged in 1959.[71] This cult teaches that all religions lead to God, the Bible contains errors, and the impossibility of miracles.[72] Since this cult denies inerrancy, the best approach for the apologist to take is to use historical evidences to argue for the deity of Christ (chapters 25 to 27) and the inspiration and inerrancy of the Bible (chapter 28). Mastering the information found in chapter 22 (which deals with the possibility of miracles) of this work will also be helpful when dealing with this cult.

CONCLUSION

The last two chapters were not meant to be exhaustive. There are many religions and cults that have not been mentioned, and the ones that have been mentioned were not covered in great detail. Therefore, the Christian apologist will have to refer to other works in order to learn more about false religions and non-Christian cults (see Appendix H). The Christian apologist will want to read not only works done by Christian scholars which refute heretical views, but also the writings of the cults and false religions themselves. (Some of these works are also listed in Appendix H.) This will give the defender of the faith a first hand knowledge of the systems of belief.

ENDNOTES

1Martin, *The Kingdom of the Cults*, 11.

2Ibid.

3Gordon B. Hinckley, *Truth Restored* (Salt Lake City: The Church of Jesus Christ of Latter-day Saints, 1979), 1-30.

4Ibid., 102-103.

5Walter Martin, *The Maze of Mormonism* (Santa Ana: Vision House, 1978), 45.

6Ibid., 48.

7Ibid., 47.

8Archer, 509-512.

9Martin, *The Maze of Mormonism*, 59-69.

10Ibid., 59.

11*Doctrines and Covenants* (Salt Lake City: The Church of Jesus Christ of Latter-day Saints, 1982).

12*Pearl of Great Price* (Salt Lake City: The Church of Jesus Christ of Latter-day Saints, 1982).

13McDowell and Stewart, 68.

14Bruce R. McConkie, *Mormon Doctrine* (Salt Lake City: Bookcraft, 1966), 576-577.

15Ibid., 577.

16Ibid., 238-239, 577.

17Daniel H. Ludlow, ed. *Latter-day Prophets Speak* (Salt Lake City: Bookcraft, 71-79.

18McConkie, 129.

19Ibid., 669-672.

20Ibid., 669.

21Ludlow, 183-189.

22McConkie, 72-73.

23Ibid., 577-579.

24Martin, *Kingdom of the Cults*, 38-46.

25Mather and Nichols, 158.

26Martin, *Kingdom of the Cults*, 47-48.

27Mather and Nichols, 158.

28*New World Translation of the Holy Scriptures* (Brooklyn: Watchtower Bible and Tract Society of New York, Inc., 1961), 1151.

29Martin, *Kingdom of the Cults*, 71-83.

30McDowell and Stewart, 47-49.

31*Let God be True* (Brooklyn: Watchtower Bible and Tract Society, Inc., 1946), 34-35, 37, 88, 91.

32Ibid., 89.

33*Reasoning from the Scriptures* (Brooklyn: Watchtower Bible and Tract Society, Inc., 1989), 334-335.

34*Let God be True*, 185-188.

35Ibid., 189-192, 208-209.

36Ibid., 297-301.

37Ibid., 57-67.

38Ibid., 68-80.

39Ibid., 226-242.

40Ibid., 21-32.

41Ibid., 189-190.

42Martin, *Kingdom of the Cults*, 133.

43Mary Baker Eddy, *Science and Health with Key to the Scriptures* (Boston: The First Church of Christ, Scientist, 1971), 113, 115, 293, 336, 447, 468, 472, 480, 482, 584, 586, 587.

44Ibid., 468.

45Ibid., 473, 583.

46Ibid., 588, 590, 593.

47Ibid., 23-25, 45-46.

48Martin, *Kingdom of the Cults*, 279.

49Ibid., 284-286.

50Ibid., 284-285.

51Ibid., 286.

52Ibid.

53Ibid., 286-287.

54Ibid., 338-339.

55McDowell and Stewart, 101.

56Ibid.

57Ibid.

58Ibid., 103.

59Ibid., 102.

60Ibid., 103.

61Victor Paul Wierwille, *Jesus Christ is not God* (New Knoxville: The American Christian Press, 1975).

62Walter Martin, *Cults Reference Bible* (Santa Ana: Vision House, 1981), 78.

63Mather and Nichols, 311.

64Ibid., 251.

65Ibid., 252.

66Ibid., 253.

67Martin, *Kingdom of the Cults*, 348-349.

68Ibid., 501.

69Ibid.

70Mather and Nichols, 295.

71Martin, *Kingdom of the Cults*, 501.

72Mather and Nichols, 286-288.

# CHAPTER 33
# THE OCCULT

The Occult deals with the secret or hidden arts.[1] It concerns that which goes beyond the five senses; it is the supernatural realm.[2] Occultic practices are forbidden in the scriptures. The God of the Bible commands His people to come to Him alone for information not attainable through natural means (Isaiah 8:19). It should be noted that the art of illusion is not part of the genuine world of the Occult.[3] In genuine occultic phenomenon, demonic intervention often occurs. The Bible commands believers to "test the spirits to see whether they are from God" (1 John 4:1). For "every spirit that does not confess Jesus is not from God" (1 John 4:3). Not all spiritual experiences are from God.

There are many different branches in the world of the occult. This chapter will examine a few of these branches and offer a scriptural refutation of their main tenets.

ASTROLOGY

Astrology is the belief that the position of the stars and planets directly influences people and events.[4] The future is thought to be determined by these heavenly bodies. The Bible declares astrology to be a false religion. The prophet Isaiah emphatically proclaims that astrologers cannot save themselves, let alone their followers (Isaiah 47:12-15). The Bible also forbids the worshiping of the stars (Deuteronomy 4:19). Astrology, in its most primitive form, worshiped the heavenly bodies.[5]

The Word of God informs its readers that the stars and planets do not control the future. It is God who controls the destinies of men and women; therefore, people should turn to Him rather than to the stars. He promises to work everything for the good of believers (Romans 8:28), and He calls people to Himself for salvation and rest from their worries (Matthew 11;28; Isaiah 45:22). All should place their trust in the personal God, not in the impersonal stars.

## PARAPSYCHOLOGY

Parapsychology is an attempt to give the supernatural a scientific explanation.[6] The two main subdivisions of Parapsychology are Extrasensory Perception and Psychokinesis.[7] Extrasensory Perception (ESP) is knowing something without the help of the five senses.[8] It includes telepathy (mind reading), clairvoyance (perception of objects not influencing the senses), and precognition (the predicting of future events).[9] Psychokinesis is the manipulation of objects without touching them.[10]

Jean Dixon and Edgar Cayce both claimed to have Extrasensory Perception. They both claimed to have the ability to predict the future.[11] The Bible shows both Dixon and Cayce to be false prophets. Many of their prophecies have failed (Deuteronomy 18:22), and their prophecies do not bring glory to Jesus (Revelation 19:10). Much of parapsychology appears to be demonic counterfeits of several gifts of the Holy Spirit. These gifts would include the gift of prophecy, a word of knowledge, a word of wisdom, the gift of healing, and the effecting of miracles (1 Corinthians 12:4-10).

## REINCARNATION

Many occultists believe in the doctrine of reincarnation. Reincarnation teaches that at death the soul of a person or animal passes to another body (person or animal). This is repeated over and over again until all negative karma is gone. At that point, the individual soul will be united with the World Soul.[12] According to this view, all will eventually be saved. There is therefore no need for a Savior.

The Bible rejects the notion of reincarnation. It declares, "it is appointed for men to die once, and after this comes judgment" (Hebrews 9:27). Jesus taught that the dead do not get a second chance

(Luke 16:19-31). He also claimed to be the only way through which a person could be saved (John 14:6). The Word of God teaches that Jesus alone suffered for the sins of man (John 1:29; Hebrews 1:3; 10:14; 1 Peter 2:24; 3:18; 1 John 1:7-10). The Bible teaches resurrection, not reincarnation. Believers will be raised to everlasting life; nonbelievers will be raised to everlasting torment (John 5:25-29; 1 Thessalonians 4:13-18; 1 Corinthians 15:50-53; Revelation 20:1-15).

## TRANSCENDENTAL MEDITATION

Transcendental Meditation is the introduction of Hinduistic forms of meditation into the western culture.[13] It differs greatly from scriptural meditation. Scriptural meditation is practiced by dwelling on the principles of God's Word (Joshua 1:8; Psalm 1:1-2). This is necessary for a believer to renew his or her mind (Romans 12:1-2), and to put on the mind of Christ (1 Corinthians 2:16).

In contrast to biblical meditation, the goal of Transcendental Meditation is to completely empty one's mind, thus surrendering control of one's own mind to possible demonic influence.[14] Single syllable chants called "mantras' are repeated during this type of meditation.[15] Several mantras have been shown to be names of Hindu deities.[16] Thus the goal of transcendental meditation is to unite the practitioner with the Hindu god called Brahman.[17]

Transcendental Meditation is a very dangerous practice. For those who practice it surrender control of their minds and invite, whether they know it or not, demonic beings to take control (1 Corinthians 10:19-20). Though many of its leaders have claimed Transcendental Meditation to be nonreligious, United States courts have ruled otherwise and Christian scholars have shown that Transcendental Meditation is religious.[18]

## FORTUNETELLING

Occultic attempts to predict the future through fortunetelling, palm reading, crystal balls, tarot cards, and numerology are forbidden by the Scriptures.[19] The purpose of true prophecy is to bring glory to Jesus (Revelation 19:10). The Lord forbids His people to consult occultists in search of information (1 Chronicles 10:13-14; Isaiah 8:19). It is God's will that His people turn to Him alone for supernatural wisdom. If He does not reveal the requested information, believers should take comfort in the fact that their God is in control and works everything for their good (Romans 8:28).

## PSYCHIC SURGERY

Psychic surgery is the performing of supernatural surgical operations without medical instruments or training.[20] Counter-cult researchers often disagree in their conclusions drawn from their investigations into this phenomenon.[21] Some believe these surgeries are entirely fraudulent; others accept the possibility of genuinely supernatural events occurring during these "surgeries." Whatever conclusion one draws, it is clear that these practices are forbidden by Scripture. Anytime a person receives supernatural abilities from any source other than God, that person has stepped outside of God's will and has become vulnerable to demonic influence. The Bible points out that the Antichrist (the end-time demon-possessed world ruler) and his right-hand man (the false prophet) will be able to perform miracles (2 Thessalonians 2:3-10; Revelation 13:13).

## SPIRITISM

Spiritism is attempted communication with the dead.[22] In the past, spiritism was usually practiced by mediums at seances.[23] Currently, however, channeling has become the most common form of spiritism.[24] This occurs when a person invites the spirit of a deceased person to possess his or her body for the purpose of channeling a message through that person.[25]

The Bible emphatically forbids communication with the dead (Deuteronomy 18:9-12; Isaiah 8:19). When King Saul enlisted the services of the Witch of Endor to call up the spirit of the deceased prophet Samuel, God allowed Samuel to return (1 Samuel 28:6-19). However, this appears to be the exception rather than the rule, for the Bible teaches that the dead cannot communicate with the living (Luke 16:19-31). In the case of King Saul it appears that God granted his wish to hear from the prophet Samuel. Still, God displayed His displeasure for the occultic practices of King Saul by using Samuel to pronounce the death of Saul (which occurred the next day).

Since God normally forbids the spirits of the dead to communicate with the living, it would seem to indicate that spiritism is either fraudulent or demonic in nature. Unclean spirits called demons do communicate with people and may even indwell people (1 Timothy 4:1; 1 John 4:1-3; Luke 8:27-33). Thus, if a specific case of spiritism is genuine, it is probably a demon that is conversing with or speaking through the medium (Acts 16:16-18).

## DEMON POSSESSION

Demon possession occurs when a person is indwelt with and controlled by one or more demons.[26] The Gospels contain eyewitness testimonies that attest to numerous episodes of demon possession (Matthew 17:18-21; Mark 1:23-28, 34; 3:22-27; 7:24-30; Luke 8:2; 27-33). Eyewitness testimonies of demon possession cases have occurred throughout history to the present day.[27] Walter Martin himself performed several exorcisms. The eyewitness accounts of these exorcisms are still in print today.[28]

The Bible teaches that Jesus has given believers authority to cast out demons out (Luke 10:17-20). The Holy Spirit indwells all true believers (1 Corinthians 6:19). He is more powerful that Satan and his demons (1 John 4:4). Still, some demons are so powerful that they will not depart unless the exorcist has prepared for the encounter through prayer and fasting (Matthew 17:18-21).

It cannot be overemphasized that the defender of the faith should not attempt to cast a demon out of a person unless there exists strong evidence that the person actually is possessed.[29] Many psychological and biological abnormalities can be mistaken for demon possession.[30] Great harm can be done by attempting to exorcise demons from persons who are not possessed.[31] An investigation should precede any attempted exorcism. Unless supernatural phenomenon (such as clairvoyance, psychokinesis, speaking in an ancient extinct language previously unknown to the victim, super human strength, levitation) are observed, one cannot be sure that possession has occurred (unless the exorcist has the spiritual gift of discerning of spirits).[32]

## WITCHCRAFT

Witchcraft (also called "Wicca") is the ancient pagan religion that worships the elements of nature and/or seeks power from nature.[33] Though some witches swear allegiance to Satan, this is not usually the case.[34] Witchcraft attempts to utilize the hidden powers of nature. When a witch uses magical powers for the supposed good of mankind, this is called "white magic."[35] "Black magic" is when a witch uses magical powers for destructive purposes, usually to cause others harm.[36] The Bible condemns all forms of magic. In magic the existence of the true God is rejected, and the creation is worshiped instead (Romans 1:18-23). Any genuine supernatural power found in witchcraft can be credited to Satan and his demons. Modern witches worship the "Mother Goddess."[37] That is, they worship the earth as a female deity.

## SATANISM

Whereas witchcraft worships Satan indirectly by worshipping nature, Satanism is the direct worship of Satan.[38] Modern Satanism is more liberal in its thought than is traditional Satanism. Modern Satanism is best represented by Anton LaVey, the founder and high priest of the Church of Satan located in San Francisco, California. LaVey is the author of the Satanic Bible.[39] He denies the existence of a literal, personal being named Satan. LaVey believes that Satan is merely symbolic for anything that orthodox Christianity categorizes as sin. LaVey's views could be classified as a sort of ritualistic hedonism in which each person is free to do as he pleases.[40] LaVey is a moral relativist whose views were influenced by the writings of the German philosopher Friedrich Nietzsche.[41]

Traditional Satanists worship a literal Satan and believe that he will someday overthrow Christ.[42] Satanists celebrate the Black Mass, which is performed in honor of Satan at the witches' Sabbath. The Black Mass is a deliberate mockery of the Roman Catholic Mass. Upside down crosses are utilized, and the "Our Father" is recited backwards. The drinking of animal or human blood and the eating of animal or human flesh are often practiced at Black Masses. Participants engage in gross immorality during this mass; some speculate that human sacrifices still occur as well.[43]

## THE AUTHORITY OF THE BELIEVER

When combating the world of the occult, believers must exercise the authority that is available to them through Christ. Josh McDowell and Don Stewart have offered a helpful illustration.[44] A police officer does not have the physical strength to stop a vehicle moving towards him at a high rate of speed. Though in himself he lacks this power, the law has invested him with its authority. Because of the authority of the law, the driver will stop his vehicle when the officer orders him to stop. Just as the police officer represents the law and is invested with its authority, so also believers represent Christ and are given His authority over the demonic realm.

Satan and his demons do not fear mere human beings. Even Michael the Archangel does not intimidate Satan (Jude 8-9). However, Satan and his demons greatly fear Christ (Mark 1:23-27; James 2:19). For this reason, Jesus gives His followers His authority over Satan and his demons (Luke 10:17-20). Still, the believer must utilize this authority by putting on the full armor of God (Ephesians 6:10-18). The believer must live a life of truth and sincerity (the belt of truth). He must live a righteous life through the power God has given him (the breastplate of righteousness). The believer must always be ready to share his faith (the shoes of the preparation of the gospel of peace). A follower of Christ must always walk in faith (the shield of faith), and he must know he is saved (the helmet of salvation). Believers must master the only offensive weapon in their arsenal, the Word of God (the sword of the Spirit). Finally, a believer must pray at all times in the Spirit (Ephesians 6:18). All Christians should wear the full armor of God at all times. Only then will they have access to the authority of Christ over the demonic realm.

Believers must combat Satan and his demons in humility.[45] They must recognize that in their own strength they have no power over Satan. But, if the believer trusts in the Lord Jesus Christ for the victory, Satan and his demons will retreat.

In conclusion, there is genuine supernatural power in the world of the occult. Even the magicians of Egypt were able to turn their staffs into serpents. Still, it must be remembered that demonic power is limited, but God's power is unlimited. This is why the serpent that came from Aaron's rod was able to devour the serpents that came from the Egyptian occultists' staffs (Exodus 7:10-12). There is power in the world of the occult, but the God of the Bible is all-powerful. He is the God who sits enthroned. The day will come when all creation will acknowledge the Lordship of Jesus Christ; even Satan and his demons will reluctantly bow before Christ's throne (Philippians 2:9-

11). Therefore, when dealing with the world of the occult, followers of Jesus must exercise the authority Christ has given to them.

ENDNOTES

1McDowell and Stewart, 149.

2Ibid.

3The art of illusion involves trickery and slight of hand, and not evil spiritual power. When used for purposes of entertainment, it is not inherently evil. This would include magicians such as David Copperfield and Doug Henning. Still, many involved with the art of illusion do eventually move into the genuine world of the occult, as was the case with Houdini. Houdini attempted to contact the spirit of his deceased mother on numerous occasions.

4McDowell and Stewart, 160.

5John Ankerberg and John Weldon, *Astrology, Do The Heavens Rule Our Destiny?* (Eugene: Harvest House Publishers, 1989), 44.

6McDowell and Stewart, 210.

7Ibid., 213.

8Ibid.

9Ibid.

10Ibid.

11Ibid., 169-174, 181-185.

12Ibid., 171-174.

13Ibid., 80.

14Ibid., 83.

15Ibid., 85.

16Elliot Miller, *A Crash Course on the New Age Movement* (Grand Rapids: Baker Book House, 1989), 94.

17McDowell and Stewart, 81.

18Mather and Nichols, 278.

19McDowell and Stewart, 190-195.

20Ibid., 218.

21Ibid., 220.

22Ibid., 240.

23Ibid., 240, 243.

24Miller, 141.

25Ibid., 140-141.

26McDowell and Stewart, 177.

27T. K. Oesterreich, *Possession, Demonical and Other, Among Primitive Races in Antiquity, the Middle Ages and Modern Times*, trans. D. Ibberson, (New Hyde Park, N. Y.: University Books, 1966).

28McDowell and Stewart, 179.

29Ibid., 180.

30John Warwick Montgomery, ed. *Demon Possession* (Minneapolis: Bethany House Publishers, 1976), 282.

31Ibid., 292-295.

32Ibid., 286.

33Mather and Nichols, 312.

34Ibid.

35McDowell and Stewart, 204.

36Ibid.

37Mather and Nichols, 315.

38McDowell and Stewart, 236.

39Anton Szandor LaVey, *The Satanic Bible* (New York: Avon Books, 1969).

40McDowell and Stewart, 237-239.

41Mather and Nichols, 244.

42McDowell and Stewart, 236.

43Ibid., 167-168.

44Ibid., 277.

45Ibid., 278.

# CHAPTER 34
# THE NEW AGE MOVEMENT

The New Age Movement is growing rapidly in America.[1] It is probably the biggest threat Christianity faces going into the twenty-first century.[2] Therefore, Christian apologists must be able to dialogue with New Agers and be able to refute their teachings.

The New Age Movement is the immersing of western culture with eastern thought.[3] It is largely responsible for the current revival of ancient occultism in the United States.[4] New Agers believe in a coming new age of spiritual enlightenment and peace towards which man is evolving.[5] New Agers seek a one world government and the destruction of nationalistic barriers between the peoples of the earth.[6] The New Age Movement is not a conscious conspiracy (on the human level) to take over the world, though its thrust towards a one world government may be demonically inspired.[7] Rather, it is a network of numerous groups who share similar beliefs and goals.[8]

## HISTORY OF THE NEW AGE MOVEMENT
The New Age Movement had its roots in the ancient occultism (secret arts) of Sumeria, India, Egypt, Babylon, and Persia.[9] However, its move into western culture has been fairly recent. The Theosophical Society is responsible for bringing the New Age Movement to America.[10] Founded by Helena Blavatsky in 1875, this cult promoted seances, spiritism and Hindu thought in the United States.[11] The Theosophical Society had three primary goals. First, it sought to declare the universal brotherhood of all mankind. Second,

it desired to teach others the unity of all religions. Third, it encouraged others to tap into the spiritual powers within man.[12] This led to the current interest of many Americans in the New Age Movement.[13] The Theosophical Society taught that the world is awaiting many avatars (manifestations of God who reveal spiritual truth to the world).[14] Blavatsky considered Jesus, Buddha, and Mohammad to be avatars.[15]

Annie Besant and Alice Bailey were later leaders of the Theosophical Society.[16] Their books are still popular today within new age circles.[17] Bailey claimed to have communicated with several spirit guides.[18] Her books are published through a company called "Lucis Trust," formerly known as the "Lucifer Publishing Company."[19]

American culture had been dominated by the Christian world view from about 1620 to 1860.[20] After Charles Darwin published his *Origin of Species*, American culture began to take on more of a secular mindset (1860-1960). Though most Americans rejected philosophical atheism (the belief that no God exists), they accepted practical atheism. In other words, they lived like no God existed. They rejected the traditional morality taught in the Bible. Moral relativism became popular. Still, Americans were not satisfied with materialistic pleasures; they longed for spiritual experiences. Even so, they did not want an authoritative God who would forbid some of their practices. This left many Americans open to eastern influences. This may also partly explain the "hippie culture" and the widespread experimentation with hallucinogenic drugs. The 1960's were famous for large-scale rebellion against materialism and authority. With many Americans starving for a religious experience, this country abandoned its secular outlook and opened the door to the occult. It was in this context that the New Age Movement became popular in America.[21]

## COMMON NEW AGE BELIEFS

The New Age Movement is antithetical to Christianity. The New Age Movement accepts a pantheistic world view, the belief that God is the universe.[22] God is thought to be an impersonal force by New Agers.[23] Obviously this contradicts Christianity, for the Bible teaches that God is not identical to the universe; rather, God created the universe (Genesis 1:1; John 1:1-3; Colossians 1:15-17). God is therefore separate from the universe. The God of the Bible is not impersonal. He is a personal God who loves the people He has created and has communicated to them in His Word (John 3:16; 2 Timothy 3:16-17; 2 Peter 1:20-21).

New Agers teach that all humans are God since they are part of the universe (which they equate with God).[24] On the other hand, the Bible states that man is not God (1 Samuel 15:29; Ezekiel 28:1-2, 9-10; Matthew 19:25-26). In fact, the lie that humans are or can be god was originated by Satan (Genesis 3:1-7; Isaiah 14:12-14). Since New Agers believe they are God, they see no need to be saved.[25] The Bible, however, teaches the need for all people to be saved (Romans 3:10; 23; 6:23; John 3:16-18; 14:6). New Agers refuse to acknowledge the reality of sin.[26] However, the Bible teaches that sin is real. All are sinners. All need the Savior, the Lord Jesus (Romans 3:10, 23; 1 Peter 2:24; 3:18; 1 John 1:8-10).

New Agers accept the doctrine of reincarnation.[27] Reincarnation teaches that the individual soul passes through the cycle of death and rebirth. The soul reanimates a different body (whether animal or human) after death until all negative karma is done away with. Then the individual soul is absorbed into the world soul.[28] This is in direct opposition to biblical teaching. The Bible proclaims that "it is appointed for man to die once..." (Hebrews 9:27). Jesus' story of Lazarus the begger and the rich man illustrates that man does not get another chance beyond this life (Luke 16:19-31). Rather than reincarnation purging a soul from sin, Jesus alone paid for the sins of mankind (John 1:29; Hebrews 1:1-3; 1 Peter 2:24; 3:18).

Many New Agers believe the external world is merely an illusion; it does not exist.[29] Still, they live as if it does exist: They clothe and feed themselves. They do not jump off of high buildings. A belief system that cannot be consistently lived should be seriously reconsidered.

New Agers are often moral relativists. They deny there is right and wrong.[30] Obviously, the Bible disagrees for the scriptures teach absolute moral laws that are above all mankind (Exodus 20:1-17; Micah 6:8; Isaiah 5:20; 1 John 1:8-10). New Agers do not live consistently with their belief in moral relativism. They do live as though some things are wrong. They protest the production of nuclear weapons.[31] They march to save the whales, seals, and other endangered species.[32] They are determined to save the earth from global warming.[33] Though most New Agers deny the existence of universal moral values, they clearly judge certain things as being "wrong." If New Agers were consistent with their moral relativistic leanings, then they could not even judge the barbarous actions of Adolph Hitler.

New Agers commonly teach that there is no absolute truth.[34] However, this is a self-refuting statement. If the belief that there is no absolute truth is true, then it would be an absolute truth (universally true). Therefore, it is self-refuting, and it must be false. Hence, some things must be universally true.

New Agers seek the establishment of a one-world government.[35] They believe that man himself will bring a new age of peace to the earth.[36] However, God wants the world divided into separate nations until Jesus returns to rule (Genesis 11:1-9). A man-made, one-world government may eventually lead to the global dictatorship headed by the antichrist (Revelation 13:3-7). The Bible teaches that there will be wars until the end, and that mankind will not be able to establish peace on earth by himself (Daniel 9:26; Matthew 24:6-7). Jesus taught that in the last days the love of man would grow cold (Matthew 24:12). Only Jesus, the true Prince of Peace, will be able to bring lasting peace to the planet (Isaiah 9:6-7; Revelation 11:15; 19:11-16). A one-world human government will only expedite man's self-destruction.

New Agers believe mankind is evolving and getting better. But, history agrees with the biblical depiction of man as eroding morally. In fact, this century has been the bloodiest century in human history. New Age optimism about the future is clearly unwarranted. Man is not getting better; he is getting worse.

New Agers often say that all religions lead to God.[37] Again, this contradicts the teaching of Scripture. Jesus taught that salvation comes only through faith in Him (John 3:16-18; 14:6; Acts 4:12). Jesus taught that those who reject Him and do not have a saving relationship with God the Father (Luke 10:16). Thus, the Bible denies that all faiths lead to God.

New Agers deny that Jesus is uniquely God.[38] They deny that salvation comes only through Jesus and that man is lost without

Him.[39] The New Age Movement is not compatible with biblical Christianity.

## COMMON NEW AGE PRACTICES

Two common New Age practices are channeling and eastern meditation.[40] Channeling is the practice whereby a person voluntarily allows himself to be possessed by a spiritual entity who then speaks through the possessed person. The spirit entity is thought to be the spirit of a deceased human.[41] The Bible forbids people to attempt to communicate with the dead (Deuteronomy 18:9-12; Isaiah 8:19). The Word of God also indicates that the dead cannot communicate with the living (Luke 16:19-31). Therefore, the spirit entities that possess and speak through people are probably demons; they are not spirits of dead humans. The Bible commands men and women to test the spirits (1 John 4:1-3). The apostle Paul predicts that in the last days men will fall prey to doctrines taught by demons (1 Timothy 4:1). The content of channeled messages contradicts the gospel message of salvation only through faith in Jesus.[42] Paul stated that any human or angel who brings a message that contradicts the gospel is accursed (Galatians 1:8-9).

New Agers commonly practice eastern meditation.[43] Eastern meditation encourages a person to empty his mind of all rational thought. This is believed to create an environment in which a mystical union with the impersonal god can take place.[44] Eastern meditation differs essentially from biblical meditation. In biblical meditation, the person's mind is emptied of sinful desires. Still, the mind is focused on principles from God's Word (Psalm 1:1-2; Joshua 1:8). Therefore, in biblical meditation, the mind is never left completely empty. On the other hand, eastern meditation is content-less. One surrenders control of one's mind by the cessation of rational thought. Once a person looses control of his mind, demonic control may take place. Mantras are repeated during New Age meditation.[45] A mantra is a one syllable word that, when repeated over and over, is designed to remove all content from the mind. This practice is in direct disobedience to the teaching of Christ. Jesus prohibited His followers from engaging in the vain repetition which was common among pagan worshippers (Matthew 6:7). The mantras have been shown to have been derived from the names of Hindu deities (false gods).[46] Therefore, eastern meditation invites demon possession through the communion with false gods (1 Corinthians 10:19-21), as well as through the surrendering of the mind.

## CONCLUSION

The New Age Movement is not Christian. It competes with Christianity for the hearts of men and women. Therefore, defenders of the Christian Faith must be prepared to refute the doctrines of the New Age Movement.

## ENDNOTES

1Walter Martin, *The New Age Cult* (Minneapolis: Bethany House Publishers, 1989), 7-8.

2Ibid.

3Ibid., 13.

4Ibid., 15.

5Ibid., 33-34.

6Douglas R. Groothuis, *Unmasking the New Age* (Downers Grove: InterVarsity Press, 1986), 116-117.

7Miller, 202.

8Ibid., 14-16.

9Martin, *The New Age Cult*, 15.

10Ibid., 15-17.

11Ibid., 15.

12Bob Larson, *Larson's Book of Cults* (Wheaton: Tyndale House Publishers, 1982), 327.

13Martin, *The New Age Cult*, 15.

14Ibid.

15Ibid.

16Ibid., 16-17.

17Ibid., 17.

18Ibid., 16.

19Ibid., 129.

20Geisler and Anderson, *Origin Science*, 82-83.

21Groothuis, *Unmasking the New Age*, 37-56.

22Ibid., 18-21.

23Ibid., 20.

24Ibid., 21-22.

25Martin, *The New Age Cult*, 29-30.

26Ibid.

27Ibid., 32-33.

28Norman L. Geisler and J. Yutaka Amano, *The Reincarnation Sensation* (Wheaton: Tyndale House Publishers, 1986), 28-30.

29David K. Clark and Norman L. Geisler, *Apologetics in the New Age* (Grand Rapids: Baker Book House, 1990), 151-155.

30Ibid., 71.

31Martin, *The New Age Cult*, 65.

32Ibid.

33Miller, 107-111.

34Douglas Groothuis, *Confronting the New Age* (Downers Grove: InterVarsity Press, 1988), 72-76.

35Miller, 111-127.

36Ibid.

37Groothuis, *Unmasking the New Age*, 27-29.

38Douglas Groothuis, *Revealing the New Age Jesus* (Downers Grove: InterVarsity Press, 1990), 17-21.

39Ibid.

40Miller, 36, 141.

41Ibid., 141-142.

42Ibid., 169-174.

43Groothuis, *Confronting the New Age*, 23-24.

44Ibid.

45Miller, 94.

46Ibid.

# PART NINE

# CULTURAL APOLOGETICS

# CHAPTER 35
# THE IMPACT OF RELIGION
# ON GOVERNMENT

Cultural apologetics deals with defending the Christian faith from the consequences of a religion on a society or government. If Christian apologists can show that Christianity is the one religion that makes for a peaceful, orderly society and promotes freedom more than any other religion, then the case for Christianity will be greatly strengthened. In this chapter, we will examine the impact that different religions have had on societies and governments. In the final chapter, we will argue that, if Western Civilization does not return to the God of the Bible, the West will go the way of all other civilizations—it will crumble from within. We will now discuss the impact different religions have had on governments and cultures.

Though we have all heard the liberal rallying cry of "separation of church and state," the fact of the matter is this: human government cannot exist in a spiritual vacuum. Human government must be based upon certain presuppositions about man and the universe in which he lives. In short, political and economic theories must be based upon a religious foundation. Thomas Jefferson, the author of *the Declaration of Independence*, recognized this when he penned the words, "all men are created equal." Even the atheists who signed the first *Humanist Manifesto* acknowledged man's reliance upon religious ideas by stating that, "nothing human is alien to the religious."[1] Human beings are incurably religious, and their governments must have a religious foundation as well.

## THE JUDEO-CHRISTIAN WORLD VIEW

The United States government was founded upon the Judeo-Christian world view (i.e., the Bible).[2] Our founding fathers believed that all men were created equal and in God's image, and that all men have God-given rights that could not be taken away. God instituted human government to protect these unalienable rights.

According to our founding fathers, the need for human government is twofold. First, because man was created in God's image, human life is sacred and therefore worth protecting. Second, because man is in a fallen and sinful state, human life needs to be protected, for some humans infringe upon the God-given rights of other humans. Thus, the need for human government is based upon the biblical doctrines of Creation and the Fall.

Our founding fathers took seriously the sinfulness of mankind. They recognized that since human governments are ruled by sinful humans, government power must be limited. No man or group of men should be allowed to have their sinful lust for power go unchecked. Our nation's founders heeded Lord Acton's advice— "power corrupts, and absolute power corrupts absolutely." Therefore, *the Declaration of Independence* and the *United States Constitution* limited the power of government officials in several ways. First, God and His laws were recognized as existing above human government and its officials. Government officials are not above the law; they are answerable to God. Second, global government was rejected. A global government limited in power is an oxymoron. Third, a system of checks and balances and separation of powers (federal and state governments & the three branches of the federal government) were established to prevent the unleashing of a unified assault against the American people and their freedoms. Fourth, the people's rights to worship as they saw fit, elect many of their government officials, peacefully protest the government's actions, and bear arms were protected.

The Constitution does not force Americans to become Jews or Christians, but, because it is based upon the Judeo-Christian world view, it protects a person's freedom to worship according to the dictates of his or her conscience. The form of government America has and the freedoms we enjoy are due to the Judeo-Christian world view. Our founding fathers acknowledged the biblical view of government and morality in their political and economic thought. Political liberals may not like this fact, but it is a historical fact nonetheless. Although political liberals wish to change the religious presuppositions of our government, the alternatives are not very promising. And we must never forget that governments must have a religious base. We will now look at some of the alternatives to the Judeo-Christian basis for human government.

## ATHEISM/SECULAR HUMANISM

In *Humanist Manifestos I and II*, atheist leaders proposed to save this planet by working towards a one-world socialistic government based upon the foundation of the atheistic world view.[3] However, in this century we have witnessed the horrors produced by governments based upon atheism. The totalitarian regimes of the Soviet Union and Red China together have systematically slaughtered more than 80 million of their own people in this century alone.[4]

Atheism, by denying belief in God's existence, is a world view that has no basis for the sanctity of human life. Man is merely molecules in motion, having no intrinsic worth. Since atheists also reject a historical Fall of mankind, man's lust for power is left unchecked. A survival of the fittest mentality is allowed to run rampant among government leaders. While claiming to have the best interests of the populace in mind, government officials are answerable to no one as they seek to increase their power.

Consistent atheism not only entails a rejection of traditional values, but also a complete denial of any absolute moral laws. Therefore, there is no such thing as right and wrong; the end (the goals of those in power) justifies the means (even if millions are slaughtered). Atheism fails to supply the moral foundation necessary for good government. Therefore, if the Judeo-Christian world view is rejected, we must look elsewhere for an alternative religious base for human government.

## ISLAM

In the militant Islamic world view of Iran, the government leader (the ayatollah) is viewed as the infallible spokesman for God.[5] This is the Shi'ite branch of Islam. It perverts the Judeo-Christian world view by allowing a sinful man to stand in the place of God. The results can be the same as that of the atheistic world view since the atheist denial of God's existence causes its government leaders to attempt to replace God as the highest authority. The power of the government leader is not held in check. Whenever a human leader (other than the Lord Jesus who is fully God and fully man) stands in the place of God and claims to speak infallibly for God, oppression will almost surely follow. This was seen during the Carter administration when Ayatollah Khomeni took innocent Americans hostage for 444 days. The militant wing of Shi'ite Islam is known as Hezbollah.

The violent side of Islam is not only found in the Shi'ite Islam of Iran, but also in the Sunni Islam of other Muslim countries. Most Muslims in the world are Sunni Muslims. Within the Sunni branch of Islam, two movements deserve our attention. The Wahhabi movement originated in Saudi Arabia in the eighteenth century, and the Deobandi movement began in India in the nineteenth century and is currently popular in Pakistan.[6] Both branches of Sunni Islam are reform movements within the Muslim world. These groups literally interpret the Koran (the Muslim holy book written by Muhammad) and the Hadith (early and authoritative Muslim traditions). Therefore, they take seriously Muhammad's commands to slay the idolaters or infidels (Surah 9:5; 5:34-35, etc.). They often use force and violence to purify the Islamic faith. This entails terrorist attacks on liberal or modern Muslims as well as acts of unprovoked violence against the non-Muslim world. The Al-Qaida terrorist network, the Taliban, and Osama Bin Laden have links with both Deobandi and Wahhabi Islam. The terrorist attacks against America on September 11, 2001 were the work of Bin Laden and his followers.

Though some would argue that violent Muslims, whether of the Shi'ite or Sunni type, are perverting the peaceful and tolerant religion of Islam, the facts tell a different story. Though most Muslims are probably peace-loving people, the Koran and the Hadith call for the slaying of non-Muslims wherever they are found. Muhammad meant Jihad (a holy war fought in the name of Allah, the Muslim God) to be taken literally; he himself conquered non-Muslims with the sword. In fact, whereas the first three centuries of Christianity saw thousands of defenseless Christians persecuted, the first three hundred years of Islam were characterized by Islamic military conquests of non-Muslim lands. Professing Christians who kill innocents in Jesus' name pervert the teachings of Christ; Muslims who commit terrorist acts in the name of Allah are following Muhammad's example and obeying the teachings of Muhammad as found in the Koran as well as the Hadith. A "back to the Bible" movement usually leads to religious freedom, while a "back to the Koran" movement will always lead to bloodshed and violence. It is no coincidence that every government heavily influenced by the Islamic faith offers no religious freedom to non-Muslims. In Middle-Eastern Muslim countries, non-Muslims can be executed for trying to convert a Muslim, and in the Sudan more than 2 million professing Christians have been killed by Muslims since the 1950's.

POLYTHEISM

Many tribal peoples in Africa and South America hold to the belief in many gods, called polytheism. The animism (the belief that all nature is animated with spirits) of American Indians was very similar to polytheism. History has shown that polytheism and animism leave their adherents in occultism, superstition, poverty, and anarchy. Human sacrifice is often practiced (i.e., Incas, Aztecs, Mayas). Polytheism offers no unified code of ethics to unite its people, since the gods are often opposed to one another. Ancient dictators were more than willing to bring in their own unifying principle (usually the enforced worship of the emperor or ruler as the superior god) while using polytheism to aid them in suppressing the rights of their people. In short, polytheism often produces a society that lacks a unified direction, thus making that society easy prey for potential dictators. The finite gods of polytheism are not able to sustain a society.

OTHER-WORLDLY PANTHEISM

Pantheism is the belief that God is the universe, and that, since man is part of the universe, man is God. In India, the society and government are based upon this world view due to India's most popular religion—Hinduism. But this type of Hindu pantheism in India is an *other-worldly* pantheism—the emphasis is not on this life, but on future reincarnations. This lessens the incentive of Hindus to alleviate the suffering of others, for the suffering person is working off negative karma. To alleviate his suffering would be to force him to return to this world, in a different body, and to suffer again to work off the negative karma. Thus, helping alleviate a person's sufferings is viewed as a hindrance to that person's spiritual progress. This is why many of the health care workers in India are Christian.

The caste system in India is another consequence of other-worldly pantheism. It is almost impossible for a person to leave the caste (or class) into which they are born, since the person is thought to be in that caste due to the karma he has brought from a former life. Usually, it is assumed that a future incarnation is the only way for a person to move out of their caste. Due to the other-worldly pantheism of India, suffering people are often neglected since they are thought to be working off negative karma.

It should be noted that any reform movements in India attempting to change the caste system are actually contrary to the doctrines of Hindu Pantheism. On the other hand, reform movements in America, such as the abolition of slavery, were actually bringing American life more in conformity to the Judeo-Christian world view.

## THIS-WORLDLY PANTHEISM

In contrast to the other-worldly pantheism of India is the *this-worldly* pantheism of Nazi Germany.[7] In early twentieth century Germany the leadership of the German Church had all but apostacized. In earlier decades, German theologians and philosophers had attacked the authenticity and reliability of the Bible, causing many professing Christians in Germany to lose their confidence in the traditional Christian world view. The German Volk religion filled the void left by the church's apostacy. It became the dominating religious perspective of Germany's leadership.

The German Volk religion was a pantheistic ideology which held that the Aryan race is divine and that the German leader (Hitler) was the fullest manifestation of the divine. Non-aryan races were viewed as "sub-human." These races were seen as a threat to human progress, for it was feared that they could pollute the pure genetic make-up of the Aryan (master) race. The emphasis of the pantheism of the German Volk religion was on this life and the supposed future spiritual evolution of the Aryan race. The undesirable "sub-human" races had to be weeded out in order to usher in a "new age" of spiritual enlightenment.[8]

Thus, the holocaust, which took the lives of more than 6 million innocent Jews, was motivated by the this-worldly pantheism of Adolph Hitler and the Third Reich. The present-day version of this-worldly pantheism is the New Age Movement. Both the New Age Movement and the German Volk religion were greatly influenced by the occultic beliefs of Theosophy, a cult founded by the Russian mystic Helena Blavatsky.[9] The New Age Movement, if it continues to grow in popularity, may produce another holocaust; however, this holocaust may cover the entire earth. New Age leader and author Barbara Marx Hubbard believes that not everyone is ready for the coming New Age of peace and spiritual enlightenment. In fact, she believes that traditional Christians, Jews, and Muslims are holding back the spiritual evolution of mankind because they refuse to acknowledge that man is God. Therefore, reasons Hubbard, one-fourth of mankind needs to be exterminated in order to usher in the New Age.[10]

Pantheism (in both its this-worldly and other-worldly forms) teaches that God is an impersonal force, not the personal God of the Bible. Being an impersonal force, the God of pantheism is beyond the moral categories of right and wrong. Therefore, ultimately, there are no moral absolutes; what is right for one person is not necessarily right for another person, and visa versa. Usually this moral relativistic view translates into a toleration of willful, immoral behavior (i.e., homosexuality, abortion, euthanasia, sexual immorality, pornography, etc.), as well as an inconsistent lack of toleration of traditional values and beliefs (i.e., the Judeo-Christian world view). Unfortunately, that which a this-worldly pantheistic world view cannot tolerate it usually exterminates. For although the concept that man is God appears to be a high view of man, it is actually devalues human life since it entails the weeding out of undesirables who hold back human progress. (For the New Age Movement the undesirables include traditional Christians and Jews, as well as patriotic Americans who hold to traditional values.)

## WHAT ABOUT THE INQUISITION AND THE CRUSADES?

Christianity is often blamed for the terrors of the Inquisition and the bloodshed of the Crusades. In reference to the Inquisition, several things need to be clarified. First, the Inquisition was primarily a killing & torturing of those who opposed the Bishop of Rome. In other words, it should not be viewed as an indictment on traditional, protestant Christianity (i.e., Bible-based Christianity). When the church and the Roman Empire merged, it was the empire that corrupted the church, not the other way around. Second, much of the inquisition dealt with torturing and killing Jews merely because they were Jews and they would not convert to "Christianity." But, true Christians cannot hate Jews. Jesus was Jewish. The apostles were Jewish. The Bible (Old and New Testaments) is Jewish. True Christians pray for Israel and love the Jewish nation since it is God's chosen nation. Jesus said "not everyone who says to Me 'Lord, Lord' shall enter the Kingdom of Heaven, but he who does the will of My Father in heaven" (Matthew 7:21). Third, Bible-believing Christians defend Jesus, not the actions of a fallible church. We do not believe the church is infallible, nor do we believe that the Bishop of Rome (i.e., the Pope) is infallible when he speaks for the entire church in areas of faith or practice. Protestants acknowledge that professing Christians have committed horrors in the name of Christ, but we believe that their actions prove them to be outside the true faith, for "faith without works is dead" (James 2:26). Fourth, during the Inquisition many true Christians were tortured and killed because they refused to submit to the Bishop of Rome. Often, the Inquisition was characterized by professing Christians killing true Bible-believing Christians as well as Jews.

The Crusades involved the waging of war in behalf of the Church of Rome. The early crusades were fought in defense of the Eastern Church as she was being attacked by Muslim invaders. Still, later Crusades morally deteriorated to the point where there is simply no way to justify them. Again, we must remember that these actions were ordered by the Roman Catholic Church. Protestants argue against the church hierarchy having that kind of authority;

Protestants reject the notion of papal infallibility. Like the Inquisition, the Crusades show that not all professing believers are genuine Christians.

In a book entitled *Christianity on Trial,* authors Vincent Carroll and David Shiflett sum up the issue well:

> Whatever Christianity's role in the conflicts of the last two millennia, its hands were clean during the bloodiest century on record—the one just past. The body count from the two great barbarisms of the twentieth century, communism and Nazism, is extraordinary enough on its own. Communism's toll ran to perhaps 100 million...Adolph Hitler's death machine was equally efficient, but ran a much shorter course...Communism was and is proudly atheistic, while Nazism...embraced a form of neopaganism. Both were hostile to the organized religions in their midst, and neither genuflected before any power other than man himself. Yet these movements exterminated their victims with an efficiency that clearly exceeded the most grisly achievement of states produced by Christian zealotry. In that sense, they were worthy heirs to the French Revolution, which erected altars to the Goddess of Reason before the backdrop of a guillotine.[11]

CONCLUSION

Government cannot be separated from religion. Every government must have a doctrine of man and his place in the universe, and it is here that government and religion overlap. If a government rejects the faith of our founding fathers (the Judeo-Christian world view), then it will accept an alternative world view. But the consequences of that alternative world view will infringe on man's freedom and eventually result in great loss of life, for the dethronement of God is not without consequences. Contemporary man's flight from God will inevitably lead him down the dark, bloody road to tyranny.

## ENDNOTES

1Paul Kurtz, ed. *Humanist Manifesto I & II* (Buffalo: Prometheus Books, 1972), 9.

2It is true that not all of our founding fathers were Christians. Some were deists; they denied the miraculous elements of Christianity. Still, the founding fathers who were deists were *pro-Christian deists*. They were politically conservative and held to the biblical view of government and morality. On the other hand, *anti-Christian deists* could be found among the leaders of the bloody French Revolution. Anti-Christian deists are politically liberal—they believe that big government has all the answers to man's problems, and that man, through his reason, can save this planet. Anti-Christian deists reject the biblical view of limited government as well as the biblical view of morality. Modern deists usually fall into the anti-Christian deist camp. They often have more in common with secular humanists (i.e., atheists) than with adherents of the Judeo-Christian world view.

3Kurtz, 8, 10, 21.

4R. J. Rummel, *Death by Government* (New Brunswick: Transaction Publishers, 1994), 8.

5Timothy Demy and Gary P. Stewart, *In the Name of God* (Eugene: Harvest House Publishers, 2002), 58-59.

6Ibid., 59-62, 80-82.

7Richard Terrell, *Resurrecting the Third Reich* (Lafayette: Huntington House Publishers, 1994), 49-61, 145-168.

8Ibid., 50.

9Ibid., 49, 151-153.

10Tal Brooke, *One World* (Berkeley: End Run Publishing, 2000), 197. Hubbard is an insider with the United Nations and the United Religions Organization. She is not alone in her thinking. Her idea that a large portion of the world's population needs to be exterminated is shared by Cornell Professor David Pimentel. In 1994, he argued before the American Association for the Advancement of Science that the total population of the world should not exceed 2 billion people. Since the world's current population is about 6 billion, Pimentel apparently would like to see 4 billion people "disappear." Pimentel's wild idea was treated with respect by the *Los Angeles Times*. See William Norman Grigg, *Freedom on the Altar* (Appleton: American Opinion Publishers, 1995), 109.

11Vincent Carroll and David Shiflett, *Christianity on Trial* (San Francisco: Encounter Books, 2002), 109.

# CHAPTER 36
# THE DEATH OF MAN:
# THE COMING DEATH OF
# WESTERN CIVILIZATION

As the twentieth century comes to a close, we must properly diagnose the disease that has caused the unprecedented wars, bloodshed, and genocide which this century has experienced. In this paper I will discuss the prophetic insights of the German atheist Friedrich Nietzsche, as well as the prognostication of Christian thinkers C. S. Lewis and Francis Schaeffer, concerning the future of Western civilization. I will show that the nineteenth century's death of God has led to the twentieth century's death of both universal truth and absolute moral values, and that this in turn will lead to the death of man in the twenty-first century if the tide is not reversed.

## NIETZSCHE: PROPHET FOR THE 20TH CENTURY
Friedrich Nietzsche (1844-1900) proclaimed that "God is dead."[1] By this he meant that the Christian world view was no longer the dominant influence on the thought of Western culture. Nietzsche reasoned that mankind had once created God through wishful thinking, but the nineteenth century man intellectually matured to the point where he rejected God's existence.[2] Intellectuals throughout the world were embracing atheism as their world view,

and the ideas of these intellectuals were beginning to influence the common people throughout Western civilization. According to Nietzsche, scientific and technological advances had made belief in God untenable.

But Nietzsche saw a contradiction in the thought of these intellectuals. Though he agreed with their atheism, he rejected their acceptance of traditional moral values. Nietzsche argued that, since God is dead, traditional values have died with Him.[3] If the God of the Bible does not exist, reasoned Nietzsche, then the moral values taught in the Bible should have no hold over mankind.

Nietzsche viewed existence as a struggle and redefined the good as "the will to power."[4] This was a logical outgrowth of his acceptance of the Darwinian doctrine of the survival of the fittest. Nietzsche called for a group of "supermen" to arise with the boldness to create their own values.[5] He proposed that, through their will to power, these "supermen" replace the "soft values" of Christianity with what he called "hard values." Nietzsche believed that the "soft values" of Christianity (self-control, sympathy, love for enemies, human equality, mercy, humility, dependence on God, etc.) were stifling human creativity and progress; these values encouraged mediocrity. But the "hard values" of the supermen (self-assertion, daring creativity, passion, total independence, desire for conquest, etc.) greatly enhance creativity.[6] Nietzsche considered the soft values a slave morality, and the hard values a master morality, and he promoted the latter.

Nietzsche rejected the idea of universal, unchanging truths. He viewed truths as mere human creations, as metaphors mistaken for objective reality.[7] Therefore, Nietzsche showed that, since God is dead, universal truth, like absolute moral values, is dead as well.

Nietzsche predicted that the twentieth century man would come of age. By this he meant that the atheist of the twentieth century would realize the consequences of living in a world without God, for without God there are no absolute moral values. Man is free to play God and create his own morality. Because of this, prophesied Nietzsche, the twentieth century would be the bloodiest century in human history.[8] Still, Nietzsche was optimistic, for man could create his own meaning, truth, and morality. Set free from belief in a non-existent God, man could excel like never before. Nietzsche viewed the changes that would occur as man becoming more than man (the superman or overman), rather than man becoming less than man.

Nietzsche was the forerunner of postmodernism. A key aspect of modernism was its confidence that, through reason, man could find absolute truth and morality. Postmodernism rejects this confidence in human reason. All claims to having found absolute truth and morality are viewed by postmodernists as mere creations of the human mind.[9]

The history of the twentieth century has proven Nietzsche's basic thesis correct. Western culture's abandonment of the Christian world view has led to a denial of both universal truth and absolute moral values. The twentieth century has proven to be the bloodiest century in human history.[10] Hence, the Christian thinker must object to the optimism of Nietzsche. The death of God is not a step forward for man; it is a step backward—a dangerous step backward. If God is dead, then man is dead as well.

The comments of Roman Catholic philosopher Peter Kreeft are worth noting:

> One need not share Nietzsche's atheism to agree with his historical, not theological, dictum that "God is dead"—i.e., that faith in God is dead as a functional center for Western civilization, that we are now a planet detached from its sun. One need not share Nietzsche's refusal of morality and natural law to agree with his observation that Western man is increasingly denying morality and natural law; that we are well on our way to the Brave New World.[11]

## C. S. LEWIS: THE ABOLITION OF MAN

The nineteenth century brought the death of God to Western culture. The twentieth century brought the death of truth and morality to Western culture. Two twentieth century Christian thinkers, C. S. Lewis (1898-1963) and Francis Schaeffer (1912-1984), argued that the death of man will follow, unless of course man repents.

A Christian thinker should not be content with rightly analyzing and critiquing current ideas. A true thinker should also attempt to foresee the probable future consequences of ideas. In this way, a Christian thinker performs the role of a watchman by warning his listeners of future dangers (Ezekiel 33:1-9). C. S. Lewis and Francis Schaeffer had the courage to fulfill this role.

Lewis, in his prophetic work *The Abolition of Man*, critiqued an English textbook, written in the 1940's, which was designed for school children. Lewis found that more than English was being taught in this book, for the authors rejected objective truth and traditional values and proclaimed a type of moral relativism.[12] Lewis expressed concern for two reasons. First, the children who read this textbook would be easy prey to its false teachings.[13] Second, this would lead to a culture built on moral relativism and the rejection of objective truth, something that, according to Lewis, has not existed in the history of mankind.[14]

Lewis not only refuted the fallacious views of the authors, but also predicted the future consequences of this type of education. He argued that teaching of this sort would produce a race of "men without chests."[15] By this he meant men without consciences. According to Lewis, this would mean an entirely "new species" of man and "the abolition of man."[16]

Lewis argued that the practical result of such education would be "the destruction of the society which accepts it."[17] The rejection of all values leaves man free to recreate himself and his values.[18] When this power is placed into the hands of those who rule, their subjects will be totally at their mercy.

Lewis also saw in this rejection of traditional values a new purpose for science. In a sense, science is like magic in that both science and magic represent man's attempted "conquest of nature." However, science will become an instrument through which a few hundreds of men will rule billions of men,[19] for in man's conquest of nature, human nature will be the last aspect of nature to surrender to man.[20] Science will be used by future rulers to suppress the freedoms of the masses.

Lewis refers to the future rulers as "the man-moulders of the new age" or the "Conditioners."[21] It will be the job of the Conditioners to produce the rules, not to obey the rules.[22] The Conditioners (i.e., Nietzsche's supermen) will boldly create the laws the conditioned must obey. The role of education will become the production of artificial values which will serve the purposes of the Conditioners.[23] The Conditioners, through their Nietzschean "will to power" and motivated by the thirst to satisfy their own desires, will create their own new values and then force these "values" on the masses.[24]

According to Lewis, the rejection of traditional values and objective truth will lead to the same mentality in future rulers as that of "the Nazi rulers of Germany."[25] Traditional values will be replaced by the arbitrary wills of the few who rule over the billions,[26] and this will "abolish man" and bring about "the world of post-humanity."[27]

## SCHAEFFER: THE POST-CHRISTIAN ERA & THE DEATH OF MAN

Francis Schaeffer proclaimed that Western culture is now in a "post-Christian era." By this he meant the same thing Nietzsche meant when he declared "God is dead." Schaeffer was saying that the Christian world view was no longer the dominant presupposition of Western culture. Now, a secular humanistic view of reality permeates the thought of the West.[28] Due to this change in world view, modern man has fallen below what Schaeffer called "the line of despair."[29] Schaeffer meant that, by throwing the God of the Bible out of the equation, modern man, left to himself and without divine revelation, could not find absolute truth and eventually gave up his search for it. According to Schaeffer, modern man no longer thinks in terms of antithesis (i.e., the law of non-contradiction); he now views truth as relative. And, since he believes there are no absolutes, modern man has rejected universal moral laws and has embraced moral relativism.

Schaeffer wrote concerning America, "our society now functions with no fixed ethics," and "a small group of people decide arbitrarily what, from their viewpoint, is for the good of society at that precise moment and they make it law."[30] Schaeffer compares this present climate of arbitrary lawmaking to the fall of the Roman Empire. The finite gods of Rome where not sufficient to give a base in law for moral absolutes; therefore, the Roman laws were lax and promoted self-interest rather than social harmony. This eventually led to a state of social anarchy as violence and promiscuity spread throughout the empire. To keep order, the Roman Empire had to become increasingly more authoritative. Due to Rome's oppressive control over its people, few Romans believed their culture was worth saving when the barbarian invasions began.[31] Schaeffer saw that America, like ancient Rome, had turned to arbitrary laws which have led to an increase in crime and promiscuity, which in turn has led to ever-increasing government control. Schaeffer stated this principle as follows:

> The humanists push for "freedom," but having no Christian consensus to contain it, that "freedom" leads to chaos or to slavery under the state (or under an elite). Humanism, with its lack of any final base for values or law, always leads to chaos. It then naturally leads to some form of authoritarianism to control the chaos. Having produced the sickness, humanism gives more of the same kind of medicine for the cure. With its mistaken concept of final reality, it has no intrinsic reason to be interested in the individual, the human being.[32]

Schaeffer also noted that most American leaders no longer consider themselves subject to God's laws. They often view themselves as answerable to no one. They do not acknowledge "inalienable rights" given to each individual by God. Instead, American leaders play God by distributing "rights" to individuals and by making their own arbitrary laws. Schaeffer quotes William Penn who said, "If we are not governed by God, then we will be ruled by tyrants."[33]

Schaeffer saw the 1973 legalization of abortion as a by-product of man playing God by legislating arbitrary laws and by the few forcing their will on the many.[34] But, according to Schaeffer, this is just the beginning, for once human life has been devalued at one stage (i.e., the pre-birth stage), then no human life is safe. Abortion will lead to infanticide (the murdering of babies already born) and euthanasia (so called "mercy-killing").[35] Christianity teaches that human life is sacred because man was created in God's image, but now that modern man has rejected the Christian world view (the death of God), the death of man will follow (unless modern man repents) and man will be treated as non-man. Schaeffer documents the erosion of respect for human life in the statements of Nobel Prize winners Watson and Crick. These two scientists, after winning the Nobel Prize for cracking the genetic code, publicly recommended that we should terminate the lives of infants, three days old and younger, if they do not meet our expectations.[36]

In his response to behavioral scientist B. F. Skinner's book *Beyond Freedom and Dignity*, Schaeffer argued that Western culture's rejection of God, truth, and God's moral laws will lead to the death of man. Written in 1971, Skinner's book proposed a "utopian" society ruled by a small group of intellectual elitists who control the environment and genetic makeup of the masses. Schaeffer stated, "We are on the verge of the largest revolution the world has ever known—the control and shaping of men through the abuse of genetic knowledge, and chemical and psychological conditioning."[37] Schaeffer referred to Skinner's utopian proposals as "the death of man,"[38] and wrote concerning Skinner's low view of C. S. Lewis:

> Twice Skinner specifically attacked C. S. Lewis. Why? Because he is a Christian and writes in the tradition of the literatures of freedom and dignity. You will notice that he does not attack the evangelical church, probably because he doesn't think it's a threat to him. Unhappily, he is largely right about this. Many of us are too sleepy to be a threat in the battle of tomorrow. But he understands that a man like C. S. Lewis, who writes literature which stirs men, is indeed a threat.[39]

Schaeffer understood not only the failure of secular humanism, but he also realized that Eastern pantheism offered no escape from the death of man. Only a return to the Christian world view could save the West from the death of man. He stated:

> Society can have no stability on this Eastern world-view or its present Western counterpart. It just does not work. And so one finds a gravitation toward some form of authoritarian government, an individual tyrant or group of tyrants who takes the reins of power and rule. And the freedoms, the sorts of freedoms we have enjoyed in the West, are lost. We are, then, brought back to our starting point. The inhumanities and the growing loss of freedoms in the West are the result of a world-view which has no place for "people." Modern humanistic materialism is an impersonal system. The East is no different. Both begin and end with impersonality.[40]

Schaeffer called upon evangelicals to sound the alarm, warning the church and society to repent, for the death of man is approaching:

Learning from the mistakes of the past, let us raise a testimony that may still turn both the churches and society around—for the salvation of souls, the building of God's people, and at least the slowing down of the slide toward a totally humanistic society and an authoritarian suppressive state.[41]

CONCLUDING REMARKS

Nietzsche wrote that Western culture's rejection of God would inevitably lead to the rejection of absolute truth and universal moral values. Allan Bloom confirmed that this has indeed been the case when he began his epic book *The Closing of the American Mind* with these words: "There is something a professor can be absolutely certain of: almost every student entering the university believes, or says he believes, that truth is relative."[42] Still, Nietzsche wrongly believed that this rejection of truth and morality would improve humanity by ushering in the "overman."

Lewis and Schaeffer agreed with Nietzsche's death of God, truth, and morality hypothesis, but, since they were Christians, they argued that this would not be an advancement for man. Instead, this would bring about the death of man. Though I believe that Lewis overstated his case by asserting that the death of man would create a "new species," I agree that, apart from Western culture's repentance, some type of death of man is inevitable. Man is presently being treated as non-man throughout the world (i.e., abortion, infanticide, euthanasia, religious persecution, genocide, violent crimes, etc.), and this trend will continue to increase apart from a return to the Christian world view.

As I see it, the death of man will involve spiritual, social, and psychological aspects. The death of man will be characterized by man being further alienated from God (the lost becoming harder to reach with the Gospel), from others (mankind becoming more and more depersonalized), and from himself (the light of man's moral conscience and his thirst for God will be dimmed). People, especially those in positions of authority, will treat other people as less than human. Man's love for man will grow cold.

To prevent, or at least slow down, the death of man, Christian thinkers must defend the reality of God, absolute truth, absolute moral values, as well as the dignity of man and the sanctity of human life. Still, we must do more than refute current ideologies; we must also proclaim to a complacent church and world where those ideas will take us in the twenty-first century if we refuse to repent. Like Lewis and Schaeffer, we must resist the temptation to pick dates for Christ's return or dogmatically declare that these are the last days, for we do not see the future with certainty—maybe Western culture will repent. Therefore, like Lewis, Schaeffer, and the Old Testament prophets, we must call our culture to repent. We must tell our generation that the nineteenth century gave us the death of God, and the twentieth century gave us the death of truth and morality. Without widespread repentance, the twenty-first century will bring the death of man. Just as the removal of God from our schools has all but destroyed our public school system, the removal of God from the reigning ideas of Western culture will surely destroy our civilization. The death of God will ultimately lead to the death of man, if we do not turn back to the God of the Bible. Unless trends are reversed and the Christian world view is restored as the dominant perspective in Western culture, the twenty-first century will surpass the twentieth century in tyranny, violence, and ungodliness.

Though only God knows if we are actually in the final days, the words of our Savior warn us that someday the death of man will come:

> And this Gospel of the kingdom shall be preached in the whole world for a witness to all the nations, and then the end shall come…. for then there will be a great tribulation, such as has not occurred since the beginning of the world until now, nor ever shall. And unless those days had been cut short, no life would have been saved; but for the sake of the elect those days shall be cut short (Matthew 24:14, 21-22).

ENDNOTES

1Friedrich Nietzsche, *The Portable Nietzsche*, ed. Walter Kaufman (New York: Penguin Books, 1968), 124, 447.

2Ibid., 143, 198.

3Norman L. Geisler and Paul D. Feinberg, *Introduction to Philosophy* (Grand Rapids: Baker Book House, 1980), 408.

4*The Portable Nietzsche*, 570.
5Geisler and Feinberg, 408.

6Ian P. McGreal, ed. *Great Thinkers of the Western World* (New York: HarperCollins Publishers, 1992), 409-410.

7*Portable Nietzsche*, 46-47.

8Frederick Copleston, A *History of Philosophy*, vol. VII (New York: Doubleday, 1963), 405-406.

9Stanley J. Grenz, *A Primer on Postmodernism* (Grand Rapids: William B. Eerdmans Publishing Co., 1996), 83.

10R. J. Rummel, *Death by Government* (New Brunswick: Transaction Publishers, 1997), 9. Rummel estimates that, in the twentieth century alone, between 170 and 360 million people have been killed by their own governments during times of peace. (This does not include the millions of unborn babies who were aborted in this century.)

11Peter Kreeft, *C. S. Lewis for the Third Millennium* (San Francisco: Ignatius Press, 1994), 107.

12C. S. Lewis, *The Abolition of Man* (New York: Collier Books, 1947), 23.

13Ibid., 16-17.

14Ibid., 28-29.

15Ibid., 34.

16Ibid., 77.

17Ibid., 39.

18Ibid., 62-63.

19Ibid., 69, 71.

20Ibid., 72.

21Ibid., 73-74.

22Ibid., 74.

23Ibid.

24Ibid., 78, 84.

25Ibid., 85.

26Ibid.

27Ibid., 85-86.

28Francis Schaeffer, *A Christian Manifesto* (Westchester: Crossway Books, 1981), 17-18.

29Francis Schaeffer, *The Complete Works of Francis A. Schaeffer*, vol. I (Westchester: Crossway Books, 1982), 8-11.

30Schaeffer, *A Christian Manifesto*, 48.

31Schaeffer, *Complete Works*, vol. V, 85-89.

32Schaeffer, *A Christian Manifesto*, 29-30.

33Ibid., 32-34.

34Ibid., 49.

35Schaeffer, *Complete Works*, vol. V, 317. see also vol. IV, 374.

36Ibid., vol. V, 319-320.

37Ibid., vol. I, 381.

38Ibid., 383.

39Ibid., 382-383.

40Ibid., vol. V, 381.

41Ibid., vol. IV, 364.

42Allan Bloom, *The Closing of the American Mind* (New York: Simon & Schuster, 1987), 25.

## APPENDIX A

## FURTHER RESOURCES FOR AN INTRODUCTION TO
## APOLOGETICS

### INTRODUCTION TO APOLOGETICS

Craig, William Lane. *Apologetics, An Introduction.* Chicago: Moody Press, 1984.

Geisler, Norman L. *Christian Apologetics.* Grand Rapids: Baker Book House, 1976.

Lewis, Gordon R. *Testing Christianity's Truth Claims.* Lanham: University Press of America, 1990.

Moreland, J. P. *Scaling the Secular City.* Grand Rapids: Baker Book House, 1987.

### HISTORY OF APOLOGETICS

Cairns, Earle E. *Christianity Through the Centuries.* Grand Rapids: Zondervan Publishing House, 1981.

Clark, Gordon H. *Thales to Dewey.* Jefferson: The Trinity Foundation, 1985.

Copleston, Frederick. *A History of Philosophy.* 9 vols. New York: Image Books,1985.

Dowley, Tim, ed. *The History of Christianity.* Oxford: Lion Books, 1977.

Sahakian, William S. *History of Philosophy*. New York: Harper Collins Publishers, 1968.

## SYSTEMATIC THEOLOGY

Chafer, Lewis Sperry. *Systematic Theology*. 8 vols. Grand Rapids: Kregel Publications, 1993.

Erickson, Millard J. *Christian Theology*. Grand Rapids: Baker Book House, 1985.

Hodge, Charles. *Systematic Theology*. 3 vols. Grand Rapids: William B. Eerdmans Publishing Company, 1989.

Ryrie, Charles R. *Basic Theology*. Wheaton: Victor Books, 1986.

Thiessen, Henry Clarence. *Lectures in Systematic Theology*. Grand Rapids: William B. Eerdmans Publishing Company, 1979.

## APPENDIX B

## FURTHER RESOURCES FOR TESTIMONIAL APOLOGETICS

Cruz, Nicky. *Run Baby Run*. Plainfield, New Jersey: Logos Books, 1968.

McDowell, Josh. *Evidence that Demands a Verdict*. San Bernardino: Here's Life Publishers, 1979, 325-367.

Morison, Frank. *Who Moved the Stone?*. London: Faber and Faber, 1958.

Saint Augustine. *Confessions*. (translated by R. S. Pine-Coffin). New York: Penguin Books, 1961.

## APPENDIX C

## FURTHER RESOURCES FOR PRESUPPOSITIONAL APOLOGETICS

Clark, Gordon H. *A Christian View of Men and Things*. Jefferson: The Trinity Foundation, 1991.

. *Clark Speaks From the Grave*. Jefferson: The Trinity Foundation, 1986.

. *An Introduction to Christian Philosophy*. Jefferson: The Trinity Foundation, 1993.

. *Religion, Reason and Revelation*. Jefferson: The Trinity Foundation, 1986.

. *Three Types of Religious Philosophy*. Jefferson: The Trinity Foundation, 1989.

Frame, John M. *Apologetics to the Glory of God*. Phillipsburg: Presbyterian and Reformed Publishing Company, 1994.

Lewis, Gordon R. *Testing Christianity's Truth Claims*. Lanham: University Press of America, 1990, 100-150.

Van Til, Cornelius. *Christian Apologetics*. Phillipsburg: Presbyterian and Reformed Publishing Company, 1976.

. *The Defense of the Faith*. Phillipsburg: Presbyterian and Reformed Publishing Company, 1967.

## APPENDIX D

## FURTHER RESOURCES FOR PSYCHOLOGICAL APOLOGETICS

Kreeft, Peter. *Christianity for Modern Pagans*. San Francisco: Ignatius Press, 1993.

Lewis, Gordon R. *Testing Christianity's Truth Claims*. Lanham: University Press of America, 1990, 210-284.

Morris, Thomas V. *Making Sense of it All*. Grand Rapids: William B. Eerdmans Publishing Company, 1992.

Pascal, Blaise. *Pensees*. (translated by A. J. Krailsheimer). New York: Penguin Books, 1966.

Schaeffer, Francis A. *Trilogy*. Wheaton: Crossway Books, 1990.

Zacharias, Ravi. *Can Man Live Without God?*. Dallas: Word Publishing, 1994.

APPENDIX E

FURTHER RESOURCES FOR PHILOSOPHICAL APOLOGETICS

Geisler, Norman L. *Christian Apologetics*. Grand Rapids: Baker Book House, 1976, 11-259.

, and Winfried Corduan. *Philosophy of Religion*. Grand Rapids: Baker Book House, 1988.

, and Paul D. Feinberg. *Introduction to Philosophy*. Grand Rapids: Baker Book House, 1980.

, and William D. Watkins. *Worlds Apart*. Grand Rapids: Baker Book House, 1989.

Hick, John, ed. *The Existence of God*. New York: The Macmillan Company, 1964.

. *Philosophy of Religion*. Englewood Cliffs, New Jersey: Prentice-Hall, Inc., 1963.

Martin, Michael. *Atheism—A Philosophical Justification*. Philadelphia: Temple University Press, 1990.

Miethe, Terry and Antony Flew. *Does God Exist?*. San Francisco: Harper Collins, 1991.

Moreland, J. P. and Kai Nielsen. *Does God Exist?*. Nashville: Thomas Nelson Publishers, 1990.

Saint Thomas Aquinas. *Summa Theologiae, A Concise Translation*, ed. Timothy McDermott. Westminster: Christian Classics, Inc., 1989.

APPENDIX F

FURTHER RESOURCES FOR HISTORICAL APOLOGETICS

Archer, Gleason L., Jr. *A Survey of Old Testament Introduction*. Chicago: Moody Press, 1974.

Blomberg, Craig. *The Historical Reliability of the Gospels*. Downers Grove: Inter-Varsity Press, 1987.

Carson, D. A., Douglas J. Moo, and Leon Morris. *An Introduction to the New Testament*. Grand Rapids: Zondervan Publishing House, 1992.

Habermas, Gary R. *Ancient Evidence for the Life of Jesus*. Nashville: Thomas Nelson Publishers, 1984.

. *The Resurrection of Jesus*. Lanham: University Press of America, 1984.

, and Anthony Flew. *Did Jesus Rise From the Dead?*. San Francisco: Harper and Row, 1987.

Martin, Michael. *The Case Against Christianity*. Philadelphia: Temple University Press, 1991.

McDowell, Josh. *Evidence that Demands a Verdict*. San Bernardino: Here's Life Publishers, 1979.

, and Bill Wilson. *He Walked Among Us*. San Bernardino: Here's Life Publishers, 1988.

Wilkins, Michael J. and J. P. Moreland, eds. *Jesus Under Fire*. Grand Rapids: Zondervan Publishing House, 1995.

## APPENDIX G

## FURTHER RESOURCES FOR SCIENTIFIC APOLOGETICS

Ackerman, Paul D. *It's a Young World After All*. Grand Rapids: Baker Book House, 1986.

Darwin, Charles. *The Origin of Species*. New York: Mentor Books, 1958.

Geisler, Norman L. and J. Kerby Anderson. *Origin Science*. Grand Rapids: Baker Book House, 1987.

Huse, Scott M. *The Collapse of Evolution*. Grand Rapids: Baker Book House, 1983.

Johnson, Phillip E. *Darwin on Trial*. Downers Grove: Inter-Varsity Press, 1991.

Lubenow, Marvin L. *Bones of Contention*. Grand Rapids: Baker Book House, 1992.

Moreland, J. P., ed. *The Creation Hypothesis*. Downers Grove: Inter-Varsity Press, 1994.

. *Christianity and the Nature of Science*. Grand Rapids: Baker Book House, 1989.

Morris, Henry M. *The Biblical Basis for Modern Science*. Grand Rapids: Baker Book House, 1984.

*Science and the Bible*. Chicago: Moody Press, 1986.

Peacock, Roy E. *A Brief History of Eternity*. Wheaton: Crossway Books, 1990.

Ross, Hugh. *Creation and Time*. Colorado Springs: NavPress, 1994. *The Creator and the Cosmos*. Colorado Springs: NavPress, 1993.

*The Fingerprint of God*. Orange, California: Promise Publishing Company, 1991.

Sagan, Carl. *Cosmos*. London: Futura Publications, 1980.

## APPENDIX H

## FURTHER RESOURCES FOR COMPARATIVE RELIGIOUS APOLOGETICS

### RELIGIONS AND CULTS (GENERAL)

*Eerdmans' Hanbook to the World's Religions.* Grand Rapids: William B. Eerdmans Publishing Company, 1982.

Larson, Bob. *Larson's Book of Cults.* Wheaton: Tyndale House Publishers, 1982.

Martin, Walter. *The Kingdom of the Cults.* Minneapolis: Bethany House Publishers, 1985.

Mather, George A. and Larry A. Nichols. *Dictionary of Cults, Sects, Religions and the Occult.* Grand Rapids: Zondervan Publishing House, 1993.

McDowell, Josh and Don Stewart. *Handbook of Today's Religions.* San Bernardino: Here's Life Publishers, 1983.

Smart, Ninian. *The Religious Experience of Mankind.* New York: Charles Scribner's Sons, 1976.

Tucker, Ruth A. *Another Gospel.* Grand Rapids: Zondervan Publishing House, 1989.

## ISLAM

Geisler, Norman L. and Abdul Saleeb. *Answering Islam*. Grand Rapids: Baker Book House, 1993.

*The Koran*. (translated by N. J. Dawood). London: Penguin Books, 1990.

Morey, Robert. *The Islamic Invasion*. Eugene: Harvest House Publishers, 1992.

Shorrosh, Anis A. *Islam Revealed*. Nashville: Thomas Nelson Publishers, 1988.

## BUDDHISM

Gard, Richard A., ed. *Buddhism*. New York: George Braziller, Inc., 1962.

*The Teaching of Buddha*. Tokyo: Buddhist Promoting Foundation, 1984.

Watts, Alan W. *The Way of Zen*. New York: Vintage Books, 1957.

## HINDUISM

*Bhagavad-Gita*. (translated by A. C. Bhaktivedanta Swami Prabhupada). New York: The Bhaktivedanta Book Trust, 1972.

Renou, Louis, ed. *Hinduism*. New York: George Braziller, Inc., 1961.

## MORMONISM

*The Book of Mormon*. Salt Lake City: The Church of Jesus Christ of Latter-day Saints, 1981.

*Doctrine and Covenants & Pearl of Great Price*. Salt Lake City: The Church of Jesus Christ of Latter-day Saints, 1982.

Ludlow, Daniel H., ed. *Latter-Day Prophets Speak*. Salt Lake City: Bookcraft, 1948.

McConkie, Bruce R. *Mormon Doctrine*. Salt Lake City: Bookcraft, 1966.

Martin, Walter. *The Maze of Mormonism*. Santa Ana: Vision House Publishers, 1978.

## JEHOVAH'S WITNESSES

Bowman, Robert M., Jr. *Jehovah's Witnesses, Jesus Christ, and the Gospel of John*. Grand Rapids: Baker Book House, 1989.

*Let God Be True* Brooklyn: Watchtower Bible and Tract Society, 1946.

*New World Translation of the Holy Scriptures*. Brooklyn: Watchtower Bible and Tract Society, 1961.

*Reasoning From the Scriptures*. Brooklyn: Watch Tower Bible and Tract Society, 1989.

## THE NEW AGE MOVEMENT

Clark, David K. and Norman L. Geisler. *Apologetics in the New Age*. Grand Rapids: Baker Book House, 1990.

Groothuis, Douglas R. *Unmasking the New Age*. Downers Grove: Inter-Varsity Press, 1986.

Martin, Walter. *The New Age Cult*. Minneapolis: Bethany House Publishers, 1989.

Miller, Elliot. *A Crash Course on the New Age Movement*. Grand Rapids: Baker Book House, 1989.

## SATANISM

Larson, Bob. *Satanism, the Seduction of America's Youth*. Nashville: Thomas Nelson Publishers, 1989.

LaVey, Anton Szandor. *The Satanic Bible*. New York: Avon Books, 1969.

Montgomery, John Warwick, ed. *Demon Possession*. Minneapolis: Bethany House Publishers, 1976.

## APPENDIX V

## BIBLIOGRAPHY

BOOKS

Ackerman, Paul D. *It's A Young World After All*. Grand Rapids: Baker Book House, 1986.

Ankerberg, John, and John Weldon. *Astrology*. Eugene: Harvest House Publishers, 1989.

Archer, Gleason L., Jr. *A Survey of Old Testament Introduction*. Chicago: Moody Press, 1974.

Ayer, A. J., and Jane O'Grady, eds. *A Dictionary of Philosophical Quotations*. Cambridge, MA: Blackwell Publishers, 1994.

Basinger, David, and Randall Basinger, eds. *Predestination and Free Will*. Downers Grove: Inter-Varsity Press, 1986.

Baugh, Carl E., and Clifford A. Wilson. *Dinosaur: Scientific Evidence That Dinosaurs and Men Walked Together*. Orange: Promise Publishing. Inc., 1987.

*Bhagavad-Gita*. (translated by A. C. Bhaktivedanta Swami Prabhupada). New York: The Bhaktivedanta Book Trust, 1972.

Blomberg, Craig. *The Historical Reliability of the Gospels*. Downers Grove: Inter-Varsity Press, 1987.

*The Book of Mormon*. Salt Lake City: The Church of Jesus Christ of Latter-day Saints, 1981 ed.

Bowman, Robert M., Jr. *Jehovah's Witnesses, Jesus Christ, and the Gospel of John*. Grand Rapids: Baker Book House, 1989.

Brooke, Tal. *When the World Will Be as One*. Eugene: Harvest House Publishers, 1989.

Bruce, F. F. *Paul: Apostle of the Heart Set Free*. Grand Rapids: William B. Eerdmans Publishing Company, 1986.

Cairns, Earle E. *Christianity Through the Centuries*. Grand Rapids: Zondervan Publishing House, 1981.

Calvin, John. *The Institutes of the Christian Religion*. Grand Rapids: William B. Eerdmans Publishing Company, 1989.

Camus, Albert. *The Plague*. New York: Vintage Books, 1948.

Carnell, Edward John. *The Case For Orthodox Theology*. Philadelphia: The Westminster Press, 1959.

Carson, D. A., Douglas J. Moo, and Leon Morris. *An Introduction to the New Testament*. Grand Rapids: Zondervan Publishing House, 1992.

Chafer, Lewis Sperry. *Systematic Theology*. 8 vols. Grand Rapids: Kregel Publications, 1993.

Charlesworth, James H. *Jesus Within Judaism*. New York: Doubleday, 1988.

Charnock, Stephen. *The Existence and Attributes of God*. Grand Rapids: Baker Book House, 1979.

Clark, David K., and Norman L. Geisler. *Apologetics in the New Age*. Grand Rapids: Baker Book House, 1990.

Clark, Gordon H. *A Christian View of Men and Things*. Jefferson: Trinity Foundation, 1991.

. *An Introduction to Christian Philosophy*. Jefferson: Trinity Foundation, 1993.

. *Clark Speaks From the Grave*. Jefferson: Trinity Foundation, 1986.

. *Language and Theology*. Jefferson: Trinity Foundation, 1993.

. *Religion, Reason and Revelation*. Jefferson: Trinity Foundation, 1961.

. *Thales to Dewey*. Jefferson: Trinity Foundation, 1989.

. *The Philosophy of Science and Belief in God*. Jefferson: Trinity Foundation, 1987.

. *Three Types of Religious Philosophy*. Jefferson: Trinity Foundation, 1989.

Copleston, Frederick. *A History of Philosophy*. 9 vols. New York: Image Books, 1985.

. *Aquinas*. New York: Penguin Books, 1955.

Corduan, Winfried. *Reasonable Faith*. Nashville: Broadman and Holman Publishers, 1993.

Craig, William Lane. *Apologetics: An Introduction*. Chicago: Moody Press, 1984.

. *No Easy Answers*. Chicago: Moody Press, 1990.

. *The Son Rises*. Chicago: Moody Press, 1981.

Crabb, Lawrence J. Jr., *Effective Biblical Counseling*. Grand Rapids: Zondervan Publishing House, 1977.

Cruz, Nicky. *Run Baby Run*. Plainfield: Logos Books, 1968.

Darwin, Charles. *Origin of Species*. New York: Mentor Books, 1958.

Davis, John J. *Paradise to Prison: Studies in Genesis*. Grand Rapids: Baker Book House, 1983.

Descartes, Rene. *Discourse on Method and the Meditations*. (translated by F. E. Sutcliffe). London: Penguin Books, 1968.

*Doctrines and Covenants, Pearl of Great Price*. Salt Lake City: The Church of Jesus Christ of Latter-day Saints, 1982.

Dowley, Tim, ed. *The History of Christianity*. Oxford: Lion Books, 1977.

Eddy, Mary Baker. *Science and Health with Key to the Scriptures*. Boston: The First Church of Christ, Scientist, 1971.

*Eerdman's Handbook to the World's Religions*. Grand Rapids: William B. Eerdmans Publishing Company, 1982.

Elwell, Walter A., ed. *Evangelical Dictionary of Theology*. Grand Rapids: Baker Book House, 1984.

. ed. *Handbook of Evangelical Theologians*. Grand Rapids: Baker Book House, 1993.

Erickson, Millard J. *Christian Theology*. Grand Rapids: Baker Book House, 1985.

. *God in Three Persons*. Grand Rapids: Baker Book House, 1995.

. ed. *Readings in Christian Theology*. Volume I. Grand Rapids: Baker Book House, 1987.

. *The Word Became Flesh*. Grand Rapids: Baker Book House, 1991.

Ericksen, Robert P. *Theologians Under Hitler*. New Haven: Yale University Press, 1985.

Eusebius. *The History of the Church*. (translated by G. A. Williamson). London: Penguin Books, 1965.

Evans, C. Stephen. *Philosophy of Religion*. Downers Grove: Inter Varsity Press, 1982.

Ferencz, Benjamin B., and Ken Keyes, Jr. *Planethood: The Key to Your Survival and Prosperity*. Coos Bay: Vision Books, 1988.

Fernandes, Philip. *A Defense of Biblical Christianity*. Unpublished D.Min. dissertation, Bethany Theological Seminary, 1989.

Filmore, Lowell. *New Ways to Solve Old Problems*. Lee's Summit: Unity School of Christianity, 1950.

Fletcher, Joseph. *Situation Ethics: The New Morality*. Philadelphia: Westminster Press, 1966.

Foreman, Dale. *Crucify Him: A Lawyer Looks at the Trial of Jesus*. Grand Rapids: Zondervan Publishing House, 1990.

Foxe, John. *Foxe's Book of Martyrs*. Springdale: Whitaker House, 1981.

Frame, John M. *Apologetics to the Glory of God*. Phillipsburg: Presbyterian and Reformed Publishing Company, 1994.

. *Cornelius Van Til: An Analysis of His Thought*. Phillipsburg: Presbyterian and Reformed Publishing Company, 1995.

Freeman, Eugene, and John Owens, eds. *The Wisdom and Ideas of Saint Thomas Aquinas*. New York: Fawcett World Library, 1968.

Freud, Sigmond. *The Future of an Illusion*. (translated by W. D. Robson-Scott). New York: Penguin Books, 1982.

Friesen, James G. *Uncovering the Mysteries of MPD*. San Bernardino: Here's Life Publishers, 1991.

Gard, Richard A., ed. *Buddhism*. New York: George Braziller, Inc., 1962.

Geisler, Norman L. *The Battle for the Resurrection*. Nashville: Thomas Nelson Publishers, 1989.

. *Christian Apologetics*. Grand Rapids: Baker Book House, 1976.

. *Christian Ethics: Options and Issues*. Grand Rapids: Baker Book House, 1989.

. *Inerrancy*. ed. Grand Rapids: Zondervan Publishing House, 1980.

. *Is Man the Measure?*. Grand Rapids: Baker Book House, 1983.

. *Miracles and the Modern Mind*. Grand Rapids: Baker Book House, 1992.

. *Thomas Aquinas: An Evangelical Appraisal*. Grand Rapids: Baker Book House, 1991.

. ed. *What Agustine Says*. Grand Rapids: Baker Book House, 1982.

, and Abdul Saleeb. *Answering Islam*. Grand Rapids: Baker Book House, 1993.

, and Ronald M. Brooks. *Come Let Us Reason*. Grand Rapids: Baker Book House, 1990.

, and Paul D. Feinberg. *Introduction to Philosophy: A Christian Perspective*. Grand Rapids: Baker Book House, 1985.

, and J. Kirby Anderson. *Origin Science: A Proposal for the Creation-Evolution Controversy*. Grand Rapids: Baker Book House, 1987.

, and Winfried Corduan. *Philosophy of Religion*. Grand Rapids: Baker Book House, 1988.

, and J. Yutaka Amano. *Religion of the Force*. Dallas: Quest Publications, 1983.

, and J. Yutaka Amano. *The Reincarnation Sensation*. Wheaton: Tyndale House Publishers, 1986.

, and Thomas Howe. *When Critics Ask*. Wheaton: Victor Books, 1992.

, and Ronald M. Brooks. *When Skeptics Ask*. Wheaton: Victor Books, 1990.

, and William D. Watkins. *Worlds Apart: A Handbook on World Views*. Grand Rapids: Baker Book House, 1989.

Ghandi, Mohandas K. *Mahatma Ghandhi Autobiography*. Washington DC: Public Affairs Press, 1948.

Gilson, Etienne. *The Philosophy of St. Thomas Aquinas*. New York: Barnes and Noble, 1993.

Godfrey, Laurie R. ed. *Scientists Confront Creationism*. New York: Norton and Company, 1983.

Graham, Tom M. *Biology: The Essential Principles*. Philadelphia: Saunders College Publishing, 1982.

Groothuis, Douglas R. *Confronting the New Age*. Downers Grove: InterVarsity Press, 1988.

. *Revealing the New Age Jesus*. Downers Grove: InterVarsity Press, 1990.

. *Unmasking the New Age*. Downers Grove: InterVarsity Press, 1986.

Habermas, Gary R. *Ancient Evidence for the Life of Jesus*. Nashville: Thomas Nelson Publishers, 1984.

. *The Resurrection of Jesus*. Lanham: University Press of America, 1984.

, and Antony Flew. *Did Jesus Rise From the Dead: The Resurrection Debate*. San Francisco: Harper and Row, 1987.

, and J. P. Moreland. *Immortality: The Other Side of Death*. Nashville: Thomas Nelson Publishers, 1992.

Harris, Murray. *Raised Immortal: Resurrection and Immortality in the New Testament*. Grand Rapids: William B. Eerdmans, 1985.

Harrison, Everett F. ed. *Baker's Dictionary of Theology*. Grand Rapids: Baker Book House, 1960.

Harrison, R. K. *Old Testament Times*. Grand Rapids: William B. Eerdmans Publishing Company, 1970.

Hasker, William. *Metaphysics: Constructing a World View*. Downers Grove: Inter Varsity Press, 1983.

Hegel, Georg Wilhelm Friedrich. *The Philosophy of History*. (translated by J. Sibree). New York: Dover Publications, 1956.

Hick, John. *The Center of Christianity*. San Francisco: Harper and Row Publishers, 1978.

, ed. *The Existence of God*. New York: The Macmillan Company, 1964.

. *Philosophy of Religion*. Englewood Cliffs: Prentice-Hall, Inc., 1963.

Hinckley, Gordon B. *Truth Restored: A Short History of the Church of Jesus Christ of Latter-day Saints*. Salt Lake City: The Church of Jesus Christ of Latter-day Saints, 1979.

Hodge, Charles. *Systematic Theology*. Volume I. Grand Rapids: William B. Eerdmans Publishing Company, 1989.

. *Systematic Theology*. Volume II. Grand Rapids: William B. Eerdmans Publishing Company, 1989.
. *Systematic Theology*. Volume III. Grand Rapids: William B. Eerdmans Publishing Company, 1989.

Holmes, Arthur F. *Ethics: Approaching Moral Decisions*. Downers Grove: InterVarsity Press, 1984.

Hume, David. *Dialogues Concerning Natural Religion*. New York: Hafner Publishing Company, 1948.

. *An Inquiry Concerning Human Understanding*. New York: The Liberal Arts Press, 1955.

Huse, Scott M. *The Collapse of Evolution*. Grand Rapids: Baker Book House, 1983.

John, DeWitt. *The Christian Science Way of Life*. Boston: The Christian Science Publishing Society, 1962.

Johnson, Phillip E. *Darwin on Trial*. Downers Grove: Inter Varsity Press, 1991.

Josephus, Flavius. *The Works of Josephus*. (translated by William Whiston). Peabody: Hendrickson Publishers, 1987.

Kant, Immanuel. *Prolegomena to Any Future Metaphysics*. (translated by Paul Carus). Indianapolis: Hackett Publishing Company, 1977.

Kierkegaard, Soren. *Fear and Trembling*. (translated by Alastair Hannay). London: Penguin Books, 1985.

*The Koran.* (translated by N. J. Dagwood). London: Penguin Books, 1990.

Kreeft, Peter. *Christianity for Modern Pagans.* San Francisco: Ignatius Press, 1993.

, and Ronald K. Tacelli. *Hanbook of Christian Apologetics.* Downers Grove: Inter Varsity Press, 1994.

. *A Shorter Summa.* San Francisco: Ignatius Press, 1993.

Kurtz, Paul, and Edwin H. Wilson, eds. *Humanist Manifestos I and II.* New York: Prometheus Books, 1933 and 1973.

Kushner, Harold S. *When Bad Things Happen to Good People.* New York: Avon Books, 1981.

Larson, Bob. *Larson's Book of Cults.* Wheaton: Tyndale House Publishers, 1982.

. *Satanism: The Seduction of America's Youth.* Nashville: Thomas Nelson Publishers, 1989.

LaVey, Anton Szandor. *The Satanic Bible.* New York: Avon Books, 1969.

Lewis, C. S. *Mere Christianity.* New York: MacMillan Publishing Company, 1952.

. *Miracles.* New York: MacMillan Publishing Company, 1960.

. *The Problem of Pain.* New York: MacMillan Publishing Company, 1962.

Lewis, Gordon R. *Testing Christianity's Truth Claims.* Lanham, Maryland: University Press of America, 1990.

*Let God Be True*. Brooklyn: Watchtower Bible and Tract Society, Inc., 1946.

Lightfoot, J. B., and J. R. Harmer, JR., eds. *The Apostolic Fathers*. Grand Rapids: Baker Book House, 1987.

Little, Paul E. *Know Why You Believe*. Wheaton: Victor Books, 1980.

Lubenow, Marvin L. *Bones of Contention*. Grand Rapids: Baker Book House, 1992.

Ludlow, Daniel H., ed. *Latter-Day Prophets Speak*. Salt Lake City: Bookcraft, 1948.

Luther, Martin. *Commentary on Romans*. (translated by J. Theodore Muller). Grand Rapids: Kregel Publications, 1954.

. *The Bondage of the Will*. (translated by James I. Packer and O. R. Johnston). Old Tappan: Fleming H. Revell Company, 1957.

Martin, Michael. *Atheism: A Philosophical Justification*. Philadelphia: Temple University Press,1990.

. *The Case Against Christianity*. Philadelphia: Temple University Press, 1991.

Martin, Walter R. *Cults Reference Bible*. Santa Ana: Vision House, 1981.

. *Essential Christianity*. Ventura: Regal Books, 1980.

. *The Kingdom of the Cults*. Minneapolis: Bethany House Publishers, 1977.

. *The Maze of Mormonism*. Santa Ana: Vision House Publishers, 1978.

. *The New Age Cult*. Minneapolis: Bethany House Publishers, 1989.

Mather, George A., and Larry A. Nichols. *Dictionary of Cults, Sects, Religions, and the Occult*. Grand Rapids: Zondervan Publishing House, 1993.

McBirnie, William Steuart. *The Search for the Twelve Apostles*. Wheaton: Tyndale House Publishers, 1973.

McConkie, Bruce R. *Mormon Doctrine*. Salt Lake City: Bookcraft, 1966.

McDowell, Josh. *Evidence That Demands a Verdict*. San Bernardino: Here's Life Publishers, 1979.

. *Evidence That Demands a Verdict*. Vol. 2. San Bernardino: Here's Life Publishers, 1981.

. *More Than a Carpenter*. Minneapolis: World Wide Publications, 1977.

,and Don Stewart. *Handbook of Today's Religions*. San Bernardino: Here's Life Publishers, 1983.

, and Bill Wilson. *He Walked Among Us*. San Bernardino: Here's Life Publishers, 1988.

McGrath, Alister E. *Intellectuals Don't Need God and Other Modern Myths*. Grand Rapids: Zondervan Publishing House, 1993.

Miethe, Terry L., and Anthony Flew. *Does God Exist?*. San Francisco: Harper Collins Publishers, 1991.

Miller, Elliot. *A Crash Course on the New Age Movement*. Grand Rapids: Baker Book House, 1989.

Montgomery, John Warwick, ed. *Christianity for the Tough Minded*. Minneapolis: Bethany Fellowship, 1973.

, ed. *Demon Possession*. Minneapolis: Bethany House Publishers, 1976.

. *History and Christianity*. Minneapolis: Bethany House Publishers, 1965.

. *The Shape of the Past*. Minneapolis: Bethany Fellowship, 1975.

Moreland, J. P. *Christianity and the Nature of Science*. Grand Rapids: Baker Book House, 1989.

, ed. *The Creation Hypothesis*. Downers Grove: Inter Varsity Press, 1994.

. *Scaling the Secular City*. Grand Rapids: Baker Book House, 1987.

, and Kai Nielsen. *Does God Exist? The Great Debate*. Nashville: Thomas Nelson Publishers, 1990.

, and Michael J. Wilkins, eds. *Jesus Under Fire*. Grand Rapids: Zondervan Publishing House, 1995.

Morey, Robert. *The Islamic Invasion*. Euguene: Harvest House Publishers, 1992.

Morison, Frank. *Who Moved the Stone?*. London: Faber and Faber, 1958.

Morris, Henry M. *The Biblical Basis for Modern Science*. Grand Rapids: Baker Book House, 1984.

. *The Genesis Record*. Grand Rapids: Baker Book House, 1976.

. *The Long War Against God: The History and Impact of the Creation/Evolution Conflict*. Grand Rapids: Baker Book House, 1989.

. *Many Infallible Proofs*. El Cajon: Master Books, 1974.

. *Science and the Bible*. Chicago: Moody Press, 1986.

, ed. *Scientific Creationism*. (Public School Edition). San Diego: Christian Life Publishers, 1974.

Morris, Thomas V. *Making Sense of it All*. Grand Rapids: William B. Eerdmans Publishing Company, 1992.

. *Our Idea of God*. Downers Grove: Inter Varsity Press, 1991.

Nash, Ronald H. *The Concept of God*. Grand Rapids: Zondervan Publishing House, 1983.

. *Faith and Reason*. Grand Rapids: Zondervan Publishing House, 1988.

. *Is Jesus the Only Savior?*. Grand Rapids: Zondervan Publishing House, 1994.

Nietzsche, Friedrich. *Beyond Good and Evil*. (translated by Walter Kaufmann). New York: Vintage Books, 1966.

. *The Portable Nietzsche*. (edited and translated by Walter Kaufmann). New York: Penguin Books, 1982.

*New American Standard Bible*. New York: Collins Publishers, 1977.

*New World Translation of the Holy Scriptures*. Brooklyn: Watchtower Bible and Tract Society of New York, Inc., 1961.

Oesterreich, T. K. *Possession, Demonical and Other, Among Primitive Races in Antiquity, the Middle Ages and Modern Times*. (translated by D. Ibberson). New Hyde Park, N.Y.: University Books, 1966.

Pascal. *Pensees*. (translated by A. J. Krailsheimer). London: Penguin Books, 1966.

Paley, William. *Natural Theology: Selections*. (edited by F. Ferre). Indianapolis: Bobbs Merrill, 1963), 3-4.

Peacock, Roy E. *A Brief History of Eternity*. Wheaton: Crossway Books, 1990.

Pentecost, J. Dwight. *The Words and Works of Jesus Christ*. Grand Rapids: Zondervan Publishing House, 1981.

Pfeiffer, Charles F., and Everett F. Harrison, eds. *The Wycliffe Bible Commentary*. Nashville: The Southwestern Company, 1962.

Plantinga, Alvin C. *God, Freedom, and Evil*. Grand Rapids: William B. Eerdmans Publishing Company, 1974.

*Reasoning From the Scriptures*. Brooklyn: Watch Tower Bible and Tract Society, 1989.

Renou, Louis, ed. *Hinduism*. New York: George Braziller, Inc., 1961.

Ross, Hugh. *Creation and Time*. Colorado Springs: Nav Press, 1994.

. *The Creator and the Cosmos*. Colorado Springs: Nav Press, 1993.

. *The Fingerprint of God*. Orange: Promise Publishing Company, 1991.

Russell, Bertrand. *Why I am Not a Christian*. New York: Simon and Schuster, Inc. 1957.

Ryrie, Charles C. *Basic Theology*. Wheaton: Victor Books, 1986.

. *The Ryrie Study Bible*. Chicago: Moody Press, 1978.

. *You Mean the Bible Teaches That....* Chicago: Moody Press, 1974.

Sagan, Carl. *Cosmos*. London: Futura Publications, 1980.

Sahakian, William S. *History of Philosophy*. New York: Harper Collins Publishers, 1968.

Saint Bonaventura. *The Mind's Road to God*. (translated by George Boas). Indianapolis: The Bobbs-Merrill Company, 1953.

Sanford, Charles B. *The Religious Life of Thomas Jefferson*. Charlottesville: University Press of Virginia, 1984.

Sartre, Jean-Paul. *The Transcendence of the Ego*. (translated by Forrest Williams and Robert Kirkpatrick). New York: Farrar, Strause, and Giroux.

Schaeffer, Francis A. *Back to Freedom and Dignity*. Wheaton: Tyndale House Publishers, 1972.

. *A Christian Manifesto*. Westchester: Crossway Books, 1981.

. *The Complete Works of Francis Schaeffer*. Vol. 1. Westchester: Crossway Books, 1982.

. *Escape From Reason*. London: Inter Varsity Press, 1968.

. *The God Who is There*. Downers Grove: Inter Varsity Press, 1968.

. *He is There and He is not Silent*. Wheaton: Tyndale House Publishers, 1972.

. *How Should We Then Live?*. Westchester: Crossway Books, 1976.

. *Trilogy*. Wheaton: Crossway Books, 1990.

, and C. Everett Koop. *Whatever Happened to the Human Race?*. Westchester: Crossway Books, 1979.

Schaff, Philip. *History of the Christian Church.* 8 vols. Grand Rapids: William B. Eerdmans, 1910.

Schonfield, Hugh J. *The Passover Plot.* Toronto: Bantam Books, 1965.

Shorrosh, Anis A. *Islam Revealed: A Christian Arab's View of Islam.* Nashville: Thomas Nelson Publishers, 1988.

Smart, Ninian. *The Religious Experience of Mankind.* 2nd ed. New York: Charles Scribner's Sons, 1976.

Smith, George H. *Atheism: The Case Against God.* Los Angeles: Nash Publishing, 1974.

Smith, Gerard. *Natural Theology.* New York: The Macmillan Company, 1951.

Sproul, R. C. *If There's a God, Why are There Atheists?.* Wheaton: Tyndale House Publishers, 1978.

, John Gerstner, and Arthur Lindsley. *Classical Apologetics: A Rational Defense of the Christian Faith and a Critique of Presuppositional Apologetics.* Grand Rapids: Zondervan Publishing House, 1984.

St. Anselm. *Basic Writings.* (translated by S. N. Deane). Lasalle: Open Court Publishing Company, 1962.

St. Augustine. *City of God.* abridged. (translated by Gerald G. Walsh, Demetrius B. Zema, Grace Monahan, and Daniel J. Honan). New York: Image Books, 1958.

. *Confessions.* (translated by R. S. Pine-Coffin). London: Penguin Books, 1961.

St. Thomas Aquinas. *Summa Theologiae: A Consise Translation* (edited by Timothy McDermott). Westminster: Christian Classics, Inc. 1989.

Stevenson, Kenneth E., and Gary R. Habermas. *The Shroud and the Controversy*. Nashville: Thomas Nelson Publishers, 1990.

, and Gary R. Habermas. *Verdict on the Shroud*. Wayne: Banbury Books Inc., 1981.

Stott, John R. W. *The Authentic Jesus*. Downers Grove: Inter Varsity Press, 1985.

. *Your Mind Matters*. Downers Grove: Inter Varsity Press, 1972.

Swinburne, Richard. *The Existence of God*. Oxford: Clarendon Press, 1991.

*The Teaching of Buddha*. Tokyo: Kosaido Printing Company, 1966.

Tenney Merrill C. *John: The Gospel of Belief*. Grand Rapids: William B. Eerdmans Publishing Company, 1976.

, ed. *The Zondervan Pictorial Bible Dictionary*. Grand Rapids: Zondervan Publishing House, 1967.

Thiede, Carsten P. *Simon Peter*. Grand Rapids: Zondervan Publishing House, 1988.

. *Rekindling the Word*. Valley Forge: Trinity Press, 1995.

Thiessen, Henry Clarence. *Introduction to the New Testament*. Grand Rapids: William B. Eerdmans Publishing Company, 1943.

. *Lectures in Systematic Theology*. Grand Rapids: William B. Eerdmans Publishing Company, 1979.

Thurston, Herbert. *Ghosts and Poltergeists*. Chicago: Henry Regnery Company, 1954.

Tucker, Ruth A. *Another Gospel*. Grand Rapids: Zondervan Publishing House, 1989.

Unger, Merrill F. *Unger's Bible Handbook*. Chicago: Moody Press, 1966.

. *What Demons Can Do To Saints*. Chicago: Moody Press, 1991.

Van Till, Howard J., Davis A. Young, and Clarence Menninga. *Science Held Hostage: What's Wrong With Creation Science and Evolutionism*. Downers Grove: Inter Varsity Press, 1988.

Van Til, Cornelius. *Christian Apologetics*. Phillipsburg: Presbyterian and Reformed, 1976.

. *Defense of the Faith*. Phillipsburg: Presbyterian and Reformed, 1967.

Varghese, Roy Abraham, ed. *The Intellectuals Speak Out About God*. Dallas: Lewis and Stanley, 1984.

Vine, W. E. *Expository Dictionary of New Testament Words*. Grand Rapids: Zondervan Publishing House, 1952.

Watts, Alan W. *The Way of Zen*. New York: Vintage Books, 1957.

Wedge, Thomas W., and Powers, Robert L. *The Satan Hunter*. Canton: Daring Books, 1988.

Whitcomb, John C., and Henry M. Morris. *The Genesis Flood*. Phillipsburg, Presbyterian and Reformed, 1961.

Wierwille, Victor Paul. *Jesus Christ is not God*. New Knoxville: The American Christian Press, 1975.

Willmington, H. L. *That Manuscript From Outer Space*. Nashville: Thomas Nelson Publishers, 1974.

Wood, Leon J. *A Survey of Israel's History*. Grand Rapids: Zondervan Publishing House, 1986.

Woodhouse, Mark B. *A Preface to Philosophy*. Belmont: Wadsworth Publishing Company, 1984.

Zacharias, Ravi. *Can Man Live Without God?*. Dallas: Word Publishing, 1994.

. *A Shattered Visage: The Real Face of Atheism*. Grand Rapids: Baker Book House, 1990.

*The Zondervan Parallel New Testament in Greek and English*. Grand Rapids: Zondervan Bible Publishers, 1980.

## MAGAZINE AND JOURNAL ARTICLES

Adams, Marilyn McCord. "Fides Quaerens Intellectum: St. Anselm's Method in Philosophical Theology." *Faith and Philosophy* vol. 9:4 (October 1992): 409-435.

Aggassiz, Louis. "Contribution to the Natural History of the United States." *American Journal of Science* (1860): 144-145.

Beckwith, Francis J. "Limited Omniscience and the Test for a Prophet: A Brief Philosophical Analysis." *Journal of the Evangelical Theological Society* vol. 36:3 (September 1993): 357-362.

Bishop, Leigh C. "The Theodicy of Chance." *Bulletin of the Evangelical Philosophical Society* vol. 15 (1992): 26-36.

Bonansea, Bernardino M. "The Impossibility of Creation from Eternity According to St. Bonaventure." *Proceedings of the American Catholic Philosophical Association* vol. 48 (1974): 121-135.

Byl, John. "On Pascal's Wager and Infinite Utilities." *Faith and Philosophy* vol. 11:3 (July 1994): 467-473.

Chandler, Hugh S. "Divine Intervention and the Origin of Life." *Faith and Philosophy* vol. 10:2 (April 1993): 170-180.

Clark, David K. "Narrative Theology and Apologetics." *Journal of the Evangelical Theological Society* vol. 36:4 (December 1993): 499-515.

. "Is Presuppositional Apologetics Rational?" *Bulletin of the Evangelical Philosophical Society* vol. 16 (1993): 1-15.

Cowen, Steven B. "On the Epistemological Justification of Miracle Claims." *Philosophia Christi* vol. 18:1 (Spring 1995): 25-41.

Craig, William Lane. "Philosophical and Scientific Pointers to Creatio ex Nihilo." *Journal of the American Scientific Affiliation* vol. 32 (March 1980): 5-13.

. "Professor Mackie and the Kalam Cosmological Argument." *Religious Studies* vol. 20 (1985): 367-375.

. "Should Peter Go to the Mission Field?" *Faith and Philosophy* vol. 10:2 (April 1993): 261-265.

Creel, Richard E. "Agatheism: A Justification of the Rationality of Devotion to God." *Faith and Philosophy* vol. 10:1 (January 1993): 33-48.

Cuneo, Terrence. "Combating the Noetic Effects of Sin: Pascal's Strategy for Natural Theology." *Faith and Philosophy* vol. 11:4 (October 1994): 645-662.

Davis, Richard B. "Modality and Eternity: Averroes on the Eternity of the World." *Philosophia Christi* vol. 17 (1994): 15-29.

Earman, John. "Bayes, Hume, and Miracles." *Faith and Philosophy* vol. 10:3 (July 1993): 293-310.

Edelman, John T. "Suffering and the Will of God." *Faith and Philosophy* vol. 10:3 (July 1993): 380-388.

Geisler, Norman L. "Is Creation-Science Science or Religion?" *Journal of the American Scientific Affiliation* (September 1984): 149-155.

Gould, Stephen Jay. "Evolution's Erratic Pace." *Natural History* (May 1877): 14.

Groothuis, Douglas. "Kant's Rejection of Divine Preformation Epistemology." *Bulletin of the Evangelical Philosophical Society* vol. 15 (1992): 14-25.

. "Proofs, Pride, and Incarnation: Is Natural Theology Theologically Taboo?" *Journal of the Evangelical Theological Society* vol. 38:1 (March 1995): 67-76.

. "Stricken with Theism: Was Moses Rational After All?" *Philosophia Christi* vol. 17 (1994): 31-44.

Hick, John. "Religious Pluralism and the Rationality of Religious Belief." *Faith and Philosophy* vol. 10:2 (April 1993): 242-249.

Jordan, Jeffrey. "Pascal's Wager and the Problem of Infinite Utilities." *Faith and Philosophy* vol. 10:1 (January 1993): 49-59.

Keller, James A. "Michael Martin: Atheism: A Philosophical Justification." *Faith and Philosophy* vol. 10:1 (January 1993): 112-119.

Konyndyk, Kenneth J. "Aquinas on Faith and Science." *Faith and Philosophy* vol. 12:1 (January 1995): 3-21.

LaShell, John K. "Edwards, Aristotle, and Moral Responsibility— Part 1: The Natural Conscience." *Bulletin of the Evangelical Philosophical Society* vol. 16 (1993): 35-47.

. "Edwards, Aritotle, and Moral Responsibility—Part 2: Voluntary Action." *Philosophia Christi* vol. 17 (1994): 45-57.

McGrath, Alister E. "The Challenge of Pluralism for the Contemporary Christian Church." *Journal of the Evangelical Theological Society* vol. 35:3 (September 1992): 361-373.

. "The Christian Church's Response to Pluralism." *Journal of the Evangelical Theological Society* vol. 35:4 (December 1992): 487-501.

Moreland, J. P. "Humanness, Personhood, and the Right to Die." *Faith and Philosophy* vol. 12:1 (January 1995): 95-112.

. "The Rationality of Belief in Inerrancy." *Trinity Journal* vol. 7 (Spring 1986): 75-86.

O'Connor, David. "Ethical Naturalism and Evil." *Faith and Philosophy* vol. 10:3 (July 1993): 389-393.

Owens, Joseph. "The Need for Christian Philosophy." *Faith and Philosophy* vol. 11:2 (April 1994): 167-183.

Piety, Marilyn Gaye. "Kierkegaard on Rationality." *Faith and Philosophy* vol. 10:3 (July 1993): 365-379.

Robbins, J. Wesley. "Is Naturalism Irrational?" *Faith and Philosophy* vol. 11:2 (April 1994): 255-259.

Rowe, William L. "The Problem of No Best World." *Faith and Philosophy* vol. 11:2 (April 1994): 269-271.

Siemens, David Jr. "A Response to Williams' Theistic Argument." *Bulletin of the Evangelical Philosophical Society* vol. 15 (1992): 37-41.

Short, Shirl. "Exclusive Interview with Chuck Colson." *Moody Monthly*. February 1976.

Smith, Quentin. "The Conceptualist Argument for God's Existence." *Faith and Philosophy* vol. 11:1 (January 1994): 38-49.

Swinburne, Richard. "The Argument from Design." *Philosophy* vol. 43 (July 1968): 199-212.

Whitrow, G. J. "On the Impossibility of an Infinite Past." *British Journal for the Philosophy of Science* vol. 29 (1978): 39-45.

Williams, Donald T. "The Objectivity of Value: Properties, Values, and Moral Reasoning." *Bulletin of the Evangelical Philosophical Society* vol. 16 (1993): 49-58.